Administrative Practices of AEE Accredited Programs

2nd Edition

By Jude Hirsch & Deb Sugerman

Association for Experiential Education
3775 Iris Avenue, Suite 4
Boulder, CO 80301-2043
303.440.8844 • 866.522.8337
www.aee.org

ISBN: 978-0-929361-15-4

association for experiential education
A COMMUNITY OF PROGRESSIVE EDUCATORS & PRACTITIONERS

Published and printed in the United States.

Table of Contents

* This edition of *Administrative Practices of AEE Accredited Programs* is formatted to specifically reflect the contents of the *Manual of Accreditation Standards for Adventure Programs, 4th edition.* As such, starting with Chapter 4 in this Table of Contents, the name of the organization is followed by the standards to which the sample policy and procedures in this book correspond. See page 2 of this book for a copy of the Table of Contents of the *Manual of Accreditation Standards for Adventure Programs, 4th edition* (Figure 1.1).

Photo Credits

Front cover: Photo by Dave Anderson for NOLS/climbing in Fremont Canyon, Wyoming

Back cover: Photo by Mark Ames for Red Top Meadows/students study a field guide in Jedediah Smith Wilderness Area, Wyoming

Photo by Pascal Beauvais for NOLS/canoeing in Yukon, Canada

Photo by Deb Sussex for NOLS/bouldering in Cochise Stronghold, Arizona

Photo by Kyle Barrus for Red Top Meadows/three students in Red Breaks Canyon, Utah

Photo by Mark Ames for Red Top Meadows/hiking down Mt. Fitzpatrick, Wyoming

Photo by Brady Robinson for NOLS/photo of NOLS instructor Jeffrey Post

Acknowledgments

We would like to acknowledge the many people who have helped to make this book possible.

Accredited organizations of the Association for Experiential Education that submitted policies for review deserve many thanks for their willingness to share and for their belief in the importance of this project. Their names and contact information are contained in Chapter 3.

Since the inception of the Association for Experiential Education Accreditation Program in 1992, members of the Accreditation Council and AEE staff have been visionary and worked tirelessly to professionalize the field of adventure education through standards development and review. The field owes a debt of gratitude to this group of professionals including: Deb Ajango, Mark Ames, Hank Birdsong, Bob Box, Penny Elder, Mike Gass, Sky Gray, Reb Gregg, Pat Hammond, Molly Hampton, Jude Hirsch, Drew Leemon, Scott McLarty, Steve Pace, Jane Panicucci, Mark Rowland, Bob Ryan, Bob Stremba, Deb Sugerman, Tex Teixeira, Betty van der Smissen, Jed Williamson, Paul Wolfe, Henry Wood, Rita Yerkes, and Bill Zimmerman.

Because we are both educators and believers in the inclusion of students in all phases of our work, many students were involved in the process of writing this text. Justin Talbot, a graduate student from the University of New Hampshire, researched much of the information used to write Chapter 2: Policy and Procedures. Much thanks goes to his efforts to provide us with a comprehensive overview of the topic.

Senior undergraduate and graduate students in outdoor education at Georgia College & State University examined the many policies that were submitted. Based on specific criteria provided by the editors, they proposed policy examples for each section in the *Manual of Accreditation Standards for Adventure Programs, Fourth Edition* (2005). Many of their selections are included in this book and their efforts helped us immensely. Special thanks to Bobby Oliver, Lindsay Martin, Lisa Marie Lombardi, Ben Strickland, Eric Sanderson, Holly Shell, Katie Schmitt, William Pritchard, Rusty Caspers, Leigh Anne Beaudreau, Sandefur Brownlow, Liz Speelman, Nat Johnson, Emily Marr, and Beth Sayers.

And as a last thought, Jude's dog, Tilly, deserves the biggest credit because without her we would not have had an excuse to take time out to walk in the Georgia woods and sit on the dock throwing balls for her to fetch, thus enabling us to have engaging conversations about many topics related to this book and our work on the Accreditation Council!

Jude Hirsch & Deb Sugerman

CHAPTER 1

ABOUT THE SECOND EDITION

The second edition of *Administrative Practices of AEE Accredited Programs* is formatted to specifically reflect the *Manual of Accreditation Standards for Adventure Programs, Fourth Edition* (Leemon, Pace, Ajango, & Wood, 2005). Since the inception of the Association for Experiential Education (AEE) Accreditation Program in 1992, the AEE Accreditation Council has been charged with developing standards for adventure programming. The fourth edition of the standards manual clarifies and simplifies the process of accreditation by combining several activities to reduce repetition and by adding several new standards that reflect what has been learned by the Accreditation Council about the accreditation process.

Chapters 4 through 8 correspond to specific chapters and sections in the standards manual. When possible, examples are provided for each section of standards; however some sections are not included if policy was not available from contributing organizations. Often a subset of policy, procedures, or curriculum was extracted from larger documents to focus on a specific area in the standards manual; therefore the reader should not assume that any example is a comprehensive indication of an organization's policy for a particular section. In some cases, for example, equipment or staffing policy and procedures are included in a specific activity policy. In these cases we may have elected to place the entire example in the relevant activity section to provide a comprehensive example of one approach to creating and implementing policy. In other cases policy, procedures, or curriculum materials that seemed to fit best in other chapters or subsections may have been used without using the remaining content in another part of the book. Figure 1.1 provides the index for the *Manual of Accreditation Standards for Adventure Programs, Fourth Edition,* which correspond to chapters four through eight in this book.

As we read documents submitted by accredited organizations, we concluded that there have been some important changes in policy format since the publication of the first edition of this book (1998). At that time policy seemed to be formatted around the external referents provided by standards. Much of the current policy submitted for this edition seems to be formatted around internal referents provided by the nature and work of an organization. AEE Accreditation Program standards are more integrated into policy now than they were earlier in the life of the Accreditation Program. In an effort to represent this change, the second edition provides an indication of the standards for which a policy may provide initial evidence of compliance. By listing specific standards, by number, prior to each policy, we hope to provide guidance for organizations in the process of conducting self-assessments of adventure programs. Our disclaimer is that we are not implying standard compliance for the particular context of any organization; the Accreditation Council holds authority for this judgment in accordance with its policy and procedures (Hirsch & Sugerman, 2005). However, we hope that this format will provide a starting point for thinking about evidence of compliance with standards contained in the *Manual of Accreditation Standards for Adventure Programs, Fourth Edition* (Leemon, Pace, Ajango, & Wood, 2005).

Gass (1998, p. v-vii) provides an excellent foreword to the use of the first edition of *Administrative Practices of Accredited Adventure Programs,* stating that four basic interactive variables will determine

Chapter 1. Philosophical, Educational, and Ethical Principles

Section 1. Philosophy and Education

Section 2. Ethical Principles

Chapter 2. Program Governance

Section 3. Program Governance

Chapter 3. Program Management, Operations, and Oversight

Section 4. Program Oversight and Management of Activities

Section 5. Human Resources: Staff Selection, Hiring, Training, and Supervision

Section 6. Transportation

Section 7. Equipment, Nutrition, and Hygiene

Section 8. Venue Selection and Appropriateness

Section 9. Environment and Culture

Section 10. International Considerations

Chapter 4. Technical Skills—Land Based

Section 11. Hiking, Camping, and Backpacking

Section 12. Climbing Activities

Section 13. Manufactured Climbing Walls

Section 14. Bicycle Touring and Mountain Biking

Section 15. Caving

Section 16. Horseback Riding and Pack Animals

Section 17. Winter Activities

Section 18. Running

Section 19. Initiative Games and Problem-Solving Exercises

Section 20. High and Low Challenge Courses

Section 21. Solos

Section 22. Service Projects

Section 23. Unaccompanied Activities

Section 24. Incidental Activities

Chapter 5. Technical Skills—Water Based

Section 40. Flat and White-Water Canoeing, Kayaking, and Rafting

Section 41. Sea Kayaking

Section 42. Sailing

Section 43. Snorkeling

Section 44. SCUBA Diving

Figure 1.1 **Contents of the *Manual of Accreditation Standards for Adventure Programs, Fourth Edition***

specific elements of "appropriate" practice: environment, activity, technical expertise, and participant profile. Growth in the field of adventure programming has challenged us to create a format for this book that reflects the diversity that Gass observed in 1998 and has continued to characterize the field of adventure programming. Therefore we have added quick reference information at the beginning of each policy example that will assist the reader in understanding the unique context in which a policy is used. Figure 1.2 provides an example of how information will appear before each policy and details about how to interpret quick reference information.

The Association for Experiential Education	
	F **Education**
	E **Rocky Mountain**
	C **Experiential Educators**
	S **1.01–1.05, 2.01–2.05**

F **Focus**

- Indicates the primary outcomes the organization seeks
- Includes recreation, education, training and development, or therapeutic settings
- Does not imply that programming is limited to this focus; see Chapter 3

E **Environment**

- Indicates the AEE region in which the organization is located
- Includes Rocky Mountain, West, Northwest, Heartland, Southeast, Northeast, Mid-Atlantic regions
- Does not imply that programming is limited to the region; see Chapter 3

C **Client**

- Indicates the primary client group with which the organization works
- Does not imply that programming is limited to this client group; see Chapter 3

S **Standards**

- Indicates standards for which the policy may be considered evidence of compliance
- Standard compliance should be assessed relative to organizational context
- Does not imply endorsement by the AEE Accreditation Program (see *Manual of Accreditation Standards for Adventure Programs, Fourth Edition*)

Figure 1.2 **Quick Reference Information**

To support quick reference information, Chapter 3 provides mission statements and contact information for accredited organizations that contributed to this book. We intend Chapter 3 to assist readers to better assess potential applications and adaptations of policy and procedures contained in this book. We cannot stress enough our gratitude to the organizations that contributed to this book. We also cannot stress enough the need to critically analyze each example in relation to the dynamic context in which it is being considered.

Standards

Because this book is closely linked to the fourth edition of the *Manual of Accreditation Standards for Adventure Programs,* it is important to understand how the Accreditation Council defines a standard. Figure 1.3 contains definitions offered by the *Merriam-Webster Online Dictionary* for "standard" and "criterion." These definitions imply key aspects that are inherent in the process by which the Association for Experiential Education Accreditation Program defines and interprets its responsibility to develop, adopt, maintain, evaluate, and revise standards. In order to ensure that standards remain current and applicable, feedback is sought from professionals, accreditation reviewers, and accredited programs.

Standard

1. Something established by authority, custom, or general consent as a model or example;
2. Something set up and established by authority as a rule for the measure of quantity, weight, extent, value, or quality;
3. A requirement of moral conduct.

Criterion

1. A standard on which a judgment or decision may be based;
2. A characterizing mark or trait.

Figure 1.3 **Definitions of Standards and Criterion**

Standards are intended to be used to help evaluate the overall quality and effectiveness of adventure-based programs. Individually, a standard may be thought of as a satisfactory, or reasonable and prudent practice, especially when that practice is compared to other adventure or outdoor organizations. For example, there are standards that apply to "hiring and using qualified staff." The standards within that section do not "tell" an organization what employee prerequisites to include; instead, it is up to the organization to prove to the Accreditation Council that it has a system in place to make sure all staff is qualified to lead activities. In this sense, the standards are not a prescriptive list that tells an organization how to function. Instead, they are broad in scope and are designed to be applicable to most, if not all, adventure-based education systems. AEE reviewers, and the Accreditation Program liaison and staff help interpret standards, compare them to a program's self-assessment study, and determine whether or not the organization's practices indeed meet the intent of each standard. Overall, the standards contained in the fourth edition of the manual are considered to be elements of effective and professional operations. They address philosophical, educational, and ethical practices; program management and program oversight; and most land- and water-based adventure activities.

Each standard is accompanied by an explanation that is intended to help readers understand the intent of a standard, or better clarify why the standard exists. Program managers are responsible for identifying that the organization is in compliance with a standard by determining specific evidence of compliance and, in the case of organizations seeking accreditation, providing proof in the self-assessment study of how the organization goes about meeting the intent of the standard. There is rarely one "right" way to do something, especially given the diversity of outdoor adventure organizations. In order for a review team and the Accreditation Council to feel confident that the organization meets all applicable standards, evidence must be compelling and verifiable by reviewing on-site documentation, conducting interviews, and observing programs and management systems.

AEE Accreditation is, to some degree, an endorsement of the quality of an organization's programs and risk management systems. However, accreditation has limits because it is an endorsement that an organization has met, or appears to have met, specific minimal requirements or standards at a given time. While many AEE standards focus on risk management practices and safety, accreditation is not a guarantee that clients or staff of accredited programs will be free from harm.

Forms

Forms support an organization's operational and management systems. They help clarify expectations and key pieces of information about accepted organizational and field practices, and other policy and procedures that are not left to staff discretion or judgment. Organizations use forms to track, communicate, and evaluate a wide range of administrative functions such as risk management, staff training and supervision, participant information, venue characteristics, equipment management, and curriculum and program planning. Effective organizations develop systems to help form users access appropriate forms for specific uses, evaluate forms to ensure that they are comprehensive and in compliance with industry standards, and integrate information collected on forms with administrative functions throughout the organization. Forms impact program quality by laying out information in a logical, concise, and user-friendly manner that is based on clearly defined and understood purposes. Forms educate administrators, program staff, participants, sponsors, and parents, often by providing a level of detail that may not be included in policy and procedures and ideally by providing data that is used to make a range of decisions at program, organizational, and professional levels. An accident/incident report form that includes data-collection needs of the Wilderness Risk Management Committee makes data submission far easier. Equipment management forms that support equipment-acquisition planning increase resource efficiency, and program design forms that provide essential information about intended and actual program delivery, route plans, and curriculum help subsequent delivery teams to avoid pitfalls and take advantage of the past experience. Examples of forms related to specific policy are included in subsequent chapters and many organizations that contributed to this book post forms on their websites. Readers are encouraged to use contact information provided in Chapter 3 to visit websites for additional examples of forms.

A Final Word

The job of selecting one policy over another for use in this book was difficult because all policy received from accredited organizations reflects a strong commitment to excellence and a willingness to further the goals of the Association for Experiential Education Accreditation Program (Figure 1.4). Our goal for this book is to provide examples of policy and procedures that have been examined by peers and determined to be in compliance with one set of industry standards. We hope the collection is comprehensive and indicative of the diversity in adventure programming.

The primary goals of the AEE Accreditation Program are to:

a. Inform and educate the public;

b. Protect the integrity of the field by advancing acceptable, prudent standards of practice; and

c. Make a reasonable assessment of organizations conducting a range of experiential programming.

Figure 1.4 **AEE Accreditation Program Goals**

Gass (1998, p. ix) clearly outlined the intent of the first edition of this book and its use. Since we could not say it better for the second edition, we offer a brief synopsis of his points:

- Appropriate and adequate practice will mean different things for different program contexts, therefore use the content of this book as a starting point for careful assessment and revision of administrative practice for the specific context in which an organization functions.
- Many exemplary practices that are occurring in the field have become evident during the AEE Accreditation Program review process, therefore "byproducts" of this process are sharing these practices and an understanding of the importance of engaging in and supporting external peer review opportunities.
- There are pivotal resources that many accredited programs use to create and sustain administrative practices; therefore know and use the expertise of professional associations and organizations (visit the Association for Experiential Education website, www.aee.org, for links to experiential education resources).

According to the *Accreditation Program Policy and Procedures Manual* (Hirsch & Sugerman, 2005), accreditation is a voluntary process of evaluation that credits an organization with conforming to a prescribed set of professional practices or standards. It attempts to serve at least three interests: the public, the industry, and the organization under review. The public's interests include having quality services from which to choose; having an objective, independent source of information about those services; and having a reasonable indication of the quality of those services. The interests of the industry include safeguarding the reputation of the field, elevating the practices of the field, providing avenues for self-governance, advocating for its members, and providing opportunities for continuing education and professional development. The organization's interests are many and include providing leadership to the field, improving the quality and performance of programs, preserving access to federal lands, preserving access to affordable insurance, and increasing the ability to attract financial and human resources.

It is our hope that this book will help students, practitioners, administrators, and participants deliver and experience the power of safe, environmentally sound, and effective adventure-based programs.

CHAPTER 2

POLICY AND PROCEDURES

This chapter provides an overview of policy and procedure development and management for adventure-based programs. It begins by offering a conceptual framework for understanding the larger context from which they derive authority and intention. It then goes on to provide an approach for writing policy and procedures (Section 2), and Section 3 focuses on enhancing capacity for managing policy.

Meaning and Context

Clarity about the meaning of policy and procedures is essential to the work of developing and managing a system for guiding the delivery of adventure-based programs and services. Testimony to the complexity of any policy initiative is that there is no one agreed-upon definition of policy. Figure 2.1 contains three definitions that highlight how policy may be used differently to regulate, frame decisions, and/or guide actions.

"A general guideline to regulate organizational action and conduct" (Campbell, 1998, p. 17).

"A philosophy, standard, or criterion that helps users exercise good judgment and discretion in the management of daily affairs" (Campbell, 1998, p. 17).

"A predetermined course of action established as a guide toward accepted business strategies and objectives" (Page, 2002, p. 2).

Figure 2.1: ***Definitions of Policy***

Policy provides the foundation on which operational procedures are built. It is revised less often than procedures because it is broader in scope. Programs that operate within larger organizations develop policy that is consistent with higher level documents and may actually defer to them when appropriate.

Procedures supplement policy by providing specific information about actions that may or should be taken to be in compliance with or reach goals inherent in policy. They are often referred to as instructions, protocols, or processes and are sometimes referred to as standard, local, or departmental operating procedures. They are written in a variety of formats such as lists, outlines, and flowcharts to illustrate sequence, relationships, or complexity. They often include actions, alternatives, consequences, examples, help sections, staff responsibilities, and forms. Sometimes procedures are written to specify or interpret higher levels of policy in an organization. Figure 2.2 contains definitions of procedures that underscore their tangible, specific, and factual nature.

"A method by which a policy can be accomplished; it provides the instructions necessary to carry out a policy statement" (Page, 2002, p. 2).

"A set of steps that must be followed to achieve the desired results" (Campbell, 1998, p. 17).

Figure 2.2 **Definitions of Procedures**

Policy and procedures create a framework for action within an organization and are meant to have some level of administrative authority and accountability. A simple way of understanding authority and, therefore, accountability is to distinguish between regulatory, obligatory, and optional factors associated with control and flexibility. Federal and state laws, ordinances, regulations, and codes are regulatory in the sense that an organization must comply with them and may be sanctioned for noncompliance. Examples include the Americans with Disabilities Act of 1990 (ADA) and the Occupational Safety and Health Act (OSHA). Administrative authority for regulating the ADA rests with the U.S. Equal Employment Opportunity Commission and for the OSHA with the U.S. Department of Labor. Organizations expected to comply with state and federal laws normally use policy and procedures as evidence of compliance and control, and flexibility is external. Accreditation standards are obligatory if they are not considered by governmental authority to be regulatory. Levels of control and flexibility are externally determined and penalties for noncompliance vary among accreditation programs. Accreditation programs may include standards that are very specific or defer to regulatory agencies and standards that can be broadly interpreted based on organizational context. Finally, policy may be optional in that the organization is not compelled by any external authority to self-regulate. Industry standards may or may not exist, and levels of control and flexibility are self-determined. In this case, if accepted or preferable industry standards exist, an organization may be held to a level of compliance after the fact of an accident or complaint. Penalty or sanction in this regard may then be determined by an external authority. It is essential to understand the larger context in which policy and procedures exist and their intended purpose in order to make decisions about their development and management. Figure 2.3 offers four reasons to develop and manage policy and procedures.

Quality Enhancement: Policy and procedures provide a consistent set of protocols that provide employees with limits, options, and general guidelines to use to make decisions that represent the organization's mission and standards of quality.

Documentation: Policy and procedure documents serve as a record of accepted actions and may help protect an organization, its employees, and the public. They also distinguish them from organizations that do not follow industry standards.

Regulation and Accreditation: Policy and procedures demonstrate compliance with regulatory and industry standards.

Integration: Policy and procedures serve as a reference point for administrative practices to ensure that they are based on a consistent value structure and set of rules.

Figure 2.3 **Purpose of Policy and Procedures**

Policy Development

Using a Systematic Approach

Establishing and maintaining policy and procedures is a systematic process. Page (2002) introduced the policy and procedures Improvement Cycle (PIPC) as a way of illustrating the constant adaptation and improvement that comes from systematic research, communication, evaluation, and revision (Figure 2.4). The stronger the systems that are put into place, the easier it will be to develop, implement, and evaluate policy and procedures.

Figure 2.4 Policy and Procedures Improvement Cycle

Putting together a team.

The first step in the process is putting together a team that will be effective in managing the system of developing, implementing, and evaluating policy and procedures. The team selected should have a variety of levels of experience within the organization (e.g., administrative, managerial, facilitative, instructional). This will give the team a diversity of perspectives from which to understand and develop policy. To aid the team in being most effective, the following should be considered:

- **Establish a Plan:** Strategize on the ultimate outcomes of the project and the process through which outcomes will be achieved. Develop a step-by-step outline of the stages of the process.
- **Establish a Timeline:** Agree on realistic deadlines for each stage of the process. Develop visuals (e.g., charts or graphs) that articulate deadlines, responsibilities, and timeframes.
- **Establish Responsibilities:** Ensure that all team members are clear on their role(s) within the team. Assign or choose responsibility for completion of stages in the process and/or sections of the documents.
- **Establish a Workflow:** Create a system of consistent feedback for tasks completed. This might include peer review, face-to-face meetings, and/or a specific system of editing documents.
- **Establish a Common Format:** Develop guidelines concerning how information will be reported. Agreement on format and writing style will ensure consistency and reduce editing time.

Gathering Information

This stage of the development process entails gathering data and information from a variety of sources that will aid in the final decision-making process of what will ultimately be included in the organizational policy and procedures. This stage involves examining both internal and external sources for documents and information.

Internal sources.

Consider information that currently exists within the organization that will impact the development of policies. Gather and review internal print sources (e.g., existing policy and procedures, training materials, internal memos, administrative documentation). Consult with organizational staff that has a variety of roles to find out what policy and procedures they currently follow and what information they think needs to be included or changed from existing documents. This information can be gathered through questionnaires, interviews, or direct observation.

External sources.

Consider research information from external sources that will strengthen and add to existing internal documents. Print sources include vendor recommendations, standards from a variety of industries (e.g., American Camping Association, American Canoe Association, American Mountain Guides Association, Association for Experiential Education, Association for Challenge Course Technology) and existing documents from similar organizations. Consult with experts (e.g., lawyers, technical skill experts) in specific areas to obtain more information and interview staff from similar organizations to acquire suggestions concerning process and content.

Determining Content

After gathering extensive data from internal and external sources, the next step is to cull the information and decide what content should be included in the policy and procedures. This should be done systematically to ensure that what is chosen meets organizational needs, goals and objectives, and stated outcomes. Several factors influence what content is included in policy documents. Consider:

- **Regulations:** regulation and accreditation standards at the local, state, and national levels that must be followed.
- **Benchmarks:** leading organizations conducting similar operations include in their policy and procedure documents.
- **Legal Issues**: legal consequences of including or excluding certain policies or procedures.
- **Current Practice:** practices and protocols currently used by staff and the organization.
- **User Groups:** the level of competence, independence, and experience of staff that will be using the documents.
- **Time and Resources:** the team's logistical abilities and limitations when deciding the breadth and depth of content.

Writing the Documents

The team will decide the type and amount of documents developed, whether the policy and procedures should be housed in one document, or whether it would be more practical to have two or more documents. Smaller adventure programs tend to have one central program manual that houses all policy and procedures. Larger programs may have a central program manual that houses general policies and procedures and separate manuals that detail policies and procedures for more specific programs (e.g., challenge course or indoor climbing wall). The team will also decide how the policy and procedures will be formatted and written. Depending on the objective of the documents, they may be formatted to follow government regulations, industry standards, or programmatic needs. Considerations for format include:

- **Developing Consistency:** Create a system that organizes, differentiates, and clearly displays information (e.g., font, margins, indentation, numbering, punctuation, use of white space), and use this system throughout all documents.
- **Developing Visual Tools:** Create a system of various visual tools to be used within the document that can quickly and easily convey information (e.g., lists, checklists, text boxes, flowcharts).
- **Reducing Redundancy:** Create a system that cross-references information applicable to a number of sections to reduce redundancy and make the documents easier to use.
- **Creating Clear Referencing:** Create a system that allows readers to reference needed information quickly (e.g., table of contents, clearly marked subsections within the document, detailed indexes and glossaries)

Once the content and general format for the policy and procedures has been established, the team will make decisions on organizing information on the micro level. A key element to keep in mind when writing policy is the concept of appropriate ambiguity; policy language should be consistent with intent. The level of ambiguity written into policies is based on the legal implications of the statement, how precisely the organization wants to control the actions of staff, the level of staff competency, and the consequences associated with not following a policy. Some situations imply a complex set of variables in which a subjective interpretation of a policy is preferred, while others entail specificity associated with external regulation. When ambiguous statements are used, criteria for professional judgment should be clear.

Using promissory statements legally binds the organization to abide to a policy. Words such as "always" or "never" mean exactly that; a single exception can open the organization to legal action. This type of language is often appropriate in relation to safety issues. The words "shall" and "will" imply a legal commitment to a given action. Qualifiers such as "under normal operating conditions" can be used to restrict the scope of promissory language allowing for exceptions in some circumstances.

The use of technical writing skills will help to make the documents clear, concise, and user friendly. Considerations include the following:

- **Use appropriate form:** Use a consistent voice and tense throughout the documents; use parallel sentence structure to express similar ideas in a similar form; and simplify words and phrases.
- **Avoid negative wording:** Write statements in a positive format as readers are more receptive to positively stated policy and procedures.
- **Use socially sensitive language:** Use language that is fair, sensitive, and respectful to the ethnicity, socioeconomic status, and the varied values of your staff and clients.
- **Define acronyms and avoid jargon:** Define acronyms and specialized terms the first time they are used in a specific section, or develop a glossary of terms. Avoid the use of field-specific jargon.
- **Use appropriate level of detail:** Strike a balance between being specific and eliminating unnecessary detail.

Policy Management

The concept of "implied contract" legally binds an organization to follow its policy and procedures in all states except Florida, Texas, and North Carolina (Campbell, 1998). Because policy is an expressed contract with an organization's constituents, implementing and managing policy is not only essential for quality control and continuous improvement, but it also serves as a reference for other administrative functions within an organization. Assuming that documents are well written for their intended use, adventure-based programs often experience the same challenges in implementation and management faced by any organization. Adventure-based programs may experience additional challenges for a variety of reasons: Field staff may be out of contact with each other across shifts; high staff turnover rates or disproportionate numbers of contract staff may occur; industry standards change rapidly across the wide range of technical activities that are typically found in adventure programming; and environmental factors demand that policy permit some degree of interpretation and judgment on the part of field staff. Experts suggest that it is important to create a system for implementing and managing policy so that employees develop a sense of continuity and are not surprised by changes that they did not anticipate. The challenge is to enhance an organization's capacity to develop, implement, and maintain policy by nurturing a culture that cultivates ownership. For the purpose of this section, implementation and management are treated separately to clearly distinguish between implementing new policy and procedures, and managing those already in use.

Implementation

Managers and staff tend to value policy documents differently and feel compelled to apply policy at different levels of use. One common reason for not implementing policy is inadequacy of procedures (Wieringa, Moore, & Barnes, 1998). Common examples of inadequacy include excessive use of obvious procedures for simple tasks, inaccurate or outdated procedures, and excessively redundant and lengthy documents. Therefore, the first step toward successful implementation is to use the team approach discussed earlier when developing policy documents. Multiple stakeholder input about issues related to levels of use and topics of concern is an essential implementation strategy.

A clear system of communication to inform and motivate users may include a variety of channels and opportunities for engagement that are required and optional. Some examples of system components are:

- **Training:** Creatively integrate new, complex, or confusing bits and pieces into training. Training offers an opportunity to identify muddy points, practice processes, develop judgment, and hear what works better than in the last version. Consistency across training is important as is documenting attendance, especially if it is difficult to conduct all-staff training.
- **Ongoing Communication:** Start with communication channels and opportunities that are already in existence such as meetings, team distribution lists, mailboxes, bulletin boards, and staff newsletters. Use technology creatively to support the system, not drive the system.
- **Support:** Adopt continuous improvement approaches to supervision, methods of awards and recognition, and the allocation of resources to enhance implementation at the individual, team, and organizational levels. Opportunities to coach, mentor, or understand another's world view about policy are both informal and formal in most organizations.
- **Redundancy:** Employ a variety of means to communicate, including using an accessible central repository (i.e., a secure area on the web), multiple means to disseminate information (electronic and hard copies), and hyperlinked cross-references within electronic documents.

- **Accountability:** System accountability begins with clear explanations about consequences for noncompliance. Building accountability into system components may be as simple as adding a signature line to a particular form or as complicated as developing assessment strategies like quizzes, skill checklists, or self-assessment requirements for specific responsibilities. Some organizations require staff to document that they have read, understand, and will implement policy and procedures in their role as an agent of the organization.

Maintain

The ongoing maintenance of policy and procedure often slips through the cracks until an incident occurs or the organization is faced with preparing for external or internal reviews. Administrators who create and integrate feedback loops into how the organization does business on a daily basis make it easier for everyone in the organization to feed data into the system. Feedback loops should include a range of review, revision, and communication activities that suit the context of the organization.

Review

Finding ways to deposit information on the right form or in the right hands so that it makes its way into the policy review system helps ensure that information is not lost or overlooked. There are numerous opportunities to create two-way communication systems that enhance ongoing policy review, including: listing standing items related to policy review on meeting agendas; establishing organized committees to review specific components of policy documents; asking staff and clients to evaluate the program; and adhering to internal and external reporting requirements set by parent organizations and accrediting agencies. Using outside evaluators to evaluate policies, training, and practice, adding an external person to an organization's risk management committee, or establishing an advisory committee able to provide external support to managers often prompts an organization to ask policy questions that might otherwise be overlooked.

Revise

Ongoing policy revisions should be based on continuous input from constituents engaged in the review processes. Some revisions require immediate implementation due to changes in regulatory or industry standards; others, like format and typos, may accumulate and be included in the regular overhaul cycle. It is suggested that an in-depth review and revision of policy and procedures should take place every 5 years at minimum. Many adventure programs conduct in-depth reviews and revisions in conjunction with new editions of accreditation standards. Some organizations structure policy documents to permit immediate revisions and to accommodate a cycle of review and revisions to primary sections by structuring policy documents so that smaller sections can be revised and replaced without having to alter page numbers or reprint the entire document.

Inform

Policy and procedure changes are communicated through the implementation channels discussed earlier. Some organizations maintain a secure web page where policy and other announcements are posted, others send announcements by a staff distribution list, clearly indicating the subject and the level of importance of the message, and others post announcements in a staff meeting room on a specific color of paper that is not used for any other purpose. Regardless of what channels of communication are used, announcements should be clear and the date of the revision as well as the demarcation in policy should be noted. Notices should include the answers to the following questions to help foster implementation, integrity, and consistency:

- **What** is the specific name and document ID for the change?
- **How** is the change different from past practices?
- **Why** is the change necessary?
- **Who** does the change directly or indirectly impact?
- **When** does the change go into effect?
- **Where** can one get additional information and assistance to implement the change?

CHAPTER 3

CONTRIBUTING ORGANIZATIONS

Currently 52 organizations or specific programs within an organization are accredited by the Association for Experiential Education Accreditation Program. All accredited organizations offer adventure-based programs, however their range of settings, clients, and intended outcomes varies considerably. Some offer recreation opportunities in higher education, community recreation, or residential camps, while others use adventure activities for teaching subject matter through direct experience at public or private schools, or outdoor education centers that offer programs and services to schools or school districts. Organizations that use experiential strategies for human resource training and development are also represented in this book, as are organizations that use adventure-based interventions to address a wide range of therapeutic issues. All organizations currently accredited by AEE were invited to participate in this project. Policy and procedures submitted by 16 organizations was selected for inclusion based on the need to align examples with The Manual of Accreditation Standards for Adventure Programs, Fourth Edition. *Selection does not imply that accredited organizations not included in the book were inferior in any way. Often their policy and procedures were aligned with the previous edition of the standards manual and may remain so until the next accreditation site visit. At this time organizations seeking initial or continuing accreditation demonstrate compliance with the current edition of the standards manual through the submission of a detailed, documented self-assessment study and interviews, an on-site document examination, and interviews and observations that take place during the site visit. Readers should use this chapter to develop an understanding of the unique context in which an organization develops and manages the administrative practices contained in subsequent chapters.*

Albuquerque Academy

Mission: We believe that children's lives change when their natural passion for learning is nurtured and transformed into habits of life-long learning and reflection. We believe that the world changes as these children learn to serve country and community with wisdom, conviction, and compassion. In light of these beliefs,

- We serve students of talent and character, offering them an education that broadens their perspectives, sharpens their minds, strengthens their bodies, and engages their hearts.
- We commit to creating a caring, inclusive, and just community, using the geography and culture of our home in the Southwest to enrich our educational programs and to foster creativity, personal balance, and a connection to the natural world.
- We devote our resources to ensure economic accessibility to our students and to support the wider community through outreach and community service.

- We entrust this mission to our graduates and successors as we preserve our resources and serve the generations of children to come.

Contact Information:

Albuquerque Academy
6400 Wyoming Boulevard NE
Albuquerque, NM 87109
(505) 828-3200
www.aa.edu

Boojum Institute

Mission: To unlock potential, promote self-discovery, and inspire growth.

Contact Information:

Boojum Institute
P.O. Box 711
Pioneertown, CA 92268
(760) 228-2311
www.boojum.org

Camp Woodson

Mission: Camp Woodson is a short-term, voluntary, Department of Juvenile Justice and Delinquency Prevention prerelease program for incarcerated youth from North Carolina. Camp Woodson uses outdoor, therapeutic, adventure-based activities designed to build self-esteem and responsible community membership.

Contact Information:

Camp Woodson
741 Old US Highway 70
Swannanoa, NC 28778
(828) 686-9595
www.ncdjjdp.org/facilities/woodson

Chadwick School

Mission: Chadwick, a K–12 school founded in 1935, is dedicated to academic excellence and to the development of self-confident individuals of exemplary character. Students are prepared through experience and self-discovery to accept the responsibilities inherent in personal freedom and to contribute positively to contemporary society. The Chadwick community is committed to living in accordance with its core values of respect, responsibility, honesty, fairness, and compassion.

The school aims to create a learning environment that is challenging, diverse, and supportive where talented, dedicated faculty and students are encouraged to interact in an atmosphere of mutual respect and trust. Students are prepared for rigorous future educational endeavors in a manner that enables them to discover the joys of learning and the importance of community.

In all of its programs, Chadwick seeks to discover and nurture the special gifts each student possesses; to deepen each student's understanding of the complexities of the world; and to inspire each to realize his or her full potential. With a clear recognition of the needs and capabilities of students of differing ages and experiences, and with the support of parents, the school implements its mission:

- By ensuring small classes that promote critical thinking, analytical reasoning, and effective communication skills;
- By encouraging students to evaluate the choices they make based on a carefully considered sense of right and wrong;
- By gradually guiding students from dependent to independent learning;
- By providing expanding opportunities for individual self-direction and creativity as a student grows and matures;
- By providing a student body that is enriched by economic, social, and ethnic diversity and by individuals who possess varying kinds of and degrees of intellectual, artistic, and physical abilities;
- By stressing high academic standards and a strong commitment to the process of learning;
- By creating an environment for learning that is stimulating, innovative, tolerant, enjoyable, and that encourages intellectual inquiry and curiosity;
- By fostering in each student a healthy self-concept and a sense of personal value through recognition and encouragement of individual potential and talent;
- By encouraging student involvement in the community and community involvement in the school;
- By aiming to achieve a balance, perhaps different for each individual, between the cognitive and affective aspects of learning;
- By teaching students to evaluate evidence and experience and to understand the dynamic between individuality and social responsibility;
- By stressing the fundamental values of integrity and trust.

Contact Information:

Chadwick School
26800 S. Academy Drive
Palos Verdes Peninsula, CA 90274
(310) 377-1543
www.chadwickschool.org

Charleston County Parks & Recreation Department

Mission: The Charleston County Parks & Recreation Commission will improve the quality of life in Charleston County by offering a diverse system of park facilities, programs, and services.

P—Provision of park and recreation facilities in an efficient and economical manner.

A—Acquisition of park land and open space.

R—Recreation services and programs to meet countywide needs.

K—Knowledge through the interpretation of the county's natural, historic, and cultural resources.

S—Stewardship through responsible management.

Contact Information:

Charleston County Parks & Recreation Department
861 Riverland Drive
Charleston, SC 29412
(843) 762-2172
www.ccprc.com

Georgia College & State University Academic Program and Georgia College Outdoor Education Center

Academic Program Mission: Outdoor education academic programs in the Department of Kinesiology in the School of Health Sciences include the B.S. in Outdoor Education, the M.Ed. in Health and Physical Education with emphasis in Outdoor Education Administration, and the minor in Outdoor Education.

The Department of Kinesiology offers outdoor education academic programs in accordance with the mission and principles of Georgia College & State University. The department is a learning community of caring, committed faculty and students dedicated to excellence in teaching, scholarship, and service within the liberal arts tradition. Its innovative curricula focus on the interactions among movement, personal growth, and wellness. Faculty and students work with diverse populations in a variety of settings in order to empower others to lead healthy lifestyles and to function more effectively in society.

Outdoor education academic programs support the mission of the Department of Kinesiology by seeking to develop students who are prepared to make professional contributions to a variety of recreation, education, training and development, and therapeutic settings. Outdoor education programs and services are used in these settings to achieve movement skills, personal growth, and wellness within diverse populations.

We serve graduate and undergraduate students, graduate assistants, and faculty through academic courses and related opportunities for professional development and service learning. We also serve the Association for Experiential Education (AEE) Accreditation Program through compliance with accredited standards and interaction with the network of AEE accredited organizations.

We are committed to teaching and learning that integrates respect for human diversity and the natural world; service to local, national, and global communities; experiential learning; and professionalism. We offer programs of study that challenge students to become excellent professional outdoor educators.

Georgia College Outdoor Education Center Mission: The GCSU Outdoor Education Center provides excellent technical training, outdoor recreation education, leadership training, and group development experiences. We serve outdoor education professionals, GCSU faculty, staff, students, and members of the surrounding community. We provide programs and services led by competent personnel in compliance with the Association for Experiential Education accreditation standards. The Outdoor Education Center seeks to enhance the mission of the state's public liberal arts university through safe, environmentally sound, and effective programs and services.

Contact Information:

Georgia College & State University
Coordinator of Outdoor Education Programs
Director of the Georgia College Outdoor Education Center
CB 065
Milledgeville, GA 31061
(478) 445-1218/4072/5186
http://hercules.gcsu.edu/~jhirsch/

National Outdoor Leadership School

Mission: The mission of the National Outdoor Leadership School is to be the leading source and teacher of wilderness skills and leadership that serve people and the environment.

Contact Information:

NOLS
284 Lincoln Street
Lander, WY 82520
(800) 710-6657
(307) 332-5300
www.nols.edu

Prescott College

Mission: It is the mission of Prescott College to educate students of diverse ages and backgrounds to understand, thrive in, and enhance our world community and environment. We regard learning as a continuing process and strive to provide an education that will enable students to live productive lives while achieving a balance between self-fulfillment and service to others. Students are encouraged to think critically and act ethically with sensitivity to both the human community and the biosphere. Our philosophy stresses experiential learning and self-direction within an interdisciplinary curriculum.

Contact Information:

Prescott College
220 Grove Avenue
Prescott, AZ 86301
(877) 350-2100
www.prescott.edu

Red Top Meadows

Mission: Our goal is to help adolescent boys improve the quality of their lives and to increase the likelihood that they will become respectful members of their community. Our students learn how to initiate positive change in their lives and discover more about themselves and their relationships with others. RTM helps our students and their families find solutions to personal problems and family conflicts.

Contact Information:

Red Top Meadows
P.O. Box 290
Wilson, WY 83014
(307) 733-9098
www.redtopmeadows.org

Santa Fe Mountain Center

Mission: We are dedicated to promoting personal discovery and social change among youth, families, and groups through the use of creative learning experiences in wilderness, community, and cultural environments.

Contact Information:

Santa Fe Mountain Center
P.O. Box 449
Tesuque, NM 87574
(505) 983-6158
www.sf-mc.com

Team Leadership Results, LLC

Mission: Our mission at Team Leadership Results is to provide quality outdoor adventure-based training tailored to organizations that seek increased productivity, quality, and innovation through collaborative leadership.

Contact Information:

Team Leadership Results, LLC
124 Vassar Lane
San Antonio, TX 78212
(210) 822-1542
www.team-leadership.com

Thompson Island Outward Bound

Mission: Thompson Island Outward Bound is a not-for-profit organization whose primary purpose is to provide adventurous and challenging experiential learning programs that inspire character development, compassion, community service, environmental responsibility and academic achievement. Our organization principally serves early adolescents from all economic and social communities of greater metropolitan Boston, and the institutions and adults who support them.

Contact Information:

Thompson Island Outward Bound
P.O. Box 127
Boston, MA 02127
(617) 328-3900
www.thompsonisland.org

University of New Hampshire Outdoor Education Program

Mission: The mission of the Outdoor Education Program is to promote the use of physical activity in outdoor/adventure environments to create healthier individuals and social change.

Contact Information:

Outdoor Education
University of New Hampshire
Department of Kinesiology
124 Main Street
Durham, NH 03824
(603) 862-2024
http://www.shhs.unh.edu/kin_oe

University of North Carolina—Carolina Adventures

Mission: The Carolina Adventures Outdoor Education Center is a center for experiential learning. Experiential learning is simply the process of learning by doing. Common goals for all Carolina Adventures programs are to:

- promote hands-on learning;
- build an increased sense of community on the UNC campus;
- empower and challenge all participants to reach beyond their personal limits—physically, mentally, and socially—resulting in increased self-confidence;
- promote minimum-impact practices and foster a greater appreciation for our natural environment;
- offer participants the opportunity to recognize and develop their leadership abilities;
- have *fun*.

Contact Information:

University of North Carolina, Chapel Hill
Carolina Adventures
UNC CB#3433
Chapel Hill, NC 27599
(919) 962-4179
http://campusrec.unc.edu/OEC/

University of North Carolina at Charlotte—Venture Center

Mission: The mission of the Venture Center enhances the overarching educational mission of the University of North Carolina at Charlotte. We foster student development using experiential, hands-on learning. We engage people in meaningful and challenging activities to address individual, leadership, community, and environmental issues.

- We strive to be a catalyst to increase participants' sense of self-worth and personal responsibility.
- We provide opportunities for the development of leadership qualities through training and positions of responsibility.
- We design activities for small groups in which participants experience a sense of community.
- We encourage teamwork and open communication.
- We regard the stewardship of our earth's resources as a crucial focus. We promote the awareness and preservation of the natural environment.
- Our ultimate commitment is to safety, quality programs, and responsible stewardship of the earth's resources.

Contact Information:

Venture
UNC Charlotte, Bonnie E. Cone Building
9201 University City Boulevard
Charlotte, NC 28223
(704) 687-2486
www.uncc.edu/venture

The Westminster Schools

Mission: Westminster is a Christian, independent day school for boys and girls, which seeks to develop the whole person for college and for life through excellent education.

Contact Information:

The Westminster Schools
1424 West Paces Ferry Road, NW
Atlanta, GA 30327
(404) 609-6202
www.westminster.net

Wilderness Treatment Center

Mission: It is the mission of Wilderness Treatment Center to assist young men in their recovery from drug addiction. It is our goal to introduce the young men and their families to a way of life free from drugs and alcohol with an increased self-esteem and feeling of empowerment. Through our innovative program, incorporating the principles embodied in the 12 Steps, we instill motivation and hope for the future. Blending traditional and experiential therapies, the young men and their families create a new beginning, a new freedom, and a new happiness.

Contact Information:

Wilderness Treatment Center
200 Hubbard Dam Road
Marion, MT 59925
(406) 854-2832
www.wildernessaltschool.com

CHAPTER 4

PHILOSOPHICAL, EDUCATIONAL, AND ETHICAL PRINCIPLES

This chapter corresponds to Chapter 1 in the Manual of Accreditation Standards for Adventure Programs, Fourth Edition, *which focuses on standards that are applicable to the educational design of a program's activities. Compliance indicates that activities are experiential in nature, based on sound objectives, sequential, and conducted ethically. Philosophy and education standards address mission alignment, instructional goals and outcomes, experiential education principles, and the nature and limits to the confidentiality of participants. Ethics standards were developed with the assistance of the American Psychological Association (APA) and the American Association of Marriage and Family Therapy (AAMFT). These standards address the nature and limits to the confidentiality of participants and the need for staff to conduct their work in a responsible, honest, competent, respectful, and caring manner. As is often the case, policy and procedures related to the philosophical, educational, and ethical principles by which an organization manages its practice are difficult to separate into clearly defined units that relate to specific standards. Therefore, the reader will find a range of examples that integrate several standards into one or more sections of policy.*

Camp Woodson	*F* **Therapeutic**
	E **Southeast Region**
	C **Incarcerated Youth**
	S **1.01–1.05**

Camp Woodson Is a Therapeutic Adventure-Based Wilderness Program

There has been a proliferation of therapeutic camping programs in the U.S. over the past 20 years. Camp Woodson is unique in that we also add adventure-based" and "wilderness" to the formula. In 1976, Camp Woodson was founded on the idea that the wilderness provides a unique environment for learning, change, and personal growth. As our student population has changed to include more serious offenders and more seriously emotionally disturbed children, our focus has necessarily become more therapeutic. Throughout this evolution, however, we have maintained a wilderness focus.

The wilderness environment is particularly applicable to delinquents, as the intensity of the experience facilitates cooperation, trust, and a healthy outlet for adolescent "machismo." The wilderness provides "appropriate" means for adolescents to prove themselves, to make a rite of passage, and to find an adrenaline rush that doesn't involve drugs or breaking the law. The wilderness also provides staff a level of control and a position of authority that would not exist in conditions more familiar to students.

Adventure-Based Programs

Camp Woodson has close ties and many similarities with Outward Bound. Outward Bound espouses the following educational goals: (a) to encourage personal growth; (b) to develop courage and willpower; (c) to live efficiently and rely on one's natural resources; (d) to develop interpersonal competence; (e) to develop the desire and ability to serve others (Katz & Kolb, 1967, p. 44). Camp Woodson, like Outward Bound, uses adventure activities such as climbing, canoeing, expeditioning, ropes courses, to accomplish the above goals. The critical point is that adventure activities are not the goal—they are the means to the goal. Adventure education is our treatment modality. Adventure adds the pizzazz, the excitement, and the motivation. It makes this experience very real and oftentimes unforgettable.

Dunk 'Em and Dry 'Em

Wilderness adventure programs will have many hardships. We believe that challenge, stress, hard work, discomfort, and hardship can be appropriate and useful in building student's character and self-esteem. It's fine to push hard most of the time, but it's equally important to kick back to rest, reflect, and rejuvenate some of the time. This can be a difficult call in our program because our staff rotates in and out with the kids. It is important to check in with the program coordinator and the previous shift to get a big-picture understanding of what the group has been through. You may be rested and excited to go climbing, but the students may have gone to bed without supper and spent a wet, sleepless night dealing with thunderstorms and skunks. Flexibility is key!

> **"We are better than we know. If we can be made to see it, perhaps for the rest of our lives we will be unwilling to settle for less."**
>
> —Kurt Hahn

Square Pegs Don't Fit in Round Holes

Camp Woodson is a student-centered program that focuses on the individual needs of each student. We recognize that every student brings with him or her a unique set of challenges. Our goal is to provide life skills that enable our students to return to their communities and be productive members of society. A good number of the camp students who are selected are unable to succeed in the mainstream training school program. All have failed in their communities. Camp Woodson's unique approach and individualized, tailored treatment plan is often the key in helping these students make the changes necessary to return to their communities.

The Bottom Line—Safety and Security

Safety and security must always remain our number one concern; they are the foundation of our program. Treatment cannot occur unless we maintain a safe, secure environment, both physically and emotionally. We are at our best when we go beyond issues of safety and security and work toward our treatment goals. Ideally, the bulk of our energy and resources will go into the treatment program. However, circumstances do not always permit this, and we must always be prepared to back up and deal with immediate and pressing issues of safety and security.

Positive Relationships Between Staff and Students Is Critical for Change

This program operates on the assumption that positive, friendly, sincere relationships between staff and students can facilitate positive changes in a student's behavior. The staff/student relationship is a critical element in our success and one that each of us must work diligently toward building. The exemplary staff is one who listens well, takes kids seriously and shows respect to all kids, at all times. We use as a base Glasser's Reality Therapy/Control Theory Model. It all begins with the first step—becoming a friend. The best way to negotiate the many barriers toward creating this friendship is to make sure you *have fun* with your students and show them that you really care about their personal needs. Administer karmic repair and Band-Aids liberally.

Our program is designed to provide both individual and group counseling. Group meetings in a positive peer culture can be very powerful for students. When used inappropriately group meetings can turn into volatile group disturbances. Staff must develop the art of knowing when to "divide and conquer" and when to call a group and turn up the heat. Facilitating a group takes skill and experience but is one of the most effective tools we have when used appropriately. We must take the responsibility to set the boundaries and teach the skills for students to interact appropriately in a group counseling session. This skill is not emphasized in training school. Students can have group meetings in their tent groups, in an activity group or with the entire group. Our staff-to-student ratio far surpasses any other program in the DJJDP system and allows us many options.

> **"If the teacher carries out the role properly, students will accomplish more than they ever could on their own. Yet if the approach is truly student centered, they may not be aware the teacher had a role at all."**
>
> —Chapman, *Journal of Experiential Education, 15*(2), p. 17

Trust Without Trusting

Trust is a critical component of any relationship. Our students may confuse trust with love. New staff frequently falls into a trap of trusting our kids too much, too soon. Let us not confuse our love or caring for a child—that is unconditional. Trust should not automatically be given to any adolescent. Adolescents may not admit it, but they are aware, at some level, of their incompletely developed coping abilities and find security in rules, structures, and limits. If we are too trusting we will unintentionally increase the adolescent's anxiety through lack of limit setting and structure. The result is acting-out behavior.

It is important to make a distinction with our kids between trust and trustworthiness. Trust is our willingness and ability to place faith in another individual's trustworthiness. Trustworthiness has two parts: First is the measure of predictability in general or unknown situations; second is the match between a person's verbal commitment and his or her behavior? Both require a track record to develop. Trust should be earned by the adolescent's ability and willingness to engage in trustworthy behavior. (*Adolescent Counselor,* July 1991, p. 20).

Student: "Don't you trust me?"

Staff: "I would like very much to trust you. Let's discuss how you can show me you are trustworthy."

Empowering Your Students

Our goal is to empower students to make good choices in their lives. So how do we empower? A 17-year-old runaway named Greg published this in the Michigan Runaway Network News (*Adolescent Counselor,* July 1991, p. 24) "Empowerment is not something that you can give me; it is an inside out job. Instead, here are some other really good E words that you can use to help youth."

"Encourage: Show me and tell me that you believe in me."

"Envision: Help me to see all the possibilities."

"Excite: I really do want to feel positive about my future."

"Elevate: Help me to help myself rise above adversity."

"Example: Be the change that you're trying to create."

"Endure: Help me remember that change takes time."

"Enable: Give me the chance to try."

"Enrich: If I help to improve another life, it enriches my own."

"There is, in every child, the wherewithal to succeed at something if someone just respects them, believes in them, encourages them, challenges them, gives them a chance—and if they are able to believe this themselves."

—Conrad, *Journal of Experiential Education, 15*(2), p. 14

The Reason for Freezin'

Adventure education is based on the belief that shared adventure and hardship brings a group together as an effective team. It removes the veneer that people hide behind and brings out one's true character. It provides a natural setting (rather than a contrived, sit-in-my-office-and-tell-me-your-problems type approach) to bring out positive and negative behaviors. It also provides students the opportunity to change undesirable behaviors, to leave behind their past and become the persons they would like to be. Adventure experiences supply an ample amount of natural consequences to both reward and reprimand students for their actions. "Skunk therapy" can teach a tent group of students to hang their food much more effectively than any counselor commentary. It allows the staff to be a supportive friend while Mother Nature hands out the consequences. Shared adversity brings people together and heightens the group's level of trust and understanding.

Staff must control the physical and emotional safety of our activities while at the same time allowing students to feel an appropriate level of adventure. Adventure involves challenge, risk, real and perceived danger, dealing with the unknown and pushing one's personal limits. Adventure is both exciting and scary at the same time. It brings out feelings and emotion and all the spice in life. Skilled staff will be able to control the stress meter by dialing it up or down when appropriate. Do we off-trail hike or take the road? Do we make camp or push on to our destination in the rain and dark? This is the art of instructing. It takes skill, experience, and an intuitive connection with the staff, students, and environment to make good calls. We must allow students to experience perceived danger while at the same time ensuring the real danger is kept at safe and acceptable levels.

> **"I am glad I did it, partly because it was well worth it, and chiefly because I shall never have to do it again."**
>
> —Mark Twain

Epic adventures can provide incredible learning opportunities for students. Epics can take the form of horrendous off-trail hikes, bear or skunk encounters, downpours, blizzards, etc. These unplanned and impactful challenges often teach unforgettable lessons that will stay with a person for the rest of his/her life. Staff may avoid epics out of their own insecurities or desire to avoid discomfort. Epics tend not to be fun or comfortable, but they can be the most powerful learning experience you ever give students. Look at epics as incredible learning opportunities. Learn to allow your students the opportunity to experience epics without stepping outside the safety boundaries of our program.

The Adventure-Based Learning Process

The adventure-based learning process is physically and psychologically demanding and used to promote interpersonal and intrapersonal growth. First, students engage in an experience that causes a state of disequilibrium by being placed in a novel setting and a cooperative environment. Students are then presented with a unique problem-solving situation that is designed to lead to feelings of accomplishment. The experience is augmented by processing, which promotes generalization and transfer to future endeavors (Nadler and Luckner, 1992).

Processing Is Key in the Experiential Learning Cycle

Processing is an activity that is used to encourage individuals to reflect, describe, analyze, and communicate what they have recently experienced. It forms the cornerstone of an effective adventure-based learning experience. The four phases of a learning cycle are experience, reflection, processing, and application. Reflection involves structuring time for individuals to look back and examine what they saw, felt, and thought during the event. We miss the boat and disrupt opportunities for learning if we just barge right into another experience without completing this cycle. Processing involves sharing what they saw, felt, and thought during the event. Our intent is to help students figure out what happened at a cognitive, effective, and behavioral level before, during, and after the activity. It is at this stage that students begin to intellectually transfer leanings to similar occurrences in other settings. Application is the final part of the learning cycle. Application involves applying what they have learned during the experience to actual situations in which they are involved in the woods or at home or school. The question is "now what? What did you learn and what are you going to do differently?" It is a time to make specific plans for experimenting with different ways of thinking, feeling, and behaving (Nadler and Luckner, 1992).

Staff Consistency

The glue that holds our program together through the challenges, crises, and epics is staff consistency. Our students are excellent manipulators and will look for opportunities to divide us or play us against each other (i.e., Student: "But Tex said we could cuss at each other." Staff: "I find that hard to believe, but we'll ask Tex what he said. Do you understand that I'm telling you cussing is unacceptable and needs to stop?"). If mom doesn't give them what they want, they'll go to dad. It is very important that we communicate clearly with each other and that we support each other in front of the students. It is fine to have a disagreement with another staff, but it's best to work this out behind the scenes. Avoid blaming or badmouthing other staff or shifts in front of kids. We need to handle our inevitable disagreements as professionals.

If Your Only Tool Is a Hammer, Everything Begins to Look Like a Nail

Educating children is not a one-size-fits-all proposition. Every student is unique and every situation is different. To work at maximum effectiveness we must have the resources to generate multiple alternatives in any given situation. Some people refer to this as a "Bag of Tricks." If what you are doing isn't working, consider trying something else. "I've told him 1,000 times, blah, blah, blah." Will telling him 1,001 times make a difference? Probably not. We need to be consistent, and we need to acknowledge when we are being ineffective and try something new and creative. Develop a creative repertoire of responses to every situation.

"Would you tell me please which way I ought to go from here?" asked Alice.

"That depends a good deal on where you want to go ," said the Cat

"I don't much care where," said Alice

"Then it doesn't matter which way you go," said the Cat.

"—so long as I get somewhere," Alice added as an explanation.

"Oh you're sure to do that," said the Cat, "if you only walk long enough."

(Carroll, 1916, *Alice's Adventures in Wonderland*)

Design—The Compass That Guides Us

We can easily feel like Alice in the story above if we don't have a clear goal or outcome in mind at all times. Our shift notes tell us what we should be doing (i.e., hiking from A to B). That's the easy part. We must keep in mind why we are hiking and focus on attaining those goals we hope to attain while hiking (i.e., teamwork, communication, leadership, decision making). Be prepared to gather staff for a discussion and change the design if the desired learning is not taking place.

So What Is Experiential Education?

Bill Proudman stated it eloquently:

> Good experiential learning combines direct experience that is meaningful to the student with guided reflection and analysis. It is a challenging, active, student-centered process that impels students toward opportunities for taking initiative, responsibility, and decision making. An experiential approach allows numerous opportunities for the student to connect the head with the body, heart, spirit, and soul. Whatever the activity, it is the learning

and teaching process that defines whether a learning experience is experiential. Further, an experiential learning process can be conducted almost anywhere and with any type of activity or learning medium.

Experiential education engages the learner emotionally. Students are so immersed in the learning that they are often uninterested in separating themselves from the learning experience. It is real and they are part of it. Rather than describing experiential learning as "hands-on" learning (an insensitive and offensive term connoting that one must have hands to learn experientially), maybe we should think of experiential education as emotionally engaged learning.

—Proudman, *Journal of Experiential Education, 15*(2) p. 20

"Whatever the activity, it is the learning and teaching process that defines whether a learning experience is experiential."

—Proudman, *Journal of Experiential Education, 15*(2) p. 20

Crisis—The Catalyst for Change

You can almost count on there being a crisis when working with our population. Staff must develop the skills to respond to the emotional needs of students in crisis in a therapeutic and professional manner. Crisis can be very positive in that it can serve to "unstick" a student and impel him/her to change. We can use crisis to begin to change old habits, destructive responses, and maladaptive behavior patterns. It provides an opportunity to facilitate growth and change. We can't change a student who doesn't want to change. Crisis may help the student decide it is time to change.

The Wrestling Match—Not!

What do you do when a student is belligerent, disrespectful, disruptive, and refuses to cooperate? Get creative, because we do not restrain kids for these reasons. There are times when we may like to strangle a student, but we do not interact on a physical level with a student unless it is absolutely necessary to protect the safety of yourself or a student. We go for years at a time without a single restraint in our program. In most cases we can give choices, divide and conquer, bring in different staff who are not directly involved, or play the waiting game. In fact, we have waited for three to four hours for a kid to decide to get in the truck for a ride back to training school. We have time on our side. Eventually the student will get tired, hungry, cold, scared, etc. I would rather wait all night than wrestle a student into a vehicle.

If we have reason to believe the potential for restraint is high, D-shift and/or DHR police are called to assist. To avoid the wrestling match, always give a student at least two choices. Empower him/her with some sense of control. Remove yourself from the situation if you are angry and losing control. Don't back him/her into a corner because s/he may come out swinging. If it does become necessary to back a student into the corner, have enough beefy staff on hand to make the student feel hopelessly overpowered. If the situation seems hopeless, s/he will likely comply.

Self-Preservation

Working as a staff here can be very stressful. To survive amid all this crisis and physical and emotional discomfort, staff must find ways to meet their own needs outside of work. You'll do far more giving than receiving while on the job. Come to work well rested and refreshed. Deal with other staff directly, honestly, and immediately. Don't take comments personally from the students. We are tested by the students to determine if we are worthy of their trust; they will challenge us, threaten us, and cuss at us. Our job is to show them there is a respectful professional response. They are used to something quite different. When we pass their tests we earn trust and respect and can operate on a level that we can all be proud of. One useful survival tip is to distance oneself from our student's problems. It is important to empathize with students, but it's an unfair burden to carry the weight of other people's problems home with us after shift. It's your job to give students choices. It's their responsibility to make good choices and to live with the consequences.

> **"While society tempts many educators to market a cookbook approach, I believe that experiential educators, like all good educators, are artists using a pallet of tools and abilities that are ever expanding and changing. As artists, it is dangerous to ever become complacent about how we define and perform our work."**
>
> —Proudman, *Journal of Experiential Education, 15*(2), p. 23

Red Top Meadows	*F* **Therapeutic**
	E **Rocky Mountain Region**
	C **Adolescent Males**
	S **1.01–1.05**

Philosophy

Red Top Meadows Wilderness Program is an integral component of our overall therapeutic program. It has been a useful tool in helping our students initiate positive change in their lives by addressing the following philosophical beliefs. People can make changes in their lives when they:

- See the need to make changes, have hope that change can occur, and are willing to take some action;
- Believe that they have something to contribute, see value in making contributions, and are given opportunities to contribute to something greater than themselves;
- Live in an environment that encourages responsibility, honesty, and respect;
- Engage in experiences that give meaning to their thoughts, concepts, and goals;

- Believe that happiness and success are connected to the quality of the relationships in their lives, including their relationships with neighborhoods, towns, country, and the world;
- Are provided with a safe environment, both physically and emotionally.*

*It is widely understood that much of the value in wilderness programming is achieved by placing students in situations where there is a greater perceived risk. This is true for many of the activities at Red Top. It is also our belief that our students should be informed of the actual risks involved with each activity and be reassured that their physical and emotional well-being is a priority.

Our history tells us that wilderness experiences can accelerate the therapeutic process. We have found that, through the combination of the wilderness environment, the adventure activities, and the sense of community formed by living closely, wilderness trips facilitate change by offering a number of elements enumerated below.

A wilderness environment offers the opportunity for:

- Natural and logical consequences to take place;
- Witnessing natural phenomenon and beauty that can be conducive to personal reflection and spiritual awareness;
- Direct educational and teachable moments;
- Students to see themselves differently and an opportunity for a fresh start;
- Feeling good from eating healthy foods and getting regular exercise.

Adventure activities such as camp skills, backpacking, climbing, and river crossings provide opportunities for students to:

- Develop new skills and gain a sense of accomplishment;
- Push beyond perceived limits and see themselves as more capable;
- Be responsible and contribute to the safety and well-being of the group;
- Be exposed to new and different activities, and possibly discover new personal strengths.

Living and working together in a small group, such as a 10-person wilderness crew, facilitates:

- More access to staff, and time for meaningful conversation and attention;
- The development of trust and communication;
- An atmosphere conducive to self-disclosure, and the flow of both positive and constructive feedback;
- The process of conflict resolution for the benefit of the group;
- Full participation, which is necessary for the group's success;
- Making contributions to something beyond themselves.

Albuquerque Academy	*F* **Education**
	E **Rocky Mountain Region**
	C **Students Grades 6–12**
	S **1.01–1.05**

Educational Philosophy

As academy faculty we commit to educating the whole student, including the student's development of the appropriate habits of head, hand, and heart. We are willing to involve ourselves, therefore, in many of the aspects of a student's school life, whether our role be that of advisor, teacher, coach, sponsor, or mentor. We intend to foster a balanced maturity in students that includes a wise blend of intellectual, physical, aesthetic, and moral capacities. Therefore, when we work with a student for only part of the day, as our specialty may require, we strive to keep the whole student in mind. We believe in emotional, aesthetic, physical, and intellectual intelligences, and so we give students frequent opportunities and ample guidance to develop all of those capacities in the classroom and beyond. In all of our professional efforts at the academy, we intend to prepare our students for advanced study and for meaningful lives.

Teaching

Good teaching always, instinctively or consciously, acknowledges the uniqueness of each learner. It understands that learning takes place in trustful environments where students see significance in what they are learning and when they can make sense of knowledge by relating it to their own experiences, including what they already understand. Good teachers appreciate that knowledge is fragile, incomplete, and often personal, and that it is very much a human endeavor. By sharing that awareness with her/his students, the educator builds a base of trust from which s/he engages students, each of them in the educational act of searching, investigating, understanding, sharing, performing, growing, looking inward, and reaching out. The challenge for the teacher is to encourage each student to shape and build her/his own capacities for learning, including that of making connections among seemingly disparate events and peoples, the kinds of connections that the specialist's perspective often ignores or avoids. Throughout the relationship the teacher models the learning, the enthusiasm, and the wisdom that s/he would see in her/his students. In that kind of educational context, students learn that knowledge is to be practiced and lived in community. Too often we educators talk of the real world as something other than school. Too often the classroom is divorced from moral and practical issues. Education is most effective when it brings the student and the world together in a thoughtful, meaningful, encouraging, and developmentally appropriate fashion.

Purpose of the Department of Experiential Education at Albuquerque Academy

The primary responsibility of the Experiential Education program is to offer outdoor and experiential education within the context of the schoolwide curriculum. A theme running throughout the department's offerings is that of being a citizen of the Southwest. By exploring the natural and human history of the area roughly framed by the Four Corners states, we discover a sense of place within this unique landscape, increase awareness of the complexity of human and natural systems, and seek to broaden our students' relationships to themselves, their classmates, and their environment. Most of the programs take place away from campus at locations ranging from the academy's site in Bear Canyon to Trail End Ranch in the Gila National Forest to wilderness areas throughout New Mexico and nearby states.

Experiential Education Program Goals

We think in terms of three programmatic goals that weave throughout the curriculum in grades 6-12: intrapersonal, interpersonal, and environmental. We hope these three goals intertwine to anchor each student in a sense of person and place. These universal goals are defined below.

- **Intrapersonal goals:** Basic concepts include increasing self-awareness; understanding personal boundaries, values, and challenges; confronting fears; and accepting responsibility for personal well-being.
- **Interpersonal goals:** Basic concepts include increasing awareness of self in relationship to the group; acknowledging the interdependent nature of human systems; demonstrating respect, empathy, and compassion for others; and accepting personal responsibility for the health of the group.
- **Environmental goals:** Basic concepts include creating a sense of place while visiting the natural world, adopting a minimum-impact or Leave No Trace ethic; building basic and technical skills; increasing confidence and competence while traveling in the natural world; and accepting personal responsibility for the health of the environment.

Georgia College & State University	
	F Education
	E Southeast Region
	C University Outdoor Education Students and General Population
	S 1.01–1.05, 2.01–2.05

Outdoor Education Academic Program: Philosophy of Teaching and Learning

The outdoor education academic program engages students in a process through which they construct knowledge, skill, and value from **direct and purposeful experience**. These experiences take place in the classroom, on field trips, in nationally recognized professional training courses, and in a variety of service learning and leadership opportunities in which students engage over the course of the outdoor education program. Constructivist theorists, brain-learning researchers, and the work of educators like Kolb (*Experiential Learning*, 1984) and Gardiner (*Multiple Intelligences: The Theory in Practice*, 1993) who have so clearly focused us on the **importance of diversity** in learning styles and intelligences provide foundations for a comprehensive, interwoven program of studies. McTighe and Wiggins (*Understanding by Design,* 2004) suggest six facets of understanding, including, explanation, interpretation, application, perspective, empathy, and self-knowledge. These, together with Bloom's cognitive, psychomotor and affective hierarchies of skill acquisition (*Taxonomy of Educational Objectives*, 1956) comprise a road map for maximizing student learning through **carefully considered course goals and assignment objectives**.

Throughout the outdoor education academic experience at GCSU, carefully constructed experiences are supported by **reflection, critical analysis, and application.** Students take initiative, make decisions, and are accountable for results. They pose questions, investigate alternatives, solve problems, and construct meaning in **dynamic environments that offer significant opportunities for learning** and supplement rigorous courses taught in more traditional formats. The outdoor education program engages students emotionally, soulfully, physically, and socially in powerful experiences that include the possibility to learn from natural consequences, mistakes and successes.

Faculty select and implement suitable experiences, posing problems, setting boundaries, supporting learners, ensuring physical and emotional safety, and facilitating the learning process. They recognize and encourage **spontaneous opportunities for learning**, as well as those that are defined by course syllabi. **Relationships**—the development and nurturing of the learner to self, learner to others, and learner to the world at large—are central to the program of studies. **Positive interdependence, responsible interaction, and individual and group accountability** are cornerstones of ignition experiences in the graduate and undergraduate programs in an intensive, largely field-based technical cohort.

Learning about **ecosystem and ekistic relationships**, and their importance to a sustainable society, is incorporated in all courses. Similarly, **writing, research, professional and community service, and leadership** are integrated across programs of study. Students create elements of a **professional web page** in every course, highlighting key examples of their work and artifacts of professional importance such as a résumé, a trip log, a service log, and their land use ethic.

We believe, with some acknowledged bias, that outdoor education is the **consummate application of a liberal arts education.** Substantively, pure and applied sciences, humanities, and the arts inform the curriculum. Therefore, direct experience, to be educative, must draw on these foundations. **We are recognized as one of the best outdoor education programs in the country and we strive to attract students that come here because they want to be the best they can be.**

Ethical Guidelines

Georgia College & State University is Georgia's designated Public Liberal Arts University. At GCSU we value:

- **Respect for self and others, emphasizing balanced lives:** *a commitment to diversity, ethics, integrity, wellness, and an open mind;*
- **Reason, including intellectual curiosity, creativity, and deliberative dialogue:** *a commitment to intellectual rigor, inquiry, analysis, and a passion for learning;*
- **Relationships and collaborations:** *a commitment to building a caring community that works with others on issues within and across disciplines;*
- **Responsible citizenship that enhances leadership:** a commitment to fostering a spirit that keeps us engaged with the local/global community and with our political/social/ecological systems.

Outdoor Education Principles

1. Facilitators will do their best at all times to operate according to the ethical standards for the profession and represent the outdoor education profession and GCSU in an exemplary fashion.
2. Facilitators will acknowledge that there is always a need for good judgment, and there should always be room to apply good judgment in relation to professional standards and the PPM and CCFH.

3. Facilitators will acknowledge that they are role models for participants, program sponsors, and other staff and therefore, must demand of themselves what they ask of others.

Code of Ethics

Professional Integrity

1. Promote integrity in the practice of outdoor education. Be fair, honest, and respectful during interactions with participants and other professionals.
2. Avoid making statements that are false, misleading, or deceptive when describing or reporting qualifications, services, products, or fees.
3. Strive to be aware of personal belief systems, values, needs, limitations, and the effect of their impact on participants and other professionals.
4. Avoid situations where personal problems or conflicts may impair work performance or judgment.
5. Represent personal and professional competency honestly and in a way that is appropriate to context.

Professional Responsibility

1. Clarify roles and responsibilities with other staff.
2. Accept responsibility for personal behavior and decisions.
3. Adapt methods to the needs of participants.
4. Begin and continue only if it is reasonably clear that the participant will benefit from the experience.
5. Conduct programs in a manner that has minimal impact on the environment.
6. Stay current about information in the field, and participate in ongoing professional efforts to maintain knowledge, practice, and skills.
7. Provide programs within the boundaries of competence, based on education, training, supervision, experience, and practice.
8. Comply with GCSU outdoor education policy and procedures as written in the current version of the Policy and Procedures Manual and the Facilitator Handbook.

Respect for People's Rights and Dignity

1. Respect the fundamental rights, dignity, and worth of all people.
2. Respect participants' right to privacy, confidentiality, and self-determination within the limits of the law.
3. Strive to be sensitive to cultural and individual differences—including age, gender, race, ethnicity, national origin, religion, sexual orientation, disability, and socioeconomic status.
4. Do not engage in sexual or other harassment or exploitation of participants.
5. Respect participants' right to make decisions and understand natural consequences.
6. Respect a participant's right to refuse or consent to services or activities.

7. Provide participants with appropriate information about the nature of programs, their rights, the actual risks associated with the activity, and the responsibilities of the provider.
8. Provide the opportunity to discuss the results, interpretations, and conclusions of the experience with participants.
9. Respect participants' rights to decide the extent to which confidential material can be made public, except under extreme conditions (e.g., when required by law, to prevent a clear and immediate danger to a person or persons, if permission has previously been obtained in writing).

Concern for Welfare

1. Do not exploit or mislead participants.
2. Be sensitive to participant and coworker needs and welfare.
3. Avoid dual relationships with participants that could impair professional judgment (e.g., sexual relationships, inappropriate physical contact).
4. Provide for the physical needs of participants (water, nutrition, clothing, shelter, rest, or other essential needs) and monitor the appropriate level of emotional and physical risk.
5. Recommend that participants needing outside services beyond the scope of OEC or academic programs obtain assistance from GCSU Student Services or seek medical advice.
6. Make reasonable attempts to avoid canceling programs.
7. Plan experiences with the intent that decisions made during and after the experience are in the best interest of the participant.

Social Responsibility

1. Be aware of professional responsibilities to community and society.
2. Avoid the misuse and misrepresentation of the profession.
3. Be aware of inappropriate language and humor.
4. Tactfully and appropriately deal with inappropriate behavior from others.
5. Ensure that participants understand anything that they are signing.
6. Obtain permission or permits to use land from private land or land managers as appropriate.
7. Comply with any regulations or laws in the region.

Santa Fe Mountain Center	*F* Therapeutic
	E Rocky Mountain Region
	C Youth and Families
	S 2.01–2.05

Code of Ethics

Preamble

This code is intended to serve as a guide to the everyday conduct of the employees of SFMC and as a basis for the resolution of issues in ethics when the conduct of employees is alleged to deviate from the standards expressed or implied in this code. It represents standards of ethical behavior for employees in professional relationships with those served, with colleagues, with employers, with other individuals and other professions, and with the community as a whole. It also embodies standards of ethical behavior governing individual conduct to the extent that such conduct is associated with an individual's status and identity as a SFMC employee.

This code is taken almost verbatim from the National Association of Social Worker's Code of Ethics, which is based on the fundamental values of the social work profession that include the worth, dignity, and uniqueness of all persons as well as their rights and opportunities. It also is based on the nature of that profession, which fosters conditions that promote these values. Professionals in the fields of experiential education and mental health share these same ideals, thus SFMC is adopting a similar code of ethics.

In subscribing to and abiding by this code, the SFMC employee is expected to view ethical responsibility in as inclusive a context as each situation demands and within which ethical judgment is required. The SFMC employee is expected to take into consideration all the principles in this code that have a bearing upon any situation in which ethical judgment is to be exercised and professional intervention or conduct is planned. The course of action that the SFMC employee chooses is expected to be consistent with the spirit as well as the letter of this code.

In itself, this code does not represent a set of rules that will prescribe all the behaviors of SFMC employees in all the complexities of professional life. Rather, it offers general principles to guide conduct, and the judicious appraisal of conduct, in situations that have ethical implications. It provides the basis for making judgments about ethical actions before and after they occur. Frequently, the particular situation determines the ethical principles that apply and the manner of their application. In such cases, not only the particular ethical principles are taken into immediate consideration, but also the entire code and its spirit. Specific applications of ethical principles must be judged within the context in which they are being considered. Ethical behavior in a given situation must satisfy not only the judgment of the individual SFMC employee but also the judgment of an unbiased jury of professional peers.

The ethical behavior of employees results not from edict, but from a personal commitment of the individual. This code is offered to affirm the will and zeal of all employees to be ethical and to act ethically in all that they do as employees of SFMC.

In subscribing to this code, SFMC employees are required to cooperate in its implementation and abide by any disciplinary rulings based on it. But, this code should not be used as an instrument to deprive an employee of the opportunity or freedom to practice with complete professional integrity; nor should any disciplinary action be taken on the basis of this code without maximum provision for safeguarding the rights of the employee affected. SFMC employees should be ready to defend and assist colleagues unjustly charged with unethical conduct, as well as to take adequate measures to discourage, prevent, expose, and correct the unethical conduct of colleagues.

Employees' Conduct and Behavior

1. *Behavior:* SFMC employees should maintain high standards of personal conduct and behavior in their capacity or identity as SFMC employees.
2. *Competence and Professional Development:* SFMC employees should strive to become and remain proficient in professional practice and the performance of professional functions.
3. *Service:* SFMC employees should regard as primary the service obligation of SFMC.
4. *Integrity:* SFMC employees should act in accordance with the highest standards of professional integrity.

Employees' Ethical Responsibility to Clients

1. *Primacy of Clients' Interests:* SFMC employees' primary responsibility is to clients.
2. *Rights and Prerogatives of Clients:* SFMC employees should make every effort to foster maximum self-determination on the part of clients and insure a guarantee of their legal and ethical rights.
3. *Confidentiality and Privacy:* SFMC employees should respect the privacy of clients and hold in confidence all information obtained in the course of professional services.
4. *Fees:* When setting fees, SFMC should ensure that they are fair, reasonable, considerate, and commensurate with the service performed and due regard for the client's ability to pay.

SFMC Employees' Ethical Responsibility to Colleagues

1. *Respect, Fairness, and Courtesy*: SFMC employees should treat colleagues with respect, courtesy, fairness, and good faith.
2. *Dealing with Colleagues' Clients:* SFMC employees who serve the clients of colleagues during a temporary absence or emergency should serve those clients with the same consideration as that afforded any client.

Employees' Ethical Responsibility to Employers and Employing Organizations

1. *Commitments to Employing Organizations:* SFMC employees should adhere to commitments made to the employing organizations.
2. *Development of Knowledge:* SFMC employees should take responsibility for identifying, developing, and fully utilizing knowledge for professional practice.
3. *Community Service:* SFMC employees should assist the profession of this field in making services available to the public.
4. *Dual Relationships:* SFMC's staff will not exploit or mislead participants, as well as others, during

or after professional relationships, so as to not impair boundaries. This includes but is not limited to: (a) business or close personal relationships; (b) sexual relationships; (c) inappropriate physical contact. In the event that an emotional, sexual relationship occurs with an adult client who is not a part of a treatment or mental health group (e.g., a corporate group), the staff will inform her/his supervisor in order to clarify the best course of action.

University of North Carolina at Charlotte—Venture Center	
F	Recreation
E	Southeast Region
C	University Students and General Population
S	2.01–2.05

Ethical Issues

General Principles

Staff will act in a manner that is within the boundaries of their competence, will act with integrity and responsibility, and will respect the rights, dignity, and welfare of all individuals.

Dual Relationships

Leaders need to be aware of their influential position with respect to participants and avoid exploiting the trust and dependency of such persons. Because of this, leaders make every effort to avoid dual relationships with participants that could impair professional judgment (e.g., intimate, romantic, or business relationships with participants). When dual relationships exist, professionals take appropriate precautions to insure that judgment is not impaired and no exploitation occurs.

1. Sexual intimacy with a participant is prohibited during a trip.
2. Some specific expectations: Staff will not initiate or encourage romantic involvement with a participant during a trip (e.g., no "hitting on" participants).
3. Leaders who subsequently engage in sexual intimacy with a past participant bear the burden of proving that there is no form of exploitation.
4. If a relationship exists prior to a trip, staff will not focus extra attention or energy on this partner during a trip. It would be expected that the other participants would not even be able to tell that there is a romantic relationship.
5. If the relationship is at a point where it needs a great deal of energy or work, it is probably not appropriate for both parties to participate on the trip. If this is a concern, please talk with the director.

Confidentiality

Staff respects the right of participants to decide the extent to which confidential material is made public—except where otherwise mandated by law or to prevent a clear and immediate danger to a person or persons. Confidential information includes but is not limited to:

1. Health status (significant illness, HIV, etc.)
2. Mental health
3. Sexual orientation
4. Academic performance
5. Traumatic experience (i.e., rape)

CHAPTER 5

PROGRAM GOVERNANCE

This chapter corresponds to Chapter 2 in the Manual of Accreditation Standards for Adventure Programs, Fourth Edition. *Program governance standards aim to assess an organization's stability and soundness. Compliance indicates that the organization's mission is in alignment with program activities, that its business license or incorporation documents are in place, and that its board of directors or organizational leadership, in the case that the program is a subset of a larger organization, is familiar with the adventure activities the program conducts. Standards in this chapter address qualities that affect an organization's ability to provide well-managed adventure activities that are characterized by effective communication between management levels, avoidance of financial conflict of interest and dual relationships, and ethical marketing practices. A clearly defined organizational chart, supported by reporting procedures and evidence that people know who and how information flows throughout the system, often reflects effective program governance. Examples for standard 3.01 are not provided in this chapter because mission statements for all contributing organizations are provided in Chapter 3. Examples for standard 3.04 are not included in this section because they are found in the statutes and governing principles documents for governing bodies and advisory boards of an organization.*

Georgia College & State University
F Education
E Southeast Region
C University Outdoor Education Students and General Population
S 3.02, 3.03, 3.05

Outdoor Education Organizational Chart

Dr. Dorothy Leland
President

Dr. Anne Gormly
Vice President for Academic Affairs

Dr. Sandra K. Gangstead
Dean of School of Health Science

Dr. Jim Lidstone
Chair of the Department of Kinesiology

Dr. Jude Hirsch	Mr. Jeff Turner
Coordinator of Outdoor Education Academic Programs	Coordinator of Outdoor Education Technical Cohorts
Director Georgia College Outdoor Education Center	Assistant Professor of Outdoor Education
Professor of Outdoor Education	

Graduate Assistant	Graduate Assistant	Graduate Assistant	Graduate Assistant
Academic Programs	GCSU Outdoor Education Center	GCSU Outdoor Education Center	Academic Programs
Administrative Assistant	Program Coordinator	Equipment and Facilities Coordinator	Technical Cohort

Reporting

Reports to various administrators that provide oversight to the academic program and the Georgia College Outdoor Education Center provide an important opportunity to support an informed and effective administration. Annual reports prepared by faculty and staff include:

- *Georgia College Outdoor Education Center Annual Report* to the Department of Continuing Education.
- *Outdoor Education Academic Program Annual Report* to the Department of Kinesiology.
- *Outdoor Education Accreditation Annual Report* to the Association for Experiential Education Accreditation Program and the Outdoor Education Safety and Risk Management Committee, Department of Legal Affairs
- *Outdoor Education Annual Program Review* to the Office of Department of Kinesiology, the School of Health Sciences, and the Office of the Vice President for Academic Affairs.

6

CHAPTER

PROGRAM MANAGEMENT, OPERATIONS, AND OVERSIGHT

This chapter focuses on standards that relate to program oversight and management of activities, including: staff selection, hiring, training, and supervision; transportation; equipment, nutrition, and hygiene; venue selection and appropriateness; environment and culture; and international considerations. It corresponds to Chapter 3 (sectioms 4–10) in the Manual of Accreditation Standards for Adventure Programs, Fourth Edition.

Organizations are expected to demonstrate that appropriate management systems are in place for each area of operation mentioned above, and that there is a system for objectively evaluating performance on an ongoing basis through the use of a risk management committee and periodic reviews. It should be noted that regardless of which or how many activities a program conducts, an organization is required to demonstrate compliance for all standards in this and the two previous chapters. Together these chapters indicate what a review team and the Accreditation Council will expect regarding an organization's foundation and operating systems. The chapter includes seven sections and provides examples of policy and procedures across recreation, education, training and development, and therapeutic settings for selected standards.

SECTION 4

PROGRAM OVERSIGHT AND MANAGEMENT OF ACTIVITIES

Red Top Meadows	*F*	Therapeutic
	E	Rocky Mountain Region
	C	Adolescent Males
	S	4.12–4.14

Emergency Procedures

General

An emergency is considered to be any major accident, injury, or incident that would require the evacuation of a student from the field or prompt action to reduce the risk to individuals or the group. This would include:

- A medical injury or illness serious enough that continuing on the trip would create a significant risk to the student or the group;
- A behavioral or personal problem that creates an unmanageable risk;
- An environmental or logistical problem with equipment, supplies, or itinerary that could affect the safety of the group;
- A missing or lost student.

In each situation, the action taken will be determined through a combination of thorough data collection, the team's assessment, clear communication, and the use of sound judgment and common sense. Following is a set of guidelines that will help in the decision-making process. Each situation will require a response from the instructor team appropriate to the emergency and all the variables involved. The basic plan of action for emergencies would be:

1. *Scene safety:* Stabilize the situation, prevent any further incidents.
2. *Assessment:* Get a picture of what happened by gathering information from the group, individuals, and staff. Variables to consider are:
   - Students treatment issues/history
   - Immediate physical environment
   - Present situation
   - Emotional environment (How has the group been doing? How many students are involved?)
   - Staff (strengths and weaknesses in your staff group)
3. *Plan:* Create a plan of action based on your assessment by brainstorming and choosing the best option.
4. *Contact* on-call staff or other appropriate support staff (i.e., doctor, therapist).
5. *Document* your actions and fill out appropriate forms.
6. *Reevaluate* and make a new plan if conditions change.

Communications

Incident Command

The first person on the scene of an incident or accident is in charge of the incident until a person with a higher level of training and/or authority arrives. At this time the responsibility of incident commander should be transferred to the person with more authority or training. First-aid and patient care responsibilities should remain with the person with the highest level of first-aid training (this may not be the incident commander). RTM staff should not transfer care or responsibility to a non-RTM staff unless it is clearly evident that they have a higher level of expertise and training.

Phone Use

1. The use of phones in the wilderness is a controversial subject for many people. It can be argued that possessing a phone in the backcountry:

a. Can give instructors a false sense of security in dealing with emergency situations;
b. Can influence a student's trip by affecting the "remote" feeling of being in the wilderness;
c. Could create an avenue for manipulation for a student who is scared or unhappy;
d. Could be misused for personal business.

2. These are all valid concerns, but the most important consideration is the safety of the staff and students in the field. The use of phones in adventure programs has become a widely accepted safety practice. RTM supports this practice by sending phones on all our wilderness trips. To minimize any adverse effects of having a phone in the field, staff should:

    a. Use the phone only for emergency situations, or scheduled call-in times;

    b. Not consider it a substitute for good judgement, skills, or training;

    c. Keep the fact that we are carrying a phone low key to avoid any unnecessary distraction for the students.

3. Emergency and on-call staff phone numbers are in the trip packet materials.

Communication Protocol

1. For communication at scheduled check-in times, support or in the event of an emergency, staff should:

    a. Call RTM if it is during business hours and talk with one of the on-call staff.

    b. If it is the weekend or nonbusiness hours, call the person on the on-call schedule. If there is no answer at their home, leave a detailed message on their answering machine and then call their cell phone. Make sure to set a time that you will call back or, if your phone will receive calls, when someone should call you

    c. If for some reason you cannot reach the on-call person, try the next person on the on-call list starting with the program director.

    d. If the situation calls for immediate attention, call the most appropriate emergency service, and then continue to try RTM.

2. Before placing a call, make sure you have written down all the important information, which may include:

    a. Nature of the emergency;

    b. Students or staff involved and their current status;

    c. Location of the group;

    d. Your phone number;

    e. Action that has taken place and a clear statement of your needs.

Notification of Significant Other People

Any time there is a serious incident or accident, evacuation, or lost student, it is imperative that the program director is notified as soon as possible and given all pertinent information. It is her/his responsibility to notify the appropriate people and/or agencies. This may include but is not limited to:

- Parents or legal guardians
- A student's caseworker
- The police
- A student's judge
- Department of Family Services
- A student's therapist

The Media

Staff should refer all media to the program director to avoid any problems with student confidentiality. The director and/or board of directors will handle all media contact according to protocol.

Sending a Runner

There are times when the cell phones won't work because of mechanical failure or your location. In this case it may be necessary to send a runner to the nearest phone or emergency vehicle. It is always safer to send a group of three or four to run for help, but this is seldom possible. One RTM staff should run and, depending on the situation, the team may decide to send one or more capable students with the staff. The staff team should choose the best route by reviewing the maps and evaluating the terrain, weather, time of day, and abilities of the running party. It is imperative for the running party to take extra caution not to create another emergency. Runners need to remember to bring the following:

1. Supplies they will need to be comfortable and safe while they're gone (food, water, warm clothes, maps, sleeping gear);
2. Detailed incident information or SOAP note if the problem is medical;
3. Written directions to pinpoint the location of the incident;
4. Emergency phone number list and some quarters;
5. A travel plan, so the remaining staff knows approximately when s/he will return with help or receive a phone call.

Missing Student

There are many reasons that someone could be considered missing in the field. A student may be lost or have run away, but it is also possible for a student to be hiding or just have wandered out of sight and sound. At the point when you discover that someone is missing you should:

1. Stay calm and briefly interview staff and students to gain information, which would lead to the whereabouts of the missing person. Questions to pose include:
   a. Had the student been talking about running away?
   b. Was the student homesick?
   c. Had the student been in a fight or disagreement lately?
2. Perform a hasty search of the immediate area.
   a. One staff should stay with the group to keep students calm and occupied.
   b. The other two staff should take 10 to15 minutes to search the immediate area, calling out the student's name or blowing the safety whistle. Listen for a response.

3. If the student is not found:
   a. The staff team should have a conference to gather more information and discuss possible scenarios. Factors to consider may include:
   - Location and distance from the trailhead
   - Student's behavioral history
   - Type of terrain
   - What the student was wearing
   - Last spot where the student was sighted
   - Time of day
   - Current weather conditions
   - Student's recent mood
   - What gear the student was carrying

Lost Student

If the team decides that the student is most likely lost or is hiding, they should make plans to systematically expand the search. Staff should utilize the group and split up into search teams. Teams should coordinate how long to search, how far they should go, and when to regroup. If the student is still not found, the staff team should contact RTM or on-call staff (communication protocol) to assist with coordinating with Search and Rescue. Staff should have available all the pertinent information from the missing persons report form to give to the appropriate persons. Depending on the circumstances the group or a staff member should camp as close to the last place the student was seen.

At any time the student is found the staff team should meet with the student to:

1. Make sure they are okay and provide any necessary first aid.
2. Process how the situation happened.
3. Contract on expected future behavior to avoid the situation happening again.
4. Make sure to contact the on-call staff and/or Search and Rescue to let them know that you've found the student.
5. Fill out the appropriate paperwork (incident report).

Runaways

1. If the staff team decides that the student has run away, they should:
   a. Call RTM or on-call staff to report the runaway.
   b. Send a staff runner in the most likely direction to find and follow the student (see Send a Runner procedures).
   c. Create a travel plan for the runner that communicates:
      i. Which direction s/he will be traveling.
      ii. How far s/he plans to traveling.
      iii. When s/he will return if s/he has not found the student.

2. If the staff runner finds the student s/he should stay with him/her.
3. Call RTM or on-call staff to arrange help from a search-and-rescue team or the local sheriff's department with any updated information.
4. Fill out appropriate paper work (incident report and missing persons report form).

Runaway on the road.

1. If a student disappears from a bathroom stop or restaurant while travelling to or from a wilderness trip, the staff should:
   a. Quickly interview other students for helpful information.
   b. Perform a 10-minute hasty search of the immediate area.
   c. Call RTM or on-call supervisors.
   d. Call the local sheriff's department or police department.
   e. Fill out an incident report and missing persons report form.

Medical Emergencies

General

1. In the event of a medical emergency due to injury or illness, the staff will:
   a. Provide all necessary first aid to the level of their training.
   b. Gather all pertinent information and write a thorough SOAP note. Be prepared to give a verbal SOAP over the phone.
2. Depending on the extent of the injury or illness and all the variables, the staff will need to make a plan and be prepared to reevaluate.
3. Depending on the situation, the staff may need to:
   a. Provide first aid and move on because there is no risk of further injury.
   b. Provide first aid and wait to see if the condition improves. This may require changing the itinerary and calling RTM.
   c. Provide first aid and make plans to evacuate the student. Check the evacuation guidelines for the types of injuries that would require evacuation.
4. Make a plan to keep the rest of the group safe, occupied, and supervised.
5. Fill out an incident report: An incident report should be filled out any time the injury or illness requires more than minor first aid, will require follow-up care, or results in a lost day in the field. (See also Section 9–Incident Reporting).

First-Aid/Medical Information

Staff can refer to the back of the SOAP notes for first-aid protocols or refer to the wilderness first-aid booklet located in the first-aid kit. Staff in the field can also call the emergency room at St. John's Hospital and talk with an on-call doctor for help in diagnosing a particular problem.

Evacuations

It is the policy of the RTM Wilderness Program to perform our own evacuation only when the person can walk out without creating further injury or endangering the group. Any evacuation that requires someone to be carried out on a litter is the job of the search and rescue team or another emergency service. Staff may get some help with this decision by calling a supervisor or doctor, but ultimately it is a judgement call for the staff in the field. Request a helicopter only when there is a definite threat to life or limb. Any time a student is evacuated from the field, an RTM staff should accompany the student until they are transferred to another RTM staff or the student's family. There may be an exception to this if it creates a safety issue for the group or an individual.

Walk out.

1. If the person being evacuated can walk out, the staff team will need to:
   a. Decide who to send to provide first aid, help carry gear, and be supportive.
   b. Write a detailed SOAP note to send out with them. Remember to send the student information packet.
   c. Make sure that the walkers have all the necessary clothing and gear to stay safe, including food, water, first-aid supplies and shelter. Be careful sending gear that may be needed by the group.
   d. Contact someone from RTM so that there is a person to meet when you come out of the field.
   e. Make a plan of where and when the walkers will rejoin the group.
   f. Document your decisions and actions.

Carry out.

1. If you know that you are going to need assistance to transport the injured person, call as soon as possible so that search-and-rescue efforts can get started.
2. Make sure you have all the necessary information ready, including:
   a. Your exact location and the incident information (what happened, where, and how);
   b. Patient information including injuries, care given, and vital signs.
3. Continue good patient care, keep the patient comfortable, and make provisions for them to eat, drink, and go to the bathroom.
4. Take a set of vital signs regularly.
5. Keep the rest of the group busy setting up tarps, making hot drinks and food, or organizing gear, etc.
6. Consider sending someone to meet the rescue team at the trailhead or a trail junction.
7. Assist the rescue team when they arrive. Send out all the appropriate paperwork.
8. If at all possible, have a staff member stay with the student until another RTM staff takes over.
9. Document all your decisions and actions.

Helicopter.

Do not take a helicopter evacuation lightly. Any time a helicopter flies in the backcountry, the pilot and crew is taking a risk. Helicopters do not fly in bad weather, and they need a good landing zone that may not be near your patient. At the time of contacting 911, inform the emergency personnel of the landing site location and condition as well as the proximity to the group and patient. If a helicopter is coming for the patient, the staff will need to:

1. Brief the students regarding expectations and safety procedures.
2. Choose, clear, and mark a landing zone, adhering to the following guidelines:
    a. Choose an area that is at least 100 feet in diameter and long enough for the helicopter to approach and take off at a 15-degree angle. (Helicopter pilots like to be able to take off pointed downhill and against the wind, if possible.)

    b. Clear all obstacles that could blow into the rotors.

    c. The site's long axis should face into the wind.

    d. Hang a brightly colored wind sock in plain view.

    e. Mark a firm, flat spot with something bright that won't blow away.
3. Direct the pilot by having one person stand at the far end of the landing zone with his/her back to the wind and arms extended toward the landing area.
4. Prepare the patient for air travel by dressing her/him warmly. Ear plugs, safety glasses, helmet, and gloves are also appropriate if available.
5. Be prepared to have to sever contact with the student as you might not be able to ride along. Have all pertinent student/patient information ready to send with the student/patient.
6. Be safe around the helicopter rotors by not approaching it until the pilot signals and keeping your head low. Never approach the helicopter from the rear.
7. Keep camp and all other students 150 yards away from the landing zone.
8. Remember that a pilot will make her/his own decisions of when and where to land safely depending what s/he sees at the time.
9. Follow all the instructions of the pilot or crew.
10. Accompany the student if possible.
11. Document all your decisions and actions.

Evacuation routes.

General guidelines for evacuation routes for each of the course areas are in the trip packets. These are intended to be helpful in terms of providing information on proximity to towns and emergency services, avoiding known problematic areas, etc.

Medications

If staff knows or suspects that a student's normal medication regime has been altered to the point of being a safety issue (i.e., refusal, checking, overdosing) or that there are contraindications due to the activity or the environment, they should consult with on-call staff and/or the on-call doctor as soon as possible. If the staff is unsure whether it is a safety issue, they should call.

Fatality in the Field

1. In the event of a fatality in the field it is extremely important that the staff:
   a. Not disturb the accident scene or the body until the legal authorities show up and provide guidance and instruction.
   b. Take care of the emotional, mental, and physical well-being of all the members of the group.
   c. Keep communication with others factual and avoid offering opinions, judgments, or speculations.
   d. Notify the program director as soon as possible.
2. The program director is responsible for:
   a. Notifying next of kin and other appropriate people and filling out next-of-kin form.
   b. Making arrangements to deal with the authorities and the media according to protocol.
   c. Setting up debriefings to deal with the trauma to the group, staff, family, and friends.

Medical Emergency/Critical Incident Debriefing

Losing someone from the group can be a traumatic experience for both the staff and students. Field staff and support staff should make a decision on what type of debrief is appropriate for the situation. RTM may want to send a therapist into the field to help assess and debrief the group. Travel plans may need to be altered to have more time to meet the emotional needs of the group.

Behavioral Emergencies

General

1. Remember that the protocol for dealing with behavioral issues is similar to any other emergency. Be sure to do the following:
   a. Check scene safety.
   b. Assess situation.
   c. Make and carry out a plan.
   d. Contact RTM if necessary.
   e. Evaluate plan and start over if necessary.
   f. Fill out an incident report.
2. The following is a list of possible behavioral incidents and some information that should be considered when assessing the seriousness of the situation and making a plan. This is not meant to take the place of treatment with a trained mental health professional. Whether a student should stay in the field or not is a treatment team decision.

Student threatening suicide.

1. Any time a student is talking about or threatening to hurt or kill him/herself, it should be taken seriously. It is a fact that if a student wants to commit suicide, the wilderness

is an easy place to pull it off. If you suspect that a student is suicidal you should:

a. Call RTM or on-call staff and alert them of the situation.

b. Talk with the student honestly and ask her/him directly whether s/he is thinking about hurting or killing him/herself.

2. If the student answers "yes" then a staff should talk with the student to assess the how serious the threat is.

   a. Does the student have any personal or family history with suicide?

   b. Does the student have a plan of how and when it would happen? How detailed is the plan?

   c. How in control is the student?

   d. Is the student depressed, impulsive, able to listen, and understand?

   e. How prepared are the staff and the group to support and deal with this person?

3. The level of support and type of action taken from here depends on the outcome of the interview. Staff may need to:

   a. Make a contract with the student by getting a verbal agreement and handshake with eye contact. This is a formal promise from the student that s/he will not try to hurt him/herself for a stated amount of time. This contract will need to be renegotiated at the end of the stated time.

   b. Provide around-the-clock supervision.

   c. Reduce stress and provide emotional support.

   d. Make arrangements to evacuate the student if staff is unable to ensure the safety of the student.

4. These guidelines are a brief overview of the procedure necessary in dealing with a suicidal student and are not intended to take the place of more thorough staff training on dealing with this type of situation. Training on dealing with a suicidal student is a part of ongoing staff training for all RTM child care staff. (See emergency procedures for on grounds.)

Fighting.

1. Is it an isolated incident or do the student(s) involved have a history of aggressive behavior? Is this going to continue to be a safety issue for the group?

2. What is the level of intent in hurting or doing harm to another? Did the person knowingly use some sort of weapon?

Defiant/resistant student.

1. Is the situation an immediate safety issue? (For example, is this a sit-down strike on top of an exposed ridge with a thunderstorm approaching? Is this a medication refusal?)

2. Are there other students supporting the resistance? Would it be best to gather the group around or separate the group from the student?

3. What's the feeling, issue, or process that is driving the behavior? Be careful not to focus on just the behavior.
4. Take care of the group and reward them for not feeding into the problem, for being understanding and cooperative.

Defiant/resistant group.

1. Assess your own safety.
2. Secure meds, potential weapons, phone, keys, etc.
3. Call RTM or the on-call staff to give them notice.
4. Find students who are not involved or are borderline and work with them to make them feel safe and to get a realistic picture of how big a problem you have.

Inappropriate sexual behavior.

1. If there is more than 4 years difference in age between the two students involved or there was use of force, the staff should call RTM or on-call staff and make arrangements to have a therapist meet the group and evacuate the older of the two students or the student who used force. The therapist also needs to meet with the victim to assess trauma and take appropriate action to meet the needs of the student.
2. Interview students as soon as possible and separately so the students don't get a chance to create a story.
3. Rearrange sleeping groups to minimize risk of further problems.
4. Talk to the group openly and honestly to increase awareness without creating shame.
5. Review prevention plans or create new prevention plans with students.
6. Talk with students about how to abstain or find appropriate ways to meet their sexual needs.
7. Staff need to stay aware of and confront oversexualized behavior (sexual joking, exhibitionist, voyeur, etc.).

Psychiatric/mental health.

1. Scene safety: Does this feel like something you can deal with, or does it seem totally out of your league? Have you dealt with this type of incident before?
2. Is this the first incident of this type or intensity level for this student? Or is it a reoccurring situation that has a predictable outcome? What's the student's history?
3. Does this student take medication to help him with this behavior? Has a med dose been missed or altered in some way?
4. What was the triggering event (e.g., other substance abuse, fear, situation with staff, or other students)?
5. Call the on-call therapist with questions or concerns.

Eating disorder.

1. Does the student have a history of issues involving food? Or is this a new or situational behavior?
2. Is there an immediate health/safety risk. What is the actual intake of calories? Has the student been drinking water?
3. Does giving this student attention seem to make the situation better or worse?
4. Staff need to closely monitor food and water intake.

Substance abuse.

1. Scene safety: Immediately secure the substance that is being abused or get students out of danger (i.e., if there is gas in the tent, get everyone out of the tent).
2. Plan should involve searching for and securing any contraband.
3. If you feel there is a health risk involved (i.e., overdose of medication, ingestion of poison), call the most appropriate health professional (poison control, ER doctor), and have all information ready to give thorough verbal SOAP note.
4. Is this a suicidal behavior?

Fire-setting.

1. Scene safety: Put out the fire if you can safely do so or move students to a safe area.
2. Was this a one-time impulsive act or is it an obsession? What is the student's history? Was this hidden from RTM in the admissions process?
3. Get a clinical consultation from therapist.

Environmental Emergencies

General

Red Top staff should be aware of the possibility of storms, rock fall, lightning, river flooding, earthquakes, forest fires, and avalanches. Staff should be prepared to assess the dangers that these phenomenon present to the group and be able to make quick decisions and longer term plans on how to keep the group safe. Staff may need to make a phone call to gain more information or direction. The first priority is the safety of our students. Storms, rock fall, avalanches, and lightning are all semipredictable events for which staff can be prepared. Earthquakes and forest fires are unpredictable and the staff will need to make action plans on how to deal with these situations as they arise. The general rule of thumb is to remove our students from harm's way.

Avalanche

1. In the unlikely event that a student or staff gets caught in an avalanche, the staff should:
    a. Look around to see if the group is in immediate danger by looking at the snow pack above and below.
    b. Organize the group and give firm, clear directions.
2. Once you determine the scene is safe, do an immediate hasty scuff search for any signs

or visual clues (i.e., a hand, a glove, a ski pole of missing person.)

3. Someone should mark the last point where the victim was seen.
4. Look for features in the terrain, direction of flow, and deposition areas where a body might be trapped (i.e., in front of or behind boulders or trees, depressions).
5. Probe for a body in these areas.
6. Set up a probe line in the most likely spot and probe using ski poles or whatever you can work with.
7. Call 911 and ask for assistance.

Fire

1. Staff and students should prevent starting any forest fires by following all protocols involving flame (i.e., lighters, stoves, camp fires). To avoid forest fires staff should:
   a. Be briefed on current fire locations and fire danger before a trip.
   b. Call RTM or on-call staff if you suspect a new fire in your area. (Location of fires will be updated on the master maps.)
   c. Work with the administrative staff and the land use agency to reroute the group if that becomes necessary.

Flash Floods

1. During spring and fall in the canyons of Utah, there is the potential for flash flooding. Prevention is the best practice.
2. Be aware of the potential for flash flooding in the area and signs of previous flooding.
3. Know the extended forecast and the likelihood of flash floods prior to leaving RTM.
4. Exercise good judgment when selecting routes and campsites.
5. Plan possible escape routes.
6. Be aware of narrow drainages that are a part of a large drainage basin.

Extreme Weather/Temperature Extremes

1. Staff should have some idea of the weather forecast before leaving on the trip and be brought up to date at resupply or staff changes.
2. Staff may have to alter travel plans to avoid risks associated with extreme weather. Staff may also have to:
   a. Monitor food and water intake more closely.
   b. Monitor body temp of students (be tuned into early signs of hyper- or hypother mia and other heat- or cold-related injury or illnesses).
   c. Communicate with the on-call staff to make arrangements for rerouting, extra equipment to be brought in, or bringing in the group.

Bear Encounters and Lightning

1. See Section 5: Wilderness Education Curriculum.

Logistical Emergencies

General

1. Usually, logistical problems with food and equipment are not emergencies, just inconveniences.
2. Staff should only call for help when there is a risk of endangering the group or an individual. Examples of this would be:
   a. Staff becoming ill
   b. Running out of a student's medication
   c. Being so far off route or behind on the itinerary that you're not going to make the reissue on time
   d. An important piece of equipment breaking, such as a backpack or a tent
   e. Losing the first-aid kit in the river

Staffing Crisis

There are times when a staff member is unable to start or finish his/her shift in the field due to injury, illness, or personal reasons. There will be an on-call staff available to replace a field staff in the event of this kind of emergency. In the event of a family emergency, RTM will make an effort to communicate with staff in the field and arrange to have a staff replacement as long as the safety of the group or an individual is not compromised.

Late for a reissue.

1. There are many circumstances that could result in a crew being late for a reissue.
2. A crew could be delayed by:
   a. Being lost
   b. Behavioral problems
   c. Medical problems
   d. Bad weather creating slow or unsafe hiking conditions
3. In the event that a crew does not show up at the designated time and place, the staff doing the reissue should:
   a. Wait at the reissue site until dark;
   b. Contact RTM to find out if anyone has heard from the crew;
   c. Return to the reissue site the next morning.

4. If the crew does not show up or have contact in 24 hours, the reissue staff should contact the program director and the search-and-rescue team to coordinate a search party to back-track the crew's route.
5. The staff in the field should:
   a. Make an effort to get to the reissue site on time or within 24 hours.
   b. Send a staff ahead to notify the reissue staff if the crew is going to be a few hours late.
   c. Phone in from the field to notify staff of the delay if the crew is not going to make the reissue by nightfall.

Late for a hike-in reissue.

1. The reissue staff should:
   a. Wait for the crew as long as possible, leaving enough time to hike out safely.
   b. Hang the food and resupplies at the reissue site in a visible spot and mark it.
   c. Contact RTM as soon as possible to see if anyone has heard from the crew.
   d. Hike back into the reissue site the next morning if you have not heard from the crew.
   e. If the crew does not show up within 24 hours of the originally scheduled time, contact the RTM director and the search-and-rescue team.
2. The staff in the field should:
   a. Make an effort to get somebody to the reissue site on time.
   b. Make a phone call when they know they will be delayed past nightfall.
   c. Make a call after finding the reissue and/or you need someone to come back in to carry out garbage. (The crew should make every effort to carry their own garbage to the next reissue site.)

Chadwick School	F	**Education**
	E	**West Region**
	C	**Students Grades K–12**
	S	**4.06–4.09, 4.12–4.20**

General Risk Management Policies

Medical Screening

All participants in Chadwick Outdoor Education courses complete a confidential medical information form. These forms are reviewed by one or more of the following people: director of Outdoor Education, assistant director of Outdoor Education, director of Upper School, director of Middle School, a faculty representative, Chadwick School nurse, Chadwick School trainer, and Outdoor Education instructors. Any "red flags" are noted and followed up by conversations with the student, the parents, and the student's doctor. In the case of psychological problems (i.e., eating disorders), information is sought from the student's advisor and the school counselor. After consulting with the above people a decision is made as to whether or not the student will be allowed to participate.

If a student/parent submits a letter from the student's (nonparent) M.D., detailing a medical problem and stating that the student should not participate in the trip, the student is excused from the trip, and a notation is made on the student's transcript. Medical problems that may excuse students from trips include: severe allergies, recent surgery, recent hospitalization, severe asthma, frequent severe migraines, and eating disorders.

Wilderness First-Aid and Medication Use Policy and Procedures

1. All instructors working for the outdoor program will follow Wilderness Medical Society, Wilderness Medical Associates, or Wilderness Medical Institute Wilderness first responder protocols, procedures, and guidelines when teaching Chadwick courses.

2. First-aid and rescue equipment is carried by instructors and students during all activities.

3. First-aid kits, drug kits, and appropriate emergency equipment are available and are routinely checked during course orientation and restocked at the end of each course. Repair kits and appropriate spare items are available for trips beyond the facility or road head. Food, shelter, and equipment are provided for activities conducted beyond the facility or road head. In the event of an injury, illness, or extreme change in weather, staff have the skills and equipment to manage the situation until a return to the road head can be achieved.

4. Regarding prescription medications, we recommend that students bring two supplies, the second being a backup supply in case the first is misplaced. Students and/or parents are responsible for communicating what prescribed medications are being taken, their purpose, and whether the student or instructor will be responsible for administering the medications to the individual student. This information should be conveyed to the director, assistant director, or instructor of the Outdoor Education Program. These medications should be listed on the medical form with doses and time schedules included. We must also be informed about any other medications that are being carried into the field. In case of an emergency medical situation, it is extremely important that we know, at all times, what medications participants have ingested while they are on our courses.

5. We strongly discourage over-the-counter medications being carried by students. Each instructor team carries a drug kit that contains antihistamines, epinephrine, analgesics, anti-inflammatories, antifungals, decongestants, gastrointestinal medicines, antibiotic ointment, wound disinfectant solutions, and skin irritation relievers; in addition, each group carries an expedition-size backcountry first-aid kit.

6. Girls: Although our first-aid kits contain tampons and pads for feminine hygiene, you should bring your own supply. Outdoor courses can temporarily disrupt your menstrual cycle.

Course Itinerary Changes Before or During a Course

Weather, road, trail, sea, snow conditions, and changing river levels may force an itinerary or location change before or during a course. If conditions become so diminished or severe that the objectives of the course or activity cannot be achieved, then it is inappropriate to continue. It is within the instructors' judgment to curtail or stop the activity or course, turn the group around, get off the river, stop driving, etc., if they deem conditions to be too severe. Our instructors are employed for their good judgment and ability to manage risk, and they take the initiative to make courses as enjoyable and educational as possible. If changes are made before the start of a course, we will notify the families involved. If itinerary changes are made during a course, instructors will notify the on-call person as much as is practical and possible, so that the necessary information can be relayed to the parents on an as-needed basis.

Policy Regarding Students and the Environment

1. Policies on nondiscrimination, cultural/gender sensitivity, and sexual relations meet general school policy. See the part-time faculty handbook for details.
2. All Chadwick Outdoor Education (COE) courses will be completed according to accepted minimum-impact practices. Please refer to the Leave No Trace materials in the program office.

General Precourse Policy and Procedures

1. These apply to all courses:
    a. Instructors will check the adequacy of each person's clothing and personal equipment before student use.
    b. Two adult staff members will lead groups in the backcountry.
    c. Students and parents will read and sign the acknowledgement of risk and confidential medical information forms before each course.
2. Students/parents must complete, sign, and submit all forms before students may attend a course.
    a. School policy applies to any tobacco, alcohol, and nonprescription drugs found on courses.
    b. Instructors will file detailed itineraries, with evacuation plans for each day, and a detailed 5-day teaching plan with the director or assistant director.
3. The school on-call person will have copies of the course itinerary, driving directions to the course area, driving directions to medical facilities and phone numbers, course area emergency contacts and phone numbers.

General Policy and Procedure During Courses

1. Instructors will carry a completed confidential medical information form for each participant.
2. Instructors are required to keep a detailed written account of the course in a course log.
3. Instructors will keep students within sight and sound at all times, with the exception of solos. (See solo policy and procedures.)

4. Instructors will brief all students on hazards in the course area.
5. Instructors will always have ready access to a first-aid kit, drug kit, and a repair kit appropriate to the activity.
6. Instructors will ensure the terrain to be covered is appropriate for the students' skill levels and that the students have the appropriate clothing, food, and equipment for the activity involved.
7. Instructors will brief students on recognition and avoidance of hazards associated with the activity. Instructors will also teach participants how to cope with these hazards.
    a. Instructors will ascertain that the participants have understood the briefing and they respect the potential hazards of the activity.
    b. Key elements of the briefings will be recorded in the course log.
8. All participants must wear closed-toe shoes or boots during all activities.
9. Sandals are permissible—subject to instructor discretion—while wading or swimming.
10. An instructor will contact the school on-call person whenever a student comes out of the field for any reason.
11. Each student will each carry a whistle during the course.
12. Instructors will inform the director or assistant director during debrief of all injuries, accidents, and near-misses.
13. Instructors will contact the school on-call person when possible in any emergency.

Camping and health maintenance policy and procedures.

1. Except in emergencies, male and female students may not share the same tent or tarp.
2. Instructors will ascertain that all campsites are safe from falling rock, ice, or tree limbs, flash floods, or rising river levels.
3. On any course, if students are to operate stoves, instructors must teach correct stove use and students must display competence before using one without immediate supervision by the instructor.
4. Staff will instruct participants in hygiene procedures regarding water, food preparation, and clean-up.
5. Instructors will make daily checks on the health of each student, including hydration, personal hygiene, and foot care. In tick season/country, students will check themselves for ticks every 12 hours.
6. Staff will sleep close enough to students to fulfill their role as supervisors.
7. On any course, if students are to use knives, instructors must teach correct knife use and students must display competence before using one without immediate supervision by the instructor.

Solo policy and procedures.

1. Solo wilderness experiences will not exceed 72 hours.

2. Instructors will check on students at least once a day.
3. Participants will have free access to food and water and to adequate shelter and clothing. Students must bring food on solo.
4. Participants will each have a whistle. Instructors will arrange and test a workable emergency signaling system.
5. Instructors will remain in a central base camp, and all students will know the location of this camp. The camp will be within whistle range of the nearest student.
6. Travel, swimming, fires, candles, climbing, or bouldering are not allowed on solo.
7. On solo, if students are to use knives, instructors must teach correct knife use and students must display competence before using one without immediate supervision by the instructor.

General Postcourse Policy and Procedure

1. Instructors will turn in completed, detailed course log books and incident reports.
2. During the course debrief the instructor will report all near-misses and behavioral incidents.

Program Emergency Response Plans

1. An emergency is any missing person, serious accident, natural disaster, illness, or fatality during a Chadwick outdoor course.
2. All parties involved in responding to an emergency are urged to communicate information promptly, accurately, and completely.
3. In any emergency all parties will keep a written record of events and planned actions.

General Emergency Response Policy and Procedure

1. In any emergency, one instructor will assume the role of leader.
2. Designate a scribe to maintain a written log. Stick to the facts. Avoid opinions, assumptions, personal feelings, and evaluations.
3. The written log needs to contain information such as:
   a. Names of victim(s) or lost person(s).
   b. SOAP note of patient(s) and injuries.
   c. Explanation of incident (what, when, where, and how it happened).
   d. Condition and location (marked on a map) of staff, patient(s), and remaining students.
   e. Weather conditions at time of emergency.
4. Designate one person as the primary caregiver who will stay with the patient(s) throughout the incident.
5. Designate a leader for the rest of the group.

Policy and Suggested Procedure for a Response to a Missing Person

Unscheduled loss of contact with a participant in the field is considered an emergency if it extends to 12 hours. An emergency may be assumed to exist earlier than 12 hours, depending on the group and the circumstances.

1. Assess the safety and capability of available people for the search, and gather all pertinent information for the search, and determine urgency.
2. The following are suggested search procedures:
   a. Mark your map with a point last seen.
   b. Quickly set up a "confinement" system to keep the person within a finite search area.
   c. Send initial response teams to likely accident sites. (Lost people most often wander downhill.)
   d. Divide the search area into segments defined by topographic features such as rivers or ridges. Look for clues in likely places. Avoid grid searches (statistics show that they are a waste of time). Mark your map with notes on areas checked and thoroughness of the searches. Remember: People may wander back into areas already searched.
3. When a person is missing the following information will be written in the log:
   a. Time at which loss of contact began;
   b. Location of point last seen (marked on a map);
   c. Area searched and type of search done (hasty, grid);
   d. Physical condition of person lost and clothing/equipment/food/information they are believed to have.
4. If the person is found, reassess the planned activities for the course and adjust if necessary to avoid subjecting students, staff, and parents to unwarranted stress.
   a. Assess the needs of students and staff for physical and emotional support.
   b. End the course if necessary.
5. Contact the school on-call person to apprise them of the situation.
6. If the person is not found after the first search, notify the agency with jurisdiction for search and rescue if this has not already been done and continue the search.
7. Call the on-call person. Once a phone is reached, follow the "what to say" prompt list below. Make sure the on-call person receiving the information has written it down and it is clearly understood.
   a. *What to say:* Who you are. Where you are and your phone number. Explain the situation and agencies you have contacted. What you need. The number of patients. Identify the objective hazards. When you will call back, and whether you will be going back into the field.
   b. Make a communication follow-up plan.
8. When the person is found, debrief the situation, reassess the planned activities for the course, and adjust if necessary to avoid subjecting students, staff, and parents to unwarranted stress. Assess the needs of students and staff for physical and emotional support. End the course if necessary.
9. On the group's return to school, the director of Outdoor Education will communicate with Risk Management Advisory Committee and follow up with parents.

Policy and Suggested Procedure in Response to a Disabling Accident or Serious Injury

1. Assess the safety and capability of available people for the evacuation, and gather all the data needed to assist the evacuation.
2. Select the most expedient evacuation method and medical support; initiate an evacuation or stabilize the patient(s), and initiate a messenger team for an evacuation by outside agency.
3. Suggested procedures for a messenger team:
   a. The messenger team needs to carry a written record. The record should contain the following: the patient's SOAP note, condition of the group, the group's and the messenger team's plans and contingency plans, location of the group, the planned route of the messenger team (marked on a map), and all emergency contact phone numbers.
   b. Determine the closest (in time) emergency vehicle or phone and mark the route to this point on the map.
4. Once contact is made with the on-call person, follow the "what to say" prompt list below. Make sure the on-call person receiving the information has written it down and it is clearly understood.
   a. *What to say:* Who you are. Where you are and the phone number. What you need. The number of patients. Very specifically identify location of the patient(s). Using your SOAP notes, identify the patients' problem(s), anticipated problem(s) and treatment plan(s).
   b. Identify medical supplies needed. Provide information regarding access to the patient. What is the best way to get to the patient? How far in is the patient? What are the objective hazards? Where/how you can be reached? When you will call back? Will you be going back into the field?
   c. Once an evacuation plan has been initiated, it is important that all sources understand what is happening and that two rescues are not occurring simultaneously.
5. Collect witness statements when possible. Take pictures of the accident site and the patient if possible.
6. In consultation with the student's parents, arrange for transportation home of any student too badly injured to continue the course. Keep the student at base camp, drive him/her home, drive him/her to the airport, or wait for pick-up by a parent.
7. Once the injured person has been removed, reassess the planned activities for the course and adjust if necessary to avoid subjecting students, staff, and parents to unwarranted stress. Assess the needs of students and staff for physical and emotional support. End the course if necessary.
8. After the emergency has been resolved, The director of Outdoor Education and the School Risk Management Advisory Committee (SRMAC), with the school legal counsel and insurance company, will decide if an internal or external investigation is to be conducted.

a. For an internal investigation, a committee may be formed of existing SRMAC members and additional members by unanimous SRMAC vote.

b. No persons will be allowed to serve on the committee if it is deemed by the SRMAC that they have conflicting interests with the investigation and the emergency.

c. For an external investigation, an outdoor professional investigator will be appointed by the SRMAC to chair the investigative committee; s/he will work with the SRMAC.

Policy and Suggested Procedure in Response to a Fatal Accident or Illness

1. Assess the safety of the rest of the group.
2. Secure the area around the fatality site.
3. Notify the law enforcement agency.
4. Collect witness statements when possible. Take pictures of the accident site and the patient if possible.
5. Contact the on-call person. Then follow the "what to say" prompt list below. Make sure the on-call person receiving the information has written it down and it is clearly understood.
   a. *What to say:* Who you are. Where you are and the phone number. What you need. The number of patients. Very specifically identify the location of the patient(s). Using your SOAP notes, identify the patients' problem, anticipated problem, and treatment plan.
   b. Identify medical supplies needed.
   c. Provide information regarding access to the patient. What is the best way to get to the patient? How far in is the patient? What are the objective hazards? Where/how you can be reached? When will you call back? Will you be going back into the field?
6. Participate in the evacuation if needed.
7. Reassess the planned activities for the course and adjust if necessary to avoid subjecting students, staff, and parents to unwarranted stress. Assess the needs of students and staff for physical and emotional support. End the course if necessary.
8. After the emergency has been resolved, the director of Outdoor Education and the SRMAC, with the school legal counsel and insurance company, will decide if an internal or external investigation is to be conducted.
   a. For an internal investigation, a committee maybe formed of existing SRMAC members and additional members by unanimous SRMAC vote.
   b. No persons will be allowed to serve on the committee if it is deemed by the SRMAC that they have conflicting interests with the investigation and the emergency.
   c. For an external investigation, an outdoor professional investigator will be appointed by the SRMAC to chair the investigative committee; s/he will work with the SRMAC.

Policy and Suggested Procedure at Base Camp or School in Response to an Emergency in the Field

The following actions will be taken by the on-call person:

1. Keep the school administration fully informed of the situation through contact with the on-call person.
2. Supply logistical support to the group in the field.
3. Contact outside agencies for help as appropriate:
   a. In consultation with the course instructors and director of the program, reassess planned activities for the course and adjust if necessary to avoid subjecting students, staff, and parents to unwarranted stress.
   b. Assess the needs of students and staff for physical and emotional support.
   c. End the course if necessary.
4. Refer all requests for information from the media to the headmaster.
5. Ensure communication with parents to keep them apprised of situations as they develop.
6. After the emergency has been resolved, the director of Outdoor Education and the SRMAC, with the school legal counsel and insurance company, will decide if an internal or external investigation is to be conducted.
   a. For an internal investigation, a committee maybe formed of existing SRMAC members and additional members by unanimous SRMAC vote.
   b. No persons will be allowed to serve on the committee if it is deemed by the SRMAC that they have conflicting interests with the investigation and the emergency.
   c. For an external investigation, an outdoor professional investigator will be appointed by the SRMAC to chair the investigative committee; s/he will work with the SRMAC.

Team Leadership Results, LLC	*F* Training and Development
	E Mid-South Region
	C Adults
	S 4.04, 4.06–4.10, 4.1–4.20

Safety

Published Procedures

Team Leadership has this policy manual as well as a safety manual that documents and communicates expected practices and standards for activities that pose risk to the health and well-being of participants and staff. All Team Leadership staff has access to and familiarity with the policies and guidelines that are relevant to their work on the Team Leadership courses. Team Leadership has developed a 15-point risk management plan, which has been cited as a model for other programs (see Risk Management Plan at end of this section). Team Leadership's risk management plan includes written emergency procedures for the programs. (See Safety Standards and Procedures.)

Safety Committee

The program has a designated and functioning safety committee that monitors risk management and safety practices. Accident and close-call data is collected, analyzed, and acted upon. The committee has an appropriate representative mix, including an individual representing the ownership, one representing the facilitators, and one representing an outside advisor. The committee meets monthly to plan the monthly safety meeting and annually to review all facets of program safety.

Annual Safety and Risk Management Review

Team Leadership engages in an annual internal safety and risk management review, in which the safety committee examines all aspects of a program and one outside external advisor from another established program and discusses with program personnel. A final written report contains suggestions, recommendations, and observations of any necessary changes that might increase safety or quality. A copy of the internal report is made available to Team Leadership's insurance company.

Compliance With Laws

Team Leadership maintains facilities that conform to all applicable national, regional, and local laws and regulations. See letter from ACCT board member regarding meeting of standards.

Activity Sites

Team Leadership programs use appropriate activity sites. See Policy Manual, section on Properties and Venues.

Staff-Participant Ratio

Team Leadership has explicitly designated a staff ratio of one facilitator per seven (7) participants for team-building events. When the program is an Energizer of 1 to 6 hours, a ratio of 1 to 25 is acceptable. These ratios are based upon the nature of the activities that are typically selected for the two types of programs. Staffing of the zip line at Cielo Vista requires that an extra technical person be assigned to man either the top of the tower or the dismount deck.

Safety Training

This section is described in Safety Standards and Procedures.

Records

This section is described in Safety Standards and Procedures.

Life Support for Activities

Team Leadership provides adequate shelter, clothing, food, water, and equipment for the kinds of activities presented.

Shelter.

The Cielo Vista course has four discrete open-air shelters to protect participants from inclement weather. The Quail Canyon course is adjacent to the Oak Room at the top of the hill as well as the ranch's open-air dance pavilion in the event of inclement weather.

Clothing.

Team Leadership provides rain ponchos to participants when there is a threat of rainy weather. In cold weather, soft cotton gloves and knit caps are offered to participants. Often an additional outer layer or sweater can be offered to a participant experiencing chilling cold. In all types of weather, participants are issued a bandana, which can be used to protect skin from sunburn, to warm or cool the forehead or neck, to protect from burns when handling hot objects, etc.

Food.

Team Leadership orders box lunches for participants who will be on the course all day. Upon request Team Leadership arranges for midmeal snack food. On rock climbs Team Leadership provides breakfast, lunch and dinner items.

Water.

Team Leadership provides each participant with a factory-sealed bottle of spring water, which they are to carry with them at all times. In summer months these are iced to cool temperatures. These individual bottles are refilled from water coolers that are carried with the group. Powdered electrolyte drink is provided during summer weather in a dispenser, allowing each person to determine the concentration of the mixture desired.

Equipment.

All equipment needed for the program activities is provided by Team Leadership. This includes a portable locker for each individual for valuables, jewelry, cameras, snacks or medications, extra clothing, and small personal items. Team Leadership maintains its equipment by storing it in secure and dry huts and equipment rooms with covered storage containers. All ropes and harnesses are inspected regularly and maintained in good repair. Ropes use is recorded in rope logs that are maintained on each rope and these ropes are retired and replaced on a schedule based on time (5 years), exposure to UV radiation (1,000 hours), hard falls (100), or evidence of defect or significant wear, whichever comes first.

Informed Participants

The program informs participants of the nature of the activities, the potential risks involved, and the responsibilities, which are expected from participants. Team Leadership does this through its Participant Agreement (waiver) and Participant Information forms. Team Leadership offers the option of a demonstration initiative at no charge to the client in an effort to inform participants more fully about what to expect in the program. Some clients decline this option for various reasons, but it is always the client's decision.

Participant Preparedness

Participants are taught appropriate emergency skills. Team Leadership goes to great lengths to help participants to prepare proactively for effective management of emergencies. Its 15-point risk management plan includes several measures to inform participants of the inherent risks associated with adventure programming, including climbing and rappelling. Participants are given informative instruction and coached in spotting, belaying, and safety practices to help them both technically and attitudinally to become vigilant and proactive in detecting safety issues and avoiding emergency situations wherever they might arise. Team Leadership also prepares for contingencies in which things go wrong.

Team Leadership emphasizes individual thinking and collaborative judgment calls throughout its programs. Participants learn that being involved in team decisions can provide benefits from the collective intelligence brought to bear upon the problem. Participants who have gone through the experiential problem solving initiatives on the challenge course are often better prepared to let cooler heads prevail over members who might lead the group into action prematurely. Not every situation can benefit from this type of collaboration however, and Team Leadership facilitators who are placed in the leadership position must be equipped with the judgment and maturity to make difficult decisions about what might serve the greatest good independently, and to stand by these decisions as well. Gaining participants' trust through caring behavior, steadiness, technical competence, and consistency may pay off in the unexpected emergency situation. Good judgment is not as easily acquired.

Simulation Notification

If emergency medical or evacuation simulations are to be used, participants are informed beforehand. Team Leadership provides information in advance of any program that will simulate medical or evacuation situations for the purposes of training or preparedness.

Alcohol Consumption

Team Leadership programs have a policy of no alcohol or drug use during program activities, by employees when on duty and when operating any form of mechanized transportation. When clients take responsibility for their own transportation, Team Leadership does not object to the group choosing their own forms of refreshment after the close of the program day, so long as these are consumed in accordance with the laws of the city, state, county, and federal governments.

Health Screening

All Team Leadership staff and participants complete a health and physical screening in the participant registration form. This facilitates screening and helps participants to make informed decisions regarding their capacity to participate fully in the activities.

Emergency Protocols

Team Leadership has an established system for communication protocols in the event of a medical emergency or serious, life-threatening injury, illness, or lost person. (See Safety Standards and Procedures.)

Search-and-Rescue Protocols

Team Leadership has a search and rescue protocol in the event that a participant may become separated from the group. Staff is informed about this protocol.

Exception: Indoor Programs

Team Leadership has no evacuation protocol because there are no indoor spaces maintained by Team Leadership as program venues.

Notification Protocol

Team Leadership has a notification protocol, which is used in the event of an emergency or accident. Staff understands the notification protocol, to include communication with family, officials, and press in the event of an emergency or accident. (See Safety Standards and Procedures.)

First-Aid Kits

Team Leadership maintains first-aid kits stocked with items identified in the Safety Standards and Procedures. One safety meeting each year is devoted to familiarization with the contents of this kit. Team Leadership works to maintain a current record of staff certifications in basic first aid and CPR. Once a year Team

Leadership conducts a file updating procedure in which staff members whose certifications have expired are encouraged to update their training and to file a copy of recertifications at the Team Leadership offices.

EMS Protocol

All appropriate protocols established by the EMS system and accepted emergency medical training systems will be followed. Team Leadership follows all appropriate protocols established by the EMS system and accepted emergency medical training systems.

Risk Management Plan

Team Leadership's risk management plan includes the following:

1. Fully informing the participant in writing and verbally about the course environment, the types of activities, and inherent risks involved.
2. "Challenge by Choice" mandate, by which each individual defines his/her own level of participation—respected by all.
3. On-site orientations and program demonstrations as part of the preevent preparation.
4. Screening participants for medical, psychological, or health conditions that could affect their capacity to participate fully.
5. Comprehensive program planning and facilitator briefing prior to every program presentation.
6. Staffing ratio of two facilitators with every group of more than seven participants. Group size is limited to 14.
7. A course policy manual defining accepted procedures and protocols for operations that are specific to this course.
8. Three-hour safety meeting every month for facilitators. We target retraining needs and review safety issues and practices.
9. Safety committee keeping current logs and certification records, spotting trends or areas of concern, scheduling recertification training, and planning/presenting the monthly safety meetings.
10. Commercial general liability insurance ($1 million per occurrence) from the foremost underwriter of challenge course program coverage.
11. Close call and course incident logs recording instances where a participant did something that could become a safety issue.
12. Current first-aid and CPR training as a requirement for program facilitators.
13. First-aid kit for each group area on the course contains 27 items selected to anticipate first-aid priorities specific to this course.
14. Annual course inspection by ACCT certified builders.
15. Maintaining active membership in AEE and ACCT, and attending annual conferences.

Georgia College & State University	
	F Education
	E Southeast Region
	C University Outdoor Education Students and General Population
	S 4.04, 4.06–4.09, 4.13–4.20

Risk Management

Outdoor education programs and services at Georgia College & State University are not immune to the possibility of accidents or litigation. Risk management seeks to minimize these possibilities without compromising the program goals. The *Outdoor Education Policy and Procedures Manual*, Spring 2007 (PPM) and the *Georgia College Outdoor Education Center Facilitator Handbook*, Fall 2006 (CCFH) are central to risk management, and together with good judgment, training, and support provide a framework for planning and monitoring risk management procedures.

Safety and Risk Management Committee (SRMC)

Purpose

The Safety and Risk Management Committee (SRMC) is the critical link between program delivery and risk management. The SRMC is comprised of OE staff and several advisors. The committee of the whole meets as necessary to review and approve policy. Otherwise, advisors are available on an as-needed basis, and OE staff meets on a weekly basis to conduct ongoing business, review and revise policy, review incident/accident submissions, and plan program and course logistics.

Responsibilities

1. Provide specialized support and advisement to OE staff.
2. Collect, analyze, and interpret information related to safety and risk management in outdoor education programs and services offered through the GCSU Outdoor Education Center and the Department of Kinesiology.
3. Recommend and approve policy and procedures.
4. Oversee implementation of policy and procedures.
5. Oversee compliance with accreditation standards.

Membership

SRMC membership consists of OE staff, the GCSU director of Legal Affairs, the GCSU director of Student Health Services, the GCSU medical advisor, and specialized advisors as required.

Incidents/Accidents

Accident and incident reports assist the Safety and Risk Management Committee to identify trends that require immediate or future preventative action, monitor policy and procedures, evaluate program quality, and establish leadership development needs.

Definitions

An accident refers to a fatality, a disabling injury, or serious illness. Accidents normally necessitate that a participant be transported to a primary care facility; however in some cases, a participant may simply be encouraged to see a physician after the program. Accident reports must be completed. An incident is a "near miss" or minor accident that does not require primary care. Incidents may include a variety of situations that affect program quality; therefore the decision to complete an incident report is based on the judgment of the lead facilitator. Keep in mind that incident/accident reports are good indicators of ongoing program evaluation.

Reporting Procedures

1. OE or OEC staff complete the incident/accident report form.
2. Information should be complete, objective, and include a comprehensive description of relevant information. Consider that this document may be used by primary caregivers to make treatment decisions. Therefore:
   a. Use SOAP note protocol when appropriate;
   b. Write in a clear and professional manner;
   c. Do not indicate fault or responsibility.
3. Make every effort to obtain the injured party's signature.
4. In the case of an accident where a participant is transferred to EMS personnel, include on the form the name of EMS personnel and the location of the primary care facility to which the injured party is being transported.
5. If the person returns to the program, note the name of the physician giving permission to do so.
6. The lead facilitator has the authority to deny or adapt level of participation of a participant that returns to the program.

Staff Incidents/Accidents

In addition to the reporting procedures above, OE and OEC staff that are injured in the performance of duties for Georgia College & State University should:

1. Report the incident/accident to the direct OE supervisor immediately or within 31 days of the accident. The OE supervisor will immediately notify GCSU Human Resources (478-445-5596) of an on-the-job incident/accident that *does or does not* require medical attention.
2. The OE supervisor will forward to Human Resources (CBX 028) a completed OE incident/accident report and the appropriate Department of Administrative Services (DOAS) claim forms (incident report or accident investigation), along with the conformed panel

of physician form signed and dated by the GCSU employee and indicating first and second choices for follow-up care physicians. Human Resources will schedule follow-up appointments. Human Resources will submit documentation to the DOAS.

3. In the case of an emergency, a staff member may be treated at an emergency room. Follow-up with a primary care physician after release from the emergency room is required. A primary care physician is any physician on the confirmed panel of physician list, with the exception of a chiropractor.

4. To avoid fees being charged to personal insurance instead of the DOAS, do not present an insurance card to an emergency room or primary care physician personnel. A GCSU Human Resources representative will provide the medical care provider with the workers' compensation claims information.

5. Failure to seek treatment for job-related injuries from the conformed panel of physicians list may jeopardize payment of medical bills and other charges under workers' compensation.

6. Submit physician's diagnosis, medical bills, verification of rehabilitation, prescriptions, and any correspondence relating to the workers' compensation claim in a timely manner to Human Resources. Failure to do so may delay payment of medical services rendered.

Safety

General Guidelines

1. OE and OEC staff is responsible for participants and other staff. Participants look to staff for informed, professional instruction and guidance so that they can participate in our programs and services in reasonable safety. The greater the degree of risk an activity holds, the greater the facilitator's obligation to anticipate and avoid potential dangers.

2. Participants should be made aware of the nature and scope of risks involved in an activity before the activity commences. Several procedures are used to accomplish awareness, these include:

    a. Participants sign appropriate informed consent and assumption of risk forms. Informed consent means that participants have been informed of and understand risks associated with an activity, and that they are participating in the activity voluntarily. OE and OEC staff shall state that these forms are important documents, review relevant information out loud, answer questions, and allow time for participants to read and sign the forms;

    b. OE and OEC staff shall conduct safety briefings in accordance with the PPM or CCFH.

3. The PPM and CCFH contain standards by which OE and OEC staff conduct is assessed. Decisions to deviate from these standards should be defensible.

Safety Briefings

Safety briefings inform participants and staff about risks and safety procedures on site before engaging in potentially hazardous activities. They are an opportunity to discuss dangers and risks and ensure that staff is confident that participants understand and voluntarily assume risks before participating in an activity. Good judgment is crucial, especially when dealing with hesitant participants. Reinforce confidence and provide opportunity to practice as appropriate. Avoid forcing a participant to engage in an activity by using challenge of and by choice unless the safety of the participant, other participants, or staff is compromised.

1. The lead facilitator is responsible for ensuring that members of the facilitation team are familiar with and able to execute safety plans, including conducting appropriate safety briefings.
2. A safety briefing should establish a climate of safety and caution before undertaking potentially hazardous activities.
3. A safety briefing should include, but is not limited to, the following information:
   a. Inherent dangers in the area, along with preventative information (flashflood, poisonous flora and fauna, lightning and other weather-related dangers, widow makers, and natural disasters, etc.);
   b. Inherent dangers in the activity, along with preventative information (water safety, site management, accident prevention, etc.);
   c. Program goals and plan overview;
   d. Participant and staff responsibilities related to the conduct of the activity and emergency procedures;
   e. Safety equipment use and location.
4. The lead facilitator is responsible for checking that all participants hear and have an opportunity to ask questions about the safety briefing.

Common Safety Considerations

1. Determine appropriate staff **roles and responsibilities.** Check and recheck!
2. Assess participant **readiness** to participate in an activity. Use ongoing assessment techniques such as GRABBSS, APPLE, and CHANGES. Never assume!
3. Provide appropriate levels of **supervision**. As the degree of risk increases so must the level of supervision!
4. Implement **transportation** policy and procedures.
5. Complete, disseminate, and carry appropriate **documentation** including, but not limited to risk management and program administration documents. Document, document, document!
6. Inspect **equipment** prior to and during programs and make staff and participants know how to do so, as appropriate, and use it properly.
7. Carry an appropriate **first-aid kit** and make sure staff and participants know where it is and how to use it. Depend on it!

8. Maintain good **hygiene.** Wash or disinfect hands before cooking or sharing food and after urinating or defecating.

9. Maintain appropriate levels of **hydration and nutrition.** Ensure and monitor for adequate nourishment and hydration for all participants—including the staff!

Exposure Control

Hepatitis B and hepatitis C are infections of the liver that are caused by the hepatitis B virus (HBV) and hepatitis C virus (HCV) respectively. These viruses are found in the blood of persons who have this disease. HIV (human immunodeficiency virus) is the virus that causes AIDS. Many people have no symptoms; however they are still capable of transmitting the virus. All of these viral infections can be transmitted through unprotected sexual contact and by parenteral, mucous membrane, and nonintact skin exposures of staff to bloodborne pathogens. None are transmitted by casual contact (i.e., kissing, hugging, using the same toilet). No reasons exist for excluding people who are infected with HIV from wilderness outings (Wilkerson, 1992)[2].

Most approaches to infection control are based on a concept called *universal precautions*. It requires that staff administering aid consider every person and all blood and body fluids, to be a potential carrier of infectious disease. An exposure that might place a staff member or participant at risk for HBV, HCV, or HIV is defined as a percutaneous injury (e.g., a needle stick or cut with a sharp object such as a knife) or contact of mucous membrane or nonintact skin (e.g., exposed skin that is chapped, abraded, or afflicted with dermatitis) with blood, tissue, or other body fluids that are potentially infectious.

In addition to blood and body fluids containing visible blood, semen and vaginal secretions also are considered potentially infectious. Although semen and vaginal secretions have been implicated in the sexual transmission of HBV, HCV, and HIV, they have not been implicated in occupational settings. The following fluids also are considered potentially infectious: cerebrospinal fluid, synovial fluid, pleural fluid, peritoneal fluid, pericardial fluid, and amniotic fluid. The risk for transmission of HBV, HCV, and HIV infection from these fluids is unknown and the potential risk for occupational exposures has not been assessed. The likelihood of an outdoor education staff member being exposed to such fluids is highly unlikely. Feces, nasal secretions, saliva, sputum, sweat, tears, urine, and vomitus are *not* considered potentially infectious unless they contain blood. The risk for transmission of HBV, HCV, and HIV infection from these fluids and materials is extremely low (CDC, 1988).[3]

Avoiding blood exposures is the primary way to prevent transmission of HBV, HCV, HIV in outdoor education settings. However, hepatitis B immunization and postexposure management are integral components of a complete program to prevent infection following bloodborne pathogen exposure and are important elements of staff safety.

Guidelines for exposure control.

1. Use protective barriers (gloves, masks, and protective eyewear) to prevent exposure to blood, body fluids containing visible blood, and other fluids to which universal precautions apply. The type of protective barrier(s) should be appropriate for the procedure being performed and the type of exposure anticipated:

    a. Wear gloves when anticipating contact with blood, body fluids, tissues, mucous membranes, nonintact skin, or contaminated surfaces. Gloves should be removed and properly discarded after contact with the patient.

    b. Wear an impervious gown or apron if splattering of clothes is likely.

c. Wear appropriate protective equipment at all times including a mask and eye protection if splattering is likely to occur when attending to an injured person.

d. Whenever possible, use a pocket mask provided in the first-aid kits for mouth-to-mouth resuscitation.

e. Use general-purpose utility gloves (e.g., rubber household gloves) for tasks involving potential blood contact such as instrument cleaning and surface decontamination procedures.

2. Persons with open cuts or lesions on their hands should refrain from dressing a wound for another person, regardless of whether s/he is wearing gloves.

3. Immediately and thoroughly wash hands and other skin surfaces that are contaminated with blood, body fluids containing visible blood, or other body fluids to which universal precautions apply.

4. Use caution to prevent needle stick injuries when using, cleaning, or disposing of needles or other sharp instruments. Do not recap used needles by hand; do not remove used needles from disposable syringes by hand; and do not bend, break, or otherwise manipulate used needles by hand. Place used disposable syringes and needles and other sharp items in puncture-resistant containers for disposal.

5. Disposable articles contaminated with blood or other body fluids should be wrapped in gauze, taped, and placed in a suitable biohazard container for storage and transportation back to GCSU. Designated GCSU personnel will dispose of containers as per university policy. Contact Public Safety at (478) 445-4400.

6. Report immediately all needle stick accidents, mucosal splashes, or contamination of open wounds with blood or body fluids.

7. When indicated, CDC guidelines for the management of occupational exposures to HBV, HCV, and HIV and recommendations for postexposure prophylaxis (PEP) will be implemented. In regard to HIV, the U.S. Public Health Service emphasizes adherence to HIV PEP when indicated for an exposure, expert consultation in management of exposures, follow-up of exposed staff to improve adherence to PEP, and monitoring for adverse events, including seroconversion. To ensure timely postexposure management and administration of HIV PEP, occupational exposures should be considered as urgent medical concerns (CDC, 2005).[4]

a. HBV: Recommendations for HBV postexposure management to any person who sustains an occupational blood or body fluid exposure includes possible initiation of hepatitis B immune globulin (HBIG) and/or hepatitis B vaccine series after evaluation of the hepatitis B surface antigen status of the source and the vaccination and vaccine-response status of the exposed person (CDC, 2001).[5]

b. HCV: Immune globulin and antiviral agents (e.g., interferon with or without ribavirin) are not recommended for PEP of hepatitis C. For HCV postexposure management, the HCV status of the source and the exposed person should be determined, and for those exposed to an HCV positive source, follow-up HCV testing should be performed to determine if infection develops (CDC, 2001).

c. HIV: Antiretroviral agents from five classes of drugs are currently available to treat HIV infection. These include the nucleoside reverse transcriptase inhibitors (NRTIs), nucleotide reverse transcriptase inhibitors (NtRTIs), nonnucleoside reverse transcriptase inhibitors (NNRTIs), protease inhibitors (PIs), and a single fusion inhibitor. Only antiretroviral agents approved by FDA for treatment of HIV infection are included in the CDC guidelines. The CDC recommendations provide guidance for two-or-more drug PEP regimens on the basis of the level of risk for HIV transmission represented by the exposure. Special circumstances such as a delayed exposure report, unknown source person, pregnancy in the exposed person, resistance of the source virus to antiviral agents, and toxicity of PEP regimens are also discussed in the guidelines (CDC, 2005).[6]

8. If a person reports that s/he has HIV, AIDS, hepatitis B, or hepatitis C before or during an Outdoor Education program, consider the following guidelines in effect:
   a. Reassure the person that this information will be kept confidential. Offer to listen to the participant's concerns, such as fear of having this virus, fear of being ostracized, fear of telling loved ones.
   b. Privately counsel the person about proper infection control measures (means of transmission and acceptable procedures) and obtain a verbal commitment that s/he understands this information and will abide by it during the activity.
   c. Address the participant's concerns, such as fear of spreading the infection to other participants or staff. Reassure the person that the likelihood of infecting anyone else is extremely low provided the correct procedures are followed.
   d. If there is reason to believe that the infected person may have engaged in behavior that would have exposed another participant or staff during the activity, consult the appropriate administrator as soon as possible.
   e. Maintain confidentiality unless otherwise instructed by legal counsel.
   f. Refer to HIV counseling services and the National AIDS Hotline at the CDC (1-800-CDC-INFO) as appropriate.
9. Participants and staff should refrain from sharing "community items" (i.e., water bottles and eating utensils). Although the risk of transmitting HIV, HBV, and HCV is low, many more common pathogens can be transmitted in this manner. Participants and staff should avoid direct mouth-to-mouth contact.

Emergency Response

The lead facilitator will manage an emergency situation. If the lead facilitator is injured, an assistant facilitator will manage the situation. Although autocratic leadership style is the norm in emergency situations, flexibility and sensitivity to the needs of the group should be exercised.

General Procedures

1. Survey the situation. Do not panic. Decide exactly what steps to take before acting.
2. Ensure the safety of everyone involved. Remove a dangerous situation, remove people from a dangerous situation, and/or follow the following guidelines:

a. Carefully complete an initial patient assessment, following exposure control guidelines (see Risk Management: Exposure Control);

b. Apply first aid as required;

c. Complete detailed patient assessment and documentation (i.e., SOAP notes);

d. Develop an action plan taking into account the nature of injuries, size of group, terrain, weather, time and distance from help, etc.

3. Notify GCSU primary backup (see Risk Management: Backup System).

Scene Management

1. Treat symptoms in order or simultaneously if possible: airway, breathing, circulation, severe bleeding, shock, and stabilize the neck when appropriate.
2. Attend to environmental hazards.
3. Maintain body temperature and make the patient as comfortable as possible.
4. Attend to the physical and emotional needs of group members (set up a temporary camp, keep the group informed, etc.).
5. Assess and record vitals at regular intervals.
6. Monitor the victim at all times and administer first aid as appropriate; consider the anticipated time of rescue.
7. Try to keep group members safe and busy to reduce the anxiety level.
8. At an appropriate time, obtain written statements from possible witnesses to the accident.
9. After an evacuation, and especially in the case of serious injury or death, refer to accident notification procedures (see Risk Management: Notification Protocol).
10. In the event of a fatality, do not remove the body unless instructed to by legal authority.
11. Process the event with the group.
12. Request that the primary backup contact the GCSU counseling center at (478) 445-5331 for assistance as appropriate.
13. Complete appropriate forms.
14. After the emergency the lead facilitator or designate should follow up on patient status, and contact the primary backup to review the situation and discuss subsequent plans for program continuation or cancellation (see Risk Management: Backup System).

External Assistance

1. Implement program plan emergency procedures using cell phone or radio, or if communication by cell phone or radio cannot be established, send at least two people, three if possible, to the most effective point of communication.
2. Leave at least one medically qualified person with the patient.

3. The messenger party should:
    a. Take flashlight, matches, compass, and map showing where the victim is, vehicle keys, telephone money and numbers, protective clothing, copy of SOAP note, credit card number if possible, food, and water;
    b. Hurry, but do not risk injury or split up;
    c. Constantly observe the countryside so you know how to return to the site;
    d. Conserve energy to lead the rescue party back.
4. If phone contact is possible, call 911 and ask for the necessary emergency personnel, then notify appropriate land manager (ranger, forester, etc.).
5. Notify GCSU primary backup (see Risk Management: Backup System).

Rescue Philosophy

When responding to an emergency, keep in mind leadership priorities. Maintaining the safety of participants and staff is imperative. Manage bystanders to avoid complications. Attend to injured parties. In the case of multiple patients, triage the patients to determine who to help first. The decisions of triage should be based on two criteria: (1) do no harm to victims, and (2) do the most good for the most people. After everyone has been attended to, think about equipment recovery as appropriate.

Decisions about how to perform a rescue should be weighed according to three criteria including speed, safety, and simplicity. Generally, the faster, safer, and simpler an option is, the better it is. It is possible to categorize most rescues, regardless of activity or environment, into one of four levels[7] that are normally implemented in sequence. There may be cases in which the decision to proceed to a more complex response is appropriate. Use these levels as a tool to aid decision making in a rescue situation. Remember, the first line of defense is prevention. The best rescue is the one that is not needed.

Rescue Procedures

Level I.

A Level I rescue is an assisted self-rescue. The responder provides psychological support to a person, from a position of relative safety, in order to help them help themselves, normally by providing verbal emotional or technique support to increase the victim's ability or desire to self-rescue.

Level II.

A Level II rescue is an assisted self-rescue. The responder provides physical or material support to a person, from a position of relative safety, in order to help them help themselves, normally by providing equipment to aid self-rescue.

Level III.

A Level III rescue increases the complexity, time to respond, and relative safety of responders, who make physical contact with the patient/victim to provide a mechanism for moving the person to a safer place.

Level IV.

A Level IV rescue increases further the complexity, time to respond, and relative safety of responders, who make physical contact with the person to provide a mechanism for rescue that involves greater risks for both the rescuer and the victim.

Rescue Examples

Level	Examples
I	• **Verbally** encouraging a challenge course or rock-climbing participant to trust his/her belay system and be lowered, or to gain a position from which s/he can continue. • Verbally encouraging a capsized paddler to swim aggressively to an eddy or shore.
II	• **Sending** an etrier out to a participant who has fallen off a cable and cannot regain the foot cable. • Throwing a rope to a capsized paddler to bring him/her to shore quickly. • Applying a vector pull to a belay system to help a rock climber reach a hold and continue climbing.
III	• Moving out on an element to a stuck challenge course participant, attaching a rescue belay system, **removing** his/her initial belay system, and then lowering him/her safely to the ground. • Going out in a boat to bring back a capsized paddler who is separated from his/her boat. • Rappelling to a stuck rappeller to help release a jammed rappel device.
IV	• Moving out on an element to a stuck challenge course participant, attaching a rescue belay system, **cutting away** his/her initial belay system, and lowering him/her to the ground. • Wading into surf to bring back a distressed swimmer capsized by surf. • Performing a belay escape and climbing self-belayed to a pinned climber.

Notification Protocol

General Procedures

1. An accident normally necessitates a visit to a primary care facility.
2. In the event of a fatality, it is the responsibility of the lead facilitator or designate to notify the primary backup (see Risk Management: Backup System) who will notify public safety personnel, the director of University Communications, and the appropriate administrator.
3. If the accident occurs **on campus**, it is the responsibility of the lead facilitator or designate to inform the contact person listed on the Medical Information form and to notify the primary backup (see Risk Management: Backup System) who will contact the appropriate administrator.
4. If the accident occurs **off campus**, it is the responsibility of the lead facilitator or designate to notify the primary backup (see Risk Management: Backup System) who will then notify the family and the appropriate administrator.
5. Some general guidelines and suggestions to be used when speaking with others are:
   a. Be sensitive to the feelings of the family;
   b. Think through what you will say before you make contact;

c. Have the facts organized and be accurate in conveying them;

d. Convey condolences when appropriate to do so;

e. Details may be conveyed in a follow-up telephone call as appropriate;

f. Anticipate possible questions and prepare yourself;

g. Be prompt, delays may lead to difficult feelings or inappropriate conclusions;

h. Provide the names and telephone numbers of contact people.

Information to Press

1. Information about an accident *will not be released to the press without the consent of the director of University Communications.*
2. Normally an appointed representative of Georgia College & State University will communicate with the press.
3. Should contact with the press be unavoidable, avoid speaking about:
   a. Assessment of fault or criticism of conduct;
   b. Assessment of GCSU policy, equipment, or facilities;
   c. Information regarding the nature of the injury or illness prior to a diagnosis by a licensed medical doctor;
   d. Names of victims prior to notification of next of kin;
   e. Estimates of property damage.

Medical Evacuations

Medical evacuations are systems that may involve staff, participants, and/or EMS authorities to transport injured or sick people to primary care facilities. Basic wilderness evacuation systems are developed and implemented by staff and participants based on equipment available and the nature of the medical emergency. EMS authorities will manage the evacuation system from the point of transfer. Staff should be prepared to continue to assist with the evacuation as requested by EMS authorities. In the case that a motorized vehicle is necessary to facilitate an evacuation, staff will follow local EMS protocols. EMS will establish if a helicopter is needed and if one is available for medical evacuation.

Helicopter Evacuation

1. Keep participants clear of the landing zone.
2. Approach the aircraft only as directed by the crew.
3. Approach the aircraft from the side, be aware of the rotors and keep low. Try to signal or make nonverbal contact with the crew.
4. Face away from the helicopter during landing and take-off to protect from rotor wash. Wear eye protection if possible.
5. Take instructions from the crew. Do not argue. The crew is legally in charge of the situation once contact is made.

Backup System

Primary Backup Pager for Non-Challenge-Course-Programs is: (478) 451-2415
Primary Backup Pager for Challenge Course Programs is: (478) 451-8244
Alphatext Message: pageme@gagta.com
Codes: **1234567: indicates the primary backup is "on belay"** **7654321: indicates the primary backup is "off belay"** **911 (before phone number): indicates an emergency** **104 without a phone number: indicates an affirmative response**
86 without a phone number: indicates a negative response

Purpose

The emergency backup system helps to ensure that in the event of a field emergency or the need to communicate new information from the group to the University or from the University to the group, a contact person is available on a 24-hour basis. Academic classes will use (478) 451-2415 and OEC programs will use (478) 451-8244, unless alternative arrangements are made in advance. The OEC program coordinator or designate will be the primary backup for OEC programs. OE staff or designate will be the primary backup for academic classes.

Conditions for Success

1. The primary backup person must be accessible on a 24-hour basis.
2. Technological failure due to climatic or geological factors must be considered.
3. The primary backup person must possess appropriate emergency response competencies.
4. The system must comply with OE and institutional policy and procedures for emergency response.
5. Resources must be available to implement the system.
6. Backup personnel must be physically and mentally able to deal with an emergency situation.

Roles and Responsibilities

Lead facilitator.

1. Negotiate a competent, primary backup person who is accessible on a 24-hour basis to manage the backup system.
2. The primary backup person will be employed by GCSU or approved by the coordinator of outdoor education programs.
3. Review the completed backup file with the primary backup at least 48 hours in advance of departure.
4. Include, at minimum, in the backup file (additional items may include menus, budget, equipment lists, etc.):
    a. Master Program Checklist;
    b. Program Plan;
    c. Original medical information forms (copies to be carried with the group);
    d. AR/IC forms;
    e. Curriculum outline;
    f. Weather report;
    g. Maps.
5. Contact the primary backup upon departure from Milledgeville or at the beginning of the program.
6. Contact the primary backup about significant changes to the contents of the program backup file (route, campsite, program, etc.) that may impact location in the event of an emergency in the field or at GCSU.
7. Check for messages at least once a day to receive emergency information for group members.
8. Contact the primary backup upon arrival in Milledgeville or at the conclusion of the program.
9. Contact the primary backup in the event of an emergency.
10. Communicate emergency procedures to staff and group members.
11. Obtain the backup file from the primary backup to prepare the completed program file for submission to the OEC program coordinator (copied medical information forms replace original medical information forms that are returned to the master file and a program file summary form is completed and attached to the contents of the backup file).
12. Submit completed incident/accident reports to the coordinator of outdoor education programs.

Primary backup.

1. Review and revise as necessary contents of the backup file with the lead facilitator.
2. Carry the backup file at all times.

3. Negotiate a competent, secondary backup person(s) who is accessible to the primary backup on a 24-hour basis and able to go into the field.
4. Provide the chair of the Department of Kinesiology and the Director of Public Safety the following information in advance (normally 24 hours):
   a. Name, location, and dates of program;
   b. Estimated time of departure and arrival;
   c. Names of facilitation team;
   d. Names of participants;
   e. Primary backup contact information.
5. In the event of an emergency, assess the situation in cooperation with field personnel to determine appropriate course(s) of action.
6. Implement emergency and communication procedures in accordance with GCSU outdoor education policy and procedures and the specific emergency needs of the situation.
7. Implement emergency procedures if not notified within 2 hours of the estimated time of arrival indicated on the program plan, or at the conclusion of the program.
8. Manage emergency debrief needs.

Secondary backup.

1. Be accessible to the primary backup person on a 24-hour basis.
2. Assist the primary backup person as necessary.
3. Be ready and able to go into the field.
4. Replace the primary backup person if necessary.

Alcohol and Drugs

Alcohol and Illegal Drugs

1. There will be no alcohol or illegal drugs used by participants or staff during outdoor education programs.
2. Facilitators should be aware that legal drugs, if used inappropriately, present a variety of health and safety issues, and should maintain appropriate vigilance regarding their use.
3. In addition to the obvious risks associated with the use of alcohol and illegal drugs in the outdoors, GCSU is a drug-free workplace.
4. The best defense is prevention. A behavioral contract should be developed and agreed to by participants and staff prior to the program. Sometimes it is appropriate to develop a behavioral contract with a group, and other times it is appropriate to state the rules. In any case, the lead facilitator is responsible for ensuring that policy is clear and that participants are willing to comply with this policy.

5. In the event that alcohol or illegal drugs are taken or used on an outdoor education program the following steps should form the basis for action:
    a. Report the situation to the primary backup to discuss options;
    b. Attempt to dismiss the offender from further participation in the program as quickly as possible and to escort him/her to a safe place;
    c. Determine program options and discuss them with the group;
    d. Complete an incident report form.
6. Infractions are subject to GCSU disciplinary procedures, including dismissal from OE academic programs. Grievance procedures are detailed in Student and Faculty Handbooks.

Prescription Drugs

Prescription drugs must be appropriately labeled and used only by the person in whose name the prescription was issued. Current use of a prescription drug should be indicated on the medical information form. The confidential sharing of information among staff may be necessary. Facilitators will carry prescription drugs for minors, except those necessary for immediate care (such as asthma inhalers and Epi-Pens) which may be carried by a participant, if appropriate. Staff may carry an extra set of prescription drugs for backup purposes.

Nonprescription Drugs

Facilitators will be responsible for carrying all nonprescription drugs for minors. Facilitators should be aware of nonprescription drugs carried by adults and when they are taken.

Forms and Documentation

Forms serve several purposes that necessitate they be complete, administered according to policy, reviewed by lead facilitators and/or administrators, and filed in the appropriate location for future reference. Forms are used to:

1. Provide documentation that the academic program and the GCSU Outdoor Education Center are in compliance with accredited policy and procedures;
2. Support program planning and implementation by providing information about participants and program sponsors or organizations, which assist in the planning process, checklists and guidelines for lead facilitators to follow, and information to be communicated to participants.
3. Communicate administrative, equipment management, and logistical information to staff or other university departments.
4. Document graduation requirements and supervision of OEC staff.

Procedures

Forms fall into five categories. Within each category a specific form may or may not be a requirement for a program (see Program Administration: Program Definitions), and responsibility for completing and/or submitting a form may rest with the lead facilitator, participant, faculty, or staff. Know what is expected for each role, for a given program. Forms should be completed in an appropriate manner including correct, complete, legible information that is written in ink. Missing information should be added prior to the start of a program, and changes should be initialed by the participant and the lead facilitator. Forms should be submitted in a timely fashion to the appropriate person.

Access to Forms

All forms, policy, and syllabi are available at http://hercules.gcsu.edu/~jhirsch/ in Word or Adobe format. Click on the appropriate sidebar to access index pages.

Outdoor Education Student Forms

1. *Service Hour Report*—completed by *undergraduate and graduate outdoor education majors* and submitted to the coordinator of outdoor education academic programs for submission to the GCSU Experiential Transcript.
2. *Facilitation Hour Report*—completed by graduate outdoor education majors to the coordinator of outdoor education academic programs pre- and postfacilitation hours for submission to the GCSU Experiential Transcript.
3. *Student Use of Personal Vehicles IR/IC*—completed by undergraduate and graduate outdoor education majors and submitted to the coordinator of outdoor education academic programs prior to the use of personal vehicles for academic classes that take place off GCSU campus sites.

Personnel Forms

1. *GCSU Challenge Course Facilitator Checklist*—completed by **OE staff** in conjunction with GCSU Outdoor Education Center training.
2. *PPM and CCFH Review*—completed by **OEC staff** on a yearly basis in conjunction with GCSU Outdoor Education Center training requirements.
3. *Facilitator Feedback*—completed by **OEC staff** after OEC programs as determined by the OEC program coordinator.
4. *Staff Medical Information*—completed by **OEC staff** and updated as necessary. Copies are placed temporarily in program files for access during program and transferred to personnel file at the completion of the program.
5. *Assumption of Risk and Insurance Certification and Waiver of Liability and Covenant Not to Sue*—completed by **OEC staff** and placed in personnel file.
6. *Informed Consent*—completed by **OEC staff** and placed in personnel file.
7. *Personnel File Record*—completed by **OEC staff** and updated by **OEC staff and the OEC program coordinator** as appropriate. **Professional training certificates placed in the student academic file are recorded in the OEC personnel file.**

Program Administration Forms

1. *Accident/Incident Report*—completed by **OE or OEC staff, signed by the injured party;** and submitted to the coordinator of OE programs (See Program Administration: Risk Management: Incident/Accident Reporting).
2. *Program File Summary*—completed by **lead facilitator** and submitted with the program file to be used as an internal reference for OE staff.
3. *Program Evaluation*—completed by **capable participants** in OEC programs and submitted with the program file in accordance with the Board of Regents requirements.
4. *Client Intake Assessment*—completed by the **OEC program coordinator,** given to the lead facilitator, and submitted with the program file.
5. *Program Design Summary*—completed by the **lead facilitator** and submitted with the program file.
6. *Master Program Checklist*—completed by the **lead facilitator** (or designated students in ODED classes) for trips and some workshops, reviewed by the supervising faculty, staff, or primary backup, and submitted with the program file.
7. *Program/Route Plan*—completed by the **lead facilitator** (or designated student in ODED classes) for trips and appropriate workshops, reviewed by the supervising OE staff and primary backup, and submitted with the program file.
8. *Pretrip Meeting Record*—completed by **lead facilitator** for trips only to be submitted with the program file for OEC programs that meet once prior to the program.

Participant Forms

1. *Assumption of Risk and Insurance Certification and Waiver of Liability and Covenant Not to Sue (group and individual)*—on both group and individual Assumption of Risk Forms to be completed by **the participant or legal guardian**, to be **reviewed by lead facilitator** prior to signature, and submitted with the program file. Group or individual forms may be used for classes and clinics; individual forms are used for workshops and trips.
2. *Informed Consent*—completed by the **participant** or legal guardian, to be **reviewed by lead facilitator** prior to signature, and submitted with the program file. May be used in conjunction with a Group Assumption of Risk Form for classes and clinics; individual forms are used for workshops and trips.
3. *Medical Information*—completed by the **participant or legal guardian, reviewed and signed by the lead facilitator or designate**, and submitted with the program file or returned to the OE student master medical form file. Copies are taken on trips and off-site workshops; originals are placed in the backup file for transfer to the appropriate location (master file or program file) upon completion of the program.

Equipment Forms

1. *Challenge Course Inspection*—completed by **OE staff** and submitted to the OEC equipment and facilities coordinator.
2. *Equipment Reservation*—completed by **faculty, staff, OE students or renter** to reserve equipment and submitted to the OEC equipment and facilities coordinator.
3. *Tent Group and Program Reservation*—completed by **faculty, staff, or instructors** on an as-needed basis for equipment used for teaching purposes.
4. *Challenge Course and Tango Tower Equipment Reservation*—completed by the **lead facilitator** and submitted to the OEC equipment and facilities coordinator.
5. *Group Development Activities Equipment Reservation*—completed by the **lead facilitator** (or student for OE classes) and submitted to the OEC equipment and facilities coordinator.
6. *Rock Climbing Equipment Reservation*—completed by the **lead facilitator** and submitted to the OEC equipment and facilities coordinator.
7. *Water Equipment Reservation*—completed by the **lead facilitator** (or student for OE classes) and submitted to the OEC equipment and facilities coordinator.
8. *Equipment Inspection and Maintenance* (forms for specific equipment)—completed by **student and staff inspecting or maintaining equipment** and submitted to the OEC equipment and facilities coordinator.

GCSU Forms

1. *Request for Compensation*—completed by the **OEC program coordinator** and **submitted to the OEC director.**
2. *Request for Extra Compensation*—completed by the **OEC program coordinator** and **submitted to the OEC director.**
3. *Facilities Request Form*—completed on the web by **OE staff** and **submitted to the appropriate facilities manager.**

SECTION 5

HUMAN RESOURCES: STAFF SELECTION, HIRING, TRAINING, AND SUPERVISION

Chadwick School	*F* Education
	E West Region
	C Students Grades K–12
	S 5.01

Instructor Information

Chadwick Outdoor Education Instructors and Instructional Methods

Instructors use many different styles of teaching and instructing. Instructors understand the many facets of group development and the dynamics that run within groups. Their expertise allows them to adjust the level of experience to foster a group's process of development. Instructors use many hands-on techniques during courses, including demonstration of techniques, question and answer, practice, evaluation and more practice. Instructors use experiential learning and learning by doing in combination with critical reflection in many aspects of the program.

Because of the nature of outdoor education, the teachable moment is a widely used strategy. Often on an outdoor course, animals, plants, people or situations present themselves at opportune (and inopportune) moments that make for a powerful teaching situation. Instructors also use facilitation, the cornerstone of effective adventure-based learning. Instructors guide the growth and learning experiences that occur on courses and facilitate the transference of the learning back to the home and school environment. Facilitation is done formally and informally, through discussion, front loading and journaling on subjects such as leadership, followership, feelings, cooperation, trust, decision making and closure.

A fundamental aspect of instructors' work is to impel students into adventures while keeping actual risk to a minimum and providing a combination of support and challenge, so students will take physical and emotional risks. This is the crux of the job. The ability to produce challenges that will be taken and to provide support that will be accepted relies on the ability to connect with the students and to win their respect. Making connections and earning respect require a high level of integrity.

Instructors meet with the director and the assistant director of Outdoor Education for two to four days of planning and orientation before each course. During this time staff share ideas, review risk management policy and procedures, and refine their abilities as leaders and educators. After each course, each instructor team meets with the director and/or assistant director of the Outdoor Education Program to debrief their course experience.

Instructors follow a written syllabus for each course and adhere to a detailed set of risk management policies, outlined in the instructor manual. This document also details emergency procedures, lists emergency contacts, and gives directions to medical facilities for each of our course areas. All instructors have CPR and wilderness first aid certification.

The program uses a combination of cell phones, satellite phones and/or two-way radios as part of the emergency response. Instructors carry different devices for different course areas based on terrain and coverage of communication devices.

Staffing Process and Hiring Timeline

In order to be hired as a part-time employee at the Chadwick School, potential instructors must apply to the Outdoor Education Program with a resume and references. If it is determined that the applicant will make a good fit with the program, interviews take place and written notes are added to the file, references are then contacted to reflect accuracy and support for applicants experience and background.

Following the initial process mentioned above, the applicant must complete a significant amount of paperwork, pass a TB test, complete a DMV check, and fingerprint livescan. The OE assistant director works closely with the school's controller throughout this process, this includes an annual update of paperwork instructions and forms, which make up the initial hiring packet. The paperwork completed to become a Chadwick School part-time faculty member is housed in the business office, while additional paperwork required by the outdoor program is housed in the Outdoor Education office. OE office files include: instructor resume and references, emergency card contact info, copies of WFR and CPR certifications, staff medical form, and an acknowledgement of receipt of the Instructor's Manual and the part-time staff handbook. The files also include any correspondence received by the instructor and copies of present and past contracts. We also have a binder for instructor contact and data base information.

A checklist for all paperwork (required by the business office and outdoor program) has been developed to record all paperwork received, and the checklist binder is kept in the OE office since paperwork is received in a piecemeal fashion. The business office does not have a full-time personnel manager, and requests have been made that we keep paperwork until files are complete.

Prior to working courses, instructors are informed if their WFR and CPR certifications have expired, to insure they are current in their certifications while working Chadwick Outdoor Education courses. Email has greatly increased the ability to communicate more readily with instructors. Instructors also receive precourse information, orientation schedules, and course curriculums several weeks prior to each course via email, to allow for more effective preparation and course planning.

Recruiting takes place through word of mouth and via the program's newsletter, which is sent out three times per year. Hardcopies are sent out to approximately a hundred programs to be posted for their instructors to access. Email newsletters are sent out to several hundred recipients. Through this process, and with the effectiveness of email, we have been able to access more staff who are interested in working for the Chadwick Outdoor Education Program, which has increased our instructor pool and increased our effectiveness in communication with instructors.

Hiring Policies for Instructors

The following experience and attributes will be taken into consideration when offering instructors courses to work. The more experience and ability in any and all these areas the more consideration will be given in offering instructional work. COE requires:

- Instructors with quality experience teaching in a variety of settings, such as the outdoor environment, in particular areas in which the course is operating, experience teaching prior COE courses, and teaching in a classroom setting.
- Instructors with quality experience teaching the 7–12 grades, particularly Chadwick students or within an independent school setting.
- Instructors with the experience to recognize and act on appropriate and inappropriate student behavior. The ability to manage student-to-student and instructor-to-student

relationships in order to help students develop and grow during outdoor courses and consequently back at school/home is paramount. This includes giving positive and negative feedback and dealing with conflict and stress.

- Instructors with the technical ability in the particular activity taught; also required is technical knowledge coupled with good risk management skills for institutional settings. Instructors are required who want to improve their abilities to teach a technical subject in an institutional setting while also developing the whole person.
- Instructors who are good environmental role models with a sound knowledge of natural history of the particular environment of the course area.
- Instructors need a current WFR and CPR certification.
- Instructors need to have and maintain a safe driving record, with experience driving large passenger vans.

Responsibilities of Instructors

- All instructors are responsible for maintaining and updating the program with all required certification, such as wilderness first responder and CPR certificates.
- All courses begin with a 1- to 4-day precourse orientation. Orientations generally begin at 8:00 a.m. Instructors are to be punctual and prepared and should have set aside personal business for the duration of the orientation and course.
- For each course instructors are to produce a written log detailing the following: each day's activities, lessons, and camp locations; all accidents, incidents, near misses, any first aid administered, course area information, and itinerary recommendations.
- All instructors must read, know, and follow the Chadwick Outdoor Education risk management policies and follow the written syllabus for the course.
- Instructors will make sure all Chadwick equipment, including items rented or lent to students is returned at the end of the course.
- Instructors may be required to complete a written comment on each student that is in their group while out on a course.
- Courses end with a debrief between instructor pairs or single instructors or instructors as a group and the director or the assistant director or both. The course log is reviewed, any risk management concerns, accidents, behavioral incidents or near miss information is noted and added to the course report. Instructors will complete a WRMC incident report form for each incident. Instructor performance will be discussed. Instructors need to bring all applicable paperwork, including a detailed course log, to turn in at the debrief.

Instructor Compensation

- Instructors will receive a contract for work they are being offered. The contract will outline orientation dates, the course dates, course location, and conditions of employment.
- Positions available are:
    - Lead instructor (works solo, with faculty or with an assistant instructor).

- Assistant instructor (works with a lead or specialist instructor).
- Co-instructor (works with another co-instructor).
- Logistics (runs equipment and food logistics).
- Specialist instructor (a certified raft guide, ACA instructor or AMGA instructor).
- Trainee instructor (works with any of the above in a student noncontact role).
- Instructors new to the program will start at a base rate of $80 for student contact (instructional) days and 75% of that rate for noncontact days. After working two Chadwick courses, prior instructional experience will be taken into account regarding placement on the salary scale. For each instructional year (160 student-contact field days) of prior experience, instructors will advance one level on the scale. Instructors pay rate will then increase in increments according to the scale below, based on the number of days with Chadwick Outdoor Education.

- Lead instructor, assistant instructor, and co-instructor positions will be designated when working in instructional teams on courses, determined by the individual instructor's placement in the salary scale.

Salary scale for instructors.

- The entire course is paid at the new rate when an instructor's pay rate changes during a course.
- Student noncontact days are paid at 75% of the instructional rate. These days are not counted in calculating an instructor's pay rate.
- As a school employee, instructors are covered by worker's compensation insurance. Taxes will be deducted.
- Chadwick provides all food and housing during orientations.
- If a course is canceled within 30 days of the start, instructors will receive 30% of their pay rate.
- Instructors who work six or more courses at least 5 days long per academic year will be eligible for up to $300 toward further instructor training (a FIT award). For example awards may be given toward WFR training, AMGA training, ACA training. The program is committed to the training and development of instructors in the following areas; technical skills, risk management skills, instructional and teaching skills, including methods, models, group development and dynamics, individual behavior and motivation and facilitation, leadership skills including judgment, decision making, and problem solving.
- The program is able to purchase outdoor equipment for instructors at wholesale prices from many suppliers. An additional charge of 5% over the wholesale price is made to cover shipping expenses to Chadwick.
- If mail is to be forwarded to Chadwick School during the course, instructors will advise the director or assistant director. Chadwick School takes no responsibility for lost mail.
- Instructors can store equipment at the school while out on the course.

Job Description for Chadwick Outdoor Education Instructors

Description of job: Outdoor Education instructors will instruct backpacking courses to age 7–12 students. Instructors are required to teach a core curriculum for all courses and additional backpacking curriculum for various courses. Maintain a detailed course log. Be able to drive large passenger vans. Have excellent risk management skills.

Location of job: Chadwick School and a wide variety of course areas in CA

Salary and benefits: See instructor compensation.

Qualifications: Experience and attributes are sought in the following areas:

1. Instructors with quality experience teaching in a variety of settings, such as the outdoor environment, in particular areas in which the course is operating, experience teaching prior COE courses, and teaching in a classroom setting.
2. Instructors with quality experience teaching the 7–12 age groups, particularly Chadwick students or within an independent school setting.
3. Instructors with the experience to recognize and act on appropriate and inappropriate student behavior.
4. The ability to manage student-to-student and instructor-to-student relationships in order to help students develop and grow on outdoor courses and consequently back at school/home is paramount. This includes giving positive and negative feedback and dealing with conflict and stress.
5. Instructors with the technical ability in the particular activity taught; also required is technical knowledge coupled with good risk management skills for institutional settings.
6. Instructors are required who want to improve their abilities to teach a technical subject in an institutional setting while also developing the whole person.
7. Instructors who are good environmental role models with a sound knowledge of natural history of the particular environment of the course area.
8. Instructors need a current WFR and CPR certification.
9. Instructors need to have a driver's license and maintain a safe driving record, with experience driving large passenger vans.

Available: Year round

Job Description for Chadwick Outdoor Education Specialist Instructors

This is a description for specialists required for rock climbing, kayaking (sea and/or white-water) rafting, mountaineering, etc.

Description of job: Outdoor Education instructors will instruct in the specialized activity courses to age 7–12. Instructors are required to teach a core curriculum for all courses and additional specialized activity curriculum for various courses. Maintain a detailed course log. Be able to drive large passenger vans. Have excellent risk management skills.

Location of job: Chadwick School and a wide variety of course areas in CA

Salary and benefits: See instructor compensation.

Qualifications: Experience and attributes is sought in the following areas:

1. Instructors with quality experience teaching in a variety of settings, such as the outdoor environment, in particular areas in which the course is operating, experience teaching prior COE courses, and teaching in a classroom setting.
2. Instructors with quality experience teaching the 7–12 age groups, particularly Chadwick students or within an independent school setting.
3. Instructors with the experience to recognize and act on appropriate and inappropriate student behavior.
4. The ability to manage student-to-student and instructor-to-student relationships in order to help students develop and grow on outdoor courses and consequently back at school/home is paramount. This includes giving positive and negative feedback and dealing with conflict and stress.
5. Instructors with the technical ability in the particular activity taught; also required is technical knowledge coupled with good risk management skills for institutional settings.
6. Instructors are required who want to improve their abilities to teach a technical subject in an institutional setting while also developing the whole person.
7. Instructors who are good environmental role models with a sound knowledge of natural history of the particular environment of the course area.
8. Instructors need a current WFR and CPR certification.
9. Instructors need to have a driver's license and maintain a safe driving record, with experience driving large passenger vans.
10. Proficient skills in the technical activity so that instructors can comfortably teach the activity to students. Certifications in the particular activity (i.e.. ACA instructor training and swift-water training for kayak courses, AMGA certifications for rock climbing and mountaineering courses).

Available: Year round

Red Top Meadows	F Therapeutic
	E Rocky Mountain Region
	C Adolescent Males
	S 5.01, 5.04, 5.05, 5.07,

Wilderness Staff

Red Top uses our residential childcare staff as field staff for all our wilderness programs with the exception of the special summer programs. Those trips employ a combination of ex-Red Top senior staff and additional staff hired on contract.

Skill Set

1. Conducting adventure-based activities with a group that has therapeutic needs requires staff to have both solid backcountry wilderness skills as well as good "people" skills.
2. Red Top strives to ensure that each instructor team possesses a balance of these skills.
3. Instructor teams at RTM should be able to perform the following skills:

Wilderness skills.

- Navigate safely in the backcountry (have solid map and compass skills);
- Teach students the necessary wilderness skills (see hard skills section);
- Foresee and evaluate potential hazards;
- Assess students' abilities and limitations;
- Respond to an emergency in a professional manner;
- Develop and implement an evacuation plan;
- Follow procedures for search and rescue in the event of a lost or runaway student;
- Provide necessary first aid to the level of their ability and improvise as needed in a wilderness setting;
- Instruct students in proper care and use of equipment and repair equipment in the field;
- Complete all required paperwork such as point sheets, journals, and incident reports;
- Understand personal and professional liability;
- Exercise good judgment and common sense.

Soft skills.

- Practice good listening;
- Be empathetic of others' feelings, thoughts, and situations;
- Be willing to give and receive feedback;
- Be willing to hold students accountable for their behavior;

- Help students solve problems and resolve conflicts;
- Observe the process of the group's dynamics, as well as the content;
- Understand student treatment plans (the goals and skills they're working on);
- Help students relate their wilderness experience to their daily lives by drawing parallels, using metaphors, and asking questions;
- Have a sense of humor, play, and have fun.

Wilderness Staff Qualifications

Determining when a staff is ready to lead is a decision made by the treatment/administration team based on the self-assessment of the staff and recommendations of senior staff who have witnessed competencies during training and in the field.

Level 1—new staff.

- Meets the basic criteria for being a RTM staff (interviewed, 21 years of age or older, signed appropriate forms, etc.);
- Has completed a 2-day orientation to the RTM residential program and has basic knowledge of the philosophy and policy and procedures of the RTM;
- Has read the residential program staff manual, student manual and other orientation materials;
- Has a minimum of Basic First Aid and CPR;
- Has completed an orientation training for the RTM Wilderness Program;
- Has read the Wilderness Manual and has a basic understanding of the goals and objectives of the Wilderness Education Curriculum;
- Has basic camping skills and can take care of themselves in a wilderness environment.

Level 2—assistant.

- Meets all criteria for Level 1 staff;
- Can perform and practice policy and procedures outlined in the Wilderness Education Curriculum;
- Has solid backcountry skills (See Wilderness Manual);
- Has wilderness first aid (WFA) or wilderness first responder (WFR) certification;
- Has been in the field as a third for RTM or has equivalent prior experience in another wilderness program;
- Has ability to teach wilderness curriculum classes in the classroom;
- Has completed Mandt training;
- Has ability to understand and carry out student treatment plan;
- Has ability and willingness to plan and facilitate group wrap-ups and circle-ups.

Lead staff.

- Meets all the requirements of Level 2 staff;
- Has a minimum of 40 field days or equivalent experience in a wilderness type program;
- Has the willingness and confidence to take on leadership role and responsibilities;
- Demonstrates the ability and has experience responding effectively to student's emotional and behavioral crisis;
- Has ability to manage risk in the field by foreseeing/evaluating hazards, carrying out policy and procedures and being able to develop and execute an effective evacuation plan;
- Has demonstrated sound judgment.

First-Aid Qualifications

It is the goal of the RTM program to have all of our field instructors at a WFR (wilderness first responder) or equivalent level of training. At the present time it is our policy to have a minimum of one WFR or equivalent and one WFA (wilderness first aid) per instructor team in the field.

Staff-to-Student Ratios

It is the belief of the RTM program that individual, group, and program goals are more likely to be met when there is appropriate supervision and the group size is not too large. For these reasons it is Red Top policy to have a maximum of eight students on a trip and a minimum of two staff. RTM usually operates with three staff for a crew of seven students.

Staffing Patterns

Most of the RTM residential staff are expected to participate in the wilderness component of the program. The treatment/administration team is in charge of selecting teams. When choosing instructor teams the following variables are considered:

- Who is qualified to be a lead staff
- First-aid training
- Seniority
- Hard skill/soft skill balance
- Personalities
- Staying close to staff schedule to keep people's hours balanced

Staff Training

1. Staff training is spread throughout the year in staff meetings, staff retreat, in-service training, reading assignments, etc.
2. An annual schedule for all the topics for both residential and wilderness programs, with an estimation of # of training hours, is posted in the office.
3. During the months of April, May, and June, additional training days are scheduled to cover specific wilderness skills.
4. Depending on the needs of the staff, topics may include:

- Rock site management
- Challenge course facilitation
- Map and compass skills
- First-aid recertification
- Emergency response review
- Wilderness education curriculum review
- Processing/Facilitation techniques
- Games and initiatives
- Treatment issues
- Case studies

5. All training should be documented in the staff training log.
6. Staff planning on working the wilderness program needs to attend these trainings.
7. If for some reason a staff member cannot attend, they will need to make special arrangements with the wilderness director to make up the material.
8. The arrangement will depend on the circumstance and the amount of training and experience the staff member has.

Supplemental training days.

Prior to each wilderness trip there will be time set aside to review information specific to that trip. This may include but is not limited to:

- Specific program goals
- Student cases—goals, treatment issues, medications, strategies
- Trip logistics, including travel, permits, reissues, emergency vehicles, extra materials or equipment
- Environmental concerns
- Potential hazards and first-aid highlights
- Emergency procedures specific to that trip

Do-it-yourself training.

- During the year, training materials will be made available for the staff to read on their own.
- These assignments are in a file box in the staff room.
- Staff are responsible for completing the assignment and signing the sheet next to their name. Understanding of these materials may be discussed in monthly all-staff meetings.
- Training subjects vary from readings to practical assignments.

On-the-job training.

RTM has a history of retaining senior staff for a number of years. Much of a new staff member's training and evaluation happens on the job and in the field. Senior staff members are responsible for assessing new staff members' skills and working with them to improve those skills.

First-aid training.

RTM will sponsor a WFA/WFR recertification at RTM every 2 years. Staff unable to attend this training will be responsible to find their own course before their certification expires.

Conferences and networking.

Each year, some staff members attend workshops and trainings of various kinds. Also, being located in a small town, it is common to discuss trends in the adventure field with other professionals in the area. Information gathered at trainings or informally is passed on to the RTM staff through discussions, meetings, and/or written materials.

Instructor Teams

On each RTM wilderness trip the instructor team will consist of one lead instructor, one instructor, and a third staff member who might be an instructor in training or a more experienced staff. It should be made clear by the program director or the wilderness director who the lead instructor is for each trip. The lead instructor is responsible for making final decisions in the event of disagreement in the team. Instructor teams should take time before the trip to prepare and discuss how they are going to present themselves and handle certain aspects of the trip. Instructors should talk about team unity, specific roles, communication, and vulnerabilities.

Team unity.

It is important that instructors present themselves as a unified team to the students. Students need to see instructors as being organized, competent, and in agreement on issues regarding policy and procedure. This is important in order for students to have trust and confidence in their instructors' abilities to lead them safely on their trip. For this reason, instructors should:

- Work out as many details as possible regarding policy and procedure prior to the trip;
- Handle disagreements and discussions in the field privately;
- Be flexible on small issues of personal preference;
- Allow the lead instructor to make final decisions for the sake of unity.

Roles.

Wilderness instructors in general need to be multitalented. It is their job to be teachers, counselors, repair persons, first aiders, and risk managers among other things. For the sake of organization and to prevent getting overwhelmed, instructors should have designated roles. This means that each instructor has certain functions for which they are the primary person in charge. Distinguishing roles does not mean that only one person does repairs or first aid, but having one person in charge can reduce confusion and allow instructors to focus on fewer things. Possible roles may include:

- First aid and medications;
- Repair of equipment and clothing;
- Group facilitator or therapeutic person (someone that keeps track of student and group goals);
- Safety person in charge of scouting out potential hazards.

It is also important for staff to stay aware of the roles of authority. If one instructor is always doing the confronting and offering consequences for negative behaviors, it may lead to problems in how the team is viewed by the students.

Communication.

In order for instructors to be an effective team and cover all their responsibilities, they must communicate clearly with each other. It is essential for instructors to know where all the students are and what they are doing at all times. Instructors should make it a point to check in with each other frequently regarding the status of the group.

On a more personal level, instructors should take time on a regular basis to talk about how they are doing as a team and share how they are doing personally. It is critical to take time to give positive feedback to each other, as well as constructive criticisms. Personal issues between staff need to be dealt with in a respectful and responsible manner. Resentments amongst staff can have a strong negative affect on the group.

Personal gift.

Wilderness instructors are all required to know a specific set of skills and possess a personal quality that enables them to lead students safely in the field. The personal gift is the extra interest, hobby, skill or quality that each instructor possesses and brings to the course to share with others. It is the mixture of the gifts brought to a course that makes each course unique, educational, and fun. Instructors are encouraged to think about what their talents are and bring a gift to share.

University of New Hampshire	*F*	**Education**
	E	**Northeast Region**
	C	**University Outdoor Education Students and General Population**
	S	**5.01**

General Personnel

This policy and procedures manual is written for the faculty, staff, participants, clients, and participants of the UNH Outdoor Education Program and is intended to describe some of the expectations and responsibilities of people connected to the option. Each of these groups is defined below:

- **Faculty:** individuals who are either full-time or adjunct members of the faculty of the University of New Hampshire. An updated list of approved faculty is on file in the Kinesiology Department office. The rights and responsibilities of faculty members associated with the Outdoor Education Program are contained in the UNH Faculty Personnel Policies.
- **Staff:** for the purpose of this manual, a staff member in the OE Program is defined as anyone in a designated leadership role while conducting an activity sponsored by the UNH Outdoor Education Program. In some instances, staff members are permanent employees of the University community, as in those staff who work at the Browne Center. In other instances, the term *staff* refers to contract leaders whom, while not permanently employed at UNH, are temporarily hired to conduct a program. The term *staff*

also refers to UNH participants (graduate and undergraduate) who are in leadership positions during an activity or trip. Staff members are accountable to both the general University policy and procedures, and the specific policies of the unit in which they work (e.g., The Browne Center). All staff connected to the OE Program, including the Browne Center, use the policy and procedures detailed in this manual.

- **Participants:** part-time and full-time enrolled UNH participants. The conduct and privileges of UNH participants are contained in The Participant Rights, Rules, and Responsibilities Policies and the Participant Handbook.
- **Client and/or Participant:** attendees on sponsored OE Programs and activities. The behavioral expectation will be clearly described for clients/participants. These expectations will vary depending upon the activity.

Team Leadership Results, LLC	*F* Training and Development
	E Mid-South Region
	C Adults
	S 5.01–5.10

Staff and Human Resources

General

Team Leadership administers and presents its programs through the contributions of the following human resources:

1. Full Time:
   a. Program director
   b. Program coordinator/office administrator
2. Part Time:
   a. Consultants
3. Contracted:
   a. Program facilitators

Qualifications and Selection

Contracting.

The program hires staff that is qualified for the activities and participants they will be involved with, and the program has a system of supervising, training, and assessing staff. Team Leadership contracts staff that is qualified for the activities and participants they will be involved with. (See Facilitator Selection.) Team Leadership has a system for training, supervising, and assessing staff performance. (See Employee Development.) Team Leadership has published the following resources:

1. Team Leadership Safety Standards and Procedures
2. Team Leadership Policy Manual
3. Team Leadership Facilitator Training Manual (Low Elements)
4. Team Leadership Facilitator Training Manual (High Elements)

Through these means, staff knows what is expected of them and what the organization's policies and standards are.

Selection.

Selection of facilitators to work any specific program is left to the discretion of the program director. Many considerations play into this decision, most of which have to do with matching the profile of the facilitator with the profile of the participant group and the goals and objectives of the program. Team Leadership also considers the currency of the facilitator's experience and attendance at the monthly safety meeting when selecting facilitators to work. Team Leadership has published a list of considerations used for selection to work its programs.

Contract.

All part-time challenge course facilitators are required to have a completed and signed facilitator contract on file at the Team Leadership business office.

Staff Training and Development

Basic requirement.

All part-time challenge course facilitators are required to have completed a structured program of challenge course facilitator training approved by the program director. When the program includes high elements, staff will be selected who are specifically qualified through a structured program of high element challenge course training.

Team Leadership periodically conducts facilitator training programs for certification in both the low elements and the high elements. Each program consists of 40 hours of experiential training and awards certificates of completion based upon a practical grade and a written exam covering program content. Enrollment requirements include a minimum age of 18 and no significantly limiting physical or psychological conditions.

Team Leadership also recognizes facilitator training certification from certain other providers, though not all programs are considered to provide sufficiently equivalent training. In such cases Team Leadership reserves the right to require additional training prior to selection for employment.

Employee development opportunities.

Team Leadership provides opportunities for employees to attain higher levels of professional and personal development. These opportunities include:

1. **Safety Meetings:** Monthly safety meetings focus upon safety concerns and experiential networking around best practices for challenge course initiatives.
2. **Library:** Access to a collection of publications and subscriptions to several monthly publications of professional interest to experiential training facilitators. These publications are accessible at the Team Leadership business office.
3. **Workshops:** Advanced training workshops in which Team Leadership hosts a presenter or presenters from the network of nationally recognized professionals in the field.

4. **Conferences:** Team Leadership facilitators and staff may obtain discounts on conference fees and support for travel to professional conferences.

Professional currency.

Team Leadership program staff keeps up to date with changes in technology and procedures for program activities. (See Employee Development.)

First-Aid and CPR.

All challenge course facilitators are required to have current documentation of first-aid and CPR training on file in the Team Leadership business office.

Grievance Procedure

Description.

Team Leadership suggests the following procedure for any employee:

1. Schedule a private conference with the person with whom you have the grievance. If the grievance is with the organization, schedule a private conference with the CEO/ program director.
2. If no satisfaction is achieved from this measure, schedule a mediated conference with the same party that will include a neutral mediating volunteer who is acceptable to both parties in this role.
3. If no satisfaction is achieved from this measure, schedule a ready circle in which both parties to the issue may invite an equal number of Team Leadership associates (the total number should not exceed 12). The meeting should be held in a meeting area acceptable to both parties.
4. If no satisfaction is achieved from this measure, then mediation through legal counsel is suggested.

Records.

All personnel records are maintained in the Team Leadership business office files.

Knowledge of Environment

Program areas.

Team Leadership staff is familiar with program areas where activities are conducted so that their focus can be on the participants and the program goals. Team Leadership staff gets to know the Team Leadership program areas through attending the facilitator training programs and the monthly safety meetings.

Weather knowledge.

Team Leadership staff is skilled in observing, interpreting, and predicting basic weather patterns. Because of the policy of using co-facilitators, Team Leadership facilitators benefit from the knowledge and experience of a partner and cohort in making assessments and judgment calls. Team Leadership attempts to staff each program with facilitators who have lived in the central and south Texas region long enough to recognize the customary signs of approaching weather. Staff is encouraged to check weather forecasts as program dates approach. When inclement weather conditions are predicted facilitators are to pack special equipment and plan alternative initiatives that will allow participants to be unhampered in the pursuit of their program objectives.

Site orientation.

Team Leadership staff are skilled and effective at navigating in the program areas encountered. New facilitators will become familiar with the challenge course environments in the facilitator training, the safety meetings, and during early assignments of program co-facilitation. Other challenge environments are scouted by staff in advance of the program when there is no familiarity with the site and its topography.

Hazard awareness.

The program and staff are familiar with the identification, avoidance, and treatment of any specific environmental hazard in the program area. Team Leadership staff and the risk management program acknowledge the existence of environmental hazards specific to the program areas. Participants are briefed at the start of each program on the presence of Africanized bees, stinging scorpions, common wasps and hornets, Black Widow and Brown Recluse spiders, four varieties of poisonous snakes, and deer ticks that carry Lyme disease. Facilitators are taught first aid for snakebite and other injected poisons based upon the most current state Department of Health procedures.

Poison oak and poison ivy, different varieties of cactus, stinging nettles, and various other thorny species of plant life are common to certain areas of program activity. Staff is aware, and they caution participants about these. Given appropriate caution, few problems are encountered. Allergies due to plant allergens are common in this area and facilitators are aware of the most problematic.

Cold and hot weather contingencies have been described in Safety Standards and Procedures.

Site terrain.

Staff is capable of conducting operations appropriately in the terrain where activities occur. Team Leadership staff is professionally trained by a recognized challenge course training provider. The great majority has been through Team Leadership's facilitator training and all are included in the monthly safety meetings. Team Leadership's training program and monthly meetings take place on the terrain used for the great majority of programs. Facilitators develop sufficient familiarity with the terrain that they can focus upon the participant's experience and address changes in weather, lost resources, emergent safety concerns, or other unforeseen program changes.

Participant Awareness

Participant health information.

Program and staff are aware of relevant medical and psychological histories and health needs as disclosed by the participant. Team Leadership uses a health screening form (part of the Participant Registration form) that is a confidential disclosure of health and psychological limitations as perceived and reported by the participant or, in the case of minors, by the parent or guardian.

The screening includes a section on cardiac risk factors, medications, psychological conditions, allergies, pregnancy, recent injuries or surgery, blood sugar problems, etc. (See Participant Registration.) These screenings are provided to the program facilitators at the earliest possible opportunity, but at the latest on the day of the program.

Participants are also asked to check in physically and emotionally on the day of the program. This provides an opportunity to publicly declare any condition, which may limit one's participation so that team members may adjust their expectations downward for those who need that consideration.

Utilization of participant information.

Staff selects activities based upon participant skill levels, physical abilities, and psychological or emotional readiness. For Team Leadership staff safety consciousness includes emotional safety. This is stressed in Team Leadership's facilitator training programs, in the Facilitator Training Manual, and in the monthly safety meetings. Activity sequencing, team check-in, facilitator briefings, the participant health screening and client interviews all contribute to the assessment of client skill and ability levels.

The ability of Team Leadership facilitators to rely upon a co-facilitator in making judgment calls about participant group's readiness for the program elements that were planned allows facilitators to flex and adapt the program in progress with a measure of confidence that would not be available to a facilitator working solo with a group.

Participant psychological information.

Staff have an appropriate level of training to identify and cope with the anticipated psychological needs of participants. Team Leadership staff varies in their experience and in formal certification to work with special populations. When psychological insights are the primary objective of the program, Team Leadership works to schedule facilitators with appropriate backgrounds. All Team Leadership staff have college backgrounds, and a number have training in working with special populations. (See Facilitator Bios.)

Risk Management and Response

Staff preparedness.

Staff have skill and experience to conduct stated program activities and meet the risk management, operational, and curriculum expectations of the program. Team Leadership staff is trained to effect simple and complex rescues both within the facilitator training program, and in the monthly safety meeting. Team Leadership facilitators are taught to be resourceful and to draw upon the capacities of the co-facilitator and of members of the participant group to manage risks associated with unexpected situations. The monthly safety meeting offers opportunities to consider other participant outcomes than the ones customarily seen. In this way facilitators become proactive in spotting problem potentials. The logging of close calls is another helpful resource in preparing facilitators. When close calls are examined, a group of facilitators can often identify contributing elements that set up unsafe situations and thereby avoid an accident.

Hygiene, first aid, and safety.

Staff is skilled in improvising to meet food and water needs in case of emergencies. They know how to prevent contamination under such conditions and how to treat any consequences of the same. Team Leadership staff is trained in basic first aid and safety. Some have additional training in medicine and nursing. In addition, all have college education and a mature awareness of the consequences of contaminated foodstuffs, water. The general policy is to dispose of any food or water that is of doubtful quality or purity. Because most Team Leadership programs last only a day, most of the concern for contamination has to do with the proper cleaning of water jugs and the timely consumption of box lunches delivered to the challenge course, and staff are aware of these concerns.

Clothing and shelter.

Staff is skilled in improvising to meet clothing, equipment, and shelter needs in case of emergencies. Team Leadership staff is in general people who spend time in the great outdoors and possess fundamental competence and sound judgment based upon personal experiences in this environment. They are provided with supplies and equipment sufficient to meet both predictable and unexpected contingencies.

Staff that guide rock-climbing participants are led by someone with rock site management training. Team Leadership has contracted to provide two of these training programs for its facilitators from Outward Bound and from the International Mountain Guides Association during the 7 years of its operations.

Team Leadership works to assure that adequate water, food, and shelter are available for all its programs. When inclement weather is predicted, Team Leadership provides special equipment as a proactive measure.

Exposure control.

The program has a Hazard Communication and Exposure Control Plan. Team Leadership complies with appropriate legal statutes by including in its first-aid training a section on occupational exposure to blood-borne pathogens. Each first-aid kit is supplied with latex gloves, which are to be used in any case where one is treating external bleeding. See Hazard Communication and Exposure Control Plan.

Emergency care and transport.

Staff has had theoretical and practical training in emergency medical care. Team Leadership staff are required to have the appropriate level of first-aid and emergency care training for the kinds of participants, programs, and activities they encounter. Team Leadership provides an emergency first-aid kit that is carried with each group on the challenge course. A phone is available for each program coordinator should the EMS need to be activated. Team Leadership refreshes facilitators on first-aid practices during the monthly safety meeting. Emergency protocols are practiced during high-element rescues in the same context.

In the majority of cases where transport to medical facilities is called for, Team Leadership staff is to manage the patient until professional emergency responders can arrive at the scene. Therefore the staff may remove the injured victim from an environment that may cause immediate further harm, maintain an airway, stop external bleeding, immobilize and treat for shock, recognize and treat environmental emergencies, make all reasonable efforts to determine when an injury or illness necessitates evacuation and mentor and record vital signs, recording all pertinent information needed for the victim and the Safety Committee's records.

Georgia College & State University	
	F Education
	E Southeast Region
	C University Outdoor Education Students and General Population
	S 5.01

Personnel Administration

Faculty

Roles and responsibilities for faculty extend beyond academic programs to responsibilities associated with the GCSU Outdoor Education Center (OEC). One faculty will serve as the coordinator of outdoor education programs and director of the OEC. The other faculty will serve as the coordinator of technical cohorts. Both will serve as needed in all aspects of academic and service programs, supervise graduate assistants, develop and implement policy and procedures, maintain compliance with accreditation standards, serve the university and the profession, and engage in scholarly activity.

Outdoor Education Staff

Outdoor education staff (OE staff) is a collective term used to refer to faculty, graduate assistants, and undergraduate or graduate students completing directed projects or practicum courses under the supervision of outdoor education faculty or OE graduate assistants. OE staff are a subcommittee of the Outdoor

Education Safety and Risk Management Committee (SRMC), and as such will meet weekly or biweekly to address matters related to the administration of outdoor education programs at GCSU. Safety and risk management matters may be referred to the appropriate advisor on the SRMC on a needs basis. Graduate assistantship staff includes the following positions:

Georgia College OEC equipment and facilities coordinator.

1. Manage equipment areas at Lake Laurel Campus (water, land, and challenge course equipment).
   a. Input acquisition and maintenance records into database in compliance with industry standards and AEE accreditation requirements;
   b. Complete a detailed inspection of equipment on a yearly basis;
   c. Develop an equipment acquisition plan and procedures for receiving equipment;
   d. Submit commitment requests to the coordinator of outdoor education programs;
   e. Complete a detailed inspection of the challenge course prior to the beginning of each semester;
   f. Fill equipment requests for academic and service programs;
   g. Provide maintenance to equipment.
2. Manage permits, licenses, and regulatory requirements for vehicles, trailers, and USFS sites used for OEC programs and academic classes.
3. Manage GCSU facilities.
   a. Oversee outdoor education facilities and submit work requests to Physical Plant as necessary;
   b. Complete regular inspections of attractive nuisance facilities and report incidents to the coordinator of outdoor education programs.
4. Manage medical supplies in compliance with WFR protocols, industry standards, and AEE accreditation.
   a. Maintain three WFR kits;
   b. Maintain first-aid kits for on-site locations;
   c. Develop and implement a system for reporting use of contents of WFR and first-aid kits;
   d. Liaison with student health services;
   e. Dispose of toxic waste in accordance with GCSU policy.
5. Manage a professional equipment acquisition program for outdoor education students, faculty, and staff.
   a. Liaison with equipment vendors regarding contact information and ordering procedures;
   b. Communicate with outdoor education students regarding procedures for ordering equipment;
   c. Maintain price and product information;
   d. advise students, staff, and faculty about equipment options.

Georgia College OEC program coordinator.

1. Manage contracts for programs and services offered by the GCSU Outdoor Education Center in compliance with AEE accreditation standards.
   a. Develop contract specifications (terms and responsibilities) for GCSU student, faculty, and staff groups; and community and professional groups;
   b. Maintain program and site files in accordance with accreditation standards and GCSU policy;
   c. Manage billing and payment systems for staff and clients;
   d. Reserve facilities, arrange for support services as requested by clients;
   e. Assess client goals for program development;
   f. Liaison with client representative.
2. Manage OEC staff.
   a. Establish and maintain current and complete OEC personnel files;
   b. Provide supervision and feedback to staff based on program evaluation feedback from clients and facilitator feedback from co-facilitators;
   c. Assist with the development and implementation of a staff training;
   d. Recommend staff for lead, assistant, and technical status to outdoor education faculty and staff;
   e. Liaison with staff about changes in policy and procedures, training, work assign ments, etc.
3. Develop and implement marketing strategies to GCSU students, faculty, staff, and the general community.
   a. Review and revise marketing plan on an ongoing basis;
   b. Maintain distribution lists;
   c. Develop and implement promotional materials.
4. Maintain the GCSU Outdoor Education Center web page.
   a. Update information on an ongoing basis;
   b. Liaison with GCSU technology services;
   c. Maintain forms and related information on the web page;
   d. Review and revise web page design on an ongoing basis.
5. Manage the GCSU Outdoor Education Center office.
   a. Return messages;
   b. Copy program, participant, risk management, etc. forms as required;
   c. Develop components of the annual report for submission to the Board of Regents.

Georgia College OEC technical cohort assistant.

1. Plan and implement logistics for outdoor education class expeditions and trips.
   a. Coordinate transportation and lodging arrangements for technical skills class trips;
   b. Develop site-specific resources to create "land full" interactions with trip environments;
   c. Guide students through process of developing appropriate risk management tools for trip and program implementation.
2. Develop skill development sessions throughout academic term for outdoor education students to review and practice skills learned in technical classes.
   a. Develop a calendar of skill development sessions that meet student needs;
   b. Coordinate facility and equipment needs for sessions with faculty and OEC staff;
   c. Monitor skill sessions;
   d. Serve as a resource throughout session as students review skills.
3. Assist with technical skill instruction and assessment for academic courses included in the graduate and undergraduate technical cohorts in compliance with accreditation standards.
   a. Conduct skill assessment sessions for technical cohort students;
   b. Coach students through skill acquisition process;
   c. Provide group supervision in technical skills classes.
4. Assist with third-party vendor contracts for professional technical training in outdoor education classes with regard for industry standards.
   a. Coordinate logistics and program design/curriculum in conjunction with GCSU preparation.

Georgie College academic administrative assistant.

1. Manage academic database for B.S. and M.Ed. in compliance with accreditation standards and degree requirements.
   a. Liaison with administrative support staff to develop and maintain current databases;
   b. Forward service and facilitation documents to the Office of Experiential Education.
2. Manage the review, revision, and development of policy and procedures documents.
   a. Coordinate process for outdoor education faculty, OEC staff, and the Outdoor Education Safety and Risk Management Committee to complete and approve revisions to the PPM and the CCFH;
   b. Compile data for AEE accreditation annual report submission and accreditation self-studies.
3. Serve as secretary to the Outdoor Education Safety and Risk Management Committee.
   a. Schedule meetings of the SRMC as necessary;
   b. Record and distribute minutes for weekly staff meetings.

4. Assist OE faculty with research and publication initiatives that are directly related to the OE academic program of study.
5. Manage the Outdoor Talk listserve.
   a. Develop and maintain student roster and list membership;
   b. Post weekly announcement message to Outdoor Talk.
6. Manage outdoor education web page.
   a. Update information related to current courses, policy, internships, and employment announcements, etc.
7. Assist with academic course logistics (in nontechnical areas) as required.
8. Assist with market planning and implementation of promotional materials for academic programs.

GCSU Outdoor Education Center Staff

GCSU Outdoor Education Center staff (OEC staff) is a collective term used to refer to faculty, graduate students, undergraduate students, and alumni who work or volunteer to facilitate OEC programs. They are referred to as facilitators, a term which will encompass a range of responsibilities including instruction, teaching, and leadership. Outdoor education students may elect to establish a personnel file after successful completion of the technical cohort. Students who do so will be initially designated as assistant facilitators and may be recommended for lead facilitator status with approval of OE staff. On occasion a student may be approved to become OEC staff without completing the technical cohort based on previous experience, training, and performance.

Outdoor Education Interns, Directed Project, and Practicum Students

On occasion, GCSU Outdoor Education Center and outdoor education academic programs will sponsor student internships and practicum or directed project courses. Job descriptions, required skills, and supervisory responsibilities are developed on a per case basis. Contracts are developed by faculty and approved by the coordinator of Outdoor Education Programs and the chair of the Department of Kinesiology.

GCSU Leadership Certificate Program

The GCSU Leadership Certificate Program offers select GCSU students an opportunity to obtain leadership knowledge and experience in select programs that are GCSU mission related. The OEC is a partner in this program. Students who have completed academic core requirements for the program may apply to complete experiential leadership requirements with the OEC. Students accepted to do so must complete appropriate technical training and are approved for assistant or lead facilitator status by OE Staff.

Facilitator Qualifications

Academic Courses

The instructor of record for an academic course will be the lead facilitator and may designate roles and responsibilities to graduate assistants and students as appropriate.

OEC Staff Approval

Potential staff may establish a personnel file with the OEC, normally at the conditional status of assistant challenge course facilitator, upon successful completion of ODED 3020 or 5520, successful completion of challenge course training requirements for the GCSU Leadership Certificate Program, or by permission of the director of the GCSU Outdoor Education Center.

Facilitator Designation and Advancement

Facilitator designation may be at the lead, assistant, or technician level for challenge course pursuits (group development activities, low challenge course, and/or high challenge course), land pursuits (rock climbing, land navigation, tree climbing, camping, and/or backpacking), or water pursuits (flat-water canoeing, moving or white-water canoeing, kayaking, or rafting, and/or coastal kayaking). Personnel may be designated for one or more activities within each of these categories.

The OEC program coordinator may recommend a change in designation for approval by OE staff based on factors such as, but not limited to, attendance at OEC staff training, prior training and experience, facilitator evaluation, technical training associated with ODED courses beyond the technical cohort, and feedback from lead facilitators. OEC staff that meet minimum qualifications for lead facilitator status will typically be required to "shadow" a designated lead facilitator and then "be shadowed" in the role of lead facilitator by a designated lead facilitator.

Training and Professional Development

OEC staff must attend staff training at the beginning of each academic year in order to maintain a current personnel file. Additional optional professional development opportunities may be offered by the OEC or in conjunction with OE courses.

Qualifications

Lead facilitator.

Lead facilitators will meet minimum requirements for approval, as indicated above, possess current CPR, first-aid and Epi training, WFA, or WFR (wilderness context); and complete additional requirements as established by OE staff on a per case basis.

Assistant facilitator.

Assistant facilitators will meet minimum requirements for approval as indicated above and possess current CPR, first-aid and Epi training.

Technician.

Technicians are approved by permission of the OEC program coordinator or OE staff and may not hold responsibility for participant safety systems unless directly supervised by an assistant or lead facilitator.

Facilitator Responsibilities

General Responsibilities

1. Maintain a complete and current OEC personnel file.
2. Place copies of professional training certificates associated with OE classes in the student file as required by Department of Kinesiology and copies of all other professional training certificates in the OEC personnel file.

3. Possess a current and functional understanding of the instructional principles, requisite skills, laws, regulations, equipment, and programs associated with each activity.
4. Be aware of and ensure that the group adheres to rules and regulations, as well as access and legal statutes of the area in which the activity is conducted.
5. Recognize the presence of diminished operating conditions and limit or adapt program activities as necessary.
6. Maintain staff/participant ratios and provide appropriate levels of supervision to participants.
7. Provide or develop group operating norms and individual and group goals.
8. Communicate the philosophy of challenge-of-and-by-choice to participants.
9. Manage group behavior.
10. Adjust program design and specific activities according to client intake information and ongoing assessment.
11. Set activity characteristics such as psychological level or traveling speeds that are appropriate to the type of activity, physical setting, and group characteristics.
12. Establish systems to enhance group supervision and observation, and communication between staff, group members and staff, group members, and staff and primary backup.
13. Attend program planning and assessment meetings.
14. Share learning goals and negotiate relevant roles and responsibilities.
15. Review relevant PPM and CCFH topics as necessary.
16. Assist the lead facilitator and other staff as required.
17. Complete necessary forms as required by the PPM or CCFH.
18. Represent GCSU outdoor education programs in a professional manner.

Teaching

1. Teach appropriate sequences of skills, safety procedures, and equipment management.
2. Provide structured and semistructured opportunities for practice and feedback.
3. Take advantage of teachable moments to emphasize primary program, group, and individual goals.
4. Conduct appropriate warm-ups and stretches prior to engaging in activities.
5. In addition to activity-specific technical skills and information, the curriculum may include:
    a. Appropriate gear and clothing selection, use, and management for expected terrain and weather;
    b. Environmental impact and interpretation;
    c. Health, hygiene, first-aid, and emergency procedures;

d. Individual and group behavior and team effectiveness;

e. Hydration and nutritional requirements.

Safety and Environment

1. Select program areas that are appropriate to participant skill levels, program activities and goals, logistical constraints, and leadership abilities.
2. Develop familiarity with program areas (site files, print and electronic resources, past program files, or by visitation).
3. Be aware of site-specific natural and cultural heritage, and utilize appropriate environmental educational and Leave No Trace principles to limit group impact.
4. Conduct safety briefings about relevant environmental issues/hazards (access points, physical hazards, harmful flora and fauna, and weather) and emergency prevention and response procedures (i.e., missing person, lightning drill, injury response) prior to and during the activities.
5. Review emergency procedures, roles and responsibilities, and site-specific information.
6. Communicate information about first-aid procedures and supplies to staff and participants.
7. Exercise the right to disallow any individual from participating in a program if they are inadequately prepared to do so safely.
8. Ensure that participants have access to sufficient water and food.
9. Assess potential diminished environmental conditions and make appropriate adaptations or arrangements to limit impact on participants and programs quality.

Clothing and Equipment

1. Review personal clothing and equipment requirements with participants.
2. Teach basic heat management principles as appropriate (i.e., layering, fabric suitability, proper footwear, and equipment use).
3. Carry activity-specific field repair and emergency response equipment and supplies.
4. Approve personal equipment for program use on a case per case basis.
5. Inspect program equipment prior to use and throughout the program (i.e., when putting a harness on a participant).
6. Manage equipment according to the PPM or CCFH during a program and at the conclusion of the program (inventory, storage, and rope logs).
7. Inform the equipment and facilities coordinator of maintenance or replacement needs for safety and first-aid equipment, program, and participant equipment.
8. Teach participants to respect equipment and report damaged, dysfunctional, or lost gear to a facilitator.
9. Use equipment according to manufacturer's specifications or the PPM or CCFH directions.

Lead Facilitator Responsibilities

Preprogram responsibilities.

1. Obtain the program file from the OEC program coordinator.
2. Obtain appropriate forms from the OEC program coordinator, the OE classroom, or at http://hercules.gcsu.edu/~jhirsch/.
3. Consult with the OEC program coordinator about the composition of the facilitation team.
4. Review the program file contents (intake information, contact information, risk management forms, etc.).
5. Contact the program sponsor to make introductions and finalize program goals, obtain client information, communicate program logistics and other arrangements (personal equipment, etc.).
6. Meet with the facilitation team to review client characteristics and program goals, develop the program design, assign roles and responsibilities, establish individual facilitation goals, review relevant PPM or CCFH information, and review program logistics.
7. Submit appropriate equipment reservation forms in timely fashion. (See Program Administration: Equipment Management.)
8. Disseminate and collect participant forms.
9. Review participant forms with staff and adapt program design as necessary.
10. Arrange program support logistics (food, water, facilities, transportation, publicity, etc.).
11. Complete all necessary program administration and equipment management forms.
12. Obtain site and environmental condition information (i.e., weather report, road conditions, emergency contact information).
13. Conduct pretrip meeting with participants for trips (as defined in Program Administration: Program Definitions). The agenda should include, but is not limited to:
    a. Program purpose;
    b. Participant expectations;
    c. Program, group, and personal equipment requirements;
    d. Safety, environmental, and group expectations and rules;
    e. Travel and site information;
    f. Trip logistics and emergency contact procedures.
14. Arrange backup system in accordance with the PPM.

Program responsibilities.

1. Greet and orient participants to facilities and program logistics.
2. Arrange equipment and prepare site.
3. Inspect program site, facilities, and equipment prior to the program as appropriate for program activities.

4. Provide medical screening information to participants for programs that do not require the completion of individual Medical Information forms.

5. Provide oversight and supervision to program implementation, group management, site safety and security, equipment management, and staff.

6. Have course participants complete program evaluations.

Postprogram responsibilities.

1. Return equipment and completed equipment reservations forms (include rope log information and maintenance notes) to the equipment and facilities coordinator.

2. Submit the completed program file to the OEC program coordinator (OEC programs) or OE faculty (academic) within 14 days of the program. The completed program file should include, but is not limited to:

   a. Completed participant evaluation forms;

   b. Facilitator feedback forms (these may be emailed to the program coordinator; however compensation forms cannot be processed until facilitator feedback forms are submitted);

   c. Original and revised program plans;

   d. Risk management forms as appropriate;

   e. Program and route plan, weather report, site and travel documents, equipment lists, budget and menu information, site information, and risk management forms appropriate to trip programs, and Program File Summary form.

University of North Carolina at Charlotte—Venture Center
F Recreation
E Southeast Region
C University Students and General Population
S 5.08

Venture Staff Competencies

These competencies check-off lists are for staff working with the Venture Center. Checklists may be accessed at http://venture.uncc.edu/venturedownloads and include:

Cover Sheet Competency
General Trip Leader Competency Checklist
Overnight Competency Checklist
Hiking Competency Checklist
Caving Competency Checklist
Climbing Wall Competency Checklist
Climbing Outdoor Competency Checklist
Water Competency Checklist
Team Challenge Course Competency Checklist
High Team Challenge Competency Checklist
Leadership Effectiveness Competency Checklist
Involvement Log

Leadership Effectiveness Competencies

This evaluation is intended to provide instructors with specific feedback by assessing their knowledge and performance level. Please provide examples that demonstrate the level of effectiveness in each outdoor leadership component listed below. At each subsequent review, please list date and indicate current level of effectiveness.

This list focuses on the interpersonal, group management, and nontechnical aspects of leadership. Used in conjunction with the General Trip Leading Competencies and the appropriate specific activity competencies checklists, or with the TCC, HTC, and/or Wall Competencies checklists, this will provide a clearer picture of an individual's ability and readiness to take on the specific leadership roles required in these positions.

- To be an *Instructor*, staff will have met a minimum of Level 3 in at least seven of the Leadership Effectiveness Competencies including all the ** items, and no competencies will be at level 1
- To be *Trip Leader,* staff will have met a minimum of Level 4 in at least seven of the Leadership Effectiveness Competencies including all the * and ** items, and no competencies will be at Level 1 or 2

SCALE:

5. Highly effective—skill is highly developed and can serve as a benchmark
4. Effective—skill is very good, yet room for improvement
3. Somewhat effective—skill is acceptable as an assistant, yet fair amount of potential for growth
2. Not effective—has potential, but needs more time and training to develop OR not yet observed
1. Adversely effective—lacks potential

(*Developed by Sarah Fox—modified from Indiana University*)

Please provide examples that demonstrate the level of effectiveness.

** Maturity/Responsibility/Integrity

- Well respected by participants and staff
- Sees tasks through to completion, follows through on commitments
- Has a plan and a contingency plan, able to adjust
- Aware that trip leaders are representing the program and is good role model
- Models socially responsible behavior and promotes same from others
- Awareness of and ability to manage own emotions

This is a requirement for Instructor (minimum Level 3) and Trip Leader or Senior Staff positions (minimum Level 4)

	Level
date:	1 2 3 4 5
date:	1 2 3 4 5
date:	1 2 3 4 5
date:	1 2 3 4 5
date:	1 2 3 4 5
date:	1 2 3 4 5
date:	1 2 3 4 5
date:	1 2 3 4 5

** Safety Conscious	Level
• Knowledge of risk management plan	date: 1 2 3 4 5
• Knowledge of dynamics of accidents model	date: 1 2 3 4 5
• Is active in preventing emergency/survival situations	date: 1 2 3 4 5
• Follows proper vehicle safety procedures	date: 1 2 3 4 5
	date: 1 2 3 4 5
	date: 1 2 3 4 5
This is a requirement for Instructor (minimum Level 3) and Trip Leader or Senior Staff positions (minimum Level 4)	date: 1 2 3 4 5
	date: 1 2 3 4 5

Please provide examples that demonstrate the level of effectiveness.

** Positive Member of Leadership Team	Level
• Gives, receives, and applies constructive criticism graciously and compassionately	date: 1 2 3 4 5
• Sets goals for the trip in collaboration with co-leaders	date: 1 2 3 4 5
• Leads or contributes to staff debriefing and completes leadership evaluations after the trip	date: 1 2 3 4 5
• Works cooperatively with fellow staff	date: 1 2 3 4 5
• Takes initiative for doing fair share of teams work and looks for ways to contribute.	date: 1 2 3 4 5
This is a requirement for Instructor (minimum Level 3) and Trip Leader or Senior Staff positions (minimum Level 4)	date: 1 2 3 4 5
	date: 1 2 3 4 5
	date: 1 2 3 4 5

Please provide examples that demonstrate the level of effectiveness.

* Teaching Ability	Level
• Effective teaching techniques (able to explain and demonstrate skills)	date: 1 2 3 4 5
• Able to discuss and apply knowledge of learning styles and strategies to engage different styles	date: 1 2 3 4 5
• Effectively uses hands-on, active learning, and gets the participants involved	date: 1 2 3 4 5
• Able to explain and implement experiential learning, Flow, Optimal Arousal, Comfort Zone, and Challenge-by-Choice models	date: 1 2 3 4 5
• Exudes confidence and knowledge of skills, yet humble enough to admit own limits	date: 1 2 3 4 5
This is a requirement for Trip Leader or Senior Staff positions (minimum Level 4)	date: 1 2 3 4 5
	date: 1 2 3 4 5
	date: 1 2 3 4 5

Please provide examples that demonstrate the level of effectiveness.

* Communication Skills	Level
• Presents effective verbal and nonverbal messages • Able to tune in to another person's verbal and nonverbal messages and respond appropriately • Listens and responds to group concerns ***This is a requirement for Trip Leader or Senior Staff positions (minimum Level 4)***	date: 1 2 3 4 5 date: 1 2 3 4 5 date: 1 2 3 4 5 date: 1 2 3 4 5 date: 1 2 3 4 5 date: 1 2 3 4 5 date: 1 2 3 4 5 date: 1 2 3 4 5

Please provide examples that demonstrate the level of effectiveness.

* Ability to Create a Positive Atmosphere	Level
• Welcoming to all participants and shows respect for diversity • Demonstrates empathy, acceptance, and support of participant's emotions, fears, and doubts. • Understands and uses Challenge by Choice • Creates an atmosphere of openness; is available to participants and other staff • Provides a successful and fun learning experience • Knowledge of group norms and expedition behavior ***This is a requirement for Trip Leader or Senior Staff positions (minimum Level 4)***	date: 1 2 3 4 5 date: 1 2 3 4 5 date: 1 2 3 4 5 date: 1 2 3 4 5 date: 1 2 3 4 5 date: 1 2 3 4 5 date: 1 2 3 4 5 date: 1 2 3 4 5

Please provide examples that demonstrate the level of effectiveness.

* Organizational Skills	Level
• Is well prepared for pretrip meetings • Delegates tasks appropriately (without sacrificing safety) • Is effective at coordinating staff efforts • Handles logistics effectively including gear check-out/check-in • Completes necessary documentation within a reasonable time period ***This is a requirement for Trip Leader or Senior Staff positions (minimum Level 4)***	date: 1 2 3 4 5 date: 1 2 3 4 5 date: 1 2 3 4 5 date: 1 2 3 4 5 date: 1 2 3 4 5 date: 1 2 3 4 5 date: 1 2 3 4 5 date: 1 2 3 4 5

Please provide examples that demonstrate the level of effectiveness.

Flexible Leadership Style	Level
• What is this individual's primary leadership style? ________________ ________________________________	date: 1 2 3 4 5
• Uses appropriate leadership style for changing situations	date: 1 2 3 4 5
• Big picture mentality: able to focus on entire group as well as details	date: 1 2 3 4 5
	date: 1 2 3 4 5
	date: 1 2 3 4 5
	date: 1 2 3 4 5
	date: 1 2 3 4 5
	date: 1 2 3 4 5

Please provide examples that demonstrate the level of effectiveness.

Facilitation Skills	Level
• Recognizes the purpose and value of debriefing	date: 1 2 3 4 5
• Leads effective briefing (framing the day) and debriefing sessions and facilitates transfer of learning	date: 1 2 3 4 5
• Capable of debriefing after an emotionally trying incident	date: 1 2 3 4 5
	date: 1 2 3 4 5
	date: 1 2 3 4 5
	date: 1 2 3 4 5
	date: 1 2 3 4 5
	date: 1 2 3 4 5

Please provide examples that demonstrate the level of effectiveness.

Group Dynamics	Level
• Able to assess and meet participants' physical, emotional, and mental needs, conditions, and goals	date: 1 2 3 4 5
• Able to discuss and apply knowledge of basic conflict management models and techniques	date: 1 2 3 4 5
• Identifies group development stage and acts accordingly	date: 1 2 3 4 5
	date: 1 2 3 4 5
	date: 1 2 3 4 5
	date: 1 2 3 4 5
	date: 1 2 3 4 5
	date: 1 2 3 4 5

Please provide examples that demonstrate the level of effectiveness.

Servant Leadership Mentality	Level
• Exhibits selflessness through valuing the needs of the group over-personal interests and shows empathy toward the participants' experience • Invests in participants by talking with and getting to know them • Focuses on serving other people's highest priority needs • "Encourages collaboration, trust, foresight, listening, and the ethical use of power and empowerment" Robert Greenleaf	date: 1 2 3 4 5 date: 1 2 3 4 5 date: 1 2 3 4 5 date: 1 2 3 4 5 date: 1 2 3 4 5 date: 1 2 3 4 5 date: 1 2 3 4 5 date: 1 2 3 4 5

Please provide examples that demonstrate the level of effectiveness.

Committed to the Program and Motivated to Learn and Grow	Level
• Understands and is able to articulate and support program's philosophy • Shows initiative to learn new things • Willing to mentor new leaders and contributes to the learning and development of apprentices	date: 1 2 3 4 5 date: 1 2 3 4 5 date: 1 2 3 4 5 date: 1 2 3 4 5 date: 1 2 3 4 5 date: 1 2 3 4 5 date: 1 2 3 4 5 date: 1 2 3 4 5

Please provide examples that demonstrate the level of effectiveness.

SECTION 6
TRANSPORTATION

National Outdoor Leadership School	*F*	Education
	E	Rocky Mountain Region
	C	Various Populations
	S	6.01

Transportation Policy

Revised February 17, 2006

The NOLS transportation policy provides guidance and requirements for the operation of NOLS vehicles, staff/driver training, and expectations for driving behavior. This policy applies to all NOLS vehicles and any personal vehicles carrying students. NOLS vehicles are intended for NOLS business only. All use of NOLS vehicles must have approval by the appropriate branch school manager.

This policy is based on U.S. laws and regulations and serves as a basis for NOLS transportation policy worldwide. Specific laws and regulations in other countries may preempt parts of this policy.

Driver Requirements and Training Policies

1. The vehicle driver must (for NOLS-owned or rented vehicles):
    a. Be at least 21 years of age.
    b. Have in their possession a valid driver's license.
    c. Have on file a valid, current, and satisfactory motor vehicle record (MVR). **MVRs need to be renewed every year.** MVRs may not be available for non-U.S. drivers. The following criteria apply.
        - Drivers aged 21 and 22 must have their driving record (MVR) approved by our insurance carrier. There can be no violations on their record, ever.
        - Drivers aged 23 and 24 can have no more than two moving violations during the previous 3 years.
        - Drivers aged 25 and older can have no more than three moving violations during the previous 3 years.
        - Any drivers with a violation of driving under the influence or driving while intoxicated within the last 3 years cannot drive NOLS vehicles.
        - Non-U.S. citizens under the age of 23 without the means of verifying their driving record cannot drive. Non-U.S. citizens 23 years of age or older may drive subject to other aspects of this policy.
    d. Have permission of the branch school director or other appropriate manager.
2. Completion of a defensive driving course is required for drivers transporting students. Completion of a defensive driving course is encouraged if driving responsibilities do not include transporting students. NOLS prefers that drivers complete the NOLS defensive driving course. NOLS-trained defensive driver trainers are employed at branch schools. Opportunities to receive NOLS defensive driving include:
    a. While on contract prior to working a course that requires an instructor to drive (check with the branch school).
    b. Attending regularly scheduled defensive driving courses at a NOLS branch school (check with the training department or branch school).
    c. Classes may be offered in association with some seminars; caving, rock climbing, or river.
3. The vehicle driver must have successfully completed NOLS training specific to the operation of the vehicle including loading procedures and understanding the handling characteristics of the vehicle. This is available on a case by case basis with each branch school.

4. In addition to the above, full-time transportation employees and any bus driver must hold a valid commercial driver's license, satisfactorily complete training specific to bus driving, and have annually updated physicals and MVRs.
5. International staff, such as a U.S. citizen in Australia or Australian citizen in the U.S., need to be approved for driving by the branch director or appropriate branch manager. Appropriate supervised time behind the wheel when in a different country is necessary before solo driving or driving with students. Consider allowing international staff to drive only with another local staff or in convoy led by a local driver.
6. Drivers with international licenses may have limits imposed on the number of passengers they can transport.
7. A Yukon Class 4 license or similar provincial license or a U.S. commercial driver's license is necessary for driving a van with more than 10 passengers in the Yukon.

University of North Carolina—Carolina Adventures
F **Recreation**
E **Southeastern Region**
C **University Students and General Population**
S **6.01, 6.03, 6.04, 6.10, 6.11**

Van Travel and Emergency Procedures

Van travel poses the greatest risk on any trip. In addition to the normal hazards of highway travel are the increased hazards of traveling in a large vehicle and on remote, steep, gravel roads. The following guidelines are to be followed on all Carolina Adventures trips in order to minimize the likelihood of an accident. It is the instructor's responsibility to make sure all safety and operating policies are followed and to make appropriate judgment calls, in the interest of safety if there is no policy for a given situation.

Van Policies

1. All operators must be licensed and have their driver's license with them while on the trip.
2. You must complete a driver check-out with the expedition program manager to become an eligible driver.
3. Never operate the van within 8 hours of using drugs or alcohol.
4. There should always be at least two eligible drivers on any trip in case of emergency and to relieve driver fatigue.
5. Drivers should never drive for more than 2 hours at a time.

6. Maximum van capacity is 12, including driver.
7. Route should be established and documented on Course Detail Sheet before leaving the Outdoor Education Center. This route should only be changed due to unforeseeable conditions such as road closure or if weather conditions make another route safer. Notify expedition program manager by phone if you decide to adjust your route during the trip.
8. Instructors and participants must wear seat belts while the van is moving.
9. Participants should remain calm and quiet during the trip to allow driver to concentrate and communicate with the navigator. It is the navigator's responsibility to follow the map and directions as well as insure a safe and quiet atmosphere in the van.
10. Headlights should be used whenever the van is moving.
11. Stop at all railroad crossings and look left, look right, and look left again before crossing. Never stop on railroad tracks.
12. Never exceed posted speed limits and always operate the van in accordance with all state and local laws.
13. Never talk on a mobile phone while driving.
14. Vans are not for personal use.
15. Personal vehicles are not to be used to transport participants on Carolina Adventures trips.

Van Characteristics

1. The length of the van must be taken into consideration when turning corners, changing lanes and backing. Make sure you take wider than normal turns to avoid side swiping things or running the back wheel off of the road. It is often difficult to tell if you are clear to get over especially on the right side of the van. Use your navigator to help you see and do not change lanes unless you are absolutely sure the lane is clear. * Always have someone get out and watch you while backing. It is difficult to see behind the van, especially shorter objects. If you are by yourself, get out and check behind van before backing. Always blow horn prior to backing.
2. The width of the van is greater than most cars and the length of the van exaggerates this problem. Drive slowly and be aware that the shoulder is often soft on narrow mountain roads and can give way underneath you, causing the van to roll.
3. The weight of the van requires additional stopping distance. This is especially true when pulling the trailer. * Never tailgate and allow more stopping distance than you think you need. Do not pump the brakes on long descents. Instead, apply constant, even brake pressure to control your speed.

Adverse Conditions

1. Drive cautiously on slippery roads.
2. Never drive if you do not feel confident in your or the van's abilities. Camp or find a motel or another alternative before putting yourself and the passengers at risk.

3. Use snow chains when traveling in significant snow or ice and remove chains as soon as possible once you reach dry road.
4. Snow chains are to be used only to return home. Do not use chains to go further into a potentially more dangerous situation.
5. Do not jerk steering wheel or hit brakes hard on slippery roads.
6. Pump brakes gently if you begin to skid, release brakes, and gently apply again.
7. Increase distance between you and the car in front of you.
8. On gravel roads blow the horn when approaching turns that you cannot see around. Always travel slowly and avoid getting too close to the edge. Many vans have rolled on the roads we travel.

Emergency Procedures

1. In case of an accident, drivers should check on the status of all passengers.
   a. If there are injuries, appropriate staff should treat them according to standard protocols of first-aid training or Wilderness First Responder training;
   b. Once injuries have been treated, a response plan should be created including:
      i. Passengers situated in areas with reduced risk,
      ii. Exchange of insurance information with other drivers,
      iii. Document names, addresses, phone numbers, state, and license numbers of persons/vehicles involved including witnesses.
2. Do not admit fault or discuss accident with anyone other than police or Carolina Adventures staff.
3. Wait until police arrive to assess accident.
4. Notify expedition program manager of accident and establish transportation back to Outdoor Education Center if van is unsafe for travel.
5. Complete Automobile Loss Notice form located in the van emergency file.
6. In cases requiring transportation by advanced medical professionals one staff member should accompany injured participant, if possible.

Jump Starting

(Adapted from the 2003 Chevrolet Express Owner's Manual)

1. If the battery has run down, you may want to try to use another vehicle and the jumper cables to start the van. Be sure to follow the steps below to do it safely.
2. If you don't follow these steps exactly, some or all of these things can hurt you.

   CAUTION: Batteries can hurt you. They can be dangerous because:

   - They contain acid that can burn you.

- They contain gas that can explode or ignite.
- They contain enough electricity to burn you.

3. Ignoring these steps could result in costly damage to the van that wouldn't be covered by the warranty.
4. Trying to start the van by pushing or pulling it won't work, and it could damage the van.
5. Check the other vehicle. It must have a 12-volt battery with a negative ground system.
6. Notice: If the other system isn't a 12-volt system with a negative ground, both vehicles can be damaged.
7. Get the vehicles close enough so the jumper cables can reach, but be sure the vehicles aren't touching each other.
   a. To avoid the possibility of the vehicles rolling, set the parking brake firmly on both vehicles;
   b. Put an automatic transmission in *park* and a manual *transmission* in neutral before setting the parking brake.
8. Notice: If you leave the radio on it could be badly damaged.
9. Turn off the ignition on both vehicles.
   a. Unplug unnecessary accessories from the cigarette lighter or in the accessory power outlet;
   b. Turn off the radio and all lamps that aren't needed.
10. Open the hoods and locate the positive (+) and negative (-) terminal locations of the other vehicle. The van has a remote positive (+) jump starting terminal and a remote negative (-) jump starting terminal. You should always use these remote terminals instead of the terminals on the battery.
11. The remote positive (+) terminal is located behind a red plastic cover near the engine accessory drive bracket on the driver's side below the alternator. To uncover the remote positive (+) terminal, open the red plastic cover.
12. The remote negative (-) terminal is located on the engine drive bracket and is marked "GND."

    ! CAUTION:

    - Using a match near a battery can cause battery gas to explode. Use a flashlight if you need more light.
    - Battery fluid contains acid that can burn you. Don't get it on you. If you accidentally get it in your eyes or on your skin, flush the place with water and get medical help immediately.
    - Fans or other moving engine parts can injure you badly. Keep your hands away from moving parts.

13. Check that the jumper cables don't have loose or missing insulation. If they do, you could get a shock, and the vehicles could be damaged, too.

14. Before you connect the cables, here are a few basic things you should know:
    a. Positive (+) will go to positive (+) or a remote positive (+) terminal if the vehicle has one.
    b. Negative (-) will go to a heavy, unpainted metal engine part or to a remote negative (-) terminal if the vehicle has one. Don't connect positive (+) to negative (-) or you would get a short that would damage the battery and maybe other parts, too.
    c. And don't connect the negative (-) cable to the negative (-) terminal on the dead battery because this can cause sparks.
15. Connect the red positive (+) cable to the positive (+) terminal of the dead battery. Use a remote positive (+) terminal if the vehicle has one.
16. Don't let the other end touch metal. Connect it to the positive (+) terminal of the good battery. Use a remote positive (+) terminal if the vehicle has one.
17. Now connect the black negative (-) cable to the negative (-) terminal of the good battery. Use a remote negative (-) terminal if the vehicle has one. Don't let the other end touch anything until the next step. The other end of the negative (-) cable doesn't go to the dead battery. It goes to a heavy, unpainted metal engine part or to a remote negative (-) terminal on the vehicle with the dead battery.
18. Connect the other end of the negative (-) cable to a heavy, unpainted metal engine part or to a remote negative (-) terminal on the vehicle with the dead battery.
19. Now start the vehicle with the good battery and let the engine run for a while.
20. Try to start the vehicle with the dead battery. If it won't start after a few tries, it probably needs service.

Notice: Damage to the vehicle may result from electrical shorting if jumper cables are removed incorrectly. Take care that the cables don't touch each other or any other metal.

Jumper Cable Removal

1. Disconnect the black negative (-) cable from the vehicle that had the dead battery.
2. Disconnect the black negative (-) cable from the vehicle with the good battery.
3. Disconnect the red positive (+) cable from the vehicle with the good battery.
4. Disconnect the red positive (+) cable from the other vehicle.
5. Return the positive (+) remote terminal to its original position.

Notice: Once you have started the vehicle with the dead battery, leave the engine running for a while in order to charge the battery.

Securing, Loading, Pulling, and Backing Trailers

1. When hooking the trailer to the van it is important to make sure the ball makes a good connection. Lock the hitch down and secure the safety chains and lights. Test the hitch by pulling up on it, and check the lights to make sure they are working properly.

2. When loading the kayaks, never load more than one boat on each of the bottom racks. Also, make sure kayaks are secured against the trailer and not riding above the tires. Tie-downs for the bottom kayaks should be looped around bar to prevent the boat from sliding over the wheels while traveling. This prevents the boats from being damaged by the tires when going over bumps.
3. At every stop, check the trailer connection and check tie-downs to make sure everything is tight. Also visually check the tires and hubs to see if everything looks okay.
4. When pulling a trailer, make sure to take wide turns to avoid sideswiping things on the inside of the turn.
5. When changing lanes, compensate for the extra length of the trailer.
6. The van is heavier when pulling a trailer, and it is important to allow extra room for stopping, especially in inclement weather.
7. Backing a trailer is tricky. The steering wheel is turned opposite from the normal way. You should be confident in your ability before attempting to back a trailer on a trip with passengers. Have your co-instructor get out and direct you.

Safety and Emergency Equipment

The following items are stored in the van at all times and should be checked before departure on any trip:

1. Emergency phone numbers and emergency driving directions
2. Emergency cash and gas card
3. Flares
4. Phone
5. Jumper cables
6. Snow chains

Santa Fe Mountain Center	*F*	**Therapeutic**
	E	**Rocky Mountain Region**
	C	**Youth and Families**
	S	**6.01–6.04, 6.08**

Program-Related Travel in a Motor Vehicle

Rules

1. Seat belts shall be available for all passengers. Driver and all passengers are required to wear seat belts.

2. No smoking in SFMC vehicles.
3. No riding outside of vehicle. Keep extremities inside.
4. Drivers shall meet insurance requirements.
5. Drivers shall be tested on van driving skills by approved staff and this will be documented in their personnel file. Drivers will be tested and authorized by designated staff prior to driving with a trailer.
6. Never allow more than 15 people to ride in a 15-passenger van.

Procedures/Considerations

1. Check fuel and all fluids, tires, spare, chains, jack, lights, seat belts, wipers, horn. If using a trailer, check lights, hitch, tie-downs, and visibility with mirrors prior to use.
2. Drive defensively; use extra caution at night; rotate drivers to stay fresh and alert (consider rotating drivers after 4 hours or whenever driver becomes fatigued).
3. Carefully supervise participants when stopping near the roadway.
4. Mountain Center participants will travel in Mountain Center–insured vehicles only.
5. Obey all traffic laws and follow land agencies' regulations.
6. Do not leave participants unsupervised in vehicles. Insure that keys are inaccessible to clients.
7. Maintain acceptable decorum while traveling.
8. When a 15-passenger van is not full, passengers should sit in seats that are in front of the rear axle.
9. When loading gear inside a van, be sure it is securely tied down.
10. Consider driving with lights on during the day for increased visibility.

Briefing

Brief participants regarding above rules and general safety consciousness.

Georgia College & State University	
	F Education
	E Southeast Region
	C University Outdoor Education Students and General Population
	S 6.03, 6.12–6.14

Personal Vehicles

Participants may use personal vehicles to transport themselves to and from outdoor education programs and courses that take place at a location other than a GCSU facility. Students may elect to arrange carpools. All drivers and passengers must complete an Assumption of Risk and Informed Consent: Use of Personal Vehicles for Outdoor Education Courses or Programs. For extended trips facilitators should obtain carpool and en route contact information in the Outdoor Education Personal Vehicle Log Book and provide complete and appropriate directions to the designated start site. Students should be encouraged to drive safely and allow adequate time to get to the site.

Rented Vehicles

The OEC or outdoor education academic programs may rent vehicles for program use. Facilitators shall use rented vehicles in compliance with the renting agency rules and regulations, and outdoor education policy and procedures. A minimum of two university employees shall be listed as approved drivers. Drivers must provide the rental agency proof of personal insurance. GCSU insurance covers students, faculty, and staff participating in academic requirements.

Outdoor Education Vehicles

The use of outdoor education vehicles shall be in compliance with institutional and outdoor education policy and procedures. Vehicles may be used for outdoor education academic courses or for GCSU Outdoor Education Center programs. An OE staff member, with an approved driver's license must drive outdoor education vehicles. Outdoor education vehicles and trailers are maintained and inspected on a regular basis by the GCSU Plant Operations staff. Maintenance records are filed by the foreman of the Automotive Shop.

Driver Permits

A student driver permit is required for any student who will be driving a Georgia College & State University vehicle. Student drivers must be on the Georgia College & State University payroll to comply with risk management liability insurance regulations. In order to be approved, student drivers must obtain a driver history from the Department of Motor Vehicle Safety (short history costs $5.00). The original report, along with a copy of the driver's license is submitted to the coordinator of outdoor education programs. The original is forwarded to the Department of Business and Finance and a copy is kept on file in the outdoor education administrative office. In addition, student drivers must drive with a faculty person who will assess driving competency and provide opportunity for appropriate practice.

Gas Purchase

1. Gas for rented vehicles may NOT be purchased with a state credit card:

    a. Gas for rented vehicles should be purchased by OE staff using a personal credit card;

    b. OE staff must complete a Travel Authorization prior to departure;

    c. Receipts must be submitted with a completed Travel Reimbursement Form.

2. Gas for GCSU vehicles may be purchased with the outdoor education gas card by outdoor education faculty at any gas station that will take a credit card:

    a. The gas card may be used for gas or other fluids necessary for the operation of the vehicle;

    b. A printed receipt must be obtained;

    c. Original receipts must be submitted to the coordinator of outdoor education programs within 5 days of the conclusion of the program;

    d. The loss of an original receipt or the gas card will result in the immediate termination of the account.

Kubota

The Kubota is to be operated only by an approved OEC staff member. The employee must be a university-approved driver, and must complete an operation training prior to using the RTV900. The Kubota is to be stored with its cover on at all times when not in use. Never leave the RTV unattended while it is running or while the keys are in the ignition.

Operation.

1. Always pay close attention to all danger, warning, and caution labels on the RTV.
2. Never remove, alter, or tamper with the roll-over protection structures (the roll bars).
3. *Always* use the seat belts provided. Do not allow persons to ride in the bed of the RTV or to ride without seat belt. No more than one driver and one passenger should ever be riding in the vehicle. Minimum passenger age is 5 years of age.
4. Never operate the vehicle while under the influence of alcohol or drugs. Never operate while fatigued.
5. Do not allow nonapproved operators around the RTV while it is in operation.
6. Never wear loose, torn, or bulky clothing around the vehicle; it may catch in moving parts and cause serious bodily injury or death. Stay away from all moving parts.
7. The maximum cargo capacity of the RTV is 500 kg (1,100 lbs). Never exceed this capacity, and reduce the capacity to match operating conditions (i.e., wet, icy).
8. Never allow cargo to be stacked high, which may change the center of gravity and lead to increased risk of a vehicle roll-over.
9. Never modify or alter the vehicle.
10. Always complete "preflight" inspection prior to operation.

Preflight inspection.

1. Look around and under the vehicle for items such as loose bolts, trash build up, oil or coolant leaks, and broken or worn parts.
2. Check to make sure the RTV has enough diesel fuel for the operation. Always have the tank filled when the gauge shows ¼ or less of a tank. Never allow the vehicle to run out of fuel. This is very damaging to the engine.
3. Check tire pressure. Tire pressure should be at 20 PSI.
4. Make sure that all levers are in the neutral position prior to starting the engine. Make sure the parking brake is engaged and the hydraulic outlet is *off*. Check the engine hand throttle and make sure it is in the *idle* position.
5. Ensure that driver and passenger seat belts are fastened.
6. Ensure that the bed lift is locked.

Operating the vehicle.

1. Keep all shields and guards in place.
2. Report missing or broken equipment to the OEC equipment and facilities coordinator.
3. Avoid sudden starts and stops.
4. To avoid the incident of a vehicle roll-over, go slowly when turning, on uneven ground, and before stopping.
5. Never use the differential lock unless the vehicle is stuck *and* in 4-wheel-drive mode. If differential lock is engaged, never attempt to turn the vehicle, as doing so may be dangerous.
6. Use low gear when traveling up and down steep hills.
7. When shifting gears, it may be necessary to stop before shifting up or down. If the gear will not shift with gentle coaxing, use the pressure release valve next to the 12V accessory plug to assist in shifting gears. Never attempt to force the vehicle into a gear.
8. *Never* use the vehicle in *4-wheel-drive* on paved surfaces.
9. Travel straight up and down hills in low gear. Avoid stopping or starting suddenly on steep hills. Never attempt to operate the vehicle sideways on steep hills. If the vehicle stops suddenly on a hill, engage the parking brake before getting out. Never make sudden changes in speed or direction while on steep hills, as this will increase the risk of a vehicle roll-over.
10. Remain alert while operating the vehicle and be aware of holes, rocks, and other hidden hazards in the terrain.
11. Always operate the vehicle at speeds that allow you to maintain control of the vehicle.
12. During inclement weather, the operator should reduce speed.
13. Avoid sharp turns at high speeds, to decrease the risk of vehicle roll-over.
14. Never attempt to exit the vehicle while in motion.
15. Keep hands, arms, and feet inside the vehicle at all times while in motion.

Operating the cargo bed.

1. Never operate the vehicle while cargo bed is open.
2. Always ensure the cargo bed is closed and locked prior to operating the vehicle.
3. To open the cargo bed, push both levers (found at the top of the tailgate) up, and pull the gate down and out.
4. To close the gate prior to vehicle operation, lift the gate and push it firmly closed. Ensure that the gate is locked by pressing down on both levers.
5. To raise the cargo bed, start the engine. Release the restricting plate, and pull up on the hydraulic lift lever to raise the cargo bed. Return the lever to the *neutral* position when the bed is in the desired position.
6. To lower the bed, press the hydraulic lift lever down until the bed comes to a complete stop. Return the hydraulic lift lever to the *neutral* position, and lock the lever with the restricting plate.
7. Always make sure nothing is in the way of the bed while it is being lifted or lowered.
8. If the hydraulic lift fails to work, press the hydraulic lift lever to the *float* position (all the way down), and operate the bed manually.

Vehicle maintenance.

The manufacturer suggests routine service on the vehicle in relation to the hours of operation. Following the first 50 hours of operation, a routine check is to be completed. A check is to be completed every 50 hours after that. Prior to each service mark, the GCSU Automotive Shop should be contacted for the routine maintenance to take place. Never attempt to service the vehicle yourself.

Boojum Institute	*F* **Education**
	E **West Region**
	C **Various Populations**
	S **6.01–6.11, 6.14**

Vehicle Manual

Vehicle Operation

Our intent with motor vehicle operation is to minimize transport while still running quality courses. Motor vehicle travel constitutes one of the greatest risks for an accident. All operation of Boojum Institute vehicles will be done with strict attention to risk management and in compliance with existing laws and the precautions outlined herein.

The following standards in the Boojum Vehicle Manual apply to all Boojum Institute owned or rented vehicles and their drivers, and to drivers and their personal vehicles when driving on Boojum Institute business. For purposes of this document, "Boojum vehicle" includes Boojum-owned vehicles, Boojum-rented vehicles, and personal vehicles used for Boojum business.

Policy

1. *Maximum Vehicle Capacities:*
   a. Fifteen-passenger vans shall not carry more than 11 people.
   b. Other vehicles should be loaded with no more than the manufacturer's recommended number of occupants.
2. *Drugs and Alcohol:* No one shall operate a Boojum or rental vehicle while under the influence of any drugs or alcohol including prescription medications that alter perception and reaction time in any way. No one who will be driving a Boojum vehicle or rental shall have any drugs or alcohol in their system 8 hours prior to driving.
3. *Headlight Use:* All vehicle headlights shall be on whenever the vehicle is in motion, day or night.
4. *Personal Use of Boojum Vehicles:* At no time shall Boojum vehicles or rental vehicles be driven for non-Boojum related business.
5. *Seatbelt Use:* Everyone riding in a Boojum vehicle shall have his/her own seatbelt and wear it any time the vehicle is in motion.
6. *Passenger Guidelines:* Passengers shall ride with their entire body inside the vehicle at all times; this includes all appendages.
7. *Speed Limit:* Vehicles shall be operated at or below the posted speed limit at all times. Be especially careful when driving on mountain roads as they are windy and can be hazardous in a loaded van. Excessive speed is a major cause of traffic accidents.
8. *Roof Racks:* On vans used for Boojum business, roof racks shall not be loaded or otherwise used, except for transporting white gas.
9. *Loads:* Loads shall not exceed the gross vehicle weight rating (GVWR) that is posted inside the vehicle door jamb. Drivers are encouraged to stay under 75% GVWR and, before approaching the limit, utilize additional vehicles. Loads will be packed in trailer and vehicle to achieve lowest center of gravity possible and a balanced side-to-side load.
10. *Driving Time:* Drivers shall not operate a motor vehicle for more than 8 consecutive hours or 10 hours in a day.
11. *License:* Drivers shall have their driver's license when driving a Boojum vehicle.
12. *Insurance:*
    a. Individuals driving on Boojum business shall adhere to regulations of Boojum vehicle-related insurance policies and shall not conduct themselves in any manner that would endanger or invalidate Boojum's vehicle insurance coverage.
    b. Insurance shall be in effect for all vehicles including for comp/collision and property and bodily harm. Verification shall be in vehicles at all times.
    c. All drivers shall be listed as drivers on the Boojum Institute vehicle insurance policy prior to driving.
13. *Driver Check-Off:* Anyone who operates an Institute vehicle shall have a completed Driver Check-Off form in Boojum files. This includes having read the Boojum Vehicle Manual, had a driving background check approved by the APD, and having passed the vehicle driving test with the APD or authorized designate.

14. *Predrive Inspection:* Drivers shall complete the Predrive Vehicle Inspection Checklist before driving (except if driving less than one mile).
15. *Manual:* A copy of the Boojum Vehicle Manual will be kept with every vehicle.
16. *Driver Responsibilily:* The driver is completely in charge and responsible for the operation of the vehicle and trailer and the safety of the passengers.

Procedures

1. *Reduced Visibility and Adverse Conditions Driving:* Drivers shall drive at a sufficiently reduced speed in such conditions that the driver can safely maintain control of the vehicle. Remember safety is our priority.
2. *Loading and Unloading Vehicles:* All persons shall lift with legs and not with back when moving heavy items into or out of the vehicles. Load heavier items first. Tie down all contents so they cannot shift when the vehicle is in motion.
3. *Dirt Driving:* Drive 25 mph or less and with care in order to be safe and prolong the life of the vehicle. For Bubba (Boojum's Ford truck with cage), drivers shall not exceed 15 mph on dirt roads or damage to the cage may occur.
4. *Braking:* When driving with a trailer or when the van is heavily loaded, try to avoid braking sharply. This could lessen stability.
5. *Equipment:* Each vehicle shall be equipped with first-aid kit, jumper cables, reflectors and/or flares, tire iron, and jack. Chains may be added for wintertime driving.
6. *Route Choice:* Routes that are the safest and most efficient, with the least hazardous roads and traffic conditions, shall be chosen for travel.
7. *A Vehicle Log* shall be kept in each vehicle.
8. *A Vehicle Maintenance/Inspection Log* shall be kept and maintained by the APD.
9. *Manual:* Boojum Vehicle Manual shall be reviewed annually by all Institute staff.
10. *Policy Review:* Policies shall be reviewed annually to insure compliance with state laws and insurance regulations.
11. *Smoking:* No one shall smoke in any Institute vehicle (owned or rented).
12. *Horseplay:* No horseplay shall be allowed while vehicles are in motion.
13. *Two Hands:* Drive with two hands on the steering wheel.
14. *Horn:* Blow horn when rounding blind curves on one lane roads.
15. *Side of Road:* If a vehicle is off to the side of the road, do not endanger participants or passengers by trying to push the vehicle back on the road.
16. *Trailers:*
    a. Check hitch is securely locked on the ball (try lifting trailer coupling off hitch ball; look up to visually inspect coupling clasp against ball).
    b. Check chains are attached to the van.

c. Check brake lights and turn signals are functioning properly.

d. Check items are secured so nothing can blow or fall out on the highway.

e. When backing, have someone in back to guide driver when possible.

Guidelines

1. Staff shall not drive when tired or under the influence of any substance that might impair vision, judgment, or ability to control the vehicle.
2. Be rested before driving. Do not drive when fatigued. Avoid driving at night. Night drivers have a three times greater fatality rate.
3. Driver shall factor in road conditions and vehicle weight to determine actual safe driving speed.
4. Anticipate stops! Brake early! Allow at least a 3-second gap between you and the vehicle in front of you. In adverse weather allow at least a 4-second gap.
5. If a disturbance occurs:
   a. *Do not:* brake, speed up, or turn the steering wheel
   b. *Do* let off the gas pedal and keep the steering wheel in a straight-ahead position, sufficient to remain within the lane of travel.
6. If the vehicle travels off the paved road, hold the steering wheel firmly. Let off the gas pedal. Do not apply your brakes or turn sharply. Slow down below 25 mph. Then gradually turn the steering wheel to get back on the road.
7. There are blind spots behind any vehicle. Do not rely on mirrors alone. Get assistance before you back up. If no assistance can be found, walk around the rear of the vehicle and make sure there are no children, pedestrians, or obstructions behind you.
8. Remember: Most accidents are caused by:
   a. Driver error
   b. Excessive speed
   c. Following too closely

Field Evacuation Vehicles

Procedures.

1. When in the field, Boojum vehicles are to be used as a last source for evacuations. It is preferable to make use of client vehicles as evacuation vehicles when possible.
2. Employees may not transport participants in their personal vehicles unless in an extreme emergency and when a Boojum vehicle is not available.
3. Keys to all vehicles shall be left in a prearranged location known to Boojum field staff.

Guidelines.

1. Evacuation vehicles can be useful in an emergency.
2. When possible, position evacuation vehicles at trailheads, parking lots, or other areas near course activities.

Road Shoulders

Procedures.

1. If the wheels of the vehicle travel off the paved roadway:
   a. Hold the steering wheel firmly.
   b. Let off the gas pedal and slow down below 25mph.
   c. Do not apply the brakes.
   d. Do not turn the steering wheel sharply.
   e. After slowing below 25 mph, gradually turn the steering wheel to get back on the road.
   f. Proceed with caution when entering traffic.

Mechanical Trouble and Breakdowns

Procedures.

1. On course, field staff is responsible for maintaining vehicles. If you experience mechanical trouble, do your best to determine the problem and fix it or have it fixed.
2. Immediately park the vehicle in a safe place, completely off the roadway. Avoid stopping on the shoulder of freeways. Drive to an off-ramp and pull onto a surface street.
3. If one must continue on the roadway to reach a safe place off the road, turn on the emergency flashers and proceed with caution. Do not hesitate to drive on a flat tire if it is necessary to reach a safe place completely off the roadway. (Drive slowly, since the scraping tire and wheel could cause a fire.)
4. If the driver can't get the vehicle well off the road and in a safe area, have the vehicle towed to a safe place for maintenance or repair (e.g., for fixing a flat tire).
5. Use high-visibility cones or flares during any mechanical trouble when pulled over to the side of the road (especially at night).
6. All individuals shall position themselves in a safe location to avoid being hit by oncoming traffic or being exposed to other hazards. If the vehicle is in a hazardous location, all individuals shall stay away from the immediate area until safety has been secured by the police or highway patrol.
7. If there will be delay in arriving at the course site or returning to the Boojum office, call to notify the office as soon as possible. Office staff may be able to help or at least inform the client.

Vehicle Accident

Procedures.

1. Get everyone into a safe location. Call a doctor or ambulance if anyone is injured.
2. Stay at the scene and notify the police. Make sure an accident report gets filled out.
3. Make no comment regarding the accident to anyone except the police, Boojum administration, or our insurance carrier. Do not plead guilty or assess or admit fault. Do not argue.

4. Call the Boojum administrator on call. He or she may direct you to call our insurance provider. If you cannot reach an administrator, call the insurance company on your own to report the accident.
5. Fill out the Vehicle Accident form if your accident involved other vehicles. An Incident Report form shall also be filled out by the driver or responsible party.
6. In the case of an injury to a Boojum employee or vehicle damage sustained in an accident, the driver or responsible party shall fill out an Incident Report with the help of other staff involved. The course director or most senior employee on site may fill it out in the absence of the driver or responsible party.
7. If the Boojum vehicle is safely drivable and everyone is uninjured, inform the office and proceed to your destination.
8. If a Boojum employee is injured in an accident, have another employee accompany him/her to the nearest medical facility and immediately notify the Boojum administration staff per the notification sequence in the emergency call guide.
9. If the Boojum vehicle is not safely drivable, immediately notify the Boojum administration so we can make other arrangements.
10. If a review determines gross driver negligence, a charge may be assessed to cover a portion of the Boojum's property damage.

Interstate Driving

All standards listed below are from the *Federal Motor Carrier Safety Administration's Rules and Regulations for Use of Commercial Vehicles.* Any Boojum Institute vehicle and its driver that crosses state lines must meet Department of Transportation Rules and Regulations, including:

1. Driver minimum age 21.
2. Driver record background check completed.
3. Driver testing completed.
4. Driver must provide a list to his/her employer of all motor vehicle traffic violations for which s/he has been convicted or forfeited bond in the previous 12 months.
5. Driver must have a current medical exam, which must be renewed every 24 months and may be subject to random drug testing.
6. Boojum Institute vehicles shall not transport alcohol across state lines.
7. Other federal rules and regulations apply, regardless of whether they are listed in the Boojum Vehicle Manual or not. Changes in the law or interpretation by the DOT, FMCSA, National Highway Traffic Safety Administration, or other legal agency will be conformed to in all interstate travel.

Winter Driving

Procedures.

1. While driving, carry appropriate clothing and gear for conditions and length of trip in case of emergency.

Guidelines.

1. Low speed is your best "avenue" to control a vehicle. Maintain slower speeds with all winter driving.
2. If weather has made traveling unsafe (deep snow, poor visibility, icy roads, significant blow-down, or landslide on the road), the trip should be rescheduled. If not possible, exercise extreme caution and your very best judgment at all times, and drive according to conditions.

Winter reminders.

1. Mountain roads can be snow covered and slippery.
2. Normal driving speeds and braking distances vary considerably.
3. When braking on icy or snow-covered roads, never lock the brakes. Remember you are only able to steer when the wheels are turning.
4. The ditch is a better alternative than hitting another vehicle.
5. Handling empty vans can be difficult compared with properly loaded ones on winter roads.

Driving Eligibility

Policy.

1. Staff shall be a minimum of 19 years of age for the operation of any Institute vehicle and shall have three or more years driving experience.
2. All staff shall have proof of satisfactory driving record on file at the Boojum Institute office as a result of a DMV driver record check initiated by Boojum before driving any vehicles on Boojum business.
3. Drivers for Boojum shall be entered into the DMV Pull Notice program where Boojum is notified of driving violations on an ongoing basis.
4. Any employee who will be driving an Institute vehicle shall have a completed Driver Check-Off sheet on file at the Boojum Institute office.
5. Every employee with driving duties must have a motor vehicle record (MVR) meeting the acceptable grading requirements stated below.
6. MVRs shall be examined prior to the start of employment and annually thereafter.

Standards for Motor Vehicle Record Checks

1. All operators must have a valid driver's license for at least 3 years
2. No Boojum employee shall be allowed to drive who has a "borderline" or "poor" MVR. MVRs will be graded based on the table below, as minimum requirements.
3. Driving records must remain "acceptable" or "clear," for continued employment in position with driving duties.
4. There should not be any DUI, DWI, or similar alcohol or drug related offenses within the past 5 years.
5. Any other exceptions to motor vehicle record requirements must be referred to the APD for written approval.

Guidelines.

1. Boojum may use the MVR as criteria for hiring for positions that specifically require driving; continued employment in a position with driving duties also requires an MVR meeting the standards. Boojum might not consider driving requirement as employment criteria in other circumstances.
2. MVR types of violations and motor vehicle grading tables are provided by the St. Paul Risk Control division as published in Fleet Exposure Management.

Privileges and Responsibility

Procedures.

1. Driving privileges may be revoked for not following the policies, procedures, or guidelines set forth in this manual or for traffic violations occurring during Boojum business.
2. All traffic tickets are the responsibility of the driver to pay. The Institute will not pay for any traffic tickets.
3. Drivers who are negligent will be responsible to pay up to 50% of the deductible of Institute's insurance to cover the cost of repairs. The maximum amount owed by the negligent driver is $500.
4. Unreported accidents are grounds for immediate termination of employment.

Personal Vehicles

Policy.

1. When Institute staff are requested to drive their own vehicle on Institute business, the following criteria shall be met:
   a. An Institute vehicle meeting the needs of the employee is not available.
   b. The employee carries insurance with the state minimum requirements for Bodily Injury and Property Damage.
   c. If during the normal course of Institute business an accident occurs or damage is sustained to the non-Institute vehicle for which the employee is negligent, the Institute has no obligation to pay any associated costs.
   d. Boojum recommends abstaining from the use of a cell phone while driving on Institute business. The Institute has no obligation to pay any associated costs of an accident that occurs as the result of cell phone use while driving an Institute or non-Institute vehicle.

Driver Training and Assessment

Policy.

1. All certified drivers will participate in a yearly Boojum driver training. Topics shall include:
   a. Fifteen-passenger vans (unique design and handling, risks, history, and causes or rollovers)
   b. Center of gravity, causes of lateral instability, understeering, and oversteering
   c. Weigh distribution, loading, and unloading

   d. Emergency handling
   e. Interstate rules and regulations
2. Use of trailers or other special equipment shall require additional training and assessment, which might include braking, hitching, trailer loading, tongue weight, safety equipment and other topics as deemed necessary by the conditions in which the trailer is operated.
3. A designated evaluator will conduct and document practical exam. Performance evaluation shall include road and driving conditions typically encountered while driving.

Procedures.

1. A written exam shall be conducted requiring mastery of topics covered during driver training.
2. Documentation shall be kept of all drivers, driver's licenses, and driving records.

Van Rollover Risk

Since 2002, the National Highway Traffic Safety Administration (NHTSA) has issued a cautionary warning to users of 15-passenger vans because of an increased rollover risk under certain conditions. The NHTSA does not state that 15-passenger vans are unsafe. These vehicles meet federal standards for passenger transportation. Their overall rollover "ratio" is acceptable. Driving more slowly and allowing space between vehicles are the most important ways the driver can positively impact driving safety.

Specifics

Recent analysis by the NHTSA revealed that 15-passenger vans have a rollover risk that is similar to other light trucks and vans when carrying a few passengers. That risk increases dramatically as the number of occupants increases from fewer than five occupants to over 10 passengers. The analysis indicated that, with 10 or more occupants, the vans had a rollover rate in single-vehicle crashes that is nearly three times the rate of those that were lightly loaded.

The physics involved in the problem are called understeer and oversteer, neither of which are so dangerous in and of themselves. They combine with design features, load distribution, road characteristics, and *speed* to cause trouble, however. The physical characteristic responsible is a top-heavy design for the vans. Understeer is exacerbated by increased van weight or by loading a 15-passenger van to its gross vehicle weight (GVW). Both understeer and oversteer are exacerbated by lateral acceleration, the side force exerted on the van as it rounds a turn or swerves to avoid an unexpected obstacle.

Understeer.

Understeer is when the vehicle's front wheels are describing a larger curve than the rear wheels. Most passenger cars are designed to understeer for safety reasons; it gives the driver greater control. When cornering too fast in a van or making an avoidance maneuver, it feels like the vehicle is plowing straight ahead in the turn despite the driver's steering input. Slower speeds minimize understeer problems. Since the van is rear-wheel drive, this has the effect of settling the van down over the front wheels and giving the driver more control.

Oversteer.

Oversteer is when the rear wheels are describing a larger curve than the front wheels. This happens during a sharp turn at high speed or an avoidance maneuver when the van's relatively high center of gravity leans the vehicle toward the outside of the curve. It feels as if the van's rear end will "kick out." This can result in spinning out, which increases the chance of rolling over. Entering a turn at slow speed decreases the negative effects of oversteer.

Fifteen-passenger vans have a higher rollover rate partly because they drive well and predictably at low speeds, and then suddenly become difficult to handle at higher speeds. When making a corner at slow speed, a heavily loaded van's understeer characteristics are similar to its lightly loaded condition. They are dramatically and dangerously different when making an avoidance maneuver at high speeds.

While cornering at high speed or instinctively overcorrecting after an avoidance swerve, the loaded vehicle will exhibit over steer, possibly resulting in a rollover. So, the moral of the story is, drive slowly and under control, and take care when loading.

Loading the van.

1. Always remember that the load should be forward and low for best stability, including:
   a. The load to consider includes passengers plus packs and other gear.
   b. The driver of a Boojum van should take responsibility for distributing the weight to optimize handling characteristics of a 15-passenger van.
   c. Everyone in the van must be secured by a seatbelt.
   d. Everything in the van must be secured so that it can't become a projectile in the event of a rollover or other loss of control.
   e. There are a variety of ways to tie cargo down inside a van. We have cargo nets and ropes, plus webbing to make it easier to tie down different size loads.

Points to consider.

1. Keep the load forward.
2. Keep the load on the back seat (or section behind the rear axle) as light as possible or leave it empty.
3. Weighing down the back seat unweights the front of the van. This situation causes handling difficulty. (The van extends far enough beyond the rear axle so that axle acts like a fulcrum.)

Securing white gas.

1. Keep the white gas out of the van if possible.
2. If there is a trailer, secure it in the trailer, away from food.
3. If there is a wooden box and a factory-installed roof rack on the vehicle, put the white gas in the box on the roof and tie it down.
4. If gas must be stored inside the van, keep the gas out of the van until departure time (but don't forget it!).
5. It should be the last thing loaded and the first thing unloaded.
6. The idea is to avoid leaving gas in a nonmoving vehicle where it can heat up.

SECTION 7
EQUIPMENT, NUTRITION, AND HYGIENE

Red Top Meadows	*F*	Therapeutic
	E	Rocky Mountain Region
	C	Adolescent Males
	S	7.01–7.07

Equipment

RTM believes that one of the ways to reduce risk on wilderness trips is to equip our students with adequate gear. Through donations, wholesale accounts, and acquiring used gear from NOLS, RTM has assembled a substantial inventory of outdoor gear and clothing. It is the responsibility of the wilderness director to work with the appropriate staff to maintain the inventory by soliciting donations, setting up new accounts, and placing orders for new gear when it is necessary.

Inventory

Staff in charge of the equipment room should make sure there is a sufficient inventory of gear prior to a trip going in the field. The inventory sheet is kept in the three-ring binder in the wilderness director's office. It is important to maintain a variety of sizes to accommodate any group of students. Equipment that needs to be repaired frequently (i.e., stoves and tents) are assigned to staff members. Staff in charge of these items must notify the wilderness director when replacement of parts or entire units is necessary.

Care and Repair

Each piece of clothing and equipment should be inspected at the time of inventory, before it goes in the field and at the end of a trip during de-issue. Students are asked to look over each piece of gear and report the general condition at the time of issue. The condition is written down on the issue sheet. At the end of a trip, during de-issue, the gear is rechecked. Damage to equipment may result in a debt for a student if the damage was caused by abuse. Debts for lost gear are also assigned at this time. Any items that need repair are labeled and put in the repair box, after washing. The instructor team that finishes a trip is responsible for the duty of washing clothes and putting them back in the appropriate place in the equipment room. Sleeping bags are brought to the laundromat after each trip. The wilderness director is responsible for making arrangements to get the necessary repairs done. This may be done at RTM or some items such as tents may need to be shipped out. Students are supervised in the cleaning of stoves, tents, packs, cook gear and vehicles.

Repair Kits

Inventory of the repair kits should be checked by a staff before being sent out in the field and clearly marked "ready to go" with a date. Inventory lists, for both day and expedition repair kits, are kept in the three-ring binder in the wilderness director's office. A staff member will be assigned the task of putting together a repair kit for ski days during the winter months.

Storage

All wilderness gear and clothing is stored in the equipment room. A tour of where everything goes should be a part of every staff's training. Trash cans, bins, and crates should all be clearly labeled with their contents. Staff should take care when replacing gear to put it into the correct container. All containers should be stored off the floor on wooden pallets or on shelves. White gas cannot be stored in the equipment room. Stoves and fuel bottles should be emptied into gas cans and stored in the gardening shed.

Staff Equipment/Pro Forms

Staff is responsible for providing their own gear for wilderness trips. Borrowing gear is acceptable only after students have been outfitted and there is a leftover supply. RTM has set up many proform accounts for staff to purchase gear at discounted prices. Please honor the rules of the pro purchase programs and use this benefit for yourself only.

Issuing

Staff starting a trip is generally responsible for issuing. They should check with the staff in charge of the equipment room regarding what equipment is good to go. A good rule thumb is: If you wouldn't use a piece of gear or item of clothing, don't send it into the field with a student. Having confidence in your equipment and liking the clothes you're wearing is important to everyone. Staff should take the time when issuing to make sure the clothing and equipment issued:

- Fits the student properly (i.e., sleeping bags are long enough and packs are fitted to the individual).
- Is functional and not in need of repair. Have students operate zippers on sleeping bags and closures on clothing. Make sure buckles and adjustments work.
- Is liked by the student. Allow students to have some personal choice when possible regarding color and style. They are the ones that have to live in it.
- Is logged carefully on the personal issue sheets. Record size, style, color, and condition. De-issue goes smoother when you can identify the piece of equipment as the same one that was issued and not one taken from another student.

Staff starting the trip is responsible for organizing their own group gear and filling out the appropriate sheet. Group gear and food should be organized and set aside to be issued just prior to going in the field.

Personal Items List

Personal clothing and other items a student needs to bring on the trip are listed on a personal items checklist. There are different checklists for summer and winter. A student should have these items checked off and gathered in a bag or crate before being issued. Staff checking students need to make sure that the clothing the student has picked out is appropriate for the trip and in good repair.

Pack Packing

A class on packing a pack will be done with students during the week before the trip (see wilderness education curriculum). Staff should help students pack as a group just prior to the trip. Group gear should be divvied up and "who is carrying what" written down in the staff log book.

De-Issue

At the end of the trip, equipment and clothing is de-issued. De-issuing entails the collecting, inspecting, and cleaning of all personal and group gear that was issued. Staff should use the de-issue checklist to make sure everything gets done. The staff de-issuing are responsible for getting everything done or clearly making arrangements for someone else to finish up.

Staff Group Gear

First-aid kits, walkie-talkies, repair kits, phones, maps, trip packets, etc. will be gathered in the wilderness director's office and labeled for each group. Staff going on the trip are responsible for figuring out tents and other personalized group gear (i.e., books, toys).

Food and Nutrition

Food is an important item to adolescent boys. Teenagers burn many calories, especially when they are active in outdoor activities. In addition, many of our students have had experiences in their lives that have resulted in security issues around food. We have found that involving students in the planning and preparation of the food is a valuable experience and can help students:

- Develop organizational and cooking skills.
- Take some responsibility in their daily lives.
- Deal with fears and food security issues directly.
- Develop relationships with their peers by sharing in cook group responsibilities and being social.
- Practice conflict resolution.

One staff member is responsible for planning the food rations for each trip and arranging a time to package it. Attention is given to nutritional requirements, variety, and amounts appropriate for each group. Prior to a trip, students should be prepped on the identification of certain foods, tips on organizing and rationing, and a general menu plan. When logistically possible, students are involved in the packaging process. All re-rations are packaged, bagged, and labeled prior to the trip. Depending on the experience level of the group, a cooking class may be scheduled into the week prior to the summer trip. A cook/kitchen schedule pairing up students with staff should be made up on the first day of a trip. Staff should supervise their cook group closely at first and spend time teaching basic cooking and kitchen skills.

Water and Hydration

One cannot say enough about the importance of staying hydrated, especially in a wilderness environment. Drinking plenty of water keeps the body functioning in many ways. Staff and students should try and drink at least 3 quarts of water a day minimum. When conditions are more extreme, more water can be helpful. Consider all water in the field to be contaminated and treat it accordingly (3 to 4 drops of iodine per quart and wait 15 to 20 minutes before drinking). Water may also be brought to a boil or pumped with a filter if time and equipment permit. RTM does not issue water filter systems.

Resupply

Every 3 to 7 days in the field, depending on the trip itinerary, a crew needs resupply. The staff responsible for resupply should check the re-ration checklist to make sure they have everything they need before leaving Red Top. Field instructors should have their group ready for resupply by having garbage and leftover food separated, peanut butter and margarine containers ready to exchange, fuel bottles ready to refill, and a list of needed equipment, first-aid, or repair items.

Maps

Laminated master maps of most of RTM's operating areas are on the wall in the main office building. Routes, campsites, and other useful information should be posted on or near these maps. Information from these maps can be transferred onto the trip maps or into the staff log. Trip maps are located in the wilderness director's office. Each group should have two complete sets of maps for each trip. The students are responsible for carrying and caring for one set and the staff is responsible for the other set. A list of the maps in the order in which they are needed is kept in the map bag. Worn out maps should be retired at the end of a trip. Any new information regarding routes, camps, etc. should be posted on the master maps.

Transportation

RTM staff should follow all the policies and procedures for vehicle use listed in the Staff Hand Book. Extra attention should be given to loading and unloading vehicles. Make sure loads riding in roof-top carriers are securely tied down. Staff driving 15-passenger vans should be aware of safety hazards associated with that vehicle. Staff driving some distance at the end of the trip should rotate drivers frequently and stay alert.

Student Health

General

Participating in the wilderness program is an integral part of a students stay at RTM. All Red Top students are scheduled for doctors appointments soon after entering the RTM program. Background health information is obtained during the admissions process. Students' health, physical condition, and medications are monitored as an ongoing part of the program. RTM has a fairly rigorous PE and group activity program that keeps the students in good physical shape. A student's doctor is consulted any time there is a concern about his/her ability to participate in the wilderness program.

Nonresidential students joining us for one of our special programs and their parents must fill out the medical questionnaire, which contains sections on emergency contact information, insurance, general health questions, a letter of participation to be signed by a physician, and a medical consent form. Additional information regarding referrals can be found in the intake materials. Students are also advised to do some pretrip conditioning. RTM may need to consult with the doctor if there is any questionable medical information.

First-Aid Kits

RTM expedition first-aid kits and resupply items are stored in the wilderness director's office. Day trip first-aid kits (in square Rubbermaid containers) are stored in the first-aid cabinet in the staff office. An inventory of what each kit contains is kept in the kit and in the three-ring binder in the wilderness director's office. In addition, there are smaller kits in each vehicle. To ensure that first-aid kits remains in good shape, all staff should observe the following guidelines:

1. RTM first-aid kits should be used only for RTM wilderness trips or off-grounds activities. First-aid supplies for use on-grounds are found in the first-aid cabinet.
2. The staff in charge of first-aid kits should check and restock kits prior to each trip. Kits ready to go should be taped shut and clearly marked.
3. Students should not be allowed to get into kits without staff supervision.
4. Foot-repair kits should be carried separately to avoid having to open and close the kits constantly.
5. Insect repellant and other solvents or contaminates should be carried separately.
6. Student medications and medication sheets should be carried separately.

Medications

Many Red Top students take daily medications prescribed by their doctor. At RTM there are written procedures for dispensing medications to the students. It is important to follow these procedures as closely as possible in the field. The following guidelines should be helpful in making this transition smooth:

1. One staff should be assigned to do a medication count prior to the trip and order enough to last the length of the trip. There should be a little leeway figured into the amounts. Remember to leave enough time to make arrangements for certain meds that require a prescription for each refill (Methylphenidate, Dexedrine, etc).
2. Since the students are about to change their environment drastically, student requests for changes in medications or dosages prior to the trip are discouraged.
3. One staff member per crew should be responsible for carrying and dispensing medications.
4. Medications and medication sheets should be carried in a waterproof bag or pouch.
5. Medications should be dispensed on time or as close as possible depending on the situation. Medication sheets should be filled out at the time medication is given.
6. Possible side effects of certain medications should be reviewed in staff training prior to the trip.
7. More severe medical conditions, such as acute asthma or insulin-dependant diabetes, will require consultation with a doctor to determine the student's eligibility for the trip.

Personal Hygiene

Many RTM students have a hard time with basic hygiene issues. Taking care of the basics in a wilderness setting can seem second nature to the staff but can be unimportant or overwhelming to the students. Personal care is important to prevent individual or group illnesses caused by dirty bodies and dishes. Staff should make sure the students:

- Brush their teeth regularly.
- Bathe critical areas regularly. Staff need to supervise and help students take billy baths. Playing in the water alone is not enough.
- Instruct students how to use and dispose of TP properly. If TP is used on a trip, it is RTM policy that it is carried out in sealable plastic bags.

- Staff need to instruct and help students wash clothes on layover days when possible.
- Students and staff should wash and sanitize hands before handling food. Just sanitizing dirty hands is not good enough.
- Staff should check students' feet on a regular basis for foot rot, blisters, etc.
- Students should be encouraged to dry their feet out whenever they get a chance (e.g. lunch breaks).
- Students should not be allowed to touch carcasses of dead animals.
- Group dishes and personal cups and bowls should be cleaned after each meal.
- Students need to be encouraged to report any health issues they might be having to staff ASAP. Prevention and early treatment of rashes, blisters, etc. is helpful.

University of North Carolina at Charlotte—Venture Center	
F	Recreation
E	Southeast Region
C	University Students and General Population
S	7.01–7.04

Preparation of Equipment for Trips

General Points

1. Keep equipment room locked when no one is there.
2. It is important that time and care goes into the preparation of equipment. Even small details, if neglected, can spoil or hinder a trip.
3. Arrange for additional staff support with preparation when needed. Example: loading canoe trailer.
4. Before prepping gear:
   a. Check to see how many people are in the workshop, including staff.
   b. Find out which vehicle to prep and prep according to checklist (Appendix A-5).
   c. Look over workshop equipment form (Appendix A-6 or A-7) from instructor.

Day Trips

1. Find out if Venture is providing lunch.
2. First-aid kit (2 blue bags + 1 mesh bag for boating and fanny pack kit for all others).
3. Associate director inventories kit(s) prior to each workshop.

Special Equipment Needs

All overnights.

1. Check all tents for fly, poles, junction tubes, stakes, and ground cloth.
2. Appropriate number of sleeping bags:
   a. Check for weak seams, faulty zippers, and cleanliness.
   b. Stuffed in plastic garbage bag inside stuff sack, with flannel liner included inside each stuff sack.
   c. Try to select appropriate bags for the weather.
   d. Cooler weather will need the new, better bags, warmer weather the older bags will work fine.
   e. Prep both regulars and longs.
3. Check condition of ensolite pads.
4. Place cup, bowl, and spoon in small mesh stuff sacks.
5. One or two white gas stoves, 3/4 full with Coleman fuel, and a case of matches with each stove. (Best stoves are Nova or MSR XGK's with their own Sigg fuel bottle.)
   a. Check that all parts and windscreen and bases are in the stove zip bag + 1 Sigg bottle (silver) of white gas for each day of the trip.
6. Check all stoves for proper burning, repair kit and all parts to the pump. (Repair person). (See pages 74–76 for stove and pump parts).
   a. Check for gaskets on Sigg bottles. If missing, they will leak.
   b. Staff may request a Trangia alcohol stove instead of, or in addition to, white gas stove.
   c. Make sure all parts are with stove.
   d. Provide 1 Sigg bottle (red) of alcohol for each 2 days of the trip.
7. Cook pots: usually 1 large pot, 1 medium pot, and 1 coffee pot and lids for each.
8. Kitchen duffel (utensil roll or bag): 1 large cooking spoon, 2 small spoons, 1 spatula, 2 sharp knives, 2 kitchen knives, 1 cutting board, 1 can opener, 1 pair of pot grips, garbage bag, and scrubby.
9. First-aid kit: (Appendix B-1 to B-6) associate director inventories kit(s) prior to each workshop.
10. Shovel.
11. Toilet paper in a plastic bag with matches or disposable lighter and coffee can.
    a. Each roll should be in its own bag with own burning tool.
12. Garbage bags.
13. Hypothermia kit as appropriate for weather conditions.
14. Cellular phone—to be signed out by senior staff.

Camping away from vehicle.

1. Tents: Four people per Timberline or NoAll. (Except sea kayaking or canoeing, which might use three per tent.)
2. Water bag: at least two (check for leaks).

Car camping (example: white-water kayak trips).

1. Tents: Three people per Timberline or NoAll.
2. Coleman lantern (extra mantels) and white gas.
3. Coleman 2-burner stove if requested.

Backpacking.

1. Packs: check clevis pins, back straps, shoulder straps, hip belt, straps for sleeping bag, and pack bag to make sure in good shape.
2. Pur water filters if requested.

Boating of any type.

1. Try to arrange equipment so that all the group equipment needed on the water is in the canoe trailer.
2. Prep the following items:
   a. Paddles: 1 per boat for canoeing; 1 per boat for kayaking plus 1 spare for trip.
   b. Paddling jackets and pants (each participant may choose set).
   c. Dry bags (as requested).
   d. Throw ropes.
   e. Water first aid kit.
   f. Water rescue kit (for white-water).
   g. Water hypothermia kit.
   h. Extra plastic bags.
   i. Bailers (for canoes) or sponges.
3. Load trailer with appropriate number of boats. Double-check that all are well tied.
4. Put keys for trailer lock and spare tire lock in vehicle.
5. White-water kayaking additions:
   a. Kayak paddles—1 per person plus 1 small break-a-part as an extra.
   b. Spray skirts: 1 per person and numbers are marked on skirts that coincide with a number on each kayak. Include at least 5 or 6 extra.
   c. Kayak helmets.
   d. Check for float bags, there should be 1 on each side in the back as a minimum.
6. Sea Kayaking additions:
   a. Sea Kayak paddles—1 per person (all the break-apart and the lightest ones first) plus 1 extra.

7. Place in duffel bags the following items:
   a. Spray skirts: Make sure they are nylon sea kayak skirts, some have suspender straps, and all are large.
   b. Paddle floats: 1 per boat.
   c. Bilge pumps: 1 per boat.
   d. Blue or black dry bags: all.
   e. Water bags, all (depending on trip, usually need 1 per person per 3 days).
   f. Storage flotation bags (blue nylon Perception ones), 1 for each old Chinook.
   g. Emergency signaling devices: flares, smoke, dye (all from director's office).
8. Repair kit: including Leatherman tool, line or cord, duct tape, wire, can of WD40, extra rudder cables, Fastex buckles, extra foot peg and track, Phillips and regular screw drivers, 2 pairs of pliers, cable clamps, extra screws and nuts, marine caulk, etc.
9. Rescue loops for staff boats.
10. Staff should bring cellular phone, weather radio.
11. If camping on beach, pack sand stakes (old tent poles): 6 to 8 per tent.
12. Outfitter wing tarp for sun shelter on beach and around 24 sand stakes for it also.
13. Map case for charts.
14. Sail (with lines) and mast for Tofino.
15. Check boats, especially rudders, rudder cables, and foot pegs. Make sure they can be adjusted and work properly.

Climbing.

1. Ropes: check with instructor as to the number and type. Check all ropes issued for weak spots!
2. Grab a 1-foot section of rope, fold it, and move it back and forth. If the section forms a smooth arch, then no damage exists. If a break appears in the arch, it's a weak point.
3. Mark all possible weak spots with masking tape and get a second opinion on the spot in question. If weak spot is in the end of the rope, the end can be cut off and the new end sealed. If weak spot is in the middle section, retire the rope. Check with climbing coordinator.
4. Sit harnesses: check for visual signs of damage.
5. Slings, carabiners, figure 8's, sticht plates or other belay devices, and prussiks.
6. Rack: check with instructor.
7. Helmets (appropriate number) check for working buckles.
8. Carpet squares to protect ropes over edges.
9. Gloves: for rappels.
10. Backboard in vehicle.

Caving.

1. Headlamps: clean and 4 batteries in each lamp. Extra batteries should be sealed in bags. If using carbide lamps: clean and make sure each lamp is in good working order.
2. Repair kit with cleaning needle, spare felts, etc., unless using headlamps.
3. Baby bottles filled with carbide, unless we will be using headlamps.
4. Plastic bag per participant with matches, candle, and extra bags to hold spent carbide.
5. Helmets with bungee to attach headlamp or brackets for carbide lamps: 1 per person.
6. Small cave packs: 1 per person.
7. Knee pads: 1 set per person.
8. Rope: 1 for building litter or hauling.
9. Stokes litter in vehicle; backboard in vehicle.
10. Cave duffels for packs: 1 per person if overnight.
11. Toilet seat with a bucket and 4 to 5 garbage bags if overnight.
12. Coleman lantern with white gas and extra mantels if overnight.

Skiing.

1. Prep 2 instructors' emergency kits with: ski tip, wire, extra bales for bindings, candy bars, small cook pot, candles, matches, wire saw (if available), whistle, compass, space blanket, bullion, tea, sugar, parachute cord, 2 to 4 large safety pins, Leatherman tools (if available).
2. One ski repair kit with: duct tape, cord, wire, and screws.
3. Ski bag with all skis and poles.
4. Ski boots.
5. First-aid kit.
6. Prep 2 mini first-aid kits with: roll 1" adhesive tape, (6) 1" Band-Aids, (1) 4" ace bandage, (1) 2" gauze roll, (4) 2x2 and (4) 4x4 gauze pads, (1) triangular bandage, small bottle betadine, and (2) Patient Assessment Form.
7. Wool hats.
8. Mittens, both wool and insulated.
9. Rain parkas.
10. Gaiters.
11. Miscellaneous equipment: anticipate expendable supply needs (e.g., Coleman fuel, lantern mantles, flashlight batteries, spare bulbs, plastic bags, garbage bags, candles, toilet paper, pins). Give list of supplies needing to be purchased to food packer.

General Packing Instructions

1. Separate individual equipment from group gear.

2. Place a supply of gear out where obvious and available for participants to pick up.
3. Check out group gear on appropriate Workshop Equipment Form.

Equipment Inventory (All Staff)

1. See equipment inventory form.
2. Inventory should be taken yearly, near the end of spring semester.

Equipment Check-Out (Trip Staff)

1. Mark number or equipment inventory number of each individual item checked out in the appropriate column of the Equipment Participant Rental Form.
2. Check and initial all group gear on workshop equipment form.
3. Each instructor is responsible for double-checking the Check-Out form. Instructors are responsible for all equipment marked "out."

Equipment Check-In (Trip Staff)

1. Equipment check-in must take place before the group departs at the end of the trip.
   a. Go down the list item by item and check that each has been returned.
   b. If any items are missing or damaged:
      i. Assess charge to the individual responsible or divide cost among the group. As the instructor, you may need to decide which is the most appropriate.
      ii. Try to collect money at that time. It is harder to collect money once people have left.
      iii. Any uncollected money needs to be reported to the associate director, along with the name and social security number of the person(s) to be charged.
2. All instructors for that workshop are liable for any items checked in but found to be missing!
3. Equipment needs to be put back where it belongs in the cage unless it is wet, dirty, or needs to be hung up.
4. Hang up wet tents, sleeping bags, rain jackets, throw rope, helmets, spray skirts, and any gear that is wet.
5. Have participants clean out sleeping bags and put stuff sack inside the sleeping bag. The stuff sack number needs to coordinate with the sleeping bag number. The sleeping bag liner is to be placed with other dirty laundry.
6. Tent parts and stuff sacks should be placed beside the table on the cage floor. Wet tents need to be hung up.
7. Duffels, large mesh bags and dry bags should be emptied and placed in a pile on the floor.
8. Have participants empty backpacks of all items and place in their appropriate location.
9. Have participants empty water bottles and place in the dirty water bottle bin.

10. Participants should wash all dirty pots, cups, bowls, spoons and cooking utensils if extremely dirty and placed in the appropriate bin (either dirty pots/pans or dirty cup, bowl, spoon bin).
11. Diver boxes should be emptied and placed in the dirty pots/pans bin.
12. Have participants take cup, bowl, and spoon out of its mesh bag and mesh bags should be placed in the dirty mesh bag bin.
13. Dirty clothes (polypropylene, hats, gloves, sweaters) and sleeping bag liners should be placed in the dirty laundry bin. If items are not dirty, they should be placed in their appropriate location.
14. Have participants put ensolite pads in their appropriate location. If pads are wet, unroll and stand up on their end.
15. All stoves should be placed back in their appropriate location, unless they need repair. Make sure pots are taken out of the alcohol stoves so they can be washed.
16. Have participants empty the canoe or kayak trailer cage of all items. Items should be returned to their appropriate location. Boats may remain on the trailer.
17. Have participants clean out the vehicle and, if dirty, sweep out the vehicle before they depart.
18. Have participants empty the trash can in the large trash receptacle.
19. Tag any equipment to be repaired and place on the repair shelf inside the building. Leave a note in the repairer's basket (in office) as to what needs repair.
20. First-aid kit is to be returned to the office. Make a note of any items used and place note in associate directors basket.
21. Put unused food in the food closet or refrigerator in the office, as appropriate. Any perishable food should be thrown away.

Equipment Clean-Up

1. On Wednesday, take cotton laundry to the equipment check-out in the gym to be washed. Pick it up on Thursday or Friday (equipment packer).
2. Take noncotton dirty items to a laundromat and wash in cold water in mild soap (equipment packer).
3. For pots, cups, bowls, spoons, and water bottles, wash in dishwasher. If extremely dirty wash by hand and then place in large sterilizing container with water and 2 cups of Clorox bleach. Leave for a minimum of 20 minutes; remove and put away (food packer).
4. Put away tents and other items, making sure that all parts are dry and in their proper places (Equipment Packer).
5. Clean up the equipment room in general. Sweep floor as needed. Empty trash can (equipment packer).
6. Put leftover food away (food packer).

Boojum Institute	*F* **Education**
	E **West Region**
	C **Various Populations**
	S **7.05–7.07**

Health Maintenance

Procedures

1. Instructors shall teach participants proper hygiene procedures regarding self care, water disinfection, food preparation, clean-up, and waste elimination.
2. Food handling plastic gloves shall be used if handling food directly while on course. Food shall be stored away from rodents. Foods shall be heated or chilled to stay out of the "Danger Zone" of 40 to 140 degrees F. In particular, warm items shall be stored in small units (for rapid cooling) on ice or in a cool area.
3. Instructors shall make daily checks on the health of each student, including hydration, personal hygiene, foot care, and general well-being. In tick season (spring/summer) and in tick-prone regions, everyone should be checked for ticks at least once daily.
4. Even though chaperones are "on duty" during the night and unstructured time, instructors should sleep close enough to their group so as to be quickly and easily reachable in case of a medical emergency. Instructors are to inform their group and chaperones of their location during free time and at night.
5. Treat cuts, scrapes, and blisters promptly to prevent infection, and follow up on them to monitor for infection.
6. Staff, students, or others who are or may be ill shall not prepare food, clean up, or otherwise spend time in the kitchen.
7. Wash hands after going to the bathroom and before meals. Position the hand-washing system near latrines and in front of the food lines to ensure compliance.
8. Cooking and eating items shall be sanitized regularly with bleach, boiling, or other approved method on a daily basis.
9. Toilet paper shall be available on all courses.

Cooking and Kitchen Risk Management

Procedures.

1. Wash hands prior to handling food.
2. Any individual directly handling food shall wear food server gloves.
3. Youth 16 years and younger will be directly supervised at all times while operating camp stoves.

Guidelines.

1. Set up a well-organized kitchen. Locate stoves and fires away from main paths of travel; a small amount of items near the stove/fire is less hazardous than a cluttered kitchen area. Have pots, pans, cooking utensils, and spices nearby.
2. Keep students not actively involved out of the kitchen area while meal preparation is in progress.
3. Active field staff supervision, especially of younger students, is critical to help prevent common kitchen injuries such as cuts from knives and burns from boiling water. Many of our students have never prepared their own meals. You may have to spend a considerable amount of time teaching the necessary skills and monitoring their progress.
4. Do not reach into food bags (such as GORP and other snacks). Instead, pour into each person's hat, cupped hands, or bowl. This will help to avoid contamination of common foodstuffs.
5. Avoid sharing eating and drinking utensils.
6. Do not assume that participants know how to appropriately and efficiently use a knife. Field staff will teach participants proper knife use and safety. The following guidelines apply:
   a. Use short controlled strokes.
   b. Do not draw a knife toward you while cutting. Cut away from yourself.
   c. Do not use your body as a cutting board.
   d. Do not throw knives.
   e. Sharp knives are safer than dull; keep knives well honed.
   f. No playing with knives allowed.
7. Make diligent and reasonable efforts to prevent contamination of all food by animals. This may mean hanging food, storing in tightly sealed containers, or placing in vehicles.
8. Where rodents are a problem (as in the Channel Islands), sealing vulnerable food inside metal pots with tight-fitting lids is recommended. Hanging may also work well.
9. Food bags may be hung in a number of ways, between trees or from sturdy limbs. When using packs to hang food, wrapping a rope around the pack, (similar to wrapping a package) will minimize wear on straps. When hanging bags or packs against bears, the lowest part of the bag should be a minimum of 15 feet above the ground, 4 feet down from a limb or guy line, and 6 from the tree. This can require some work, and care should be taken with heavy food bags.
10. While trying to protect food remember that people and their safety come first. Any situation that involves hanging heavy food bags or packs needs to be managed by field staff until students demonstrate the competency to conduct the activity on their own. Dividing heavy loads into multiple, separate hangs may be a wise precaution.
11. Base camp programs use a wash system utilizing four containers, set up as follows:
    a. First container = a garbage bin. This is for waste leftover from their meal. Encourage a thorough scraping of all leftovers and sauces to eliminate the need to change

the water in the next buckets. When practical, retain nonmeat/dairy food waste for postcourse composting at the Boojum facility compost bin.

b. Second container = soapy water bucket with sponges. Ideally, this water is heated.

c. Third container = clean rinse water to rinse off the soap.

d. Fourth container = water with liquid chlorine bleach added. This is to be used as a dip bucket for disinfection. Enough bleach should be added to create a strong smell. One hundred parts per million of bleach with a 30 second soak time is a good standard. A 1:100 bleach: water ratio may be appropriate. Cooking and eating gear should then be allowed to air dry. The wash system should be set near the kitchen so as to be convenient when people are finished eating. It should be cleaned up soon after use; strain dirty water prior to discarding.

12. On backcountry courses or where bleach is not available, sterilize eating utensils periodically by rinsing thoroughly in boiled water or by immersing for 1 minute in a large clean pot of boiling water.

Stoves

Risk management around stoves must be conscientiously conducted. Stoves, white gas, and liquid propane (LP) gas are among the most dangerous items we have with us in the field. The stoves we currently use are:

1. Coleman Peak One. White gas, for individual group use.
2. MSR Dragonfly. White gas, for individual group use.
3. Fish-cooker style (several different models). LP gas, for large group use.

Procedures.

1. Never leave a stove unattended while burning.
2. Stoves are not to be used in tents.

Guidelines.

1. Before departing for the field, staff shall check their stove(s) to ensure proper operation.
2. Allow time for a thorough stove and fuel introduction. Impress upon students the dangers and seriousness of working with stoves and fuel. For programs with youth under 16 years of age, instructors or competent chaperones shall directly supervise stove operations from the immediate area at all times.
3. Remember and remind participants that when a stove is in use, and immediately after, all metal parts of the burner assembly and generator are extremely hot.
4. Be careful regarding long hair, clothing, plastic food bags, aprons, hot pads, and other flammable items near burning stoves.
5. Be aware of and choose pots that fit the stove you intend to use. Use of pots larger than the stove can accommodate may cause spilling and subsequent injury (or at the very least loss of a meal). Building supports of rocks surrounding the pot base can mitigate tipping hazards.
6. Set up stoves in spots well sheltered from the wind on solid ground before lighting.

White gas stoves—guidelines.

1. White gas is extremely flammable; handle with great awareness of nearby open flame. Fuel vapors are invisible, explosive, and can be ignited by heat sources 15 feet away or more. Fuel vapors are heavier than air and can travel along the ground for some distance; if the vapors reach open flame they may ignite and arc back to a fuel bottle or open stove causing an explosion.
2. Be sure that all participants know which containers hold fuel.
3. If students arrive on course with aluminum bottles they intend to use as water bottles, ensure that they are clearly marked, or replace their bottle with one loaned from Boojum for the duration of the course.
4. Always fill stoves and fuel bottles outdoors. Never fill tank or loosen or remove fuel cap (of stove or gas container) near flame or other ignition sources. At freezing temperatures, white gas can cause instant frostbite if it comes into contact with skin.
5. The MSR Dragonfly and the Peak 1 are both designed to use white gas. Never use kerosene, gasohol, regular or unleaded automotive fuel in these stoves.
6. Pack fuel and stoves separately from food whenever possible. Gas should not be packed above food in a pack. Release pressure and turn upside down to check for leaks before packing. Any time you handle a fuel bottle, give the top a twist to make sure it's on tightly.

LP gas stoves—guidelines.

1. LP gas fittings use left handed threads. This means that to attach the hose to the tank, you should turn to the left to tighten and to the right to loosen - the opposite of normal use.
2. Fish cookers will be configured so that the maximum possible distance is allowed between the tank and open flame. Minimize the potential for someone tripping over the hose and tipping the stove by blocking passage near the fish cooker and tank.
3. Always store LP gas containers in an upright position away from flame, other sources of ignition, or excessive heat. LP gas tanks are equipped with pressure release valves. On a hot day if they are left in the sun the pressure release valve will open and release gas. LP gas smells like bad garlic due to an additive (mercaptan) to the odorless propane. If you become aware of this smell, extinguish any open flame and carefully move the tank into the shade.

Water Disinfection

Procedures.

1. All drinking water acquired from nonpotable water sources will be disinfected.

Guidelines.

1. Always strive to carry or have available enough water to meet the needs of your group with a bit extra remaining for unexpected situations and delays.
2. When water disinfection is necessary on an ongoing basis, participants should be taught and practice the proper procedures.

3. Teach students that precautions must be taken to treat the threads of caps and bottles if they come into contact with unpurified water. Add the treatment (iodine or chlorine) then screw the cap back on the water bottle. If using tablets, let the tab dissolve. Then unscrew the cap part-way and squeeze some of the treated water out through the threads. Let the full-strength treated water remain on the threads for the full treatment standing time.

Prefiltering guidelines.

1. If the only available water is cloudy or has suspended particulate matter, prefilter it prior to using chemical disinfectants. This will improve the quality of the treatment and make the water a bit more visually appealing. Prefiltering can simply consist of pouring the untreated water through a clean bandanna or other piece of clean fabric. Use the following water disinfection procedures as available and appropriate.

Potable Aqua for 1 Quart of Water

Water Temp	*Condition*	*Amount*	*Standing Time*
Warm >50° F	Clear or Cloudy (let tabs dissolve 5 minutes first)	2 tabs Potable Aqua	30 min.
Cold <50° F	Clear or Cloudy (let tabs dissolve 5 minutes first)	2 tabs Potable Aqua	60 min.

Tincture of Iodine 1 Quart of Water

Water Temp	*Condition*	*Amount*	*Standing Time*
Warm >50° F	Clear	5 drops iodine	20 min.
Warm >50° F	Cloudy	10 drops iodine	20 min.
Cold <50° F	Clear	10 drops iodine	20 min.
Cold <50° F	Cloudy	10 drops iodine	40 min.

Posttreatment, the water should have a faint iodine smell. Allow the Potable Aqua tablet to dissolve before starting to count the standing time. Do not use povidone iodine (e.g., Betadine), as this has not been tested or manufactured for water disinfection. Do not add Emergen-C or other Vitamin C compounds prior to disinfection, as this will neutralize the iodine disinfection action. Do not use Potable Aqua tabs that are grey and crumbly.

Boiling.

If the water is heated to a rolling boil the heat is enough to kill commonly occurring harmful microbes. The untreated water must come to a full rolling boil. Water need not stay at a boil for any length of time. In most cases we are trying to kill Giardia, which dies at 170 degrees F. Bringing water to a boil is an effective way to ensure the water has reached 170 degrees F.

The Sanitizer System (chlorine treatment).

This system utilizes a two-stage process. The initial stage purifies water with a very potent dose of chlorine. So much chlorine is added to the water that we need to remove it by adding hydrogen peroxide, an oxidizer, during the second stage. The second step eliminates the leftover chlorine.

The system includes one bottle of chlorine crystals (dry), a small plastic scoop, and a bottle of hydrogen peroxide (liquid). It may be necessary to practice with this system before you take it into the field to teach others. We have found the Sanitizer to provide good results with proper use:

1. To treat 1 quart of water with the Sanitizer:
   a. If the water is at all cloudy prefilter it before using this system.
   b. Fill the scoop with 24 chlorine crystals and add them to your water bottle.
   c. Let it stand 20 minutes.
   d. Smell the water. It must smell strongly of chlorine.
   e. Add 2 drops of the hydrogen peroxide (oxidizer) to the water.
   f. Let it stand 20 minutes.
2. To treat 5 gallons of water with the Sanitizer:
   a. Fill a jug in the middle of the river to the 5 gallon mark.
   b. Put a slightly mounded 1/8 teaspoon of chlorine crystals in the water.
   c. Let it sit for 20 minutes.
   d. Smell the water. It must smell strongly of chlorine.
   e. Add 30 drops of Hydrogen Peroxide to the water.
   f. Wait 20 more minutes.
3. Precautions and first aid for the Sanitizer System:
   a. *Chlorine:* Keep chlorine crystals dry. Highly corrosive. Causes skin and eye damage. May be fatal if swallowed.
   b. Skin contact with 30% hydrogen peroxide may result in temporary whitening or bleaching and a mild stinging sensation.
4. Precautions and first aid for iodine or Potable Aqua:
   a. Keep Potable Aqua tablets dry. Iodine may be harmful if swallowed without dilution.
   b. Avoid eye contact. Will cause severe irritation to eyes and mucous membranes.
   c. Avoid contamination of food.
   d. Wash after handling.
   e. If iodine is swallowed, drink freely a thin paste of starch or flour (2 tablespoons in water).
   f. In case of contact with eyes flush thoroughly with water.
   g. To check for expiration of Potable Aqua tablets, read the vertical stamped numbers on the label. The first numbers indicate the month, then the date of manufacture. The last numbers are the lot number. For example, 40229 is lot 29, manufactured in April 2002. Tablets are good for 6 years from manufacture, 1 year once opened. It is a good idea to write in permanent marker the date the bottle was opened, on the cap or bottle label.

Georgia College & State University	
	F Education
	E Southeast Region
	C University Outdoor Education Students and General Population
	S 7.01–7.04

Equipment Management

The quality of outdoor education classes and programs are partially dependent on the availability of properly functioning and appropriate equipment. Faculty, staff, students, and participants are expected to work together to implement various components of a comprehensive equipment management system.

1. Use appropriate equipment reservations and maintenance forms for specific activities and programs.
2. Submit requests for equipment reservation, maintenance, and replacement in a timely fashion, and include information that will assist staff to select appropriate equipment (activity descriptions, site specifications, type of rope, etc.). Available at http://hercules.gcsu.edu/~jhirsch/Forms/default.htm.
3. After a program return equipment reservation forms that include information that is necessary to maintain use logs (challenge course and climbing ropes, etc.).
4. Clean and inspect equipment before returning it to the OEC.
5. Clearly state or graphically identify maintenance and repair needs on the equipment reservation form and program summary form.
6. Teach participants appropriate procedures for using and caring for equipment.
7. Model behavior that demonstrates equipment stewardship.
8. Store equipment appropriately during a program.
9. Inspect program equipment prior to use.
10. Use equipment as it is intended to be used and according to manufacturer specifications.
11. Use GCSU equipment as though it were your own!

Rental Equipment

The GCSU Outdoor Education Center offers an equipment reservation and rental service on a limited basis. Forms are available at the OEC equipment room. Persons or programs renting or reserving outdoor education equipment will agree to the terms and conditions for equipment use, care, maintenance, and replacement as outlined on the reservation form.

Equipment for ODED Classes

Students taking outdoor education classes are expected to provide their own personal equipment (sleeping bags, packs, etc.) as per the outdoor education professional equipment list distributed prior to the technical cohort. Group and program equipment normally will be provided. The course instructor must complete the appropriate equipment reservation form. Equipment used for display purposes only is recorded on the appropriate form in the OEC equipment room.

Use of Personal Equipment

The instructor or lead facilitator must approve (prior to use) specialized and personal equipment that is not obtained from the OEC.

Communication Equipment

Radios, cellular phones, and/or beepers may be included in the emergency communication plan for a specific program. Communication equipment may be obtained through the OEC or, depending on geographical location and access to emergency assistance, the instructor or lead facilitator may use personal communication equipment. Appropriate use of communication technology is important to maintain the integrity of the wilderness experience.

Equipment Acquisition

The coordinator of technical cohorts and the OEC equipment and facilities coordinator review and revise equipment acquisition plans on an ongoing basis, based on the needs of outdoor education classes and OEC programs. The plan identifies equipment needs categorized on the basis of priority to be used by the coordinator of outdoor education programs to identify outdoor education budgets and prepare special requests for additional funding. All equipment is purchased in accordance with GCSU Materials Management and Financial Services policy and procedures. Purchased equipment is delivered to Central Receiving and processed for delivery to Centennial Center. The OEC equipment and facilities coordinator will:

1. Complete an initial inspection of equipment and supplies;
2. Match received equipment and supplies to the original purchase order available from the Department of Kinesiology administrative secretary for approval for payment;
3. Transport equipment and supplies to the OEC;
4. Enter nondisposable equipment into the master inventory, assign inventory number, prepare supplemental documents used to track equipment status such as rope logs, equipment reservation forms, and inspection/maintenance forms;
5. Put equipment into circulation.

Equipment Inspection

Outdoor education equipment is inspected based on academic class and OEC program needs. Ongoing repairs are made on the basis of regular use inspections and information submitted to the equipment and facilities coordinator by faculty and staff verbally or on equipment or program administration forms. Regular inspection and preventative maintenance is conducted according to the following schedule:

August	WFR kits, prop bags, truck, and trailers
September	PFDs, canoes, canoe accessories, water clothing, and helmets
October	sleeping bags, tarps, tents and electronics
November	challenge course, Tango Tower and challenge course equipment

December	stoves, water filters, and cooking accessories
January	WFR kits, prop bags, truck, and trailers
February	rock climbing equipment
March	PFDs, kayaks, kayak accessories
April	challenge course, Tango Tower, challenge course equipment
May–July	all inventory

Equipment Retirement

Equipment is retired based on condition, manufacturer recommendations, or discontinued use or need. Retired equipment that is not disposed of may be used in academic classes or programs for demonstration purposes or may be altered for appropriate use such as knot-practice ropes. Equipment that is not disposed of is marked with white paint or tape.

SECTION 8
VENUE SELECTION AND APPROPRIATENESS

Prescott College	*F* **Education**
	E **Rocky Mountain Region**
	C **University Students**
	S **8.01–8.02**

Field Operations

As an academic institution in the Southwest, accessing public lands (i.e, National Park Service, United States Forest Service, Bureau of Land Management, and state land) is a growing concern. Land management agencies are inconsistent with their definition of academic and educational use of our public lands, therefore making permitting an accelerating issue with Prescott College courses using these lands as a classroom. It is our responsibility as an institution of higher learning to be accountable for our use on public lands.

Permits—NPS, USFS, BLM, and State Land

All field courses across curricular areas bringing students onto federal or state managed lands or rivers, must meet with the field course support and permit Coordinator prior to any field trips to discuss permitting issues and procedures for areas both local and regional. If you are requesting to use an area the college is not permitted in, you will be asked to provide the following information, sometimes 175 days in advance (agency and area dependent):

- Dates of field component
- Location and itinerary—managing agency and specific route
- Curriculum related to area. Is this the only place you can provide the curriculum, if so, why?
- Highlighted map
- Syllabus

NPS—Educational Entrance Fee Waivers

These waivers are applied for through the field course support and permit coordinator to centralize contact with agencies. These waivers do not cover campground fees. Please request fee waivers 4 to 6 weeks in advance with the following information:

- Entrance date and location
- Exit date
- Curriculum related to the park
- Syllabus

Actual Use Reporting

All use of public lands is to be reported on the Actual Use Form found in your field packet.

Map library.

1. Inventory: Prescott College has over 1,000 topographic maps of Arizona and surrounding states. Please stop by the San Juan Equipment Warehouse and see if the map you need is available and you are free to check it out.
2. Purchasing: Maps are purchased twice a year—June and December. Give the field course support and permit coordinator a list of maps you need for a class and they will be purchased at those times. After your use, they will be inventoried and filed with the other college maps.

Kino Bay field station.

Actual use reporting is not only used for reporting to land management agencies, but also to report activities to the insurance company. All visits to Kino Bay incorporating skiff travel, snorkeling, sea kayaking, camping and hiking should be reported to the field course support and permit coordinator.

Field Course Planning Checklist

1. Prior to start of enrollment period:
    - Schedule a precourse meeting with the risk management officer or AE coordinator if this is the first time you are teaching this kind of field course, or if you want additional support and advice.
    - Check with Office of the Registrar to:
        - Make sure the students in your class are registered for that class by signing, dating, and *returning* the Official Roster (yellow) to the Registrar's Office before you

leave town. To be covered by insurance, financial aid, etc., students must be officially enrolled (i.e., listed on this roster).

- ✣ Make arrangements for students to register for the *following* term, if the class will be in the field during preregistration dates (early November for spring, mid-April for fall). Call the RDP Assistant Registrar, Ext. 1106, or the Registrar, Ext. 1101.

- Check out a copy of the RDP Field Manual (unless you already have one) from the Dean's Office.
- Copies of current WFR/CPR certifications on file with Field Operations.
- Resume on file in RDP Dean's Office.
- Van/trailer and gas card requests submitted to Transportation.
- All van drivers have completed the van safety training (student drivers included).
- Purchase requisition for cash advance submitted to RDP Dean's Office.
- Request equipment and schedule check-out/in time with equipment warehouse.
- Review contents of field packet and direct questions to 776-5208.
- Double-check that you have the appropriate permits and fee waivers in packet.
- Familiarize yourself with managing agency/access issues of course area.

2. Prior to departure:
   - Pick up, review, and update medical forms from Records and Registration
   - Pick up van keys/notebook, credit cards, and cash advance.
   - Pick up van and complete Routine Inspection Checklist.
   - Pick up equipment at scheduled time, inspect/review equipment.
   - Fill out Group Responsibility Form with equipment warehouse.
   - Submit Course Participants/Itinerary Form to RDP Dean's Office.
   - Submit Course Specific Risk Waiver (if applicable).
3. Postcourse responsibilities:
   - Return equipment clean/receive "CLEAR" check-in.
   - Return van to 220 clean and with a full tank.
   - Courses *must* submit the following (applicable) completed forms:
     - ✣ Course Report
     - ✣ Actual Use/Activity Log
     - ✣ River Based Log
     - ✣ Ideal Itinerary for next enrollment period
     - ✣ Incident Reports
   - Submit course contracts and evaluations to Enrollment Services.
   - Schedule a postcourse meeting with AE program coordinator or risk management officer if this is a new course for you or you had safety concerns on you course.

SECTION 9
ENVIRONMENT AND CULTURE

National Outdoor Leadership School	*F* Education
	E Rocky Mountain Region
	C Various Populations
	S 9.01–9.08

NOLS Expectations for Environmental Studies

Marco Johnson

The ultimate goal in teaching environmental studies is for students to become better citizens and stewards who display their compassion for the Earth. This can only happen if they feel they are an integral part of the global ecosystem, and if they see that their choices make a difference. Given this framework for environmental studies, what should the expectations be for instructors teaching in this area? Environmental studies (ES) are an incredibly large and diverse area of study. How are we to approach teaching ES and not become overwhelmed?

The environmental studies curriculum can be broken down into several key areas. Instructors should be familiar with the rudiments of each area and then try to concentrate on a couple of topics within each.

Natural science encompasses geology, astronomy, animal ID, tracks and scat, plant ID, edible and medicinal plants, and meteorology. Instructors on all course types should be able to teach basic classes in these areas. There will be exceptions, for example, winter courses will not be able to teach too much plant ID. Wilderness courses and Semester sections and the natural history course should be able to spend considerable time on these. Water-based courses should be prepared to teach river hydrology or oceanography. Background information on most of these topics is found in this book and the *NOLS Safari Guides* to specific areas.

Ecological principles include biodiversity, trophic levels, niches, nutrient cycles, and energy flow. Instructors on most course types should be able to teach these topics along the trail or in formal classes and should be familiar with the *Basic Field Ecology*, pamphlet, if you are at branches that don't yet have a *Safari Guide*. You should be prepared to delve into these topics in greater detail on semester sections and natural history courses.

Environmental ethics means helping students foster a sense of place, recognizing the inherent value in wilderness, developing a sense of responsibility to protect the environment, and building a spiritual connection to the natural world. Instructors on all course types should be able to guide students along the path to building a personal relationship with the land. While much information can be found in this book on these subjects (see John Gookin's articles on "Spirituality," "Teaching Ethics," and "Stewardship, Advocacy, and Activism," and Rob Maclean's "Sense of Place"), the most impactful place this teaching comes from is instructors role modeling and sharing their personal impressions and concerns with students.

Leave No Trace camping: Instructors on all course types are expected to teach these skills on an ongoing basis. The area-specific *LNT Skills and Ethics* booklets are the best source for this information.

Leave No Trace trainer "training": Most course types at NOLS allow for enough time for students to become certified LNT trainers. If an instructor is not familiar with what is needed to make a student an LNT trainer, she should read Darran Wells' article, "Making Your Expedition an LNT Trainer's Course." Program supervisors and the NOLS Outreach Office can answer further questions.

Land management classes encompasses who the federal agencies are and what they do, land designation (Multiple Use, Wilderness, Wild and Scenic Rivers,) and the decision processes, including how the National Environmental Policy Act (NEPA) works. Instructors on all courses should be able to explain to students what management agency oversees the area the course is using. Instructors on domestic courses should understand the U.S. land management agencies (see U.S. Land Management Lesson Plan) and instructors on foreign courses should understand what agencies oversee the land those courses are using. River courses should learn about river-specific designations and how this might differ from land designation. Wilderness course and semester course students should leave with an understanding of how they can become involved in the NEPA process.

Cultural issues encompass observing local cultures and discussing ways to respect other cultures whether students are at a gas station in rural Washington or in a Masai village in Kenya. As the student population on NOLS courses becomes more and more diverse, it is imperative that we teach cultural awareness and the issues involved with different cultures. Information can be found in Jim Chisholm's "Human Culture Outline," as well as *The Canyon Instructor's Notebook* and *The Leadership Toolbox.* Program supervisors at each branch should have branch-specific cultural information to teach in the field. Drawing on student and staff personal experience or even having local guest speakers are other powerful ways to explore these issues.

At the end of the course you should make sure that each of your students gets a copy of both the *Soft Sidewalks Handout* and the *LNT Resource Handout* along with their graduation packets. These handouts should be available at all the branches and are an important aid in transferring all the LNT work you've done in the backcountry to front country settings.

Team Leadership Results, LLC	*F* **Training and Development**
	E **Mid-South Region**
	C **Adults**
	S **9.01–9.09**

Environmental Concerns

Environmental Ethic

The program has written guidelines, which focus upon environmental ethics, and programs honor these principles. Because of the type of person attracted to this work, it can be safely assumed that Team Leadership facilitators come to this organization with an environmental ethic already in place. Categorically, these are people who enjoy nature and appreciate the need to protect natural resources from the impacts that can occur without thoughtful consideration. Team Leadership supports this ethic and these values—first, in the design and construction of the Cielo Vista course (the Guadalupe Ranch Course was already constructed when Team Leadership assumed operational responsibility for it). The Cielo Vista course was constructed with minimal clearing of flora and minimal impact on fauna. Every cutting of plant life had to be justified or it was not done. The end result is as close to wild nature as one can get with a major city center only 30 minutes away. Because Team Leadership does no overnight programs, many of the considerations regarding environmental impacts do not apply. Team Leadership does have policies on fire safety and stoves (see Team Leadership safety manual), but none on campsites, backcountry travel, use of support animals, and washing. As for shelters and tents, see Team Leadership's policies on the Native American lodge (tipi). (See Team Leadership safety manual.)

Wildlife Ethic

The program respects the wildlife of the area. Team Leadership supports this ethic and these values in the design and construction of the Cielo Vista course. The Cielo Vista course was constructed with minimal clearing of flora and minimal impact on fauna. Every cutting of plant life had to be justified or it was not done. The end result is as respectful toward wildlife as it is possible to be with a major city center only 30 minutes away. Team Leadership communicates a respect for the wildlife in the area every time its facilitators introduce a group to a Team Leadership operated challenge course. Participants are asked to consider the fact that the wild critters were here first and that any intrusion into their space is considered to be just that, with a quiet withdrawal on the part of the human in any direct face-to-face confrontation. Even and especially in regard to wildlife that could be seen as adversaries to humans—poisonous snakes, scorpions, Africanized bees, etc.—participants are asked to abstain from confrontational or aggressive tactics in relationship to these wildlife.

Cultural Ethic

The program respects the local culture, including both social and physical aspects. Team Leadership does not have many opportunities to interface with indigenous cultures, but wherever it may have such an opportunity, Team Leadership's stated position will be to honor the rules, customs, and mores of that culture and to not conduct any practice that either actually disturbs or that could be perceived by members of that community to disturb their physical space, ceremonies, artifacts, or other aspects of their culture.

Conducting Activities

The program selects routes for travel where impact to the environment is minimal. In fragile areas, routes are on trails whenever possible. Whenever a Team Leadership program takes participants above timberline, into the desert, or another area that is fragile environmentally, routes will be selected based upon impact considerations.

Toiletry Ethic

If human waste is disposed of in the natural environment, it is done so in a minimally invasive manner. If this cannot be accomplished, it is carried out. If needed, toilet areas will be constructed for the type of environment where activities are conducted. Team Leadership arranges for portable toilets to be placed on the two challenge courses, based upon the number of participants that will be on the course on any given day. The provider services these toilets weekly. In backcountry or wilderness areas where appropriate toilet facilities are not available, the program promotes the appropriate methods of waste disposal. This means that individuals ought to bury their personal waste under at least 5 inches of soil or sand and rock at least 200 feet from any water source.

Leave No Trace Ethic

All paper and packaging is disposed of according to Leave No Trace guidelines. Paper and packaging material may not be left in any natural environment. It should be bagged up and carried out. When an open fire is permitted in a natural area and a fire site is part of the program, small amounts of paper materials may be burned. Because of the possibility of uncombusted remnants, Team Leadership prefers that plastic items not be burned in the campfire.

Support Vehicles

Support animals or vehicles are used only on permitted roads, trails, and routes. In most cases this means staying on established trails and roads and obeying local land management guidelines. Team Leadership requires that when support animals or vehicles are used in a program, they will be used only on permitted roads, trails, and routes. In most cases this means staying on established trails and roads and obeying local land management guidelines.

Domesticated Animal Ethic

Domesticated animals are permitted only where their effect on the environment can be limited appropriately. Team Leadership requires that wherever domesticated animals are taken into an environment by program facilitators or participants, these animals, if permitted by local land management regulations, will be utilized in a manner so as to limit any adverse effects on the environment, whether these be overgrazing, attacking indigenous animals, defecating in water sources, etc.

Visual Impact Ethic

The program limits the visual impact of its activities. Team Leadership presents a very low profile against the landscape and topography. Instead of asphalt, Team Leadership has utilized mulch in all its parking lots. Buildings on the challenge courses have been sited away from the roads and are nestled low against the hillsides. In considering the visual impact of the exterior of these buildings, Team Leadership has chosen to clothe one building in natural reed fibers. Another building is painted green, while the building at the Guadalupe River Ranch is natural cedar.

Washing Impact Ethic

Washing—people, cookware, and clothing—is done in a manner that limits environmental impact. Team Leadership programs use Leave No Trace guidelines when programs take place in the natural, environment. Minimal use of soap is encouraged by providing antibacterial wipes to participants before meals and limiting the supply of water to that used for drinking, cooking and dousing the fire. Scouring pots and pans with sand and gravel, and brushing teeth at a minimum of 60 meters from a water source are practices encouraged at Team Leadership.

Cooking Impact Ethic

Cooking and food handling are conducted in a manner that will not affect or attract animals. When Team Leadership conducts programs in natural areas, campsites are kept clean and animals are not fed by participants or staff. Dishes, utensils, pots, and pans must be washed immediately after meals. Leftovers must be wrapped and stored in reusable containers, which are secured in an ice chest if perishable, and in a food box if still in an unopened container. Food scraps should be contained in zip-lock bags and double-bagged in a second trash sack for disposal at an appropriate place. Because Team Leadership has not operated any programs where there are bear populations, there is no standing policy on methods of thwarting bears, but the hanging of food items in bags suspended high above the ground and away from where people are sleeping is a practice that many staff members recognize as important in bear country.

Food Prep and Consumption Ethic

Food is appropriately stored, and in reusable containers when possible. Food purchased for Team Leadership programs is purchased in accordance with a reduce/reuse/recycle policy. Food is appropriately stored to protect it from the effects of heat, cold, and possible animal predation. Leftovers from meals must be wrapped and stored in reusable containers, which are secured in an ice chest if perishable, and in a food box if still in an unopened container. Food scraps should be contained in zip-lock bags and double-bagged in a second trash sack for disposal at an appropriate place. Wild dogs have been a problem on the challenge course, and Team Leadership has a policy of carrying out the garbage from box lunches consumed on the course on the same day as the program whenever this is possible.

Food Disposal Ethic

If food is not used, it is carried out. If this cannot be done, it is disposed of in a minimally invasive manner. Team Leadership does not want any food left in the environment unless it can be disposed of in a minimally invasive manner. For example, food pieces that are reduced to fingernail size bits and scattered thinly and broadly away from any camp or trail is minimally invasive. Otherwise, all food must be packed out. Leftovers from meals must be wrapped and stored in reusable containers, which are secured in an ice chest immediately after the meal if perishable, and returned to a food box if still in an unopened container. Any perishable food not placed under refrigeration or an ice chest immediately after a meal should not be considered fit for consumption. These foods and other food scraps should be contained in zip-lock bags and double-bagged in a second trash sack so they may be carried out of the natural area for disposal at an appropriate place.

Fire Ethic

Fires are used in a manner so as to limit environmental impact. Team Leadership suggests that stoves be used in place of fires when fires would adversely affect the environment and when there is an opportunity to provide participants an experience in preparing food for a potluck dinner. When teams of two members prepare a dish for consumption by the whole team, mealtime preparations become a team-building activity that is win-win.

Where Team Leadership is in an environment that has an established fire site, that site will be used. When there is no established site and the environment is one where fire would not adversely affect the environment, and then any fire site created will be cleaned up after use. This may involve using a portable firepot or fire pan for cooking. Wood gathered for such a fire would be gathered in a nondestructive manner, and the ashes from fire pans are floated if at a river site. It is recognized that building a fire to save a life supersedes this general policy.

Shelter Impact Ethic

Shelters, tents, tarps, and hammocks are utilized in a manner so as to limit impact on the environment. Team Leadership supports the idea of using tents, tarps, or hammocks rather than constructing shelters from surrounding resources as the least invasive method of providing shelter. Sand, duff, or mineral soil are the preferred foundation surface for tents and tarps—not vegetated areas. When a shelter is taken down, consideration is taken to leave the area as close to the way one found it as possible. When hanging hammocks, consider the anchor points carefully so as not to uproot, tear down, or scar any species.

Camp Woodson	*F* Therapeutic
	E Southeast Region
	C Incarcerated Youth
	S 9.01–9.08

Environmental Ethics

Safety Policy

1. Minimal-impact (Leave No Trace) hiking and camping procedures will be used by staff and students at all times.

Guidelines

1. Students will be instructed about the fragile nature of wilderness areas. Enhanced understanding will increase student's sense of responsibility for the care and preservation of wild places.
2. Campsites will be chosen that minimize our impact. In general, use well-established sites and avoid creating new ones.
3. All cooking will be done on camp stoves.
4. No soap of any type will be permitted within 50 feet of a water source. Biodegradable soaps are no exception.
5. There will be a maximum of one campfire per shift. Use only wood and kindling that is dead and down. Do not remove limbs and branches from standing trees. Use existing fire rings. Consolidate multiple rings when possible and remove and build no-trace inappropriate rings as a service project.

Human waste/supervision.

1. Students will be instructed and supervised in the proper use of cat holes for disposal of human waste.
2. Each student's cat hole must be checked by staff for the first full week of camp and longer if they have not proven themselves trustworthy.

3. It is highly recommended to check randomly throughout the session. One suggestion is to flip a coin after a student returns from their dump—heads you check it, tails you don't. This takes the pressure off you "not trusting me" and keeps students on their best behavior because they know they can be checked at any time.

Human waste/cat holes.

1. Cat holes must be a minimum of 300 feet from water, 100 feet from trails, a minimum of 8 inches deep and a maximum of 12 inches deep.
2. The area should first be swept clean of leaves, an intact plug extracted, and dirt neatly piled to one side. After toilet paper and excrement are positioned in the bottom of the cat hole, fill in reverse order.
3. The finished cat hole should be marked with two sticks for later identification by staff, but should otherwise be unidentifiable to anyone else.
4. Here's the test; do you feel comfortable sitting down at this spot to eat lunch? The answer should be yes!

Georgia College & State University	
	F Education
	E Southeast Region
	C University Outdoor Education Students and General Population
	S 9.01–9.09

Environmental Ethics and Education

Outdoor Education and Environmental Responsibility

Outdoor education programs at GCSU offer opportunities for students and participants to become environmentally conscious citizens. However, awareness of environmental issues is not enough to ensure a sustainable environment. Stewards of the environment must be prepared to be stewards of society; a sustainable environment requires a sustainable society. Outdoor education experiences have the potential to contribute to a sense of environmental responsibility through teaching knowledge about the environment, developing positive attitudes toward the environment, and influencing positive behaviors toward the environment.

Environmental Education at GCSU

Outdoor education graduate students take one required course in environmental education. Undergraduate students take two required courses in environmental education. Both may take electives in environmental sciences and outdoor education undergraduate students may complete a minor or a second major in an environmental science. Graduate students take the LNT Master Trainer course and undergraduate students take the LNT Educator course in *Just Beyond the Classroom*,[8] Knapp (1996) suggests that participation in outdoor pursuits can provide the opportunity for challenge, adventure, and excitement. Outdoor pursuits offer a chance to explore and shape values, attitudes, and behaviors toward the environment, each other, and ourselves. Educating for a sustainable society is more than adopting Leave No Trace principles; it is the inclusion of environmental education as a component of every experience.

Roles and Responsibilities

1. Facilitators obtain and share information about natural and cultural heritage in settings in which programs take place.
2. Facilitators seek opportunities to teach something about ecosystems in which outdoor pursuits take place (i.e., geology at rock sites, water quality on rivers, flora and fauna in backpacking areas).
3. Facilitators encourage participants to verbalize or think about what they are going to do to live lightly on this earth in their personal and professional lives.
4. Facilitators communicate and use LNT principles.

LNT Principles[9]

The Leave No Trace Center for Outdoor Ethics is a national nonprofit organization dedicated to promoting and inspiring responsible outdoor recreation through education, research, and partnerships. Leave No Trace builds awareness, appreciation, and respect for our wild lands.

Plan ahead and prepare.

1. Know the regulations and special concerns for the area you'll visit.
2. Prepare for extreme weather, hazards, and emergencies.
3. Schedule your trip to avoid times of high use.
4. Visit in small groups.
5. Split larger parties into groups of 4 to 6.
6. Repackage food to minimize waste.
7. Use a map and compass to eliminate the use of marking paint, rock cairns, or flagging.

Travel and camp on durable surfaces.

1. Durable surfaces include established trails and campsites, rock, gravel, dry grasses or snow.
2. Protect riparian areas by camping at least 200 feet from lakes and streams.
3. Good campsites are found, not made. Altering a site is not necessary.
4. In popular areas:
   a. Concentrate use on existing trails and campsites;
   b. Walk single file in the middle of the trail, even when wet or muddy.
5. Keep campsites small.
6. Focus activity in areas where vegetation is absent.
7. In pristine areas:

a. Disperse use to prevent the creation of campsites and trails;

b. Avoid places where impacts are just beginning.

Dispose of waste properly.

1. Pack it in, pack it out.
2. Inspect campsites and rest areas for trash or spilled foods.
3. Pack out all trash, leftover food, and litter.
4. Deposit solid human waste in cat holes dug 6 to 8 inches deep at least 200 feet from water, camp, and trails.
5. Cover and disguise the cat hole when finished.
6. Pack out toilet paper and hygiene products.
7. Wash yourself and dishes 200 feet away from streams or lakes and use small amounts of biodegradable soap.
8. Scatter strained dishwater.

Leave what you find.

1. Preserve the past.
2. Examine, but do not touch, cultural or historic structures and artifacts.
3. Leave rocks, plants, and other natural objects as you find them.
4. Avoid introducing or transporting nonnative species.
5. Do not build structures, furniture, or dig trenches.

Minimize campfire impacts.

1. Campfires can cause lasting impacts to the backcountry.
2. Use a lightweight stove for cooking and enjoy a candle lantern for light.
3. Where fires are permitted, use established fire rings, fire pans, or mound fires.
4. Keep fires small by using sticks from the ground that can be broken by hand.
5. Burn all wood and coals to ash, put out campfires completely, and then scatter cool ashes.

Respect wildlife.

1. Observe wildlife from a distance and do not follow or approach them.
2. Never feed animals because feeding wildlife damages their health, alters natural behaviors, and exposes them to predators and other dangers.
3. Protect wildlife and your food by storing rations and trash securely.
4. Control pets at all times, or leave them at home.
5. Avoid wildlife during sensitive times: mating, nesting, raising young, or winter.

Be considerate of other visitors.

1. Respect other visitors and protect the quality of their experience.
2. Be courteous. Yield to other users on the trail.

3. Step to the downhill side of the trail when encountering pack stock.
4. Take breaks and camp away from trails and other visitors.
5. Let nature's sounds prevail.
6. Avoid loud voices and noises.

SECTION 10
INTERNATIONAL CONSIDERATIONS

Prescott College	F	**Education**
	E	**Rocky Mountain Region**
	C	**University Students**
	S	**10.01–10.08**

International Courses

Courses traveling outside the United States offer unique opportunities and risks to be managed; these courses should be run within the cultural, legal, and practical context of the countries in which they operate. In order to integrate Prescott College courses with local cultures in a safe manner, the following general guidelines should be followed.

1. When leading an international course, faculty need be aware of:
   a. Changes in the political and social conditions that prevail in all of the countries through which faculty and participants travel.
      i. *Explanation:* This is best done through consulting with the U.S. Department of State and a local contact in the country that is being visited.
   b. Areas in the country that are to be avoided because of rampant crime or political unrest.
      i. *Explanation:* This is best done through consulting with the U.S. Department of State and a local contact in the country that is being visited.
   c. The medical considerations particular to the countries through which faculty and participants travel.
      i. *Explanation:* Faculty has a general knowledge of the health issues of the country and are also aware of particular plants, animals, and/or diseases that may have an effect on participants. Faculty and participants are informed of any immunizations required and CDC travel information is consulted.

d. Protocols need to be in place including notification procedures for emergencies in the country, and contacts with the appropriate U.S. and local officials need to be made ahead of time.

e. Faculty and students take the country and culture in which it is operating into consideration when planning activities.

   i. *Explanation:* These considerations include but may not be limited to: (a) being aware of and sensitive to cultural mores; (b) knowledge of local customs; (c) dress code; (d) bringing—or not bringing—certain equipment.

f. Faculty provides adequate and appropriate food and liquid for the location.

   i. *Explanation:* This includes but may not be limited to: (a) compensating for diet change because of available food in the country of travel; (b) bringing water filters or other appropriate water purification methods.

g. Faculty use good judgment when choosing transportation services.

   i. *Explanation:* Many factors go into evaluating whether to use a transportation service. These include but are not limited to: whether the company has the proper licensing and certifications, condition of the vehicles, route traveled, length of time the driver is permitted to operate the vehicle, etc.

2. To help facilitate the communication of the above information to students and the college, the faculty member in charge of the course will:

   a. Create a course guide containing the above information and other course specific information.

   b. A precourse meeting between the risk management officer and the faculty member in charge of the course will be scheduled to review the course guide and to discuss how any risks specific to the course will be managed.

National Outdoor Leadership School	*F*	**Education**
	E	**Rocky Mountain Region**
	C	**Various Populations**
	S	**10.05**

India Evacuation of Country Protocol
January 23, 2002

This document describes NOLS India evacuation of country protocols and decision processes. It is organized in three sections; Information Sources, Evacuation Methods, and Evacuation Thresholds. *This document is subject to revision at any time.*

Information Sources

Reliable information is vital to making effective decisions. NOLS uses many sources of information.

In country.

1. *NOLS India program supervisor.* With each course we inform the embassy of U.S. student and instructor names. In a crisis NOLS India would be contacted by the U.S. Embassy.
2. *Media,* primarily *The Times of India* newspaper, but also via shortwave radio while in the field.
3. *Communication network* with other foreign nationals in Uttaranchal State.
4. *Local law enforcement* personnel and government officials can provide local NOLS staff with information related to local criminal activities and events in Uttaranchal State.

In the U.S.

1. News and events in India are monitored frequently (usually on a daily or weekly basis) from a variety of sources.
2. *Overseas Security Advisory Council,* a division of the U.S. Department of State, provides current information on travel advisories and diplomatic and security information for U.S. companies conducting business overseas. OSAC provides the usual U.S. Department of State travel and security information, and NOLS has been granted access to the OSAC electronic database.
3. *Media:* The worldwide web provides ready access to many news outlets including major U.S. newspapers, news services, Indian newspapers, and the British Broadcasting Company website.
4. *The British Foreign Commonwealth Office,* similar to the U.S. Department of State, provides travel advisories for British citizens.
5. *NOLS networks with similar companies and programs* in the U.S. and in India, such as college study abroad programs.
6. *The NOLS Risk Management Committee:* Members provide insights to world situations through their personal contacts in the intelligence and security professions.

Evacuation Methods

Available Communication Systems

1. *Portable Satellite telephone* at the NOLS India headquarters and available for the field. Provides reliable phone communication.
2. *Land-line telephone* service to the NOLS India headquarters is available, though can be unreliable.
3. *Email* to NOLS India headquarters—a satellite uplink that is quite reliable and avoids limits due to land lines.

U.S. Embassy Response to Threat to U.S. Citizens (order of actions relative to severity of threat)

1. Issue a warning advising all Americans to voluntarily leave the country.
2. Issue a statement directing all Americans to leave the country. Embassy no longer responsible for Americans in India.
3. Issue instructions where to go for protection or evacuation.

NOLS Response

1. *NOLS executive director team,* risk management director, NOLS PNW branch director and India program director would determine the level of risk and decide on necessary actions. Our objective is to act before outside assistance (from embassy) is necessary.
2. Contact all courses in the field using radios or telephones. Contact NOLS headquarters in Wyoming.
3. *Return to Ranikhet* or stand fast in course location. Depending on circumstances we would bring groups back to NOLS India headquarters, Delhi, or gather in known locations in or near the specific area. At each step we would further assess the situation, possible next steps, and the need for evacuation.
   a. *Delhi:* Stay at a secure hotel or return to Ranikhet using NOLS vehicles or vehicles hired by NOLS in a convoy and choosing the route carefully.
   b. *Pindari/Milum Valleys:* Return to NOLS India headquarters by vehicle.
4. *Evacuate the country by commercial aircraft.* To the extent possible we would strive to initiate an evacuation of the country before the U.S. Embassy ordered it. This strategy gives a higher probability of using commercial airlines.
5. If commercial airlines were not available we would be prepared to assemble our students and staff at the NOLS India headquarters and wait. The headquarters is often stocked with rations. Many of our food needs can be and are met from the local community.

Details of Evacuation Transportation Options

1. *Transportation from the mountains to Ranikhet:* The course will call NOLS India Base on the satellite phone to inform which road head they are coming out at. India program supervisor will then arrange taxi's to wait there. The drive from Song (GAR road head) to Ranikhet takes 6 hours. The drive from Munsiari (HBP road head) takes 12 hours.
2. *Transportation to Delhi:* Our transportation contractors can be counted on to provide us with 100% support in terms of busses, hotel bookings, etc. Depending on the urgency of the situation, he can have a bus leave Delhi at night to arrive in Ranikhet the next morning (12 hours driving time).
   i. Similarly, depending on the urgency of the situation, NOLS India program supervisor can arrange taxis to take the course to Haldwani and meet our transportation contractor's bus there. This will save 3 to 4 hours.

ii. One other option is to hire taxis in Ranikhet to take the course all the way to Delhi. Getting taxis in Ranikhet in an emergency will not be a problem, as there are plenty of them around.

3. *Hotels in Delhi:* The Swiss International Hotel where courses have stayed during the past few years will be the first option. The YWCA International Guesthouse would be the next option. There are plenty of other hotels that will meet our requirements. The Indian Mountaineering Foundation has three dorms that accommodate up to 50 people. The absolute backup is to stay in the third floor of our transportation contractor's house, which is large enough to sleep a group of 17. April-May-June being the low season for tourists, hotel rooms are normally available easily.

4. *Flying out of Delhi:* Our experience has been that it is most efficient and simple if the change in return dates are made by our travel agency. Our transportation contractor will transport the course to the airport.

5. *Flying out of Bombay (Mumbai):* If the Delhi airport is shut for international flights (and Mumbai is open), we can travel to Mumbai either by a domestic airline, or half a dozen trains that go from Delhi to Mumbai. The flying time is 1hr. 40 min. Train time is between 19 and 24 hours depending on which one we get tickets in. The Indian railways have a scheme where foreign travelers can get reservations within 24 hours.

6. *If flying out of Katmandu is the best option:* In the current India-Pakistan scenario (January 2002), it will be prudent for everyone to get a Nepalese visa in the United States. This will potentially save many hours of waiting, getting a visa at the border. In this scenario, about 3 hours out of Ranikhet, at Haldwani, the route goes south and then east to Bareilly, Lucknow, Gorakhpur, and Raxaul. Here one crosses the border into Nepal, and Katmandu is approx 140 km. Ranikhet to Lucknow can be done in one day, and Gorakhpur to Katmandu on the next day.

   Ranikhet to Bareilly: 190 km

   Bareilly to Lucknow: 247 km

   Lucknow to Gorakpur: 266 km

   Gorakpur to Raxaul to Katmandu: 300 km

   Lucknow to Varanasi: 300 km

7. *Another option* is to go to Nepalgunj, which is a border town, approximately 4 hours from Lucknow. From here, there are daily flights to Katmandu. (I got this info from Nepal Airlines in Delhi) Some other flight options are:

   Lucknow to Calcutta to Katmandu

   Lucknow to Varanasi to Katmandu

Evacuation Thresholds

Evacuation of country thresholds are used to guide decision making. They are not hard and fast rules that state if one threshold is crossed the program will be suspended. Rather they help prioritize possible significant events. The actual NOLS response will depend greatly on the specific circumstances.

Threats to and Indicators of Regional Insecurity
TERRORISM/WAR
War declared between India and Pakistan
Widespread rioting or civil unrest in Delhi or Uttaranchal by Muslims
Violent anti-American demonstrations or rioting in India
Significant terrorist activity in Delhi or other city NOLS operates or travels in
Americans in India targeted by acts of terrorism
U.S. study abroad programs suspend operations
Issuance by the British Foreign Commonwealth Office of a travel warning advising against British citizens visiting India
Issuance by the U.S. DOS of a travel warning advising against U.S. citizens visiting India
NOLS group caught unawares in anti-American demonstration (no injuries result)
NOLS students or staff attacked, injured, or killed by demonstrators or terrorists
NOLS students or staff specifically assaulted
NOLS group or individuals held hostage
U.S. Embassy in India initiates evacuation of U.S. citizens from India.
NOLS Response

Is the threat specific and controllable or is it outside our ability to control or manage?

Options available to consider may include:

- Suspend programming in affected area.
- Do nothing. We may be most secure by remaining in program areas.
- Continue programming, but modify to more secure areas.
- Cease program and initiate Evacuation of Country Plan.

POLITICAL
Civil unrest caused by dissolution of government and announcement of new elections
Civil unrest in Uttaranchal State
Escalation of border clashes to declaration of war by India and neighboring countries
Airport closure, discontinuation of international flights
Police strike, police disbanded, police controlled by opposing party
Declaration of war by India and another country
NATURAL DISASTER
Earthquake in NOLS programming area
Flooding and associated road washouts

CRIME

Assaults or Actions Against NOLS		**Threats to and Indicators of Regional Insecurity**
Random Events	**NOLS Is Targeted**	
Course robbed while in the field.	Break in at the branch facility in Ranikhet.	Violent crime proximal to operating areas. Perpetrators at large.
Course robbed en route to field.		
NOLS vehicle stopped and robbed en route to or from airport.		

NOLS Response

Is the situation within our control? Generally we will assess the situation and take appropriate action erring toward the conservative. For both categories of events or actions taken against NOLS we may:

1. Suspend programming either all or in part.
2. Suspend ISGT or ISGT with instructors.
3. Return all students to base or appropriate location.
4. Reassess situation.
5. Continue programming in different location.
6. Suspend programming and send students home.

7 CHAPTER

TECHNICAL SKILLS—LAND BASED

This chapter includes examples of policy and procedures that correspond to Chapter 4 in the Manual of Accreditation Standards for Adventure Programs, Fourth Edition. *Standards are applicable to the facilitation of specific activities. An organization is required to demonstrate compliance with all standards that are applicable to its programming. If, for example, hiking, camping, and backpacking are conducted, compliance with standards in Section 11 of the standards manual is required. If an organization offers a wide gamut of activities, it must demonstrate compliance with all of the standards associated for each section for every activity, regardless of how infrequently activities are conducted. These standards provide assurance that a program's field practices for respective activities are in alignment with or compare well to standard operating procedures of other similar and/or reputable organizations. As in previous chapters, readers will note a wide range of content, detail, structure, and integration of curriculum. Approaches vary across activities, settings, client and leadership characteristics, and desired outcomes. Examples of general land-based policy and procedures are included, even though this heading is not a section in the standards manual, because several contributing organizations streamline repetition in policy documents by including content that applies to all land-based activities in one section. Examples for running activities are not included, and examples of both land-based and water-based incidental activities are included in this chapter.*

General Land-Based Policy

Boojum Institute	*F*	Education
	E	West Region
	C	Various Populations
	S	4.02, 4.08, 4.09, 7.01, 7.06, 7.07

General Policy—Land

1. These policies apply to all Boojum program activities.
2. Only individuals who have completed a Boojum medical history form and a participant release form will be allowed to participate.
3. Instructors shall have a complete first-aid kit with Epinephrine with them at all times.
4. Instructors shall review participant medical history forms and, if necessary, interview students or chaperones concerning past or present medical problems prior to any activities taking place on a Boojum course.
5. The field team shall at all times have ready access to completed medical history forms for each participant and the medical history forms for each member of the field team.
6. Each Instructor shall conduct a risk management briefing with his/her group as soon as possible. An example is provided on the back cover of each Boojum Course Log book. As appropriate, depending upon which hazards are present, instructors should teach how to avoid: dehydration and heat illness, hypothermia, frostbite, waterborne illnesses (such as giardiasis, caused by the microorganism Giardia lamblia), dangerous animals (such as rattlesnakes, scorpions, black widow spiders, deer hunters, bears, mountain lions), dangerous plants (such as cacti, poison oak, oleander), accidents in semitechnical terrain, lightning, earthquake, flash flooding, rock fall, avalanche, and drowning. Instructors shall ascertain that participants have understood the briefing and that they respect the potential dangers of the activity or environmental conditions.
7. Additional risk management and hazard briefings shall be given to participants whenever needed to educate them in prevention and avoidance techniques appropriate for the activity and environmental conditions.
8. All activities shall be conducted only with populations that are appropriate in terms of age and emotional maturity for the activity.
9. Instructors shall have a clear understanding of the purpose and expected benefit to the students of each activity. Prior to engaging students in any activity, instructors should make a conscious decision that this benefit is worth the risk.
10. Except as noted in the sections on independent travel and solo excursions, instructors shall accompany student groups when traveling to ensure quality risk management. Instructors shall have a group management plan for keeping track of people and managing risks if splitting the group becomes necessary.
11. All participants in general shall wear close-toed shoes or boots during all activities. Exceptions are:
    a. During nonwilderness residential programs in developed areas such as a summer camp facility
    b. In the backcountry on large, clean, broad surfaces such as smooth granite slabs occasionally found in the Sierras
    c. Swimming in deep water (such as off a boat in the middle of a body of water) or in a swimming pool

12. Sandals are permissible only in camp or as noted above. At all times staff should use their good judgment and discretion in the choice of footwear. Remember that in the backcountry, a normally minor injury can have significant logistical and medical consequences for the group.
13. Adequate food, water, and emergency equipment shall be carried during all field activities.
14. Staff shall comply with all applicable laws and rules. Required permits, licenses, tickets, and personal and organizational identification shall be carried at all times.
15. Boojum staff shall supervise students at all times in the field. Chaperone-led hikes out of the immediate vicinity of the camp area are not permitted. It is permissible for a chaperone to take active leadership roles in a hike with a Boojum staff person present to assist if needed.

Guidelines

1. Every effort should be made to conduct an appropriate debrief (or processing) session upon conclusion of an activity, or at least daily, to help participants understand and be able to consciously use information they have learned throughout each day. When and how this occurs is left up to the creative judgment of each instructor. Do not make the mistake of expecting an activity to simply "speak for itself"; make a creative effort to encourage student discussion regarding individual and group performance. Let your facilitation efforts be guided by the course goals as well as your personal observations of interaction within your group. Draw connections between what was learned and how that information may be useful to participants when they return to their home environment ("transference").
2. Instructors should use their best judgment in the event that the planned activities are interrupted by unexpected adverse weather. As a guide, remember that the instructor's first priority is concern for the physical and emotional safety of the students. Options include changing the scheduled activities to accommodate the weather and seeking a way to keep to the schedule and avoid the weather. When practical, discuss the options with other staff members or the chaperones. Students should be briefed regarding the decision-making criteria and chosen options when appropriate.
3. Travel during adverse weather should be considered an activity in itself rather than simply a means of keeping to the planned itinerary. Instructors should insure that participants are physically and psychologically ready for such travel and that clothing and equipment are adequate for the activity. This is to include chaperones and students. Prior to engaging in the experience, participants shall be briefed regarding pertinent anticipated hardships or potential hazards.

University of New Hampshire	
	F Education
	E Northeast Region
	C University Outdoor Education Students and General Population
	S 4.02, 4.06, 4.08, 4.10, 4.13, 7.01, 7.05–7.07, 8.02

General Policy—Land

The guidelines outlined in this section apply to *all* activities or courses sponsored or implemented by the University of New Hampshire (UNH) Outdoor Education (OE) Program. Following this section you will find guidelines for specific activities (i.e. rock climbing, canoeing, orienteering). Persons wishing to lead, facilitate, sponsor, or instruct any activity associated with the OE program should review *all* applicable sections of this manual. General activity guidelines are divided into the following sections:

1.1. Staffing
1.2. Minimum Qualifications for Participants
1.3. Forms
1.4. Program Design
1.5. Site Selection
1.6. Emergency Planning and Procedures
1.7. Activity Brief
1.8. Supervision
1.9. Environmental Conditions
1.10. Warm-Up Activities
1.11. Nutrition
1.12. Hygiene
1.13. Clothing and Equipment

1.1 Staffing

For the purposes of this manual, a staff member is defined as anyone in a designated leadership role while conducting an activity sponsored by the UNH OE Program. This includes but may not be limited to: OE faculty, per-diem instructors, volunteers, teaching assistants, and outdoor education students who are planning or implementing activities associated with the OE program.

Minimum qualifications for staff.

The following are the minimum qualifications for anyone who is acting as a staff member for the OE program. In some cases a person in a leadership or instructor role may not be required to have all of the minimum qualifications. For example, if two people are acting as an instructor team, then it may not be required for both of them to possess the minimum level of medical certification indicated below. All staff:

- Adhere to all OE program guidelines that are applicable to the intended activity.
- Adhere to UNH OE General and Ethical Guidelines outlined in the "General Personnel" section of General and Ethical Guidelines.
- Have appropriate level of expertise in conducting the intended activity.
- Use teaching and instruction methods that fall within the accepted practices of the UNH OE program.

Note: Students planning on leading or instructing an experience associated with the UNH OE program must obtain approval from a full-time OE faculty member prior to engaging in the activity.

Medical qualifications for all staff.

- Possess a current cardiopulmonary resuscitation certification.
- For field courses, possess a current certification as an emergency medical technician, a wilderness emergency medical technician, or a wilderness first responder or work with a second leader with those credentials.
- For facility-based courses, carry a current first-aid certification.

1.2 Minimum Qualifications for Participants

In addition to guidelines in the specific activity sections of this manual, any persons wishing to participate in an activity facilitated by UNH OE staff must:

- Register for the course or obtain permission from the course staff.
- Discuss any relevant medical or physical conditions with the staff that could be aggravated by participating in the identified course.
- Complete the necessary prerequisites for the activity as outlined in the specific activity area, or have acceptable previous experience in lieu of prerequisite coursework.
- Complete medical forms to the best of their knowledge.
- Read, understand, and sign (or have had a parent/guardian sign when the participant is under 18 or otherwise unable to self-grant permission for) an Assumption of Risk form.
- Adhere to behavioral guidelines identified by program leaders and UNH.
- Use equipment and methods that are consistent with the UNH OE guidelines and procedures, unless an exception is granted by the OE staff.
- Abide by UNH OE Program guidelines to the best of their knowledge.

1.3 Forms

Prior to allowing any participant to engage in an activity, staff must review all participants' Assumption of Risk Forms and Medical Forms (see exception).

Assumption of Risk Forms: Staff should ensure that they have received completed Assumption of Risk forms from all participants. If the participant is under 18 (or otherwise unable to self-grant permission to participate), then the form must be signed by a legal parent or guardian. Participants who do not have or have not appropriately completed an Assumption of Risk form will not be permitted to participate in any activity sponsored by the UNH OE program.

Exception: If a staff member is working for an external organization under the supervision of that organizations staff, then the organization's method for granting permission to participants will apply (e.g., when UNH OE students are fulfilling course requirements by working at the Seacoast Science Center, a UNH OE Assumption of Risk form is not required).

Medical Forms: Staff should ensure they have received completed medical forms from all participants. Medical forms should be reviewed prior to engaging in any activity. Any concerns or "red flags" should be addressed privately with the individual participant. If a participant lists an unfamiliar condition or medication, then staff should check with the participant for side affects/symptoms that may contraindicate the activity. Staff should also ask participants for any additional medical or physical concerns not included on their medical forms and determine if their participation is still appropriate. If a participant's participation may not be appropriate due to medical concerns, staff should attempt to adapt the activity or the participant's role to include the individual.

1.4 Program Design

Activities and programs are designed based on the experience of the instructional staff, the educational goals of the program, goals of the participants, and experience of the participants. Considerations for program design may include:

- Use of appropriate facilitation techniques, including framing, debriefing, etc.
- Sequencing and progression—Activities and programs are designed with an intentional progression in mind. Basic skills are introduced first and then built upon as participants demonstrate competency.
- When possible, programs are designed to include all participants.
- Staff members assess each participant's physical and emotional ability throughout the activity and adjust the pace of the experience based on the assessment.

1.5 Site Selection

The following criteria apply to the selection of *all* activity sites or course areas regardless of the intended activity. Additional site selection considerations may be found in specific activity sections of this manual.

Course areas are chosen based on these guidelines:

- *Staff Familiarity:* Staff is familiar with the intended course area and contingency sites. This familiarity may be attained through personal experience, guidebooks, maps, websites, local guides or officials, etc. Course area research may be performed directly by the staff member or by the participants depending on the goals of the program.
- *Site Investigation:* Course areas are scouted by at least one staff prior to student participation in a program. Previous experience in a course area will satisfy this requirement. Scouting a course area can provide instructors with valuable current information about a course area prior to engaging in an activity with students. The reconnaissance is important to determine if the chosen course area is appropriate for the group, the instructor's level of experience, and the intended activity. Under some circumstances a course or activity may occur in an area for which a reconnaissance has not been performed. These circumstances may include, but are not limited to:
  - Educational or program goals
  - An instructor's decision to modify intended route for risk management purposes (e.g., avalanche hazard avoidance, participant injury, physical ability)

  Note: Participants are informed of the lack of reconnaissance when an activity will occur in terrain that has not been scouted by staff.
- *Accessibility of Contingency Sites and Routes*

- *Regulation/Legal Compliance:* All activities and course areas fall within the legal parameters of the region.
- *Permitting:* Permits are secured and carried, if required, for any intended course area or activity.
- *Environmental Considerations:* All efforts are made to choose and utilize course areas in which the impact on the environment will be minimized.
- *Changing Environmental Conditions:* Through reconnaissance and site research, staff understand how changing weather conditions may affect the site (e.g., rising water levels, lightning hazard, waves, etc.).
- *Identifiable Objective Hazards:* Course areas are chosen based on their freedom from obvious objective hazards or the ability to avoid high hazard areas (e.g., unstable rock, avalanche hazard, unmanageable rip current, etc..)
- *Educational and Program/Group Goals*
- *Participant Ability:* A course area should be chosen based upon the expected physical and psychological readiness of the participants.
- *Instructor Knowledge and Experience:* Staff choose to operate courses in course areas that reflect their knowledge and experience. For example, staff with greater experience may choose to operate in course areas that are more remote or require more advanced judgment-based decision-making skills to identify hazards and appropriately manage risk.)

1.6 Emergency Planning and Procedures

Appropriate emergency planning occurs for all activities. General considerations for emergency planning include but may not be limited to:

- *First-aid or Rescue Equipment:* Appropriate first-aid and rescue equipment should be available and within reasonable proximity throughout the activity.
- *Student Briefing:* Depending on the activity, students may be briefed on emergency procedures. This may include identifying roles prior to an actual emergency situation. For example, if the group is traveling in avalanche terrain, it may be prudent to establish who will lead the search and rescue operation if the instructor is buried.
- *Evacuation Planning:* Staff should have an evacuation plan for all course areas. This is usually part of a written trip plan, but in some situations may be an unwritten plan that leaders have discussed. For example, experienced staff may not carry a formal written evacuation plan for frequently used course area in close proximity to emergency facilities or services (e.g., Pawtuckaway State Park, O'diorne State Park, both of which are within a short drive of the hospital.)
- *Emergency Communication Planning*

1.7 Activity Brief

In the past the activity brief may have been referred to as the "safety talk." Staff should recognize the importance of an organized brief prior to engaging in an activity. The depth of the activity brief will depend on the educational goals of the experience, maturity and experience of the participants, intended activity, etc. Components of an activity brief may include, but are not limited to:

- Hazards that may be encountered during the activity.
- Specific rules or parameters that all participants must follow during the experience.
- Time limits (if applicable).
- Information on the intended route or activity.
- Steps for participants to follow should an emergency arise (if applicable).
- Educational goals or objectives for the day.
- Specific activity briefing information can be found in the specific activity sections of this manual.

1.8 Supervision

All UNH OE activities operate with an appropriate level of supervision, specific or general, and participant/staff ratio based upon the following considerations:

- Instructor experience
- Participant age, maturity level, and experience
- Program goals
- Course area
- Time of year
- Medical considerations
- Legal and environmental regulations

Specific and general supervision.

Supervision is viewed along a spectrum from very specific, where an instructor may be monitoring a belay team by standing right next to them with his/her hand on the brake rope, to very general, where groups may be traveling and camping alone. The level of supervision depends upon the criteria above. In most cases, especially when OE students are leading trips, or with less mature or less skilled participants, more specific supervision is used.

If the participants are to be specifically supervised:

- Group travels together under the supervision of the staff.
- If the group separates for any reason, a staff member accompanies each group.
- With the exception of certain situations (e.g., bathroom needs, solos, and while sleeping), when participants tell staff of their location, staff is in close proximity to the participants and can generally see or hear all group members.

If the participants are to be generally supervised:

- Participants are briefed on the activity, contingency plans, goals, etc.

- Participants are taught the necessary skills prior to engaging in the activity.
- Participants have demonstrated the necessary level of competence needed to engage in the activity without direct supervision.
- Participants are given any appropriate information about the area in which they will be traveling/operating.
- Staff informs participants of environmental limits, time limits, and risk management considerations for the activity.
- A system of check-ins is developed and implemented or the participants are informed of the location of or how to contact staff.
- Meeting places and times are established.

Note: Certain medical or psychological illnesses/conditions may preclude individuals from operating without direct supervision in the chosen course area. (e.g., certain heart conditions, history of severe allergic or anaphylactic reactions to stings).

Guidelines for group size.

When students are traveling or participating in an activity that is not directly supervised by staff, group size will be determined by the criteria used for ratios and level of supervision. In general, students should be in groups of no less than three when participating in most backcountry experiences. This number may be modified depending on the participants experience, location, educational goals, emergency situations, etc.

Group organization.

- The group knows the location of the first-aid kit
- Designated sweep and lead persons and/or a buddy system may be established depending on the nature of the experience and the experience of the participants.
- The staff assesses each participant's physical and emotional ability throughout the activity and adjusts the pace of the experience as needed.

1.9 Environmental Conditions

All activities are conducted in appropriate conditions. The appropriateness of weather, sea state, surface conditions, temperature, etc., will depend on the skills and abilities of both the staff and participants as well as the educational goals of the program. Activities are suspended if changing conditions present unmanageable hazards to the instructors or group, unless the prudent decision is to continue to better manage the current risk or situation.

1.10 Warmup Activities

Stretching and cardiovascular exercises prior to most physical activities can reduce the risk of illness or injury. Staff and participants perform appropriate warm-ups prior to engaging in activities if it is prudent to do so. Warm-up activities may be formal or informal. Instructors may lead or encourage an organized warm-up/stretching session or they may encourage low-key participation in the intended activity as a warm-up strategy.

1.11 Nutrition

While not all programs run by the UNH OE program provide food for the participants, it is important to ensure that nutritional requirements of staff and participants are met. Staff should recognize the importance of proper nutrition and hydration in preventing illness and injury. Many individuals may be unaware of the relationship between extreme environmental or physically stressful conditions and the body's need for increased food and water intake. Participants should be informed of the importance of proper nutrition and hydration, and encouraged to exercise appropriate levels of self-care. Though individuals' needs may greatly differ, some general guidelines for nutritional and fluid requirements follow.

Water intake.

Please note that the recommended water intake increases with increased physical stress (e.g., individuals lose and therefore need to ingest more water when hiking at altitude with a heavy pack compared to an easy day hike).

Note: Fluid needs may increase depending on the weather conditions; any extreme temperature, humidity, or altitude may greatly increase fluid needs.

Fall, Spring, and Summer Activities (e.g., Backpacking, Canoeing, Climbing)	2 – 4 quarts per day
Winter Activities (e.g., Winter Backpacking, Skiing, Winter Climbing)	3 – 4 quarts per day
High Altitude (> 7,000 ft.)	4 – 5 quarts per day

Food intake.

A normal diet generally consists of approximately 50% carbohydrates, 25% fats, and 25% proteins. However, while engaging in strenuous activities, the carbohydrates may be increased to 60% of the individual's total diet and in winter environments the fat intake may be increased to 40%. The following are some general guidelines and are dependent on the individual, the environment, the strenuous nature of the activity, and individual metabolism:

Fall, Spring, and Summer Activities	2,500 – 3,000 calories per day
Winter Activities	3,500 – 4,500+ calories per day
High-altitude cold-weather mountaineering	4,500 + calories per day

1.12 Hygiene

Personal hygiene and group cleanliness is an important factor in preventing infection and disease during backcountry experiences. Staff should promote good hygiene habits through modeling, camp rituals, rules, etc. Prevention through good self-care is key to avoiding unnecessary evacuations, itinerary changes, or trip delays.

Considerations for promoting good hygiene:

- Wash your hands:
  - After handling any material that is likely to carry germs.
  - After going to the bathroom.
  - After caring for the sick.
  - Before and after handling any food and utensils.
- Keep your body relatively clean:
  - On extended trips it may be necessary to bath with soapy water and a washcloth following LNT guidelines.
  - Pay special attention to the feet, armpits, crotch, hands, and hair (as these are prime areas for infestation and infection).
  - Encourage dental care—it is extremely easy to neglect oral care during wilderness experiences. Oral infections can quickly become major healthcare problems requiring evacuation.
- Eating and drinking safely:
  - Do not share water bottles, bandannas, toothbrushes, razors, eating utensils, etc.
  - Do not use personal utensils to serve food.
  - Routinely clean personal eating utensils and bowls with soapy water or by boiling.
  - Share GORP and other snacks by pouring into hands rather than having multiple individuals scoop from the bag with dirty hands.
- Wash and air dry all community kitchen gear
- Anyone who is ill or appears to be ill should not participate in food preparation:
- Purify all drinking water via water filtration, chemical treatment or boiling.
- Antibacterial wipes, feminine hygiene wipes, and hand gel are useful and easy tools in the woods.

Note: LNT guidelines for bathing and waste disposal should be followed.

1.13 Clothing and Equipment

Whether clothing and equipment are provided by the UNH OE program or by participants, staff will check all gear to ensure its appropriateness for the intended activity. Please see specific clothing and equipment lists at the end of each activity section. Please also see Equipment Policies for care and usage.

- Participants and staff wear appropriate clothing and carry appropriate equipment based on the environmental conditions, length of trip, and terrain (e.g., ensolite pad if traveling above tree line).
- Participants and staff understand the concept of layering and dress according to level of exertion, weather, and fitness level.
- A first-aid kit and cell phone are taken on each trip.

SECTION 11
HIKING, CAMPING, AND BACKPACKING

Charleston County Parks & Recreation

F	Recreation
E	Southeast Region
C	General Population
S	4.10, 7.01, 11.01–11.08

Backpacking/Hiking

Program Ratio

1. Maintain a maximum of 1:6 staff-to-participant ratio and at least a minimum of two staff on any program with more than six participants.
2. Maximum number of participants dependent on specific course area.

Description of Course Environment

1. Backpacking/hiking and multiuse trails
2. May include a variety of ecosystems
3. Primarily conducted in three season conditions

Safety Concerns (specific to this environment or activity)

1. Trauma from falls
2. Environmental problems related to program area (dehydration, hypo/hyperthermia, weather, etc.)
3. Blisters and/or rashes
4. Sudden lightning storms
5. Separation from the group

Strategies for Minimizing Safety Concerns

1. Practice standard participant management techniques (maintain hydration, take frequent breaks, etc.).
2. Stop at every trail junction, whether well established or minimal. Wait for entire group to be visible.
3. Provide each participant with a whistle and instruct participants to use whistle in case of emergency or separation from group. Instruct participants to blow three blasts on the whistle at regular intervals until contact is made. Instruct participants to stay where they are.

4. Have entire group present when presenting important information (e.g., foot care, fitting packs, water treatment, hiking together, and hygiene).
5. Teach and practice lightning drill before leaving (at premeeting or at trail head).
6. Staff must remain with group at all times except in the case of an emergency.
7. Proper camp craft skills/practices must be observed, especially those pertaining to health and hygiene.
8. Trained staff leads daily equipment and personnel check.

Equipment Requirements (in addition to general equipment requirements addressed elsewhere)

1. Each group must carry a flashlight, whistle, compass, map, matches, food, water, and first-aid kit.
2. Each participant must be provided with the following equipment:
   - Backpack
   - Sleeping bag
   - Insulating pad
   - Stuff sack
   - Whistle
3. Each group should be provided with the following equipment:

Tents with ground cloths (adequate quantity for size of group)	Spice kit
2 stoves	2 trowels
Stove repair kit	Repair kit
2 fuel bottles with fuel	Tarp
Pots with lids	Biodegradable soap
Pot grips	Bleach
Frying pan	Cellular phone
Serving spoons/spatulas	
2 water bags	
2 water filters with iodine tablet backup	

Group Supervision and Organization

1. Please review the camp craft section.
2. Maintain verbal and/or visual contact with participants.
3. Staff should direct and model accepted trail etiquette and courtesy, including stopping group on one side of trail only, announcing presence to other users, etc.

4. Staff should be familiar with the area designated for the trip.
5. Staff must have a route plan, including evacuation routes.
6. Staff should use games and initiatives to enhance the learning experience in problem solving and group interaction.
7. Participants should receive a gear list and have gear checked prior to leaving for a trip (show examples of clothing/gear at premeeting).
8. Participants and staff must complete a Hold Harmless form prior to trip. Copies should be left with the program coordinator (ORC/ORS).
9. Follow local guidelines and permit requirements.
10. Tools and instruction for digging cat holes must be provided.
11. Encourage participants to sweep the campsite for trash prior to leaving.
12. Consider carefully before you build a fire—can the area absorb it and do you really need it? Fires are permitted if local guidelines permit and if an established fire ring is present. Use only downed and dead sticks for firewood. Fire must be out before retiring for the night.

Supplemental Resource Information

- Leave No Trace
- NOLS Cookery

The Westminster School	*F*	**Education**
	E	**Southeast Region**
	C	**High School Students**
	S	**4.10, 11.01, 11.04, 11.07**

Expeditions

1. Discovery will maintain a 1:6 adult faculty to Westminster student ratio when in a "wilderness" context on expeditions (effective August, 2005).
2. Groups will not divide unless it is an emergency situation, it is approved by the session director, or it is a scheduled activity such as solo. In an emergency situation, the divided groups will have a minimum of three persons in each party.
3. Each person will carry a whistle.
4. Shoes or approved footwear will be worn at all times except when inside a tent.
5. A roster of participants, directions to program site, and a schedule will be left with a predesignated individual prior to any off-campus activity.
6. First-aid kits and appropriate rescue equipment will be readily accessible.

7. All faculty members will carry emergency procedures for the area and the medical forms for the participants.
8. Students will be briefed on specific environmental hazards of the program use area and emergency procedures for that area.
9. No flames of any kind are allowed in tents, around climbing equipment, or in vehicles.
10. All faculty members will carry fire building equipment, maps of the area, compass (when appropriate), and flashlight.
11. All "student-led" groups will be led by a trained Discovery student staff member who has achieved the rank of instructor or senior instructor. As with all Discovery groups, a first-aid kit will be carried at all times, each member will wear a whistle and groups will be within visual contact of the slowest member of the group. All safety policy and procedures for the program will be followed. No instructor will be given a group who has not completed the Safety Self-Assessment and the workshop review of the Discovery Safety Policies and Procedures Manual. In addition, "student-led" groups will be within visual or hailing distance of an adult employed by the Westminster Schools (to include "part-time" Discovery faculty and others hired and under the supervision of the director of Discovery) during travel. The only exception to this policy is on a "final hike" when a Discovery adult staff member will trail the group down a previously reconnoitered trail. In this case the adult staff member will be responsible for "sweeping" the trail and assuring that everyone arrives safely at the final destination. The adult "sweeper" will also carry a first-aid kit.
12. A ratio of no more than 10 ninth graders to one faculty and at least one student staff will be maintained at all times on regular Discovery session hikes.
13. When hiking, the group will stay within visual contact of all members. The group should travel at the pace of the slowest member. If a member of the group becomes physically or mentally incapable of participating in the activities, the instructors should consider evacuating that person.

Camp Woodson	*F* **Therapeutic**
	E **Southeast Region**
	C **Incarcerated Youth**
	S **11.01–11.08**

Expeditions—Hiking and Backpacking

Purpose

1. To provide students with a therapeutic problem-solving initiative in a safe, remote, and unfamiliar setting.

2. To challenge students physically and emotionally, both as individuals, and as a group.
3. To stimulate group interaction and provide opportunities for decision making, leadership, problem solving and teamwork.
4. To provide difficult and significant challenges which, once attained, build satisfaction and a sense of pride with participants.
5. To provide students with the opportunity to assume increasing levels of responsibility as skills are mastered and teamwork is developed.

Safety policy.

1. Each hiking group must carry a first-aid kit, epinephrine, and gear appropriate for the hike (map, compass, flashlight, raingear, food and water, extra clothing, etc.).
2. All staff must understand the route plan and the evacuation routes before leaving the office. Consider coaching staff unfamiliar with the hike and carrying additional area maps.
3. All students must be under the supervision of a staff member at all times, including trail scouting.

Guidelines

1. *Route Plan Modification:* Should staff decide to unexpectedly modify or otherwise deviate from the program coordinator's planned route, appropriate efforts will be made to notify the program coordinator of such changes (leave cairn, make a phone call, send a message with a pedestrian, etc.).
2. *Dump Sites:* Student dumpsites should be checked for the first three shifts in the woods. Dumpsites should be checked randomly thereafter until we are confident all is being done properly. One suggestion is to flip a coin after a student returns from their dump. Heads you check it, tails you don't. This takes the pressure off you "not trusting me" and keeps students on their best behavior because they know they can be checked at any time.
3. Students will be out of your sight while taking a dump but they should still remain under your supervision. Establish voice contact; have them shake a tree, etc. Students are not permitted to bring their pack or any gear other than a shovel and TP. Students have been known to use this opportunity to run.
4. *Drinking Water:* During the first 2 weeks of camp, students will not be sent out of the sight of staff to get drinking water. This will be discussed and reevaluated at the mid-session meeting. Until this time, students will travel as a tent group or go under the supervision of a floater.
5. *Dividing Into Hiking Groups:* Staff may choose to divide into activity groups or otherwise hike in smaller groups. If groups are to be out of sight of each other, each group must have a first-aid kit. Consider staff coverage and plan designated rendezvous points at frequent prearranged points.

6. *Scouting:* Scout parties shall include at least three persons. If the scout party is going to leave the sight of the group, a staff member must accompany the scout party.
7. *Map Reading:* Students should be taught the skills necessary to read topographical maps. Consider working with two students at a time with a rotation schedule to include everyone. Look for "teachable moments" to introduce topics to the entire group and allow students to experience appropriate "natural consequences" in the choices they make. Minimize the students tendency to "read the staff" for the correct direction at intersections.
8. *Planning Your Day:* Build in appropriate incentives, such as swimming or a campfire at the end of the day, for good behavior and efficient hiking. If conflicts are brewing, stop the hike and deal with the issues. Use games, initiatives, and other creative activities to set the tone, break up the day, or to deal with problems.
9. *Coed Hiking:* See "Working with Coed Groups—Ideas to Structure Interaction" in the Appendix.
10. *Debriefing:* Provide opportunities to debrief both your tent group and the entire hiking group. Expect an increase in interpersonal conflicts when working as a large group. Use these conflicts as teachable moments to empower the group to learn how to work together. If our goal is to have students travel as one relatively independent group on final, we need to teach them how to work together early on. "Divide and conquer" when appropriate to maintain a controlled, safe environment. Do not use this approach merely to avoid conflict or to make your day go smoother.

Teaching Outline

Organize the expedition to allow sufficient time to teach the following skills. Remember, mastery of these skills requires repetition and individualized remedial instruction.

1. Group participation and cooperation
2. Care and use of equipment (pack adjustment, gear location, do's and don'ts)
3. Camp craft (sanitation, site selection, knots, shelters, water, use of bathroom)
4. Health and hygiene (dress, diet, foot care, personal hygiene, feminine hygiene, etc.)
5. Expedition teamwork and planning
6. Map and compass skills
7. Traveling skills (pacing, staying together, point and sweep)
8. Emergency procedures (lightning, cold weather drill, etc.)
9. Environmental hazard analysis and procedures (river crossings, cold weather, night hiking, weather and lightning)
10. Nutrition and food preparation

Wilderness Treatment Center	*F*	Therapeutic
	E	Northwest Region
	C	Adolescent Males
	S	4.10, 11.01–11.08

Hiking Policy

1. Hiking activities are a major part of WTC wilderness expeditions and recreation therapy. During spring, summer, and fall, depending on snow coverage, wilderness trips will average 50 to 100 miles. Recreation therapy activities on Thursday and Sunday afternoons often include hikes from 1 to 10 miles.
2. The lead instructor facilitating hiking activities is required to possess a high level of experience, training, and skill in hiking and orienteering techniques, procedure and safety protocol. Prior to an instructor facilitating a hiking activity, his/her qualifications, experience, and skill level are reviewed by the program coordinator.
3. Program staff assisting in the supervision of hikes is able to demonstrate a working knowledge of hiking and orienteering techniques, awareness of environmental factors, and other relevant skills. The lead instructor facilitating the activity is responsible for ensuring that assisting staff possess the above knowledge and skill.
4. Staff is required to be up to date on changes in technology and procedure for this activity. This is accomplished through continued outside training experiences and reading relevant literature. In addition, periodic in-service training sessions are conducted as a forum to share experience and skills.
5. Staff supervision is required for all hiking activities. Staff-to-patient ratio is not to exceed 1:12 for day hikes during recreation therapy and 1:4.5 for wilderness expeditions. At least two staff need to be present.
6. Hikes will be appropriate for patient's skill level and physical aptitude. Staff will not engage patients in hikes that the duration and or difficulty exceed the ability of the patients. Instructors and counselors need to be aware of the physical aptitude and mental condition of the patients and plan hikes accordingly.
7. Staff will be prepared for a rescue or medical emergency.
    a. The staff team has at least one member with current WFR or equivalent and current CPR as the minimum level of medical training.
    b. All other staff has a minimum of standard first aid and CPR.
    c. A wilderness first-aid kit will be carried.
    d. On day hikes greater than 10 miles or when deemed appropriate, the following group gear will be carried: a sleeping bag, tarp, ensolite pad, stove, pot and lid, fuel, extra food, and hot drinks.
    e. Participants will carry extra clothing. Generally this includes extra warm cloths and rain gear. This can vary depending on weather and season.

8. Staff will not engage patients in hikes that he or she is not properly trained and experienced in the handling of a rescue or medical emergency.
9. Staff is able to comprehend the therapeutic use of hiking activities and is able to integrate it into the patient's treatment. This can include leadership skills, communication, working as a group, sober fun, and physical health.

Procedures

1. Prior to use by WTC all hiking areas are researched for access, safety, cultural, and ecological concerns. New use areas need to be approved by the program coordinator and program director.
2. Potential hikes are discussed with the program coordinator and other experienced staff during the planning stage of the activity. The WTC Map Atlas, the Bob Marshal Foundation, the U.S. Forest Service, the National Park Service, and other local outfitters are often consulted at this time.
3. Patients will be provided with water and food appropriate for the length of the activity. Staff and the "leader of the day" need to check on the map for potential water sources. Extra water can be carried in the dromedary if necessary. Strive to have patients consume a minimum of one gallon of fluids (water, Kool-Aid, hot chocolate, etc.) during the day of the activity. Stress the importance of staying hydrated. Discuss the signs of being properly hydrated (clear and copious urine) and the signs of dehydration (fatigue, head aches, etc.). Generally 2 pounds of food is sufficient for a day activity. This includes breakfast and dinner. Each patient should consume 1 pound of trail food during the hike. Stop often enough that patients can keep sufficiently fueled and hydrated. Generally this is about once an hour. Staff needs to continually monitor patients' fluid and food intake along with their physical condition.
4. Patients will be provided with clothing appropriate for the environmental concerns of the activity. Refer to the winter, spring, summer, and fall rental and purchase forms for a list of clothing provided on wilderness trips. During recreation therapy day hikes, patients need to carry rain gear and extra warm clothing appropriate for the season.
5. Appropriate footwear will be provided. Hiking or pack boots (depending on the season of use) are issued before leaving on a wilderness trip. When issued, both boots need to be tried on by the patient to ensure a correct fit. The boots should have a fresh coat of Snowseal for water proofing. In addition, the patients are issued gaiters and three pairs of wool socks and polypro liners. Patients who wish to use their own hiking boots on a wilderness trip need to have them preapproved by a wilderness instructor. Any patients that do not posses appropriate footwear for day hikes during recreation therapy will be loaned a pair.
6. On the first day of a wilderness trip, discuss foot care with the patients. This includes but is not limited to: wearing liners under wool socks, putting on dry socks at night, hot spots, blisters, clipping toe nails, immersion foot, and frostbite. Instructors will provide instruction and assistance in the treatment of blisters and hot spots. Stress the importance of using moleskin and tape on hot spots before they form into blisters. Have patients tighten their boot laces before long descents. This prevents boot bang. Remind patients that if they take good care of their feet, their feet will take good care of them.

7. Perform daily foot checks and enter the results in the Wilderness Trip Log.
8. Hiking expectations that will be discussed with patients prior to the activity include but are not limited to:
   a. Carrying the appropriate clothing and equipment.
   b. Staying properly hydrated and fed.
   c. No throwing rocks or other objects.
   d. No littering, smoking or graffiti.
   e. No horse play.
   f. Staying together as a group at all times.
9. Patients will be assigned the responsibilities of "leader of the day," "point person," and "sweep person." The leader of the day responsibilities include discussing the route with an instructor, determining mileage and elevation gained or lost, locating water sources, keeping the group together, ensuring the group moves at an appropriate pace, route finding, locating camp, leading day-by-day group, and communicating with the sweep and point persons. Responsibilities of "point" include hiking at the front of the group, maintaining a good pace that the group can adequately sustain, conferring with the leader as to route direction and selection, and communicating with the sweep. Responsibilities of "sweep" include hiking in the rear of the group, ensuring the group stays together, and making sure all garbage and gear are packed up. At the end of each day the leader, point, and sweep receive feedback from the group on their strong points and areas that need improvement. Patients are generally provided with two occasions to be the leader, point, and sweep. During recreation therapy day hikes point, sweep, and leader responsibilities are normally assigned to senior peers.
10. Instructors will lead participants in appropriate warm-up activities. This normally includes stretching activities designed to loosen hamstrings, lower back muscles and other areas prone to injury from hiking activities.
11. Appropriate precautions for potential bear encounters will be exercised. This is discussed in depth in the Bear Safety Policy.
12. Be aware of changing weather. Watch for signs of lightning. Set up camp or return to the unit if appropriate. In the event of a lightning storm avoid ridges, large bodies of water, and exposed areas. Be careful in extreme cold weather. Factor in wind chill. Remember the colder the temperature, the smaller the safety margins. Exercise good judgment and always think conservatively. Refer to Weather Policy for more information.
13. Staff will be sensitive to the needs and concerns of the patients. For most patients, hiking is an entirely new experience for them. It may be very physically and mentally challenging for them. They may be beyond their comfort zones. Take time to address their concerns. Give them a chance to ask questions.
14. All activities will be recorded in Recreation or Wilderness Trip Log books.

Georgia College & State University	
	F **Education**
	E **Southeast Region**
	C **University Outdoor Education Students and General Population**
	S **4.10, 11.01–11.09**

Camping, Backpacking, Land Navigation, and River Crossing

Staff/Participant Ratios

Camping	1:10 (minimum 2)
Backpacking	1:8 (minimum 2)
Land Navigation	1:8 (minimum 2)

Activity Goals

1. Introduce unfamiliar and sometimes imposing environments in which participants confront and solve realistic problems.
2. Provide opportunities to apply newly acquired knowledge and skills.
3. Provide small group experiences.
4. Provide opportunities for leadership development.
5. Challenge participants physically, emotionally, intellectually, and socially.
6. Provide opportunities to set and achieve individual and group goals.
7. Provide group decision-making opportunities that have real and natural consequences.
8. Develop a sense of stewardship toward the environment, equipment, and facilities.
9. Teach skills for life-long recreation enjoyment.
10. Have fun while learning about oneself and others.
11. Promote trust, respect for diversity, team effectiveness, leadership development, and community.

Camping

Facilitator Responsibilities

1. Use appropriate campsite selection criteria and camping procedures for pristine vs. impacted areas.
2. Select campsites that are a minimum of 200 feet from freshwater sources.

3. Designate locations for shelters, cooking, food storage, and toilet areas (preferably 200 ft. apart from each other).
4. Inspect the site carefully for potential hazards such as loose rock, dead trees (widow makers), flash flood zones, poisonous plants, and dangerous fauna.
5. Attempt to leave the campsite better than it was found.
6. Remove all trash and fluff up ground cover to discourage others from camping in the same place.
7. Perform a final sweep of the campsite to ensure nothing is left behind.
8. Base camping (in one location) and route camping (in multiple locations) require different planning considerations (i.e., group latrine vs. cat holes).

Safety and Environment

1. Model and encourage participants to maintain appropriate personal hygiene.
2. Clean hands prior to cooking or eating, and after urinating or defecating.
3. Consider designated bathing times on longer trips.
4. Ensure that food pots, bowls, and utensils are cleaned to minimize contamination.
5. Secure food at night from animals using appropriate methods such as hanging food, locking storage containers, nearby vehicles, or kayak bulkheads.
6. Model and advise participants concerning techniques for staying warm in cooler weather.

Clothing and Equipment

1. Model appropriate use of stoves and lanterns.
2. Teach how to light stoves and how to deal with flare-ups.
3. Light stoves in a jump-back position.
4. Use only two-burner stoves on tables.
5. Minimize the number of people in the kitchen area to prevent accidents.
6. Use appropriate water treatment techniques such as boiling for 15 minutes, commercial water pumps/filters, and chemicals.
7. Always follow manufacturer directions when using water pumps and chemicals.

Backpacking

Teaching

1. Curriculum may include, but is not limited to:
   a. Hard skills
      i. Basic camping skills as noted in camping section;

ii. Nutrition and rations planning;

iii. Equipment and clothing selection/use;

iv. Weather;

v. Health and sanitation;

vi. Travel techniques;

vii. Navigation;

viii. Safety and risk management;

ix. Wilderness emergency procedures and treatment;

x. Natural and cultural history;

xi. Trip planning.

b. Soft skills

i. Decision making and problem solving;

ii. Leadership;

iii. Expedition behavior and group dynamics;

iv. Environmental ethics;

v. Communication skills;

vi. Teaching, processing, and transference.

c. Additional topics or skills associated with setting, season, or developmental needs of the participants.

2. Where appropriate, group members should be involved in planning:

a. Food service, safety and emergency procedures, logistics, environment and culture, equipment, and program may provide opportunities for involving group members in the planning process at an appropriate level of readiness.

b. Provide facilitator supervision for all components of planning.

3. Pretrip instruction may be necessary based on program goals and participant readiness.

Land Navigation

Teaching

1. Curriculum may include, but is not limited to:

a. Maps and compasses;

b. Techniques for walking a bearing (i.e., line of sight, leap frog, aiming off);

c. Location (i.e., triangulation, dead reckoning);

d. Route finding;

e. Use of additional tools such as altimeters and GPS.

2. Sequence activities to build on prior developed skills.
3. Use individual, small and larger groups to appropriately introduce techniques, permit individual skill acquisition, and build group leadership and problem-solving abilities.
4. Use teachable moments to reinforce skill development and take advantage of site-specific characteristics.
5. Introduce environmental considerations that may not be as acute on a trail (i.e,. environmental hazards) when bushwhacking.

River Crossing

General Procedures

1. Select an appropriate route during planning.
2. Monitor river conditions and weather reports prior to and during trips to areas where river crossing is planned for or may occur.
3. Prepare and supervise participants at all times.
4. Examine the option not to cross a river based on the ability of the weakest participant and river characteristics such as rate of flow, depth, riverbed and shoreline characteristics, downstream hazards, and air and water temperature.
5. Face upstream and if using a rope, cross on its downstream side.
6. Wear appropriate footwear such as tennis shoes or boots, secured sandals, or water shoes.
7. When carrying a pack, undo the waistband and sternum strap, and loosen the shoulder straps so the pack can be easily removed if necessary.
8. Shuffle feet across the bottom and do not cross or lift feet.
9. Consider having a person without a pack on each side of the crossing to lend assistance.
10. Consider stationing an instructor or strong swimmer downstream as a backup.
11. Cross alone only in water less than knee high.
12. Consider the chances and consequences of a fall when crossing on a log or rock-hopping prior to doing so.

Site Selection

1. Pick a wide, shallow stretch of water that is free from obstructions that could snag a rope.
2. The banks should not be steep.
3. The stretch of water below the fording point should be long, shallow, and free of hazards.

River Crossing Without a Rope

1. Double-Crossing: Two people face each other and hold shoulders. The larger person faces downstream to create an eddy for the smaller person. Small side-steps are taken alternately, beginning with the upstream person, each supporting the other while moving.

2. Triangle Crossing: Three people form a triangle, with the strongest person as point, facing upstream. The point calls "step right, step left" as the triangle moves across the river.
3. In-Line Crossing: At least three people form a line with the strongest person in the front facing upstream and using a long stick or paddle to support themselves. Waders carefully follow holding the shoulders of the person in front.

River Crossing With a Rope

1. Use the rope as a hand line and do not clip into it.
2. Anchor one end at least 5 feet on shore.
3. Three people cross using the triangle crossing technique holding on to the rope to anchor it to the far side at least 5 feet on shore.
4. The remainder of the group crosses using the rope for support, facing upstream.
5. The last three people untie the anchor and cross using the triangle crossing technique.

University of North Carolina at Charlotte—Venture Center
F Recreation
E Southeast Region
C University Students and General Population
S 11.09

River Crossings

Staff Responsibilities

1. Participants are not allowed to cross a river without instructor supervision.
2. Rivers crossings that are more than knee deep in more than a sluggish current will not be made without specific permission in advance by the director or the associate director.
3. This is potentially one of the most dangerous activities we encounter. Therefore, participants must be instructed and carefully supervised if a river crossing is necessary.
4. Instruct participants on techniques to use when serious consequences exist if an inappropriate approach were to be used.
5. Judgment: The first option is not to cross. Make this judgment based on the ability of the weakest participant: If s/he cannot make it, do not attempt to cross.

Safety Concerns

Choosing a site to cross.

1. Pick a wide, shallow stretch of water, free from obstructions.
2. The banks should not be steep.
3. The stretch of water below the fording point should be long and shallow.
4. Look downstream. If there are hazards that someone could be washed into, look for another crossing.
5. Crossing on a log can be dangerous if someone falls. Is the log wet? Is it a long fall? Are there hazards below or downstream? If so, don't allow students to cross.

Methods for crossing without a rope.

1. Form a triangle pointed upstream.
2. Have three or more people line up one behind another, all facing upstream. The upstream person moves first.
3. Have the whole group links arms, face the opposite bank, and wade across.
4. Use a stout stick as a third "leg" and to probe depth.
5. Cross alone only in very shallow water.

Using rope.

1. Use it only as a hand line. Participants should not clip in!
2. The instructor or strongest person and two others cross, holding on to the end of the rope, and anchor it on the far side, 5 to 6 feet above the river. They should use techniques described above in making their initial crossing.
3. The last person crosses in the same manner as the first.

In all crossings.

1. Face upstream: If a rope is used, cross on the downstream side of the rope.
2. Undo waistband and sternum strap and loosen shoulder straps so that the pack can be easily removed if necessary.
3. Wear tennis shoes or boots and remove socks.
4. Shuffle feet across. Do not cross feet or lift them.
5. Consider having a person with pack off at each shore, to steady people and ready to lend assistance if someone stumbles.
6. Boulder hopping may keep your feet dry but increases the possibility of injury.
7. Consider stationing an instructor or strong swimmer downstream as backup safety.
8. Consider the water temperature and risk of hypothermia in making your plans.

SECTION 12
CLIMBING ACTIVITIES

Charleston County Parks & Recreation	
	F Recreation
	E Southeast Region
	C General Population
	S 4.10, 12.01–12.09

Rock Climbing Trip Procedures and Guidelines

Program Ratio

- Ratios 1:6 with a minimum of two staff
- Maximum number of participants dependent on specific course area

Climbing Field Sites Currently Being Used

- See Site Plans for more details on locations and logistics at:
  - Crowder's Mountain State Park, North Carolina
  - Pilot Mountain State Park, North Carolina

Description of Course Environment

- Typically off trail: steep, rugged trails, uneven surfaces and cliffs.
- May include a variety of ecosystems.
- Primarily conducted in three-season conditions, spring, summer, and fall.
- Both staff and participants can belay depending upon goals of the group. All belaying rules apply to outdoor trips.

Safety Concerns (specific to this environment or activity)

- Trauma from falls
- Environmental problems related to program area (dehydration, hypo/hyperthermia, weather, animals, plants, etc.)
- Blisters and/or rashes
- Sudden lightning storms
- Trauma from falling objects/people
- Muscle and tendon damage
- Equipment failure

- Equipment misuse
- Improper belaying technique

Strategies for Minimizing Safety Concerns

- Practice standard participant management techniques (maintain hydration, take frequent breaks, etc.).
- Have entire group present when presenting important information (helmet areas, ledges, etc.).
- Teach and practice lightning drill before leaving (at premeeting or at trail head).
- One staff member must remain with group at all times.
- Wear approved climbing helmets when engaged in activity or resting/observing within the designated "helmet area."
- Trained staff leads daily equipment checks for both group and personal equipment.
- Check routes for loose debris.
- Stretch prior to activity.
- No person, staff included, should stand closer than 6 feet to the edge of a cliff without being tied into an anchor.
- Stay on established trails as much as possible.
- On off-trail sections follow the climber trails.
- Try to avoid areas where the travel is steeper (third class or harder).
- A hand-line can be rigged for participants to clip into.
- Consider a different access trail or have everyone rappel.
- No bouldering.
- No climbing or rappelling without a belay.

Equipment Requirements

- Equipment needs will very depending upon location, size of the group, type of activity and the needs and expectations of the participants.
- Ropes: standard single Kernmantle, dynamic UIAA certified ropes 50 to 60 meters long, 2 to 4 depending upon size of the group and the activities for that day.
- Webbing/cordelette: 1-inch tubular webbing of various lengths, cordelette 7 to 8 mm or 5.5 mm tech cord, 5 to 7 meters long. Depending upon number of ropes set up and conditions, it is recommended that the combined footage of the two be 25 to 50 meters.
- Harnesses and helmets: 1 each per participant and staff.
- Belay tools: 1 per team (1 tool per 2 climbers) plus 1 for each staff person on the trip.
- Participants can use their own personal gear subject to approval of the lead instructor.

- Locking carabiners: 1 per belay tool, 4 for each anchor system (2–4 systems required for 8–16 participants), 4 spare and 4 for rescues.
- Nonlocking carabiners: as many as are needed to carry and organize gear.
- Top rope rack in pack on gear sling (it will vary by location and needs/activities):
  - 1 to 2 sets of nuts or equivalent
  - 1 to 2 sets of hex type nuts or equivalent
- Rescue gear:
  - 4 locking carabiners
  - 1 set of prussic loops or ascenders with rigging (aiders and daisies, 2 each)
  - 1 Grigri
- Camping: see Site Plan and Campcraft section
- First-aid kit
- Travel: see vehicle use

Site Selection and Use

- All participants and staff will follow the Leave No Trace procedures.
- *Fixed anchors:* preexisting bolts can be used if the bolt and surrounding rock are inspected prior to each use and are in good condition. Two bolt anchors per anchor system are the minimum. Generally, it is not recommended to use fixed pitons unless you have tested them with a hammer.
- *Artificial anchors:* can be used if no bolts are present or are not usable
  - Minimum of three independent anchors.
  - All three must be solid and in at least two different crack systems.
  - Rock must be solid and not have any fractures or are loose.
- *Natural anchors*
  - Natural chockstones.
  - Trees are not permitted for use as anchors in NC State Parks.
  - Large unmovable well-seated rocks.
  - Use a preequalized anchor system rather than a self-equalizing system using webbing/cordelettes.
  - Rope to anchor system connection will be 2 carabiners reversed and opposed (can be locking or nonlocking).

Climbing/Rappelling Route Selection

- Select routes that meets the needs and abilities of the group, usually rated between 5.5 and 5.8.

- It is good to challenge climbers who are doing better and need a harder route.
- In rappelling areas, use a location that:
  - Will not interfere with other climbers.
  - Has suitable anchors for rappelling and belaying the rappeller (belay from top).
  - Has a "high" anchor point.
  - Has an "easy" or rounded "bowling ball" start
  - Where you can set up a releasable rappel if the rappellers hand could become trapped under the rappel rope during a rappel (most likely to happen on an abrupt edge that is undercut and free hanging).
  - Is free of loose rock, etc.
- See course outlines for specific methods for teaching and supervising climbing, belaying, and rappelling.

Emergency Procedures

- See Site Plans and Emergency Guidelines.

Group Supervision and Organization

- Please review camp craft section if overnight.
- Maintain verbal and/or visual contact with participants.
- Staff should direct and model accepted climbing etiquette.
- Staff should be familiar with the area designated for the trip and the routes.
- Staff must have a day plan, including evacuation routes.
- Staff should use games and initiatives to enhance the learning experience in problem solving and group interaction.
- Participants and staff must complete a Hold Harmless form prior to trip. Copies should be left with the program coordinator (ORC/ORS).
- Follow local guidelines and permit requirements (especially for setting anchors).
- To belay, you must have been checked out by the staff.

Supplemental Resource Information

- North Carolina Climber's Guide
- Leave No Trace

Chadwick School	*F* **Education**
	E **West Region**
	C **Students Grades K–12**
	S **4.10, 12.01, 12.03, 12.04, 12.07, 12.11**

Snow and Ice Climbing

1. Roped team climbing (where anchors are not employed) will be conducted only on terrain where a sliding fall can be easily arrested. Otherwise, running belay anchors or pitched climbing will be used.
2. All participants must demonstrate competence in the self-arrest before this technique will be relied upon.
3. When teaching self-arrest, the initial slope angle should be gentle enough that participants can stop easily; the runout should be hazard free, different positions should be taught. Participants must wear helmets and remove crampons during the self-arrest class.
4. Instructor-to-climber (actually climbing) ratio will not exceed 1:2; instructor-to-class size ratio will not exceed 1:12.
5. Sites chosen for ice climbing will be checked for objective hazards and current conditions to confirm the decision to use the routes, or not, on a given program day. Where possible historical data on the site and climbs will be collected; for example, knowing when the ice formed; the freeze/thaw cycles for the current season; what is behind the ice; what has happened to the routes in previous years.
6. The training area and routes selected are within the physical and psychological capabilities of participants.
7. Before attempting to glissade, a participant must have learned the proper use of ice-axe self-arrest.

Glacier Travel

1. Participants may not travel on crevassed glaciers without staff supervision.
2. Participants will be roped together when traveling on crevassed glaciers.
3. An instructor-to-student ratio of 1:3 will be used during glacier travel.
4. Only after a participant is in a safe area can they unrope.
5. A safe area is defined as a probed, wanded area or a crevasse-free moraine.
6. The last person into and the first person out of a safe area must be belayed.
7. When traveling on crevassed glaciers, rope teams will keep the rope fully extended between each member.

University of New Hampshire	*F* Education
	E Northeast Region
	C University Outdoor Education Students and General Population
	S 4.10, 12.01–12.09, 12.11

Mountaineering Guidelines

The following guidelines are common to all mountaineering activities conducted by the UNH OE program. The guidelines outlined here should be considered in addition to the General Activity Guidelines, General Climbing Guidelines, and Winter Activity Guidelines.

1. Minimum Staff Qualifications	6. Snow Climbing
2. Participant Qualifications	7. Ice Climbing
3. Site Selection	8. Travel in Avalanche Terrain
4. Supervision	9. Glacier Travel and Camping
5. Curriculum	

1. Minimum Staff Qualifications

At least one of the staff members on a given mountaineering expedition has undergone similar activities in the areas that are to be traveled in. All staff have experience at altitudes that will be reached, are competent in the instruction of mountaineering, and have the associated skills, including:

- Avalanche-hazard evaluation and rescue
- Steep snow, and ice climbing and descent
- Evaluation of crevasse hazard, roped glacier travel, crevasse rescue, and glacier camping
- Navigation
- Altitude-related illness

2. Participant Qualifications

- Have completed Kin 543 Winter Backpacking or have provided documentation of equivalent skill level.
- Have obtained appropriate vaccinations if the course will be run in a foreign country.

3. Site Selection

All sites and conditions fit the criteria outlined in General Activity Policies, General Climbing Policies, and Winter Activity Policies, in addition to the following concerns:

- Crevasse hazard
- Avalanche hazard
- Rock/icefall hazard
- Altitude
- Snow/ice conditions
- Accessibility of site on foot or by air
- Exposure to foreign disease

4. Supervision

- Participant medical forms are screened for medical or physical conditions, which could be aggravated by mountaineering (e.g., knee injury, previous cold injury, conditions predisposing the participant to altitude sickness).
- Participants are always with a staff member when traveling in hazardous terrain (e.g., avalanche or crevasse danger).

5. Curriculum

- Participants receive instruction in the following skill areas if applicable:
    - Avalanche hazard evaluation and search and rescue
    - Weather evaluation and forecasting
    - Steep snow and ice climbing
    - Evaluation of crevasse hazard and crevasse rescue
    - Glissading
    - Self-arresting
    - Rope team travel (stationary and running belays)
    - Navigation
    - Mountain travel
    - Altitude-related illness
    - Other technical climbing skills outlined in General Climbing Policies

6. Snow Climbing

- Participants undergo a snow school involving appropriate use of an ice axe low angle to steep conditions.
- Participants use stationary or running belays in situations of increased fall risk (e.g., steep snow where self-arrest is not possible, crevasse terrain).

- Crampons and belays should be used in icy or hard snow slopes where a self-arrest is unreliable.
- Glissading is done in areas with an adequate run-out zone and crampons should not be worn.
- Additional considerations for self-arrest practice are:
  - Participants are instructed to self-arrest only with the pick away from the chest.
  - An appropriate run-out exists in the practice area.
  - Participants will not accelerate to an inappropriate speed if they fail to arrest the fall.
  - Participants do not wear crampons when practicing.
  - Slope is free from obvious rocks or objects that participants may hit while sliding.

7. Ice Climbing

- Climbs are chosen based on their stability and group goals.
- Helmets are worn by staff and students while climbing, belaying, or while below unstable ice.
- Students should be instructed on the safe use and care of ice climbing equipment.
- Protective glasses or goggles should be worn while climbing.
- Top ropes should have reliable anchors as described in the General Climbing Guidelines; anchors used for top roping on glaciers in above-freezing temperatures should be checked frequently.

8. Travel in Avalanche Terrain

Travel in known avalanche terrain is generally avoided, but some advanced skills or courses (mountaineering, backcountry skiing, etc.) run by the UNH OE program may occur in areas with possible avalanche hazard. The following policies apply to any activities occurring in sites where possible avalanche hazard exists.

- An appropriate number of group members carry shovels and avalanche probes.
- All participants should carry avalanche transceivers in pretested working order when traveling in avalanche terrain.
- The instructor indicates when everyone should turn on and off avalanche transceivers.
- All students should be trained in the use of avalanche transceivers and should engage in avalanche rescue drills prior to traveling in avalanche terrain.
- Ski touring and mountaineering parties should follow standard travel, safety procedures, and terrain and stability analysis as outlined by the AAA.
- The group crosses questionable terrain one member at a time if possible.
- All open slopes between 20 and 60 degrees may be considered suspect and evaluated prior to further travel if deemed necessary by the staff.
- Activities may be suspended if avalanche danger is too high.

9. Glacier Travel and Camping

Supervision.

- Participants are always with a staff member when traveling in hazardous terrain (e.g., avalanche, crevasse danger).

Snow-covered glacier (above fern line).

- Staff and participants are dressed for a possible crevasse fall.
- Warm clothing is highly accessible.
- Each climber has two prussiks attached to the rope, rigged for ascending; each climber also has snow protection accessible for use in a rescue.
- When pulling loaded sleds across snow-covered glaciers, consideration is given to anchoring the rear of the sled to the trailing segment of a climbing rope.
- Suspect areas and snow bridges are probed prior to crossing.
- When crossing highly suspect terrain, participants and staff receive stationary belays.
- Camps are probed and an appropriate area is established and clearly marked. Participants and staff are belayed when they leave the probed area.
- Staff and participants travel in rope teams of three to five climbers.

Dry glaciers.

- Students are informed of the dangers of mulons, crevasses, and snow-covered patches.
- Camps should be made on moraines if possible, and tent terraces should be dismantled when leaving camp.

Curriculum.

- Participants have received adequate instruction in glacial travel and crevasse rescue techniques, including:
  - Evaluation of crevasse terrain and snow bridges
  - Probing
  - Route-finding
  - Rope team travel
  - Harness setups for glacial travel
  - Ascending techniques
  - Z drag
  - Snow and ice anchors
  - Belay systems

Wilderness Treatment Center	*F* Therapeutic
	E Northwest Region
	C Adolescent Males
	S 12.01–12.09

Rock Climbing

1. Climbing, when staffing and environmental factors permit, can be used as a component of recreation therapy.
2. Climbing activities will be conducted in a safe manner using proper techniques and skills.
3. The lead instructor facilitating rock-climbing activities is required to possess a high level of experience, training, and skill in top-rope rock climbing techniques, procedure and safety protocol. Prior to an instructor facilitating a rock-climbing activity, his/her qualifications, experience and skill are reviewed by the wilderness program coordinator.
4. Program staff assisting in the supervision of rock climbing activities is able to demonstrate a working knowledge of safe top-rope climbing systems, proper belaying techniques and procedures, awareness of environmental factors and other relevant skills. The lead instructor facilitating the activity is responsible for ensuring that assisting staff possess the above knowledge and skill.
5. Staff is required to be up to date on changes in technology and procedure for this activity. This is accomplished through continued outside training experiences and reading relevant literature. In addition, periodic in-service training sessions may be conducted as a forum to share experience and skills.
6. Top ropes with appropriate anchors will be used on all climbs. Wilderness instructors are responsible for setting up anchors and top ropes using proper techniques (Grayden, D. *Freedom of the Hills*. Seattle, WA: The Mountaineers).
7. Staff supervision is required for all rock climbing activities. Staff-to-patient ratio is not to exceed 1: 4.5 with a minimum of two staff present.
8. Climbing activities will be appropriate for patients' skill level.
9. No patients will lead climb.
10. Staff will be prepared for a rescue or medical emergency.
    - The staff team has at least one member with current WFR or equivalent and current CPR as the minimal level of medical training.
    - All other staff has a minimum of standard first aid and CPR and are familiar with the use of a rescue litter.
    - A first-aid kit and backboard will be available at the climbing site.
11. Staff will not engage patients in climbing activities that s/he is not properly trained and experienced in the handling of a rescue or medical emergency.

12. Staff is able to comprehend the therapeutic use of this activity and is able to integrate it into patients treatment.

Procedures

1. Prior to use by WTC, all climbing areas are researched for access, safety, cultural, and ecological concerns.
2. Prior to use, all climbing sites will be inspected for loose rock and other hazards.
3. All equipment will be inspected prior to use (see Climbing and Rappelling Equipment Maintenance Policy).
4. The climbing terrain is determined to be appropriate for patients skill level. Generally this includes climbs rated between 5.0 and 5.8.
5. Patients will be provided with water and food appropriate for the length of the activity.
6. Patients will be provided with clothing appropriate for the environmental concerns of the activity (refer to Clothing and Equipment Policy).
7. Rock climbing expectations will be discussed with patients prior to the activity that include but are not limited to:
   - Helmets will be worn at all times.
   - No one will be within 6 feet of the cliff edge unless properly anchored.
   - No throwing rocks or other objects at the climbing area.
   - No littering, smoking, or graffiti is allowed.
   - No horse play or running is allowed.
   - The group is to stay together in designated areas.
   - Never stand on ropes, harness, or webbing.
   - Do not drop carabineer, descenders, or belay devices.
   - No jewelry or loose clothing is allowed.
8. Instructors will lead participants in appropriate warm-up activities. This normally includes stretching and bouldering.
9. A locking carabiner and ATC or equivalent device will be used to belay all participants.
10. Climbers will tie into the end of the rope using a figure 8 follow-through, backed up by a double fishermen safety knot.
11. Staff is responsible for checking that knots are tied, carabineers locked, and harnesses are secured properly.
12. Patients need to demonstrate proper hand coordination and belay techniques prior to participating in an actual belaying situation.
13. Patients may only belay when closely supervised by staff.
14. Climbing and rapelling signals will be uniform throughout the program.

- Climber: "On Belay?"
- Belayer: "Belay On"
- Climber: "Climbing"
- Belayer: "Climb On"
- Climber: "Up Rope," "Slack," "Falling"
- Climber: "Off Belay"
- Belayer: "Belay Off"

15. Patients will be educated in the danger of loose and falling rocks. Patients will be instructed to use the signal "Rock!" in the event an object becomes dislodged.
16. Staff will discuss with participants how climbing can be used as a metaphor for their recovery.
17. Staff will be sensitive to the needs and concerns of the patients.
18. All equipment used in activities will be recorded in the climbing and recreation logs.

SECTION 13

MANUFACTURED CLIMBING WALLS

Charleston County Parks & Recreation	
	F **Recreation**
	E **Southeast Region**
	C **General Population**
	S **13.02, 13.03**

The Climbing Wall and Climbing Program Introduction

Mission Statement

The Charleston County Parks & Recreation Commission Climbing Program will improve the quality of life in Charleston County by offering diverse recreational opportunities and climbing-based adventure and educational programs.

Philosophy

The Charleston County Parks & Recreation Commission's Climbing Program is dedicated to experiential education based in an outdoor setting: including rock climbing, artificial wall climbing, and portable wall events.

Goals

- To promote awareness of safe and appropriate climbing practices.
- To increase participant knowledge base as related to rock climbing and artificial wall climbing.
- To provide the recreational experience of rock climbing for all individuals in Charleston County.
- To provide training and instruction to professionals in the field of outdoor recreation on the topic of climbing wall operations.
- To promote a positive image of climbing and help educate participants and the general public on safe climbing principals.

Skills Proficiency Check Sheet for Climbing Programs

Wall assistant proficiency exam.

Skills: Basic Knots	
	Figure 8 Follow-Through
	Tying into Climb
	Double Figure 8
	Grapevines in Opposition
	Coiling Ropes
	Bowline on a Coil
	Double-Checks for the Belayer and Climber
	Back-Up Belays
	Belay Tests for Top Ropes
	Qualify the Customer
	Test Explanation
	Climber: Proper Tie-In, Harness on Correctly, Double-Check
	Belayer: Proper Belay Tool Setup, Use of Ground Anchor, Double-Check
	Staff Double-Check for Both the Climber and Belayer
	Provides Back-Up Belay
	Pass/Fail Standard
Grigri Use	
	Grigri Setup and Use
	Teaching Grigri Use
	Supervising Belayers Using the Fixed Grigri System

Group Procedures	
	Group Introduction, Safety Talk, Rules
	Portable Wall Use and Rules
	Bouldering Use and Rules
	Top-Rope Use and Rules
	Chaperon/Belayers Supervision

Additional Notes: ____________________

____

Coordinator Signature____________________
Date__________

Skills classes and lessons proficiency exam.

	Everything in Wall Assistant
	Introductions and Safety Talk
	Harness Use, Knots, Double-Check
	Belay Tool Setup, Double-Check
	Belay Commands
	Cross-Check (Climber-Belayer)
	Hand Positions/Motions
	Back-Up Belays
	Catching Falls
	Proper Lowering
	Explain Belay Tests
Lead Climbing/Belay Lessons: Climbing	
	Introductions and Safety Talk
	Gear: Ropes/Draws
	Climber Responsibilities
	The Clipping "Standard"
	Proper Falling Technique
	Back Cleaning
Lead Climbing/Belay Lessons: Belaying	
	Belying and Belayer Responsibilities
	Back-Up Belays
	Catching Fall a Lead Fall: Dynamic vs. Static
	Lowering and Back Cleaning
	Explain Lead Belay/Climbing Tests

Rappelling Lessons	
	Introductions and Safety Talk
	Harness Use, Knots, Rappel Tool Setup, Double-Checks
	Self-Belays and Back-Ups
	Rappel Commands
	Cross-Check
	Back-Up Belays
	Rappel Rope Setup

Additional Notes: ______________________________

____

Coordinator Signature______________________

Date__________

Route setting: wall tech and wall assistant proficiency exam.

	Ascend 50′ Mechanical
	Self-Belay With a Grigri
	Proper Use of Holds/Bolts
	Use of Daisies, Fifis, etc.
	Hold Inspection
	Personal Safety and Back-Up Systems
	Route Design/Safety TR
	Route Design/Safety Lead
	Hazard Awareness

Additional Notes: ______________________________

____

Coordinator Signature______________________

Date__________

Wall technician proficiency exam.

	Everything in Wall Assistant
	Water Knot
	Prussic Knot
	Munter Hitch
	Mule Knot
	Munter/Mule Knot
	Familiarity With Other Belay Tools: Belay Plates, Grigris, Figure 8s, Munter Hitch
	Portable Wall Setup/Take Down
	Battery Charging
	Trouble Shooting
	Locking Down an Auto-Belay
	Checking Auto Belays
	Climber Use/Rules
	Emergency Procedures
	Ascend 50′ With Knots and Ascenders
	Escape the Belay
	Unweighted Belay Transfer
	Weighted Belay Transfer
	Quick Don Harness
	Counterweighted Ascent
	Standing Hip Belay
	Change Over From Ascent to Descent and Descent to Ascent

Additional Notes: ____

____

Coordinator Signature______________________________

Date____________

Portable wall technician proficiency exam.

	Must Be a Wall Tech
	Paperwork
	Vehicle Use
	Site Selection
	Cash Management
	Connecting PW to Van
	Towing PW
	Electric Brake Use
	Training Volunteers
	PW Setup
	Needed Equipment
	Emergency Procedures

Additional Notes: ____

____

Coordinator Signature______________________________

Date______________

SECTION 14
BICYCLE TOURING AND MOUNTAIN BIKING

University of New Hampshire	*F* **Education**
	E **Northeast Region**
	C **University Outdoor Education Students and General Population**
	S **4.10, 14.01–14.08**

Bike Touring

1. Minimum Staff Qualifications	5. Equipment
2. Route Selection	6. Minimum Recommended Curriculum Content
3. Appropriate Operating Conditions	7. Additional Guidelines
4. Supervision and Group Organization	8. Activity Brief

1. Minimum Staff Qualifications

- Have appropriate training for the environment and conditions where the program occurs.
- Possess appropriate maintenance/repair skills for the equipment being used.

2. Route Selection

- Course areas for bike touring generally encompass large areas and may span multiple states. Routes are chosen based on the following general considerations:
  - Legal bike routes—the intended route follows roads that legally permit bicycle traffic.
  - Appropriate route—the route is chosen based on the age, maturity, and ability of the participants as well as the experience of the staff.
  - Road width and traffic congestion.
  - Availability of bike or breakdown lanes.

3. Appropriate Operating Conditions

- Darkness—riding should not occur after dusk or before dawn.
- Diminished visibility—Riding activities should cease or be postponed in heavy rain/fog in which visibility is reduced to 500 feet or less.
- Lightning—when thunder and/or lightning are present, regroup and do not resume riding until neither is present (this also applies to other extreme weather conditions like hail and heavy winds). Refer to Lightning Guidelines.

- Rain—If there is good visibility and light traffic, riding is acceptable if participants have appropriate equipment.
- Heavy traffic and rain—consider stopping or walking.
- Note: When riding in reduced visibility all staff and participants should display a red flashing light to increase their visibility to other riders and drivers.

4. Supervision and Group Organization

- Ratio—12 participants:2 staff
- Lead and Sweep—On most experiences, staff will be in the back ("last rider") and front of the group. This procedure is rarely altered based on the competence level of the group or the presence of a lag van/support.
- The "last rider" carries the first-aid kit and bike repair kit.
- Conduct check-in stops at least once every hour.
- If deemed appropriate by the staff and participants, a participant may stop alone (e.g., for a bathroom break), but the participant must leave the bike visible from the road.

5. Equipment

- Equipment Checks—Perform a daily, individual bike check before departure, including brakes, tires, derailleurs, quick-release levers, pack straps, chain, wheel trueness, accessories, bearings (wheels, crank, headset) nuts, and bolts. This bike check will be supervised by staff according to the participant's experience level.
- Helmets—All riders are required to wear a properly fitted cycling helmet.
- Visibility—Each rider should be equipped with a reflective vest and/or a bicycle flag. Each rider should also carry a red safety light for use in reduced visibility.

6. Minimum Recommended Curriculum Content

Most participants will already have some level of recreational cycling experience in their background. They may not, however, have any experience riding a loaded bicycle within a large group of riders. For this reason it is important to review and instruct some basic skills of riding as they apply to touring. Recommended content is as follows:

- Basic riding skills including:
  - Several positions on handlebars
  - Handling road hazards (potholes, railroad tracks, etc.)
  - Riding in a pack
  - Drafting
  - Steady, even pacing (e.g., 75 rpm)
  - Smooth peddling
  - Proper shifting

    - Proper braking
    - Hill climbing/descending techniques
- Verbal communication including:
    - "Car back"—informing the cyclists in front of you that a car is approaching.
    - "Passing on your left"—informing the biker, pedestrian, horse rider, etc. that you are passing them on their left side.
    - "Brake!"—informing the person behind you if you must brake suddenly.
- Hand signals for turning and stopping
- Map reading
- Applicable traffic rules
- Proper bike loading
- Basic maintenance and repair skills including:
    - Changing/patching tires
    - Adjusting brakes and derailleurs
    - Removing and replacing wheels

7. Additional Guidelines for Bike Touring

- Oversee daily bike checks prior to trip departure.
- Perform a "shakedown" or pretrip skills check prior to the experience, which will include an assessment on braking, shifting, riding a loaded bicycle, practicing group riding procedures, discussing separated group procedures, and reviewing road rules, safety, and riding tips.
- Review specific rules that apply to intersections/crossing streets:
    - At intersections, have participants get off and walk their bikes across the road.
    - When more than two lanes of traffic exist, *always* have a leader on each side of the road, helping participants cross (with young participants, do this at intersections).
- All staff and participants adhere to all traffic rules and regulations (e.g., stop signs, traffic lights, crosswalks).
- Keep a minimum of 75 feet between cyclists and maintain visual contact with bicycle in front and back you, except to pass:
    - Passing is permitted only if a leader deems participants can judge when adequate visibility and space is available for passing.
    - Never pass on a downhill.
    - Always use appropriate verbal communication when passing.
- Ride single file with the flow of traffic, staying as close to the right side of the road as possible. If there is a separate lane specifically for cyclists, travel in that lane.

- Review rules for descending hills:
  - Participants should descend at a speed at which they feel comfortable and in control.
  - If a hill has the potential for an accident for any reason (e.g., steepness, bad shoulder, rough surface), position a person in the middle of the hill off the road to limit the participants' speed so as to prevent an accident and/or respond to an accident.
  - Excessive speed coupled with a heavy load on the rear of the bike results in lack of maneuverability and loss of control; it is very important to instruct participants on how to appropriately descend hills.
- No swerving or zigzaging while ascending.
- Whenever participants are required to walk their bikes, always make sure they are putting their bike between themselves and the road. Have participants walk their bikes in any/all of the following conditions:
  - In and through parking lots.
  - In and around towns, especially with young participants.
  - Across any busy streets or intersections.
  - When crossing over railroad tracks.
  - Walk bikes across bridges on the sidewalk, or if there is no sidewalk or if the bridge is too narrow to walk across, have both leaders ride side-by-side behind the group to cross the bridge, which enables the group to take up the whole lane so cars are unable to pass.
  - When there is a lot of water on the road, go slowly or walk around deep puddles and be aware that wet brakes do not work as well as dry brakes.
  - When crossing running water on pavement, staff assess the conditions and determine if a designated person should warn participants of running water and/or if the highly deep or fast water requires the group to walk together.
  - Grooved pavement or grids on bridges require staff to assess the riding ability of the group and decide if the participants can ride or must walk.
- Do not ride double on one bike.

8. Activity Brief

- Educational objective of the activity
- Known hazards in the course area possibly including but not limited to:
  - Traffic
  - Weather conditions
  - Bridges
  - Busy intersections
  - Passing strategies
  - Minimum distance between bikers

- Parameters for participants
  - No hitchhiking
  - Speed constraints
  - No switchbacks or zigzags on hill climbs
  - Leave bike in view of road when you stop

9. Route Review

- Emergency contact information—Every participant should carry the emergency contact information for the trip leaders and the contact person.
- What to do if you become lost.
- What to do if you or another participant becomes injured.
- Staff location or contact method during the activity.
- Location of first-aid and rescue equipment.
- Time limit.

Mountain Biking

1. Minimum Staff Qualifications	5. Minimum Recommended Curriculum Content
2. Route Selection	6. Additional Guidelines
3. Appropriate Operating Conditions	7. Activity Brief
4. Supervision and Group Organization	

1. Minimum Staff Qualifications

In addition to the staff qualifications indicated in Bike Touring Polices, staff have appropriate mountain biking experience and skills.

2. Route Selection

Course areas for mountain biking are chosen based on participant competency and the educational goals for the activity.

3. Appropriate Operating Conditions

In some cases rain and other adverse weather may add to the excitement of mountain biking for riders who have developed basic skills. Refer to Bike Touring Guidelines for additional considerations.

- Puddles caused by rain or runoff should be avoided unless the rider is intimately familiar with the terrain.

- Refrain from biking on days with heavy rain.
- Avoid late afternoon rides in areas with thick forest as it gets darker in the woods earlier.

4. Supervision and Group Organization

- Participant-to-staff ratios change and adapt with a variety of conditions, student qualifications, and staff experience. A maximum ratio to consider is 12 participants:2 staff.
- Staff position themselves in the first and last positions when biking with the group, unless conditions permit participant leadership.
- The last ("sweep") staff carries the first-aid kit and bike repair kit.
- With less precise maps, the first staff member appoints a participant to direct the rest of the group at ambiguous areas on the route. Participants can ride ahead when they have demonstrated appropriate responsibility and are given strict guidelines as to when to stop and wait for staff.
- Leave a drop (person who directs riders) in the middle of a hill to reduce participants' speed if it has the potential for an accident (e.g., severe angle, highly technical, rocky, rutted).
- It may be fine for a participant to stop on her/his own for a bathroom break or to obtain water. However, when doing so, a student must leave the bike visible from the trail and inform at least one other person. With some groups, more specific supervision may be required.

5. Minimum Recommended Curriculum Content

Verbal communication and warnings to other group members increases awareness and are used, including:

- "Biker down"—informing the cyclists that a biker has fallen.
- "Passing on your left"—informing the bikers, pedestrians, horse riders, etc., that you are passing on their left side.
- "Brake"—informing the bikers behind you that you are applying your brakes.

6. Additional Guidelines

- When passing pedestrians or horses, show respect by slowing to an appropriate speed or even stopping and walking your bike.
- When stopping alone, place your bike out of the way where it is visible to the next rider. Inform at least one other rider that you are stopping.
- Anticipate other trail users around corners or in blind spots.
- Spacing depends on the speed of the riders, the trail width, number of obstacles, etc. and thus varies when off road. The following are a few areas that require extra attention:
  - Space out up to 100 feet on inclines to prevent having to get off of your bike in the event that the person in front of you does.

    - Space out at least 50 feet on technical descents.
    - Allow ample spacing on single track.
- Riding single file is prudent in most instances (e.g., on single-track, flat dirt roads, or steep dirt roads), though abandoned dirt roads/fire roads can be conducive to riding side by side. Be alert for fellow bikers/hikers/horseback riders.
- Keep right especially on dirt roads and be aware of vehicles.
- Say "passing on the left" or "passing on the right" if you are attempting to pass someone.
- Passing should only be attempted if there is ample room.

7. Activity Brief

- Educational objective of the activity
- Known hazards in the course area possibly including but not limited to:
    - Rivers and other bodies of water
    - Human-made hazards (barbed wire, etc.)
    - Roads
    - Potential wildlife hazards (e.g., ticks)
    - Wet roots and rocks
- Parameters for participants
    - No hitchhiking
- What to do if you become lost
- What to do if you or another participant becomes injured
- Staff location or contact method during the activity
- Location of first-aid and rescue equipment
- Avoidance of private property
- Time limit

SECTION 15
CAVING

Prescott College	F	Education
	E	Rocky Mountain Region
	C	University Students
	S	4.10, 15.01, 15.04, 15.06

Caving

Horizontal Caving: minimum staff-to-student ratio is 1:8

1. Artificial mines and mine shafts are not caves and should not be entered under the guise of cave exploration.
2. Students should be screened for suitability to safely take part in the activities involved in caving, especially the ability to stay together and work as a group.
3. Helmets should be worn in a cave at all times. Footwear and clothing should be checked for appropriateness.
4. Each student should be required to have a light that can be mounted on a helmet. Each student should carry a spare set of batteries.
5. Except for caves that the instructor determines to be of a simple and straightforward nature, two additional sources of light should be required besides the light mounted on the helmet. Each flashlight should have its own set of primary and spare batteries
6. The keys to the vehicle(s) should be left in a designated hiding spot near the vehicles. Emergency phone numbers and student medical forms should be left on the driver's seat or dashboard.
7. A first-aid kit containing essential supplies should be carried by the group. A more fully equipped first-aid kit should be left outside the cave.
8. A piece of webbing for use as a hand line should normally be carried by the group. Students should be encouraged to spot one another when moving through difficulty terrain.
9. In very wet caves, a carbide lamp and space blanket should be carried by the group so that a heat tent can be rigged in case of emergency. A wool hat and sleeping bag should be left easily accessible at the vehicles or cave entrance.
10. Students should not be permitted to do any solo caving during the course.
11. There are caves or sections of caves that flood after storms, that require submersion in frigid water, that require free climbing or unsafe exposure, and similar risks that cannot be justified in a program setting. Caves with these kinds of hazards should be avoided. If the instructor is unfamiliar with a cave, the instructor should take precautions to ensure that environmental hazards be detected and avoided.

Vertical Caving: minimum staff-to-student ratio is 1:6

1. The use of ropes and vertical techniques introduces the possibility of equipment failure or human error. Above-ground practice, confidence in student's abilities, and close supervision of the activity are obviously essential.
2. One of the two additional light sources should be carried on a string around the neck or in an equally accessible location.
3. The instructor should be present during all rope work.
4. All vertical techniques should first be practiced above ground.
5. Vertical caving shall be limited to rappelling/ascending fixed lines and to down-climbing/ up-climbing while belayed from above. No lead climbing should be undertaken.
6. Helmets, harnesses, climbing systems, ropes and webbing should be inspected prior to entering the cave. Helmets used for vertical caving should be only those designed for caving or climbing.
7. All anchor systems should be rigged or inspected by the instructor. All bolts used for anchors should be backed up whenever possible.
8. Students should not share gear for rappelling and ascending but should have their own, except at the discretion of the instructor.
9. Rope ascending systems should meet generally held standards for single rope technique (SRT), so that failure of any one sling or ascender maintains the climber in an upright position. "Chicken loops" should be used to ensure that feet do not come out.
10. Whenever possible, the instructor should check the student's attachment to the rope before rappelling. A knot should be tied into the end of a rope that is being used for rappelling.
11. For long rappels: The use of rappel racks should be preferred over figure 8s. A prussik or mechanical ascender should be available for easy clipping in. A student should be positioned so as to be able to apply a bottom belay.

University of North Carolina at Charlotte—Venture Center
F Recreation
E Southeast Region
C University Students and General Population
S 15.01–15.09

Caving

Purpose

1. To provide the unique challenge of adjusting to dark, close, underground environments.

Staff Responsibilities

1. Proper prior planning is necessary for a caving trip, due to the fragile environment and unfamiliar terrain into which the participants are about to enter.
2. Staff should carry the following equipment in their packs or on their persons when caving: extra hat (for warmth), water and food that they can share with participants if needed.
3. Instructors must have a working knowledge of the cave system in which the workshop is to take place, including places where spotting is needed, places where extra caution is needed, places where a hand line is necessary, and places that should be avoided altogether.
4. Discuss at orientation claustrophobia and anxiety in tight spaces. Anticipate problems individuals may have in traveling through tight crawls. Monitor the participants while caving, looking for signs of discomfort.
5. Keep track of participants. Conduct head counts at major junctions. Consider implementing a buddy system.
6. Don't lead or guide the group through the cave. Allow them to experience the thrill of being a scout or explorer. One staff member should stay close enough to the front to monitor the lead.

Safety Concerns

1. There must be three sources of light per person (headlamp, back-up flashlight, candles).
2. A first-aid kit will be carried in the cave.
3. All participants while exploring the cave will wear helmets. Helmets may be removed when resting in large rooms.
4. Never travel with less than four people in a group.
5. Participants must be instructed in recognition, symptoms, and treatment of hypothermia before entering cave. Instructors must ensure that all participants have appropriate clothes. Extra dry clothes should be available.

6. The Stokes litter, hypo kit, and a climbing rope will be available for emergencies (usually it is best to store them in the vehicle).
7. Mention methods of travel in a cave: walking, crawling, sliding, and land climbing.
8. Emphasize accident prevention: An evacuation underground is much more difficult than on a backpacking expedition. Teach and demonstrate spotting if appropriate.
9. Warn about the possibility of dangerous passages: breakdowns, flooding, pits, loose rocks, slippery surfaces, etc.
10. Do not change Coleman lantern mantles in a cave, since during its first lighting a mantle gives off toxic fumes. Light new mantles outside.
11. Teach techniques to avoid getting lost: name your own landmarks; remember climbs, turns, etc.; look in all directions: up, down, left right; look behind you, as things look different on the way out.
12. Cavers should stay together in groups no smaller than four (except for in-place solos.) Generally one staff should be with each group.
13. If a group is lost, have a group discussion to examine options: trying to get back to last place definitely recognized, staying in one place waiting for help, and/or banging on rocks to attract help from others in the cave. It may be appropriate to teach search and rescue.
14. If setting up camp in a cave, light Coleman lantern and have participants turn off lamps, in order to conserve batteries.
15. For lightning protocols and lightning policy, see page 123 of Venture Center manual.

Teaching Outline

Safety.

- Discuss safety issues from above as appropriate.

Geology and life in the cave.

- Formation of particular caves:
  - Vadose: created by the mechanical force of moving water;
  - Phreatic: created by the chemical solution of limestone: calcite ($CaCO^3$), which is formed by deposition of sea shells, is dissolved by carbonic acid ($H2CO^3$), formed by groundwater and decomposing plant life, yielding CO^2.
- Formation growth (speleothems): The opposite of cave formation: created when carbonic acid containing calcite acid in solution hits air in passages, CO^2 dissipates, depositing calcite into stalagmites, stalactites, soda straws, and draperies. Speleothems form slowly so take great care not to destroy them.
- Cave flora and fauna.
- Recognizing active formations and taking greater care not to interfere with them.

Conservation.

- Present day ethics mandate carrying out all waste, including spent carbide and solid human waste. Carry out liquid human waste if no water source exists in the cave.
- Vandalism, such as graffiti or the destruction of rock formations, will not be tolerated.
- In winter months, bats are in hibernation. Disturbing a bat in this stage affects its ability to survive through the winter. Therefore, it is important not to touch or disturb bats with light or excessive noise or body heat.
- Touching active formations interferes with their growth processes. Wear gloves to reduce impact of body oils on the cave.
- Avoid dropping particles of food and carbide in cave.

SECTION 16

HORSEBACK RIDING AND PACK ANIMALS

Camp Woodson	*F* **Therapeutic**
	E **Southeast Region**
	C **Incarcerated Youth**
	S **16.04**

Horseback Riding

Safety Policy

The director will designate site leaders for horseback riding activities.

Horseback Riding Site Leader Roles and Responsibilities

The horseback riding site leader is ultimately in charge of the safety and quality of the student riding experience. Typically the site leader delegates work projects to other staff so they can pay full attention to the horse program. Responsibilities include checking tack in and out, ensuring it is safe and appropriate for the student and horse, planning lessons to be challenging, fun, and success oriented, and being the on-site expert to make technical equipment and safety judgment calls. Additionally, site leaders facilitate debriefs and help students make a connection between their learning experience and their life at home.

Qualifications/Minimum Skills for Site Leader

Site leader candidates should have at least 2 years general experience with horses. They should be proficient in English riding techniques and should have a strong working knowledge of horse behavior and safety management around horses. Candidates should have knowledge of the individual characteristics and personalities of horses used with the program and should be able to appropriately match horse and rider. They should have working knowledge of tack and equipment and be able to recognize missing or misplaced parts. Candidates should have an effective teaching style with knowledge of grooming techniques, riding activities, and lesson progression. They should be able to recognize physical problems with horses and be able to recognize and correct the students' riding faults.

Horseback Riding Site Leader Checkout Procedure

1. Candidate notifies the director that s/he would like to be checked out.
2. The director or designee arranges a convenient time to talk about the candidate skill level and experience. Candidate demonstrates a thorough understanding of Woodson policies, guidelines and philosophy.
3. If candidate meets above qualifications, a date is scheduled to meet and ride at the ranch.
4. Candidate demonstrates a working knowledge of the ranch, trails, and individual horses. Candidate demonstrates ability to handle horses with a variety of temperaments and demonstrates proficient English riding technique on several horses in a variety of conditions. Candidate may then schedule a time to work as "acting site leader" under the supervision of a site leader on a student riding day.
5. After successfully demonstrating leadership, management, and teaching ability with students, horses, and staff, the candidate will be notified by the director that s/he is a Woodson horseback riding site leader.

Prescott College	*F* **Education**
	E **Rocky Mountain Region**
	C **University Students**
	S **4.10, 16.01–16.10**

Equestrian Activities

Minimum staff-to-student ratios for mounted activities is 1:6.

General Guidelines

1. Helmets will be available to students for use during any activity involving direct contact with horses. SEI certified helmets will be worn during any activity where a fall would be likely to result in an injury (e.g., at any gate above a walk, on uneven or rocky terrain).

2. Participants will be instructed in and practice effective dismounts prior to any mounted work. Participants will be oriented to potential risks from working with horses.
3. Participants will be instructed on the appropriate manner to approach and move around horses.
4. Participants will receive direct instruction on each new skill (e.g., haltering, leading, tacking, mounting, two-point). For specific educational outcomes, it may be appropriate to allow for initial direct experience or experimentation, in a controlled setting, prior to direct instruction.
5. Participants will be taught to two-point or post any gate faster than a walk.
6. Participants will demonstrate an ability to have the horse bend/yield to both sides and back up from the ground prior to any mounted work.
7. When securing a horse with a lead rope it is recommended that the horse is tied to the highest secure object available. When appropriate, utilize holding or ground tying to maximize relational horsemanship.
8. Animals will be provided an ethically safe environment. Regular veterinary, dental, and hoof care will be utilized to maintain the health of all animals. The least-restrictive environment possible will be used for the housing of animals (e.g. pasture or paddocks with shelter are preferable to confinement in box stalls).

Horseback Riding Site Leader Checkout Criteria

1. Candidate demonstrates a high degree of safety consciousness. S/he must exercise an awareness of group safety at all times.
2. Candidate is able to brief students and staff on the hazards and safety precautions.
3. Candidate demonstrates their ability to teach the proper techniques for grooming and tacking.
4. Candidate demonstrates their ability to "manage" a riding lesson and trail ride. As "the person in charge," coordinate a plan with staff, oversee smooth overall communication and decision making, ensure safety for entire ride, and demonstrate ability to coach students gripped with fear, unwilling to cooperate, and acting out on a horse.
5. Candidate reacts quickly, calmly, and effectively in moments of crisis to respond to hazards.
6. Candidate provides a structured, fun, success-oriented learning environment for students.
7. Candidate is able to work cooperatively with staff and give and receive feedback on performance.
8. Candidate demonstrates an understanding of "why we ride" and communicates this understanding to staff and students.

Note: The staff overseeing the horseback leader checkout should not allow a serious incident to develop. Provide room for the candidate to recognize and correct the situation but do not jeopardize the safety or quality of the student experience.

SECTION 17
WINTER ACTIVITIES

Wilderness Treatment Center	*F* Therapeutic
	E Northwest Region
	C Adolescent Males
	S 4.10, 17.11–17.17

Winter Trip Policy

Policy

It is the policy of the Wilderness Treatment Center to make the wilderness trip a safe, positive, and achievable experience.

Procedures

1. Staff-to-patient ratio is 1:4.5 with a minimum of two staff per trip.
2. Instructors must always put the safety and well-being of the group as their top priority.
3. The first couple of days should be short in distance to allow ample time for good instruction. The success and safety of the trip often depend on starting a trip in this manner. In the winter a minimum of 2 hours of daylight should be planned for properly getting camp set up and a meal cooked. Avoid making camp in the dark.
4. Early in the trip, plan on extra time to give good instruction on trail and skiing techniques, map reading and route finding, proper food and water intake, low-impact camping techniques, setting up a good camp, proper use of stoves, proper care of equipment, tips on sleeping warm, drying out wet items, foot care, and cooking tips. Sequence activities appropriately.
5. The instructors will split up and sleep with the patients in different tents for the first five nights of the trip in order to teach and monitor the winter techniques of caring for oneself. If conditions warrant, the instructors should continue this procedure at any time during the trip. A female instructor will have a minimum of two patients with her in a tent. Good instruction on sleeping warm, drying out wet items, keeping boots from freezing, keeping morale and spirits high, and helping out one another are important. Instructors should lead by example.
6. Instructors should stress being responsible and well organized. Winter teaches a harsh lesson to those who get sloppy and careless. Minor problems can rapidly "snowball" into serious problems.
7. Although winter trips can be demanding, plan for fun activities. Push the patients when needed, but do not turn the trip into a marathon ordeal with a lot of negative feelings.

8. Safety concerns are greatly amplified by the sometimes harsh winter environment. Good instruction and monitoring of the proper use of food, water, protective clothing, and shelter can make all the difference.

9. Caloric intake needs to be greatly increased in winter. Additional calories can be added to meals by adding butter, cooking oil, cheese, powdered milk, etc. "Gorping up" at rest breaks is important.

10. Eating snacks at bedtime and during the night can help a person stay warmer. Foods high in fat content help keep you warmer over a longer period of time. Breakfast and supper should be one-pot meals for the most part. Fast meals limit the amount of down time where patients may become inactive and cold.

11. Use warm-up activities before engaging in hiking, skiing, and snowshoeing.

12. Water is very important in the winter. Dehydration greatly increases the chance of getting frostbite and hypothermia. A minimum of 4 quarts of water per person should be consumed daily. Gatorade on occasion helps put electrolytes and salts back in the body, which are most commonly lost through sweating. The color of one's urine can indicate if one is becoming dehydrated. Urine should be a light yellow color and without a strong smell. If dehydrated, urine is dark in color and smells strongly. Each meal should have several hot drinks included. Warm water is absorbed more quickly by the body than cold water. Make sure patients drink frequently on the trail to maintain hydration. Take advantage of water sources.

13. Proper use of protective clothing is very important. Use of a layering system helps control the body's thermostat. Avoid overheating as well as underheating whenever feasible. Put on more layers of clothing or take off layers to maintain a comfortable zone. Monitor the group often. Do not wear parkas while skiing; save the parkas for camp. Do not let the patients stand around in a wool sweater soaking up the falling snow or rain; have them put on rain gear. Over 50% of the body's heat escapes through the head. Have patients wear their bomber hat and neck gaiter when on rest break, standing around camp, and if sleeping cold at night. Use ensolite pads underneath oneself to keep the ground cold from robbing your body heat. Do not let people lie or sit in the snow. Go to lengths to avoid becoming wet. Keep items warm and dry by sleeping with them in the sleeping bags at night. Wet items should be put in the area from the chest to the knees; do not put wet items at the foot of the sleeping bag; items will not dry out. Avoid using camp fires to dry out items as this practice usually ends up wasting time, energy, and burns up a lot of equipment. Burned equipment can seriously jeopardize the safety of the group. Fires are only for emergency situations.

14. Proper shelter placement and construction is another important aspect of safe winter camping. Proper instruction on site selection should consider water, wind, widow makers, and avalanche hazards. A close water source can eliminate the need of melting snow for water. Placement of the campsite out of the wind is vital for safe winter camping. Avoid dead trees in the camp area if possible. Avoid camping in or near avalanche hazards. Always keep in mind that avalanches occasionally overrun their boundaries.

15. When using tents for shelter, give proper instruction to avoid broken tent poles, rips in the fabric, and broken zippers. Stress TLC on all equipment. Use skis to flatten out and

firm up a good base for the tent. Keep tent windows unzipped so that proper ventilation ban be maintained. Closed tents lead to unnecessary humidity and wetness. Try to brush off as much snow as possible when entering a tent.

16. Include boot brushes when packing tents. Wind breaks can be made by digging down into the snow, using snow blocks, and mounding snow around the tents.
17. Do not camp at or near trail heads during any phase of the wilderness trip. Plan to hike or ski at least 2 to 3 miles on the last day of the trip.
18. Snow caves are time consuming to build but offer maximum security from the hazards of winter weather. Care and detail are needed in proper snow cave construction. The group should put on rain gear as building a snow cave is wet work. Establish a boundary with markers so that someone does not accidentally step through the roof of the snow cave. A snow drift can work well as one can tunnel horizontally rather than having to dig down before going horizontally. It works best if the outside entrance is somewhat lower than the floor of the snow cave so that cold air will flow out rather than settle in the snow cave. The entrance should be shorter than the snow cave room to trap heat inside. Try to keep the entrance tunnel and room ceilings arched to avoid sagging and collapsing. The roof should have 18 inches of snow in it for proper support. A good rule of thumb is to stop digging when you can see light coming through the snow. Make sure the inside ceiling is smooth to avoid water from dripping off points onto the user. A smooth ceiling will direct the condensation and other moisture to run down the side to the floor. Use a ski pole to probe through the ceiling and create ventilation holes so carbon dioxide does not build up inside. Avoid bumping the ceiling while using the snow cave. Avoid connecting one snow cave to another cave, as this practice seems to create a "draft tube" at times. The temperature in a snow cave usually ranges from 31 to 35 degrees. Keep the entrance at least partially open for proper ventilation. Do not cook or use lanterns in snow caves as carbon monoxide buildup can be dangerous. This practice will also make the snow cave very damp and humid. After finishing construction of the snow cave, have the group change into dry, warm clothing.
19. Avalanche awareness is a must for instructors. A basic avalanche course is mandatory for lead instructors and very much preferred for other staff. Annual training opportunities will be available to WTC staff. On wilderness trips proper instruction on route selection, snow pack analysis, snow pack stability and rescue is important. (See Mountain Snow Travel Policy for detailed information on this topic.)
20. Travel together as a group. Instructors should always travel with the patients. Stress the importance of good communication between the "point person" and the "sweep person." Stop at any trail intersection or junction to make sure the group all go in the same direction. Travel only as fast as the slowest person.

Santa Fe Mountain Center	*F*	**Therapeutic**
	E	**Rocky Mountain Region**
	C	**Youth and Families**
	S	**17.03, 17.05–17.10**

Snowshoeing

Rules

1. Sufficient and properly sized equipment shall be provided or approved by SFMC. Ensure that each participant is properly equipped for the activity.
2. Instructors shall file a detailed route plan and timetable with supervisory staff.

Procedures/Considerations

1. Basic skill proficiency should be developed before travel with packs or overnight camping is combined with travel.
2. Participants should only be allowed to travel routes that are appropriate to their demonstrated skill levels.
3. Carry a repair kit for field repairs of poles, bindings, snowshoes, and clothing.
4. Ensure protection from sun and snow blindness.
5. Groups should travel terrain that is familiar to instructors.
6. Anticipate cold related injuries. Train accordingly and establish system of visual checks.
7. Participants should travel in single file and signal when person in front moves out of sight. A "sweep" instructor should carry first-aid and repair kit.
8. Consider avalanche hazard.

Briefing

1. Describe route, safety concerns, local hazards, and first-aid and health skills.
2. Teach and practice basic activity skills.

University of New Hampshire	*F*	**Education**
	E	**Northeast Region**
	C	**University Outdoor Education Students and General Population**
	S	**4.10, 17.03–17.17**

Winter and Skiing Guidelines

The following guidelines should be considered when winter and ski activities are conducted by the UNH OE program. The guidelines outlined here should be considered in addition to the General Activity Guidelines and Mountaineering Guidelines as applicable.

Winter Activities

Staffing

- OE student leaders have taken the Winter Backpacking Course and are cleared by OE faculty before leading winter programs.
- OE student leaders are competent in the instruction of the appropriate and effective use of the equipment on the winter equipment list.
- OE student leaders are competent in the instruction of appropriately and effectively using any additional equipment (e.g., skis, mountain axes).
- OE student leaders are skilled in Leave No Trace procedures for winter environments.

Participant Qualifications

- Participants have and discussed with staff relevant medical or physical conditions that could be aggravated by the intended winter activity (e.g., circulatory disorders, previous cold injury, previous knee injury, pregnancy).

Supervision

- Winter activities that are one day in length have an appropriate student-to-staff ratio depending on the proximity to a road and type of activity.
- Overnight winter activities have a 5:1 student-to-staff ratio and are conducted with a minimum of two instructors.

Site Selection

- Appropriate areas exist for group instruction.
- Avalanche terrain is avoided unless it is stable, it is necessary to travel in the area, the group is prepared for travel in an avalanche zone, and the risks associated with avoiding the avalanche zone outweigh the risks associated with travel in the zone.

Appropriate Operating Conditions

- The snow conditions are conducive to the intended activity and within the physical and psychological ability of the participants.
- The weather conditions are appropriate for the activity.

Activity Brief

- Educational objective of the activity
- Relevant individual or group goals and objectives
- Intended route
- Temperature regulation and general self-care
- Establish buddy system for monitoring participants physical condition
- Current environmental hazards (e.g. wind, surface conditions, and hypothermia considerations)
- Known hazards possibly in the course area, including but not limited to:
    - Cliffs
    - Frozen and partially frozen bodies of water
    - Snow or other surface conditions
    - Change in weather conditions due to altitude or exposure
- What to do if you become lost
- What to do if you or another participant becomes injured
- Staff location or contact method during the activity
- Location of first-aid and rescue equipment
- Appropriate Leave No Trace practices
- Time plan

Equipment

- Appropriate repair kits should be brought depending on the activity (i.e., materials to repair tents, stoves, snowshoes, and ski poles).

- Staff should familiarize students with the use and care of equipment as it pertains to use in winter conditions.

Curriculum

Recommended progression:

- Winter layering systems and methods for body temperature regulation
- Techniques for sleeping warm
- Winter nutrition and hydration
- Tools for recognizing and treating symptoms of cold-related injuries
- Tools for evaluating and anticipating changing weather conditions
- Winter route planning and route finding
- Snow camping including building kitchens and snow shelters
- Use and care of snowshoes or skis
- Use and care of sleds
- Equipment repair
- Other topics relating to the specific activity (skiing, mountaineering, etc.)
- Appropriate winter Leave No Trace practices

Backcountry and Lift-Serviced Skiing

Downhill (i.e., Telemark, Alpine, and Randonée) skiing may be conducted as an independent activity or part of an extended wilderness experience. Teaching a sequential progression that stresses speed control, how to fall and stop is used when introducing novices to skiing. Proficiency in skiing under control in gentle terrain should be demonstrated by each student before advancing to steep slopes. When skiing, staff and participants must adhere to all applicable winter activity policies, in addition to those below.

Staffing

Program staff has the necessary understanding and experience with the principles of cross-country and backcountry skiing. This includes being familiar with Professional Ski Instructors of America (PSIA) Level I certification. Staff can meet the risk management, operational, and curriculum expectations of the activity. Instructors are also up-to-date on current standards and changes in technology (equipment), backcountry touring procedures, and Telemark teaching progressions. Staff leading skiing activities at a lift service area are not required to have the above qualifications that pertain to backcountry skiing and are not required to have Telemark teaching experience if teaching Alpine skiing.

Equipment

Equipment is cared for in an appropriate manner, including inspection of equipment and associated protective gear conducted prior to participant use. An appropriate repair kit and spare items is available during the activity. The items in the kit will include but are not limited to: wire, screwdrivers, pliers, and tape.

Backcountry Skiing

The following technical skills maybe reviewed prior to or during the trip:

- Proper equipment maintenance and care
- Appropriate equipment selection and sizing
- Use of climbing skins
- Appropriate use of waxes
- Basic Nordic techniques
- Telemark and parallel turns
- Basic equipment repairs
- Cold-weather physiology and safety
- High-energy nutrition for winter activity
- Proper winter clothing and layering systems
- Winter wilderness emergency procedures
- Other applicable topics depending on course (i.e., winter and mountaineering topics)

Adapting those skills to sled hauling is handled during the trip, including being a "brake" skier for the person skiing with the sled.

Lift-Served Skiing

Considerations for conducting lift-served ski activities:

- Staff is expected to orient students to risk management considerations and trail etiquette at ski area.
- Students are given meeting places and times if unsupervised.

Nordic Skiing

Nordic skiing activities are conducted in areas such as the Brown Center, College Woods, and cross-country touring areas. Staff should be familiar with Professional Ski Instructors of America (PSIA) curriculum progression and follow these guidelines as applicable to the goals of the program. Staff should have PSIA Level 1 certification or equivalent experience. More information on the PSIA Nordic teaching progression can be found at www.psia.org/01/nordic/nordic.asp.

SECTION 19
INITIATIVE GAMES AND PROBLEM-SOLVING ACTIVITIES

Wilderness Treatment Center	F	Therapeutic
	E	Northwest Region
	C	Adolescent Males
	S	4.10, 19.01–19.08

Initiative Games

Policy

1. Initiative games, when staffing and environmental factors permit, can be used as a therapeutic component during the wilderness expedition, group therapy, and recreation therapy.
2. Initiative games will be conducted in a safe manner using proper techniques and skills.
3. Program staff facilitating initiative games is not to engage participants in activities that surpass their level of competence. Staff is able to demonstrate competence in the techniques, safety, and instruction required for the activity.
4. Staff is required to be up to date on changes in technology and procedure for this activity. This is accomplished through continued outside training experiences and reading relevant literature. In addition, periodic in-service training sessions may be conducted as a forum to share experience and skills.
5. Staff supervision is required for all initiatives. Staff-to-participant ratio is not to exceed 1:12 at the WTC facility and 1:4.5 in the wilderness.
6. Initiative game activities will be appropriate for the participants' emotional, mental, and physical needs and abilities.
7. Initiative game activities will not exceed safe spotting limits. When participants are wearing helmets the participant's feet will not exceed shoulder height of the spotters. When participants are not wearing helmets, climber's feet will not exceed the waist level of the spotters.
8. Staff will be prepared for a rescue or medical emergency.
   a. The staff team will have one member with current WFR or equivalent and current CPR.
   b. First-aid kits and backboards are available at the ranch for games facilitated there. Wilderness first-aid kits are on hand for initiative games in the wilderness.
   c. Staff member will only engage patients in initiative games when he or she is capable of handling a medical emergency that could result from the initiative.

9. Staff is able to comprehend the therapeutic use of this activity and is able to integrate it into the patients' treatment. Therapeutic benefits include but are not limited to group development, communication skills, trust, conflict resolution, and group problem-solving techniques.

Procedures

1. At the ranch, potential initiative games are discussed during morning staffing. In the wilderness, potential initiative games are discussed among the staff present. Along with weather and other environmental concerns, participants' physical, mental, and emotional abilities and needs are considered at this time.
2. Expectations discussed with patients prior to activities include:
   a. No throwing rocks or other objects.
   b. No horseplay.
   c. Respect for each other's physical and emotional safety.
   d. Participants are to be alert during activities.
3. Program staff facilitating initiative games activities will lead participants in appropriate warm-up activities prior to the activity. Activities will follow a natural progression to allow for the participants level of comfort.
4. When appropriate, participants will be instructed in the proper "spotting technique." Participants will learn the difference between "spotting" and "catching" a person.
5. Participants will be provided water and nourishment appropriate for the length of the activity.
6. Staff will discuss with participants how initiative games relate to their recovery.
7. Staff will be sensitive to the needs and concerns of the participants.
8. Initiative games will be recorded in the trip, recreation, and/or ropes course logs. Information recorded will include but is not limited to: number of participants, activities, and the names of facilitators.

Georgia College & State University
F Education
E Southeast Region
C University Outdoor Education Students and General Population
S 4.10, 4.13, 19.01–19.08

General Policy for Group Development Activities, Spotting, Initiative Tasks, Ground School, Low Challenge Course, High Challenge Course, and Tango Tower

The PPM and Facilitator Handbook

The Georgia College Outdoor Education Center (OEC) offers group development, challenge course, and Tango Tower programs for GCSU students, staff and faculty, and the local and professional community. This facilitator handbook contains Local Operating Procedures (LOPs) for OEC staff conducting these programs. It is different from the Outdoor Education Policy and Procedures Manual (PPM) in that it is focused solely on a specific set of activities for OEC program delivery. It is intended to be used in conjunction with the PPM, which contains detailed information about general administrative policy and technical activities taught in outdoor education classes. To facilitate the use of this handbook, PPM, reminders are inserted throughout.

Definitions

1. *Group development activities* include sequences of warm-ups, icebreakers, acclimatizers, and initiative tasks. They may comprise an entire program or be used to develop individuals and groups for subsequent activities.
2. *Spotting sequences* are a planned set of experiences focused on building spotting skills before taking participants "off the ground" on cable elements or initiative tasks. Off the ground is normally defined as 18 inches or higher. They may be used to prepare participants to spot on-the-ground activities based on group assessment or to enhance program goals such as trust and community building.
3. *Low challenge course elements* include permanent low ropes course components that may be used to develop individual or group competencies. Cable construction properties include dynamics that may be unpredictable and require close attention to spotting. OEC low challenge course elements are situated in various locations around the general challenge course area and on the Ground School structure.
4. *Ground School* is built on poles and is adjacent to the high challenge course. It is prerequisite to the static high challenge course, used to teach communication protocols and procedures for transfer between static elements. It may be used for teaching dynamic belay systems for the high challenge course or the Tango Tower.

5. *High challenge course elements* are built on poles adjacent to Ground School. The high challenge course offers nine dynamic-belay elements and twelve static-belay elements that are separated by a double-decker group element. The high challenge course is also connected to the tandem zip lines.
6. *The Tango Tower* is built on poles. It is a multiclimber structure that includes two artificial climbing walls, several individual and tandem climbing elements, and a processing platform. All of its components may be used together to provide a group initiative that incorporates vertical and horizontal options.
7. *Challenge of and by choice* is a concept that is used by facilitators to communicate to participants that they have a choice about their level and type of participation in program activities, as well as a challenge to stretch themselves. Challenge of and by choice should be used to support individual and group accomplishment and engagement. The concept should be introduced early on in the program and reinforced throughout the program as necessary.
8. *Behavioral contracts* are used by facilitators to help groups develop operating norms and to explain nonnegotiable rules. There are a wide range of options for integrating behavioral norms with program activities depending on program goals, client characteristics, sequence, and logistics.
9. *Goal setting* is used by facilitators in two ways. One is to encourage small groups to set goals for a specific activity. The other is to negotiate individual learning goals with program participants. There are options for integrating goals with program activities depending on program goals, client characteristics and expectations, sequence, and logistics.
10. *Buddy spotter* is the spokesperson for the spotting team and is selected by the active participant (i.e., climber, faller) to support her/him throughout the activity. The buddy spotter checks to make sure that spotters are ready to spot and interacts with the participant on behalf of other spotters. The buddy spotter supports the participant from beginning to end of an activity.
11. *Form drop box* is located outside the door in the screened-in porch at the OEC. Lead facilitators request equipment prior to a program and leave the completed form in the drop box for the equipment and facilities coordinator to process.
12. *Equipment drop box* is a holding area for equipment for programs. It is next to the yurt and the key is on the key ring given to the lead facilitator by appointment. The equipment and facilities coordinator leaves equipment in the box prior to a program and retrieves equipment from the box following a program.
13. *Metal file box* is used to hold program documents and extra forms. Emergency phone numbers are listed on the inside cover of the box.
14. *Facilitator key ring* is given to lead facilitators and provides access to challenge course padlocks (including ladders and the equipment drop box), the yurt, and Lake Laurel Lodge.
15. *The yurt* is located past the Tango Tower. It is an indoor program site adjacent to the challenge course.

Facilitator Responsibilities

Lead Facilitator Responsibilities

Preprogram.

1. Receive the client file from the OEC program coordinator and review intake assessment information.
2. Contact the program sponsor well in advance of the program to:
   a. Confirm logistics (times, location, risk management forms, etc.), and discuss program goals, program design, group and/or individual characteristics, and other topics as necessary;

   b. Communicate to the program sponsor the need for participants to wear loose-fitting clothing appropriate for the climate in general and the specific weather forecast;

   c. Communicate to the program sponsor the option for participants to bring extra clothing, water, and snacks in consideration of the duration of the program and weather;

   d. Communicate to the program sponsor the need for participants to wear closed shoes (not sandals) that are secured at the toe and the heel.
3. Design a program to meet client needs and expectations when possible in conjunction with the facilitation team. *PPM Reminder:* Forms: Program Design Summary.
4. Consult the OEC program coordinator about questions, concerns, and program design information.
5. Disseminate (unless the OEC program coordinator does so), collect, and review participant forms. *PPM Reminder:* Risk Management.
6. Meet with facilitation team members to:
   a. Establish facilitator learning goals;

   b. Communicate client needs and characteristics, program design, participant information, risk management procedures, and facility and equipment logistics;

   c. Assign roles and responsibilities for program set-up and delivery, greet participants, and conduct housekeeping and risk management requirements;

   d. Review the Emergency Action Plan and establish roles and responsibilities;

   e. Review relevant PPM sections. *PPM Reminder:* Ethical Guidelines, Program Definitions, Program Cancellation, Forms and Documentation, Exposure Control, Alcohol and Drugs, Universal Access, Service Learning, and Environmental Ethics and Education.
7. Reserve program equipment. Equipment reservation forms should be completed by the lead facilitator for all equipment needs. Blank reservation forms are located in a rack in the porch entrance to the OEC. Completed reservation forms should be submitted to the equipment and facilities coordinator one week prior to the program date. Completed forms may be placed in one of the drop boxes outside the equipment room or on the front porch of the OEC. It is helpful to include information beyond that required on the form that will assist staff in providing appropriate equipment. Equipment

reserved for weekend programs will be placed in the drop box outside the yurt. Equipment pickup and drop-off for weekday programs should be negotiated with the equipment and facilities coordinator. The metal file box contains emergency numbers, extra participant and personnel forms, the completed equipment reservation form, communication devices as requested, and other relevant documents or supplies. Inspect equipment and make any necessary repairs before use in conjunction with the OEC equipment and facilities coordinator. Do not use damaged equipment. *PPM Reminder:* Equipment Management.

8. Obtain a weather report and in conjunction with the OEC program coordinator make arrangements with the program sponsor for communicating program adaptations or cancellation to participants.
9. Pick up program equipment, metal file box, and the facilitator key ring from the equipment and facilities coordinator at a predesignated time.
10. Inspect the site and use the equipment reservation form to inspect program equipment.
11. Complete program set-up requirements with the facilitation team prior to participant arrival.
12. Assign staff to meet and greet participants near the parking lot, collect outstanding forms, and organize the group for the program.

During program.

1. Process outstanding participant forms and collect missing information on forms that were presubmitted.
2. Collect additional medical screening information as appropriate. *PPM Reminder:* Medical Screening.
3. Introduce staff and welcome participants to the Georgia College Outdoor Education Center.
4. Provide housekeeping and program-related information (rules, expectations, challenge of and by choice, goals, and behavioral expectations or contract).
5. Conduct preliminary and ongoing safety briefings. *PPM Reminder:* Safety Briefings.
6. Oversee program implementation, site safety and security, equipment, and staff. *PPM Reminder:* Personnel Administration, Program Administration, and Risk Management.
7. Oversee group management.
8. Complete incident/accident forms as necessary.
9. Conduct program closure and disseminate and collect program evaluation forms from participants. The University System of Georgia requires program evaluation forms to be completed for all OEC programs by every participant unless otherwise justifiable. At minimum the program sponsor should complete the form in cases where participants cannot or will not complete the form.

Postprogram.

1. Conduct staff debrief and program evaluation.
2. Record notes in the program file for future reference.
3. Disseminate facilitator feedback forms (electronic forms available at http://hercules.gcsu.edu/~jhirsch/ > Forms > Personnel Administration > Facilitator

Feedback) and remind staff that compensation requests cannot be submitted until completed forms are submitted to the OEC program coordinator.

4. Place completed personnel, participant, equipment, and incident/accident forms in the metal file box.
5. Inspect and clean equipment as appropriate.
6. Record first-aid kit use information on the form in the kit.
7. Record rope use information for rope logs and equipment maintenance information on the equipment reservation form and place in metal file box.
8. Return equipment to the drop box or the OEC if open.
9. Store wet ropes loosely coiled on a tarp in the yurt and tie the element bag containing hardware to one end.
10. Place keys in the metal file box and place it in drop box outside the yurt or return to OEC if open.
11. Submit the completed program file to the OEC program coordinator within 14 days of the program. *PPM Reminder:* Program Administration.

Assistant Facilitator Responsibilities

1. Assist the lead facilitator as required.
2. Attend pre- and postprogram meetings.
3. Share learning goals and negotiate roles and responsibilities with facilitation team.
4. Review relevant policy and procedures prior to program.
5. Submit facilitator feedback forms.

Technician Responsibilities

1. Assist the lead facilitator as required and according to policy limitations. *PPM Reminder:* Facilitator Qualifications: Technician.
2. Attend necessary pre- and postprogram meetings.
3. Share learning goals and negotiate role and responsibilities with facilitation team.
4. Review relevant policy and procedures prior to program.
5. Submit facilitation feedback forms.

Teaching

1. Sequence activities with consideration for client characteristics, agency or program goals, and emotional, social and physical safety issues.
2. Assess individual and group readiness for moving forward to new challenges (GRABBSS, APPLE, and CHANGES are examples of assessment models that may be useful).
3. Participate in warm-ups, ice-breakers, and acclimatizers as appropriate. Avoid participation that interferes with the group experience.
4. Observe and monitor Level 1 to 4 activities to inform processing strategies and provide an appropriate level of supervision and control.

5. Use a variety of processing approaches and techniques to encourage individuals and groups to make personal and collective meaning from experiences as appropriate.
6. Provide opportunities for individuals and groups to self-regulate as appropriate.
7. Use challenge by and of choice to encourage appropriate levels of participation and behavioral contracting to encourage groups to monitor their own process.

Communication

1. Teach and practice appropriate spotting, climbing, and communication systems.
2. Emphasize the importance of simple, timely, and clear communication.
3. Note environmental noise or lack of visual access to the system that may interfere with information flow between participant and spotters or belayers.
4. Match commands and responses within communication systems according to the activity including the following components in each:
   a. Participant readiness to spotters or belayers;
   b. Spotters or belayers readiness to participant;
   c. Participant intention to begin action;
   d. Spotters or belayers signal to start action.
5. Appoint or ask the participant to select a buddy spotter or belayer who will communicate readiness on behalf of multiple spotters or belayers.

Safety

1. Place first-aid and emergency response equipment in a location that is accessible to staff.
2. Continue visual inspections of program equipment throughout the program.
3. Maintain appropriate staff/participant ratios and position facilitators to maximize participant supervision for all activities.
4. Review current instructional and safety guidelines for all activities and discuss adaptations thoroughly with the facilitation team.
5. Set activity parameters that are safe and flexible.
6. Deal with safety issues in a meaningful way that will contribute to the emotional, physical, intellectual, and social safety of individuals and groups by using techniques such as:
   a. Clarifying instructions, purpose, boundaries, or expectations;
   b. Refocusing the group;
   c. Reviewing challenge of and by choice and behavioral contract components;
   d. Speaking with a person privately;
   e. Changing or renegotiating the activity or the program design to accommodate group readiness.
7. Consider personal competency limits, and process issues that are within the skill and training experience of facilitators.

Program Design

Staff/Participant Ratios

There will be at least two facilitators (a lead facilitator and an assistant facilitator) for most activities. Therefore, the following ratios are minimum guidelines. Modifications to these guidelines should be based on a careful assessment of client needs and characteristics, and the nature of the program activities. In most cases, if a change to these guidelines is justifiable, the ratio will decrease. In some cases it may be appropriate to include supervisory staff from the sponsoring agency in the staff/participant ratio if they are willing to participate in program delivery at an appropriate level of competency. As an example, teachers may be counted as supervisory staff for group development activities, provided the procedures outlined for group development activities in this manual are followed.

Group Development Activities	1:12
Low Challenge Course	1:10 (minimum 2)
Tango Tower	1:8 (minimum 2)
High Challenge Course–Static Elements	1:8 (minimum 3)
High Challenge Course–Dynamic Elements	1:8 (minimum 2)

Purpose

1. To use a planned sequence of group development and challenge course experiences to meet the goals of groups and individuals.
2. To provide a safe and supportive environment for individual and group learning.
3. To provide an opportunity for individuals and groups to:
   a. Work as an effective team;
   b. Communicate effectively;
   c. Solve problems collectively and creatively;
   d. Explore decision making;
   e. Foster a sense of empathy and respect for others;
   f. Provide honest, constructive feedback to group members;
   g. Resolve conflicts constructively;
   h. Manage resources effectively;
   i. Build community.

Program Design Sequence

Ignition	Introductory, warm-ups, icebreakers, and acclimatizing activities are used to ignite the program, *seed* behavioral and safety expectations, and provide the facilitator with the opportunity to *observe* individual and group behavior. They develop a foundation for group building, goal setting, behavioral contracting, and challenge of and by choice. They *set the stage and the tone* of the program.
Level 1	Level 1 activities take place *on the ground* and provide the facilitator with *goal-focused assessment* information about the group and its members and about client social, intellectual, emotional, and physical characteristics. Subsequent activities are selected, implemented, and processed based on assessment insights at this level. Goal setting, behavioral contracting, challenge by and of choice, and spotting/trust activities may be *integrated* in appropriate sequence throughout this level. Level 1 activities are *FUNN, novel, and challenging.* They *build on ignition activities.*
Level 2	Level 2 activities take place *on the ground* and provide the facilitator with opportunities to *focus on goal-related skill development.* Groups *build competency* and begin to identify and address individual and group topics. Processing may be increasingly more intentional and in depth. Activities are *more complex and challenging,* involving increasing levels of physical, social, and emotional risk. Facilitators complete goal setting, contracting, challenge by and of choice, and spotting/trust skills by the conclusion of this level. Level 2 activities *build on Level 1 activities.*
Level 3	Level 3 activities *may take place off the ground* and are used to *deepen and refine goal-related competencies,* develop realistic strategies and applications, and celebrate success. Groups begin to *self-monitor* and the facilitator's role becomes less directive. Processing becomes less facilitator driven as appropriate. The group *revisits* goal setting, contracting, challenge by and of choice, and spotting/trust skills throughout this level. Level 3 activities *build on Level 2* activities.
Level 4	Level 4 activities are the *"peak experiences"* that vary based on program goals. These activities are used to *apply learning to challenging tasks.* They may also include the development of *action plans* for application to real world settings. These experiences draw on everything the program has achieved to this point. They may include high ropes elements, demanding initiative tasks, service projects, or an expedition. Participants often *demonstrate* individual goal achievement and group effectiveness at this level.
Closure	Closure provides the facilitator, individuals, and groups with opportunities to *celebrate success,* acknowledge *relationships,* and begin the *transition* back to the real world. *Commitment* to action planning and real world *applications* of learning is central. Activities may be summary in nature, fun, and emotional—all at the same time!

Risk Management

Safety Procedures

1. Facilitators are responsible for participants and therefore have an obligation to anticipate and avoid potential dangers. Participants look to facilitators for informed, professional instruction and guidance so that they can participate in our programs and services in reasonable safety.
2. Lead facilitators should be thoroughly acquainted with participant forms prior to the commencement of a program, ensure that forms are complete, and that relevant information is disseminated to staff at a suitable level of confidentiality. *PPM Reminder:* Medical Screening.
3. Participants are entitled to know the nature and scope of risks involved in the program-specific activities before participation. All participants will sign appropriate informed consent and assumption of risk forms. *PPM Reminder:* Forms and The Safety Procedures
4. Brief all participants about on-site and activity risks and safety procedures before they engage in the activity. Do not assume that a potential danger is evident to participants. Discuss the dangers and risks with them until you are confident that each person understands and voluntarily assumes the risks involved. Judgment is crucial in this matter, especially when dealing with hesitant participants. Be as persuasive as possible in an effort to reinforce confidence and to motivate participation. However, do not force a participant to participate and use challenge-of-and-by-choice strategies to negotiate levels of successful participation.
5. Common issues that may impact program delivery include, but are not limited to, expectations that:
   a. Roles and responsibilities for staff and participants are understood—check and recheck;
   b. Instructions are clear and understood—never assume;
   c. Supervision is working—as the degree of risk increases so must the level of supervision;
   d. Equipment and facilities are suitable for a program and that staff and participants
   e. Hydration and nutrition are the responsibility of participants and facilitators—monitor closely!

Safety Briefings

1. Ensure that staff is familiar with and able to execute emergency procedures and is familiar with related information in the metal file box.
2. Brief participants about safety and the conduct of the activity, and offer opportunities to ask questions and clarify procedures.
3. Establish a climate of safety and caution including, but not limited to:
   a. Inherent dangers and preventative information in the area, such as flora and fauna, weather, other environmental hazards.

b. Inherent dangers and preventative information about activities, such as falling, spotting, buddy systems.

c. Program goals and how they relate to specific activities;

d. Challenge-of-and-by-choice options and behavioral contracts;

e. Participant responsibilities;

f. Emergency procedures;

g. Safety equipment use and location.

Emergency Action Plan

Emergency Action Plan (EAP) is a set of steps that guide emergency response by providing staff members with relevant, clear information. Every emergency situation is different and requires some degree of judgment. The following process should be used to develop an EAP that permits staff members to exercise professional judgment in the way they respond to a specific situation. The EAP should be implemented for accidents in which a participant is evacuated from the program site to primary medical care or leaves the program site on their own to seek outside medical care. Incidents that require basic first aid do not necessitate implementation of an EAP. Incidents and accidents require the completion of the Incident/Accident Form. Emergency action planning involves:

1. Prior to the program, establish emergency response roles and responsibilities including a primary responder (PR) and an emergency response manager (ERM).
2. The PR, also known as the "first-in," provides initial first aid to the patient and is a staff member with appropriate or highest, current level of medical training. *PPM reminder:* Staff Qualifications.
3. The lead facilitator may elect to be the ERM based on the qualifications of other staff members to perform PR roles and responsibilities.
4. Other staff members will manage the group to minimize risk of further harm to participants and assist the PR or ERM as necessary.
5. The ERM in conjunction with the PR will determine if primary medical or emergency response system assistance is necessary. If outside assistance is required:

   a. Call 911 and provide your name, the location of the program, the patient's name, the patient's condition, any suspected injuries, and anything else that the dispatcher may ask for;

   b. Direct emergency response personnel to meet the group at the Lake Laurel Lodge parking lot;

   c. Do not end the call until the dispatcher hangs up;

   d. Write related information clearly on a SOAP note or piece of paper to give to emergency medical personnel;

   e. Move the patient to the Lake Laurel Lodge parking lot if appropriate, based on patient assessment and a judgment that further injury is not likely during transit;

   f. Do not move a patient with a possible neck or back injury, an unstable skeletal injury, or any condition where moving the patient could worsen the situation. In such a situation, treat, monitor, and comfort patient until emergency medical personnel arrive on site to manage the situation;

g. Instruct a facilitator or client representative to wait for emergency personnel in the parking lot to provide instructions or escort to the scene and to transfer patient information;

h. Comply with emergency response personnel instructions and requests for information;

i. Make a copy of information to be transferred to emergency or primary care personnel if possible;

j. A facilitator or client representative should accompany the patient to the primary care facility;

k. The ERM or primary backup should notify the emergency contact listed on the medical form;

l. Primary backup personnel should be contacted as soon as possible using contact information in the metal file.

6. GCSU Public Safety should be contacted as necessary by the primary backup; however, if backup procedures cannot be implemented in a reasonable amount of time, Public Safety may be called at (478) 445-4400. *PPM reminder:* Contact Protocol.

7. The lead facilitator, primary backup, OE faculty, or a professional may debrief the situation as appropriate and within the parameters of facilitator competency.

8. Complete an Incident/Accident Form. *PPM Reminder:* Incident/Accident Reporting.

9. Obtain written statements from witnesses if appropriate.

10. Cancel or postpone the program in consideration of client/staff ratios or contextual factors that may be unsafe or detrimental to learning and growth. *PPM Reminder:* Program Cancellation.

11. In the case of a life-threatening injury or fatality:

    a. GCSU University Communications should be contacted by the primary backup, however, if backup procedures cannot be implemented in a reasonable amount of time University Communications may be called at (478) 445-4477;

    b. University Communications should speak directly with the emergency contact listed on the Medical Information Form;

    c. Do not remove the body unless instructed by legal authority to do so;

    d. Limit access to the scene of the accident;

    e. Attend to the physical and emotional needs of staff and other participants.

Information to Press

1. Information about an accident *will not be released to the media without the written consent of the director of university communications.* Direct contact with the press should be avoided; however, should contact with the press be unavoidable, do not speak about:

    a. Assessment of GCSU personnel, policy, equipment, or facilities;

    b. Information regarding the nature of the injury or illness prior to a diagnosis by a licensed medical doctor;

    c. Names of victims prior to notification of next of kin;

    d. Estimation of property damage. *PPM Reminder:* Information to Press.

Incident/Accident Reporting

Accident/incident reports assist the Safety and Risk Management Committee to identify trends that require future preventative action, monitor policy and procedures, evaluate program quality, and establish staff training needs.

Definitions.

An *accident* refers to a fatality, a disabling injury, or a serious illness for which a participant is transferred to emergency medical care, or visits a hospital or doctor. An *incident* requires first aid to be administered on site, and/or occurs when participation in the program is discontinued for a period of time. The Incident/Accident Form is completed for both.

Reporting procedures.

1. OE or OEC staff complete the Incident/Accident Report form.
2. Make every effort to obtain the injured party's signature.
3. Documentation should be complete, objective, and include a comprehensive description of relevant information. Consider that this document may be used by primary caregivers to make treatment decisions. Therefore:
   a. Use SOAP note protocol when appropriate;
   b. Write in a clear and professional manner;
   c. Do not indicate fault or responsibility.
4. In the case of an accident where responsibility is transferred to EMS personnel, include the *name of EMS personnel and the location of the primary care facility* to which the injured party is being transported.
5. If the person returns to the program, note the *name of the physician giving per mission* to do so.
6. The lead facilitator has the authority to deny or adapt level of participation of a participant who returns to a program and should note such decisions on the form.

Environmental Hazards

Every environmental hazard is unique; some are weather related and others are inherent in location. The decision to continue a program, move to an indoor facility on site, seek temporary shelter, or postpone or cancel a program should be made based on program goals, client characteristics, and the specific environmental conditions both on the site and for traveling to another location. A key to the yurt is on the facilitator key ring, and Lake Laurel Lodge may be requested for indoor use for any OEC program. There is no substitute for having a keen weather eye to help anticipate and prepare for inclement weather and for knowing how to recognize the presence of hazardous animals and plants.

Inspect program areas prior to use including, but not limited to signs of vandalism, dangerous or nuisance flora and fauna, weather damage, dangerous ground and overhead conditions. Establish activity boundaries that ensure safe participation that is free from hazardous ground and overhead obstacles. Inform participants about hazardous materials and objects such as nails, splinters, rocks, and surface roots.

Weather-Related Environmental Hazards

Rain.

Rain, especially heavy rain, increases the likelihood of slipping on wet poles, cables, or ground cover. Heavy rain may be accompanied by heavy winds and lightning, and on occasion produce rare weather systems like a tornado. Rain does not necessarily indicate that a challenge course program should be cancelled.

Wind.

Heavy wind may pick up debris from the ground cover making visual supervision difficult and may affect hanging structures by creating difficult situations for climbing. In such cases, the use of high challenge course elements or the Tango Tower may need to be postponed.

Lightning.

Lightning is the leading direct meteorological cause of casualties in the Untied States. Lightning presents direct danger in three ways: (1) a direct strike, (2) induced currents near a strike, and (3) ground currents. Participants should be instructed about specific lightening drill procedures during the initial safety briefing if a storm is noted. The following is a list of protection measures that the lead facilitator should utilize when possible to make a decision about lightning storm response.

1. Counting the interval between a flash and the following thunder and dividing the number by 5 may estimate the distance of lightning potential, (5 seconds = 1 mile).
2. Lightning protection measures should begin no later than an estimated 3-mile distance (15 seconds) from group location. Activity may resume when the lightning is a minimum of an estimated 3 miles away (15 seconds).
3. Groups should seek shelter in a nearby building (the yurt, Lake Laurel Lodge, Outdoor Education Center, etc.) until activity can resume.

Tornados.

The National Weather Service issues two types of information related to tornados: watches and warnings. A tornado watch indicates that conditions are likely to lead to the formation of a tornado. A tornado warning indicates that a tornado has been sighted in the area. OEC programs should be adapted or cancelled in the event of a tornado watch or warning. If a tornado appears without warning, take the following action:

1. Seek shelter in a safe building, away from windows and doors.
2. Lie down in a ditch or other low area.
3. Evacuate vehicles.

Flora and fauna.

Contact with any fauna in the wild should be avoided. Sensitivity to toxins associated with poisonous plants may vary with age, weight, physical condition, and individual susceptibility. Snakes, alligators, red ants, and ticks may be found in and around areas at Lake Laurel Campus used for OEC programs. Poisonous plants such as poison ivy, tread softly, and coral bean may be a hazard. *PPM Reminder:* Environmental Hazards: Flora and Fauna.

General procedures.

1. Adhere to LNT ethics to minimize contact with flora and fauna.
2. Move away from animals slowly, while facing the animal, if a sighting/contact takes place.

3. Know common poisonous flora for the area.
4. Inspect the site prior to use.
5. Include information about poisonous flora and hazardous fauna in safety briefings as appropriate.
6. Suggest tick checks as appropriate.

Group Development Activities

Group development activities may comprise an entire program or be used to develop individuals and groups for subsequent activities on the low or high challenge course and/or the Tango Tower. They include warm-ups, ice breakers, acclimatizers, a variety of level 1 and 2 initiative tasks, and closure activities.

They are focused on having FUNN (functional understanding not necessary) and intra- and interpersonal skills, such as: communication, problem solving and decision making, respect for diversity, constructive controversy, leadership, and goal setting. They require careful sequencing (see Section Three of GCSU Manual: Program Design: Program Design Sequence) to develop emotional, social, physical, and intellectual safety. They may be used to clarify expectations, introduce rules, establish behavioral contracts, set goals, and introduce active challenge of and by choice.

Group development activity options may be found in activity books and/or on the Group Development Activity Equipment Reservation Form. Activities are normally conducted at the open space area in front of Lake Laurel Lodge, in the parking area, in one of several appropriate spaces at the challenge course site, or on the patio in front of the OEC. Site selection should be based on factors such as the number of participants, the nature of the activity, client goals, equipment, proximity to indoor facilities, and site characteristics such as ground surface, contour, noise interference and other safety features.

Facilitators may participate in some group development activities at the beginning of a program, however, they should be cognizant of interfering with group processes as a program progresses. Facilitators should not participate in activities that require focus, such as: spotting boundaries, keeping time, monitoring the conduct of the activity, or providing backup spotting. Since group development activities are a source of information about how individuals and groups behave and interact, good observation skills from outside the group are necessary for processing experiences at an appropriate level.

General Procedures

1. Inspect sites and equipment.
2. Explain the purpose of the activity and present instructions in a clear manner.
3. Set appropriate boundaries.
4. Answer questions prior to starting the activity and throughout as they arise.
5. Review rules, expectations, behavioral contract components, and challenge of and by choice as appropriate to the sequence and activity characteristics.
6. Discuss safety considerations including using appropriate communication, keeping "bumpers up." and other relevant parameters.
7. Encourage participants to ask for what they need.
8. Monitor activities closely for unsafe behavior such as pushing or pulling, not following rules or instruction, distracting behavior, inappropriate touch, inappropriate communication sequence, or horseplay.

9. Intervene in a timely and purposeful fashion as necessary.
10. Provide backup spotting support as necessary.
11. Process the activity as appropriate.

Spotting

Spotting Skills

Spotting is a concept that is used in two ways. First, it describes a set of technical skills that are taught before participants are responsible for spotting each other off the ground. When included in a program for this purpose, a sequence of at least four activities is required (see Spotting Sequence). The entire spotting sequence may be taught at once or integrated throughout Level 1 and 2 activities.

Additionally, spotting is a concept that may also be used to describe the development of social, emotional, and physical support of individuals within a group. In this sense, facilitators are always developing spotting skills because they are central to group growth. Spotting skills may take the form of participants caring for each other, offering "put-ups" instead of "put-downs," encouraging fellow participants to perform, speak up in a debrief, or ask for what they need during an activity, etc. Facilitators often model caring, positive approaches for supporting individual and group interactions early in a program, gradually encouraging or explicitly asking group members to do so themselves. Spotting activities may also include games and initiatives that lay a foundation for a particular level of behavior that is desired.

Buddy spotters are used in both of these ways. Technically, the buddy spotter monitors the communication system on behalf of the participant doing an activity when there is more than one spotter. Supportively, the buddy spotter encourages, communicates, and engages in an experience with a participant doing an activity from start to finish. When a climber touches the ground, the buddy spotter is there to provide a steady hand, celebrate success, and help with equipment.

Spotting skills are often overlooked and yet are some of the most important skills to develop early on and throughout a program.

Spotting Sequence

1. Minimum requirements for teaching spotting skills for taking participant off the ground include:
    a. A two-person Tic;
    b. A three-person Tic Toc;
    c. Wind in the Willows;
    d. At least one additional activity appropriate to the program design and assessment of group and individual readiness. One or more of the following completes the spotting sequence: Levitation (lifting), Gauntlet (walking on a cable), and/or Magic Hat (crossing, swinging, etc.). Alternative activities may be used with permission of the program coordinator.
2. Use additional activities that provide specific skill practice as needed.
3. Teach readiness for spotting responsibilities including bumpers up, spotter's stance, and positioning in relation to movement, type of spotting structure, protecting critical areas (neck and head), and environmental conditions.

4. Require a buddy spotter as appropriate.
5. Encourage participants to ask for what they need.
6. Encourage groups to self-regulate and monitor spotted activities.
7. Emphasize communication sequences.

Spotting Structures

Spotting structures should match the spotting requirements for program activities. Participants and facilitators may provide spotting for each other as appropriate. The fourth activity in a spotting-skills instructional sequence may include one or more spotting structures.

Spotting Structure	Description	Activity Examples
Basic Spot	The basic spot is used to spot anyone who is ascending or descending, or moving along a cable traverse element. It is the "basic" spotting structure used often for any situation in which a participant may be unstable. A minimum of two spotters are positioned in each fall zone. Participants and facilitators may be spotters as appropriate.	Ladder/pole climbs Team Wall Traverses Mohawk Walk Leaning Tower of Feetza Gauntlet
Group Spot	The group spot is used when the group is engaged in an activity where individuals are connected in a way that provides stability and support to the group as a whole. Facilitators provide on-the-ground basic spot coverage. Group members may ask for additional spotting or be asked to assist with on-the-ground basic spot coverage. Participants and facilitators may be spotters as appropriate.	Mohawk Walk Swinging Log
Running Spot	The running spot is named for the action that it requires from spotters. It is used when participants move across an area where other participants are not permitted. Spotters move across the area with participants providing a dynamic basic spot. Group members may ask for additional spotting or be asked to assist with on-the-ground basic coverage.	Multiswing Magic Hat
Bridge Spot	The bridge spot is used in conjunction with the basic spot. It is used when participants are performing an activity that requires them to lean against each other to the point of falling inward. Spotters bend over placing hands on lower thighs, with head down to support and strengthen their ability to catch participants on their backs. Spotters move with the action, positioning themselves so that the strongest part of the back receives the impact. Spotters are added to the bridge as soon as space permits.	Wild Woosey Leaning Warm-Ups

Spotting Structure	Description	Activity Examples
Catching/Lifting Spot	The catching/lifting spot is used to catch a preplanned fall or lift of a person. It is used in conjunction with the basic spot as participants are moving into or from positions that require them to be caught or lifted. Formations differ according to the activity (zippers, buddy positioning, stance, etc.), however lifting using leg muscles, catching critical areas, participant readiness and strength, and faller tendencies to jackknife or flail should be addressed.	Levitation Spider's Web 3D Maze

Spotting Sequence Activities

General Procedures

1. Inspect the site.
2. Explain the purpose of the activity and present instructions in a clear manner.
3. Answer questions prior to starting the activity and throughout as they arise.
4. Review challenge of and by choice.
5. Demonstrate spotting procedures that are appropriate for the activity.
6. Discuss safety considerations, including: faller body position, spotter body position and readiness, distance parameters, and actions that promote safe spotting.
7. Discuss appropriate touch.
8. Teach appropriate spotting command systems.
9. Explain the concept of team spotting for activities that require more than one spotter to act together.
10. Encourage participants to ask for what they need.
11. Ask the faller to designate a buddy spotter to respond on behalf of multiple spotters and explain the buddy spotter role before starting the activity. Maintain appropriate distance between the faller and spotters.
12. Monitor activities closely for unsafe behavior such as pushing or pulling, inappropriate distance between the faller and spotters, distracting behavior, inappropriate touch, inappropriate communication sequence, or horseplay. Reinforce behavioral contract elements, challenge of and by choice, and other strategies for monitoring behavior.
13. Intervene in a timely and purposeful fashion as necessary.
14. Provide backup spotting support as necessary.
15. Process the activity as appropriate.

Tic

Description.

Spotting and/or catching a partner develops an understanding of body weight and movement, as well as concepts like appropriate touch. Supportive spotting and catching allows participants to develop balance, judgment, and appropriate falling posture, rather than enabling a participant to overly depend on spotters. This activity introduces a basic spotting stance and a communication system that will be adapted and used in subsequent activities. The faller crosses arms in front of body and initiates commands. The spotter(s) supports the faller as s/he leans backward a small distance toward the spotter and is then assisted back to center. Gradually, and using a progression of leans, small increases in distance are added as appropriately negotiated.

Spotter information.

1. For basic spotting technique, spotter's:
   a. Knees are bent and feet in athletic stance creating a stable base with one forward and one back;
   b. Hands are up and ready;
   c. Eyes on the participant at all times;
   d. Spotter supports by absorbing the faller's weight like a shock absorber, bending at the elbows and knees, and then extending to bring the faller upright.

Facilitator information.

Catching a fall may be taught with this activity or the Tic Toc, if the group is ready, or to prepare for low challenge course activities. When falling, the faller will likely bend at the hips. The catcher moves hands under the arms and gently rests the faller against the thigh of the forward leg as the faller is slowly brought to a sitting position on the ground. The faller is then assisted to a standing position.

Tic Toc

Description.

Two spotters are positioned to the front and back of a faller to promote an understanding of body weight and movement. Emphasize the difference between supportive spotting and enabling a faller to depend on spotters rather than developing balance, judgment, and appropriate falling posture. This activity reinforces the basic communication system that will be adapted and used in subsequent activities and may be used to introduce or review concepts such as appropriate touch. Two spotters take a spotting position in front of and behind the faller. The faller may fall forward, then be brought to center before falling backward, and brought back to center. The faller will select a controlled fall to the forward and back spotters before trying a slow, continuous forward to back motion. The faller will cross arms in front of body.

Wind in the Willows

Description.

The group forms a circle to spot and guide the faller who stands in the center of the circle and may fall at any angle, toward any direction within the circle. The activity reinforces body weight and movement, supportive spotting, the basic communication system, appropriate touch, spotting posture, the buddy spotter, and it introduces team spotting. There should be a minimum of eight spotters and a maximum number of spotters to ensure that the circle is not too big. Larger groups can form into appropriately sized smaller groups. Form a shoulder-to-shoulder circle around the faller and assume spotting posture. The faller selects a buddy spotter who will respond with verbal spotting commands for the group as a whole and return the faller to an upright position. The faller initiates the motion by starting commands and falling in any direction. The group smoothly passes the faller around or across the circle and back to center.

Gauntlet

Description.

Group members form two shoulder-to shoulder lines facing one another, approximately 3 feet across. A participant walks through the center of the lines, falling in any direction, at any time, unannounced. This activity reinforces previously learned spotting skills and introduces spotting someone who is moving along a course such as a foot cable. This is an appropriate lead-up activity for low cable elements. The faller selects a buddy spotter who will stand at the other end of the line. Spotters must react by moving into a spotting position and supporting the faller to continue walking this imaginary cable.

Levitation

Description.

This activity prepares participants for lifting another participant. It is an appropriate lead-up to the Spider's Web or other lifting-type activities and reinforces the basic communication system that will be adapted and used in subsequent activities, as well as concepts like appropriate touch, buddy spotter role, and co-spotting. One participant lies on the ground in ready position. A minimum of eight lifters place hands, palm up beneath the participant at intervals down the length of the body to support key weight and movement. The participant designates a buddy spotter who will support the head and keep it in line with the body, communicate with the lifters, help the participant up and walk the person to standing position at the end of the activity. Lifters lift the body slowly to a height that does not require lifters to change hand positions. Lifters then slowly lower the participant, either to the ground or a level that permits the feet to be lowered to the ground, and assist the participant to a standing position. The participant may close his/her eyes. Rocking and tilting should be avoided.

Participant information.

1. Communicate with the spotters while being lifted to ask for what you need (e.g., "please, support my head better").

Magic Hat

Description.

This activity is a diminishing-loads puzzle. It models a spotting structure in which facilitators, with assistance from participants as required, spot active participants through a zone in which other participants are not permitted. It prepares participants to carry each other safely and with regard for appropriate touch, individual diversity, and loading of weight. Boundaries are set with webbing approximately 25 feet apart (a larger area may be used as appropriate). The group must get from one side to the other using the magic hat to designate who can walk through the area. Each participant may use the magic hat once and it can only be returned to the other side for subsequent use by a participant returning it by walking through the area. The challenge is to get everyone to the other side with limited resources while making group decisions about order and individual needs.

Initiative Tasks

Low challenge course elements and initiative tasks are located throughout the ridge area above the OEC. The Ground School structure also offers facilitators an opportunity to design low challenge course elements that meet the needs of program goals by creating sequences of experiences that are interchangeable and temporary. Props for the Ground School structure are located in the yurt. Additional initiative tasks that are not described in this handbook may be reserved through the OEC equipment and facilities coordinator. Groups complete a spotting sequence prior to doing any activity that is off the ground and requires participants to spot each other (see Spotting Sequence Activities).

General Procedures

1. Inspect the site and element components.
2. Explain the purpose of the activity and present instructions in a clear manner.
3. Answer questions prior to starting the activity and throughout as they arise.
4. Reinforce challenge of and by choice.
5. Demonstrate spotting procedures that are appropriate for each activity.
6. Discuss safety considerations including stepping off the cable, platform, or log, and spotter body position and readiness.
7. Require appropriate spotting command systems.
8. Review the concept of team spotting for activities that require more than one spotter to act together.
9. Remind participants that they may ask for additional spotters or be asked by the facilitator to assist with spotting.
10. Encourage participants to ask for what they need.
11. Ask group to agree to attempt solutions that provide adequate spotting.
12. Be aware of the strength and body size of group members and ask for agreement not to have members lifting, supporting, or being supported in a manner in which they are not comfortable.
13. Ask the faller to designate a buddy spotter to respond on behalf of multiple spotters and explain the buddy spotter role before starting the activity.
14. Maintain appropriate distance between the faller and spotters.
15. Monitor activities closely for unsafe behavior such as pushing or pulling, inappropriate distance between the faller and spotters, distracting behavior, inappropriate touch, inappropriate communication sequence, or horseplay. Reinforce group behavioral contract.
16. Intervene in a timely and purposeful fashion as necessary.

17. Provide backup spotting support as necessary.
18. Process the activity as appropriate.

Activities

1. Activities described here require permanent structures or large props that are not stored in the equipment management area in the OEC. It is not necessary to reserve these structures.
2. Additional initiative task equipment is listed on the equipment reservation form (see Facilitator Handbook: Section 2: Lead Facilitator Responsibilities: Equipment Management).

A-Frame

Description.

This initiative task consists of a 10-foot tall wooden "A" with 12 control ropes attached to the apex of the "A." Group members use the control lines to maneuver the A-frame along a predetermined course while one group member rides the cross bar of the A-frame.

Facilitator information.

1. Provide *basic* spotting for the participant riding the A-frame.
2. Instruct riders to step off the crossbar to avoid uncontrolled falls.
3. Inform participants of safety issues, such as not wrapping the control lines around their hands.

Participant information.

1. Agree not to use excessive force to maneuver the A-frame around.
2. Agree to maintain support for the A-frame until the rider steps off of the crossbar.

All Aboard

Description.

This initiative task uses a wooden platform on which the entire group attempts to balance for a predetermined or a progressively more challenging period of time.

Facilitator information.

1. Inform participants that they cannot stack people or ride on shoulders.

Participant information.

1. Agree to assist any and all group members who might need or ask for it.

Cable Traverses, Triangle Traverse, and Group Traverse

Description.

These low challenge course elements consist of one or more single foot cables between trees or poles. They may be used as a initiative task by having groups traverse one or more cables using hand props that may be permanently or temporarily affixed to poles or trees. Hand props are sequenced by the facilitator to develop skills or may be proposed by the group. Hand props include single and multiple rope attachments that may be used to create elements such as the vine walk, single attachment, short and long hand holds, and various types of tension for two-line elements. The basic spot or group spot structure is used as appropriate.

Facilitator information.

1. Design, or negotiate with the group, element sequences based on program goals and client assessment.
2. Review basic and group spot procedures.

Participant information.

1. Participants who have not started or have finished may provide basic spotting reinforcement to a group spot as needed.

Islands

Description.

This initiative task uses three wooden platforms placed 6 to 8 feet apart. The group is given two props, one plank that is about 2 feet long and one plank that is about 1.5 feet shorter than the distance between the platforms, and asked to move the group across a series of platforms.

Facilitator information.

1. Review safety hazards associated with the board and the height of the platforms.
2. Inform the group that there is to be no jumping between platforms.
3. Spot participants as they move between platforms.

Participant information.

1. Be aware of the plank moving or hitting someone when being moved.

Multiswing

Description.

This initiative task is a multiline rope suspended from a cable between two trees or poles, or hanging from an element on the high challenge course. The group uses the rope to cross a predesignated area without touching the ground between the marked boundaries. Group may not use resources other than what they possess to accomplish the task (props are sometimes given to support a group or individual; e.g., magic hula hoop). A running spot is provided in the area between the boundaries, and a basic spot is provided as a participant prepares to swing and lands on the other side.

Facilitator information.

1. Ask participants to imagine what it will be like to spot takeoffs and landings from outside the no-entry zone.
2. Perform the running spot and ask for additional spotters as needed.
3. Ask participants not to jump, dive, or do stunts while swinging or attempting to get the rope.

4. The use of a foot loop is optional. Caution should be exercised when participants choose to use the foot loop. Participants should be asked to support swinger and assist with removing foot from loop upon landing.
5. Participants should not wrap hands, feet, or other body parts in the swing rope.

Participant information.

1. Agree not to use excessive force to swing participants across.
2. Agree to encourage and support each person's swinging effort.
3. Spot takeoffs and landings carefully.

Spider's Web

Description.

A prefabricated web strung between two trees or poles made up of many holes or open web sections that normally differ in size. The group challenge is to pass members from one side to the other using the holes and without touching anything that is part of the structure of the web. Participants may be passed through separate holes or everyone may go through one hole. The group may be asked to return to the beginning side, the person who touches may be asked to return, or the group may lose holes if a touch occurs. A lifting spot is used.

Facilitator information.

1. Review lifting spot procedures with participants.

Participant information.

1. Maintain a rigid position with arms, legs, and hands staying still while being lifted and passed.

Spotter information.

1. Do not drop or let go of a participant because the web is touched.
2. Support the head and neck while lifting a participant.
3. Pass participant face up.
4. Support the body with hands and arms while lifting with the legs, not the back.
5. Lower feet first when putting a participant down.

Fall From Height

Description.

This activity allows a participant to fall backward from a platform in a controlled fashion. This activity requires a minimum of nine spotters. One participant stands on the platform away from the edge, facing the group. The facilitator stands at or on the platform to prepare the faller and to supervise the initial stages of the activity as appropriate. Use judgment to determine most appropriate placement with each faller. A minimum of eight catchers place arms, palm up in the "zipper" spotting formation. The faller designates an additional buddy spotter who will ensure the faller is appropriately aligned and spotters are appropriately positioned, with head and shoulders back. Spotters will support faller's head after the catch and help the faller to a feet-first standing position. When spotters are ready, the faller turns backward to the spotters, moves to the edge of the platform with heels slightly over and assumes ready position, to begin the communication system. The faller falls stiffly into the arms of the catchers who return the faller to a standing position.

Facilitator information.

1. Ask for volunteers to spot the climb to the platform.
2. Encourage participants to perform different roles and responsibilities.
3. Remove personal clothing and clothing that might hamper a fall or hurt the faller or catchers.
4. Review and assess readiness for "zipper" spotting procedures with participants.
5. Assess catcher placement for catching heavier body parts and potential jack-knife falls and adjust accordingly.
6. Reinforce skills, group and faller readiness, good setup, and choice.

Spotter information.

1. For zipper spotting technique, spotter's:
   a. Knees are bent, feet shoulder width apart in athletic stance;
   b. Arms are extended, palms up and arms bent at elbow;
   c. Arms alternate with spotter across from them, with fingertips extending to the opposite spotter's elbows;
   d. Head is tilted back with eyes on the participant at all times.
2. Buddy spotter responds for group.
3. Buddy spotter needs to pay close attention to supporting the head and neck and assisting the participant to an upright position.
4. Remove jewelry and hats.

Participant information.

1. Initiate communication system.
2. Maintain an upright standing position with back to spotters.
3. Interlock hands and tuck them to the chest.
4. Maintain a rigid position while falling.

Team Wall

Description.

This initiative task uses a 12-foot, flat wall (start side) with a small platform close to the top of the other side for participants to stand on (finish side). The task is to get the group up and over the wall using no props. Participants who are on the platform may assist participants to ascend the wall. Three people are allowed on the platform at one time and normally participants must descend the platform in the same order they came over the wall. A basic spot is used to spot exits off the platform. A basic spot is used to spot climbers from behind and to the sides of the wall face, in a tight rainbow formation. A running spot with other participants closing in using a basic spot is used to spot final participants to run at the wall intending to jump and reach the hands of the people on the platform.

Facilitator information.

1. Review variations on basic and running spotting procedures with participants, emphasizing the need to spot all possible fall directions.
2. Review safety issues related to lifting and pulling participants over the wall, and supporting and pushing participants up the wall.
3. Emphasize that spotter's must keep hands up until climber is completely over the wall and standing upright.
4. Indicate that both feet of all participants on the platform must remain in contact with the platform at all times.
5. Indicate that participants who have descended the platform may provide spotting assistance, but may not, otherwise, touch a climber.

Participant information.

1. Communicate clearly with other group members.
2. Agree to spot each other from the beginning of starting the wall, while on the top, and all the way down the back side.
3. Agree to have only three people on the top of the platform and one in transition.
4. Agree that no one should be in a position where their head is below their feet.

TP Shuffle and Maybe a Rectangle

Description.

These initiative tasks take place on one or more utility poles that are on the ground. The classic TP Shuffle is a single pole and the Maybe a Rectangle is a number of different size and length logs that provide corners to maneuver. Participants are challenged to change/switch positions on the log(s) without stepping off. This may be accomplished through many variations including a variety of line-up tasks or switching ends. Variations may be used as part of a sequence that should be determined based on client assessment and program goals.

Facilitator information.

1. Review group spotting procedures.
2. Remind participants to step off if a fall is imminent.

Participant information.

1. Walk on the log, do not run.
2. Pass people in a controlled manner.

Trolleys

Description.

This initiative task involves two boards with a number of hand ropes inserted through the boards for participants to hold. The group walks on the boards over a prescribed course (straight line, with obstacles on the ground, around obstacles, etc.) with each foot placed on one trolley. Participants who touch the ground may be asked to start at the back of the trolley, or turn backwards, and ropes that are dropped may be left on the ground. Basic spot is used to spot the front person as necessary.

Facilitator information.

1. Ask participants to step off of the Trolleys and let go of ropes to avoid an uncontrolled fall.

Whale Watches

Description.

This initiative task is available in two forms. The round Whale Watch is movable and smaller than the rectangular Whale Watch. Both include a platform balanced on a fulcrum like a giant seesaw or a spinning top. The group is challenged to balance itself on the platform for a negotiated amount of time or for long enough to complete a short task that does not require them to move. The basic spot is used as needed.

Facilitator information.

1. Set up the circular platform so that the pivot point is centered on the small sheet of plywood that accompanies it.
2. Review basic spotting procedures.
3. Instruct participants to step off the platform to avoid uncontrolled falls.
4. Instruct participants to enter and exit in an established way near the fulcrum.
5. Inform participants of safety issues, such as not having toes or fingers under the platform.

Wild Woozy

Description.

This initiative task consists of two cables that form a "V." Two participants, one per cable, walk the diverging cables while maintaining physical contact to a point where they can no longer continue without falling or they reach the end. A "bridge spot" is used in the center of the cables and a "basic spot" is used outside the cables.

Facilitator information.

1. Review *basic* and *bridge* spots.
2. Inform participants not to interlock fingers during activity.

Spotter information.

1. Understand that participants may fall in any direction when first starting the activity, and *basic* spotters to the outside are particularly important for the first 10 to 15 feet.
2. *Bridge* spotters should place hands above knees to avoid injury, and should maintain position to ensure that fallers contact the upper back.
3. *Bridge* spotters should be added to the outside of spotters who are in place in a way that does not unnecessarily interfere with the progress of participants.

Boojum Institute	*F* **Education**
	E **West Region**
	C **Various Populations**
	S **19.01–19.08**

Introduction

"Keep not standing, fixed and rooted,

Briskly venture, briskly roam."

~ Goethe

This manual is designed to review the philosophy and practice of educationally powerful and safely managed challenge course and initiative activities. It is no substitute for the experience and conservative judgment of trained staff, but we offer it as a guide to thoughts and actions toward excellence in outdoor education.

Challenge activities can have a great impact on participants because of the way they combine strong emotional, physical, and intellectual responses to perceived risk, challenge, and stress. Even though most challenge course activities employ contrived rather than natural challenge, they still may create significant stress; therefore, they should be used deliberately, with great clarity of purpose. These purposes may include:

- Fostering teamwork
- Having fun with each other and experiencing heights, agility, and balance
- Developing individual and group problem-solving skills
- Focusing commitment to the group process
- Coping with fear, developing courage, and finding inner strength
- Building character and the ability to set goals and overcome obstacles
- Increasing one's sense of self-confidence
- Learning to give and receive feedback
- Increasing mutual support within a group
- Growing closer to the outdoors and the natural world

Ground-based initiatives, low elements, and high elements can all have similar, powerful effects. Many times high elements are the most dramatic and memorable and are rich in learning and growth. On the other hand, some groups prefer a focus on activities more comfortable for the group to encounter.

Boojum offers challenge courses from a half day to 5 days in length, and we often integrate initiatives and games into our outdoor education courses. Boojum maintains its own year-round challenge course facility in Idyllwild and uses other courses at or near a number of other course areas. Challenge and initiative courses may also take place on site at a school.

Boojum provides challenge courses for many youth and adult groups, including school children, college students, teachers, administrators, staff, boards of trustees, and educational professional associations.

Challenge courses are particularly effective in personal development due to the high level of perceived risk and the lower level of real risk. Nevertheless, instructors should maintain high risk management awareness throughout each activity and solicit the same from participants.

Procedures and Guidelines

Procedures—General

All safety-related and other policy and procedures in other Boojum manuals and documents apply to challenge course and teambuilding activities and artificial climbing walls.

Instructor dress code.

We ask that Boojum staff refrain from wearing clothing with logos from other outdoor programs. These logos can confuse our client about who exactly is delivering this awesome, life-changing program. We also ask that Boojum staff make a point to wear their Boojum T-shirt on the first day of any challenge course or activity.

Lightning.

Once the sound of thunder comes within 15 seconds of lightning, all participants and staff should clear the course.

- Find a large unlocked camp building and assemble inside.
- Be sure to account for all of your participants and staff.
- If no suitable building is found, initiate lightning drill procedures and position once thunder and lightning are less than 10 seconds apart.
- There is to be no use of the challenge course after a thunderstorm until the CCSM has made a close inspection of all cables and trees. The CCSM should look for signs of direct strike as well as wind damage.

Natural hazards.

Staff should be aware of and what to do in the event that natural hazards that occur. These hazards may include rain/sleet, high winds, cold temperatures, and diminished visibility. See the Field Risk Management for procedures during natural hazards.

Fire/disaster.

Idyllwild Pines uses an air horn to indicate emergencies.

- If you hear an air horn, leave the challenge course quickly and assemble the whole group at the nearest flagpole on the camp.
- Be sure to account for all of your participants and staff.

Challenge Course Pre-Use Checklist

Prior to any challenge course, qualified Boojum field staff—either challenge course site manager or designate—shall complete and document the following risk management inspection. If any equipment or elements are found to be below standards, deficient or faulty, retire them and report the details to the program director so that repair or replacement may occur.

1. Visually inspect each element scheduled for use, looking at connecting points, couplings, knots, pulleys, and anchor systems. Inspect the condition of all support systems, trees, and poles. This inspection may be conducted from the ground. Inspect for breaks or kinks in cable; present and tight or otherwise functioning cable clamps, brackets, bolts, and other hardware. Look for cut or abraded ropes; inspect splices and knots for integrity. Ensure wood platforms and structures are secured, undamaged, and snugly attached. Check ladders and trees for loose staples, splinters, protruding nails, and rot. Look for hazardous insect nests, dead limbs in the air, and tripping hazards or other ground obstacles.
2. Physically and visually inspect each rope to be used for belaying prior to use. Complete the logbook for each rope used at the end of the session, following guidelines in the logbook for use. Inspection involves visual review and running the rope through the inspector's fingers. Inspect for cuts, abrasion, soft or flat spots, lumps or protrusions, discoloration, excessive fuzziness, and other damage.
3. Inspect all harnesses for sewing, webbing, and buckle integrity prior to use. Look for cut, stained, or abraded webbing, and cracks in or burrs on buckles.
4. Inspect all helmets for cracks, webbing and internal suspension system integrity and properly functioning buckles.
5. Inspect all carabiners prior to use for cracks, rust, and stiff or otherwise improperly functioning gates or barrels.
6. Inspect all belay devices and any other hardware or equipment prior to use for cracks, deformity, or missing pieces. Inspect for cracks, burrs, rust, and stiff moving parts.

Low and Ground-Based Elements

1. The minimum staff-to-student ratio is 1:15.
2. Low ropes elements shall be inspected by a qualified challenge course site manager or facilitator before each use.
3. Facilitators will conduct a safety briefing at the beginning of the day and prior to beginning each new activity.
4. Spotting, and lifting of heavy objects or of people, shall be done using proper technique as outlined in the Field Manual.
5. There will be a cell phone with reception or other appropriate telecommunications device on course at all times.
6. For trust falls, have the faller secure her hands in her pockets and keep elbows in to avoid hitting a spotter in the head with an elbow. Crossing arms tight over chest is also acceptable.

7. Staff shall ensure that weather and terrain are appropriate for participants' level of and comfort skills. If necessary, postpone activity until weather conditions improve.
8. Staff shall be qualified by being trained on the course prior to the event.

Guidelines

1. Carefully sequence events, taking into account: course goals, overall risk involved, time limits, physical condition of individuals, age and energy level of the group, weather and the terrain, and the (hopefully) increasing skill level and teamwork ability of the group. Remain flexible and sensitive to changes in the group throughout activity sessions. Have a contingency plan as well as a "rain plan" in case your original does not go as expected.
2. Facilitators will often lead a group debrief (or processing) session after participants have concluded an activity or element. Do not expect the activity or element to "speak for itself"; make a creative effort to encourage student discussion and reflection regarding individual and group performance. Let your facilitation efforts be guided by the course goals as well as your personal observations of interaction during the activity. Draw connections ("transference") between what was learned from involvement in an activity and what could be useful to participants when they return to their home environment. Consider criteria of a successful day by attempts to try new things and work together, rather than completion of elements.

SECTION 20

HIGH AND LOW CHALLENGE COURSES

Georgia College & State University

F	Education
E	Southeast Region
C	University Outdoor Education Students and General Population
S	20.01–20.10

General Policy

Ground School

Adhere to General Policy for Group Development Activities, Spotting and Initiative Tasks as appropriate. Ground School is built on five 25-foot poles and is located adjacent to the high challenge course. The structure includes a foot cable, platforms, and two belay cables at approximately 9 feet and 17 feet. Ground

School is designed to prepare participants for the high challenge course in two ways. It offers an approximate replication of the static belay experience, including platforms, for teaching static belay transfers. It also offers a location to teach dynamic belay skills to climbers and belayers, should participants be ready and willing to belay each other based on client assessment and program design (see Section 6: Belay Procedures of GCSU manual).

Low Challenge Course Elements

Ground School is also designed to provide low challenge course elements that may be tailored to participant needs and characteristics (see Section Four: Low Challenge Course Elements: Tension Cable Traverses, Triangle Traverse, and Group Traverse of GCSU manual).

Static Belay Instruction

Static belay transfer practice is prerequisite to the use of static elements on the high course. The lower level of Ground School provides an opportunity to practice this skill in a controlled environment. Skill instruction includes an overview provided by staff of the process of belay transfers, focusing on belay transfers with appropriate communication systems, and emphasizing the responsibility of the participant for his/her own safety throughout the experience. Participants practice two or more transfers until they can demonstrate physical and emotional readiness to self-belay using lobster claws. Participants may also practice adjusting the length of the lobster claws and regaining a foot cable. The facilitation team should implement a system to ensure that all participants have completed Ground School prior to using static elements on the high course.

Dynamic Belay Instruction

Ground School may be used to teach participants to belay using a dynamic belay system. Belay ropes can be affixed to the middle cable of Ground School using a steel locking carabiner to simulate a dynamic belay system. The climber and belayer start approximately 20 feet from Ground School, where they check and double-check each other's equipment. The climber initiates the communication system and then moves toward Ground School, simulating a vertical climb, while the belayer takes in rope. Climbers may move left and right on the ground or on a foot cable if a basic spot is used to simulate traversing an element. Groups should practice using a back-up belayer, anchor, buddy and other roles that will be used in programs to promote group involvement and responsibility. Participants should practice the dynamic belay skills until they demonstrate physical and emotional readiness to belay others using a dynamic belay system.

High Challenge Course

Adhere to General Policy for Group Development Activities, Spotting, Initiative Tasks, and Ground School as appropriate. The high challenge course is designed to accommodate a variety of individual and group experiences. Three types of high challenge course elements are available including nine dynamic belay elements, twelve static belay elements, and two zip lines. The high challenge course procedures included in this handbook require facilitators to be experienced in and able to teach specific spotting and belay techniques to participants as appropriate. Most programs that include the high challenge course are sequenced to culminate in this peak experience. If at any time the lead facilitator determines that the group is not ready for the high challenge course, the program should be adapted to achieve readiness for the high challenge course or be adapted to provide alternative, developmentally appropriate activities.

The Tango Tower is an exclusive ERi, Inc. climbing structure. It challenges individuals and groups to climb to the top of a tower using various route options that support individual or paired efforts. Once at the top, participants may "top off" and enjoy the view while processing the experience individually or with their group.

Setup and Takedown

During periods of regular use, belay hardware is left on the course and lazy lines are used to string belay ropes prior to each use. All ladders when in use as access points should be securely attached to the pole by means of a cam strap or ladder cradle. At the end of programs, lazy lines and hanging element structures (e.g., hand lines) should be securely wrapped around staples at least 12 feet off the ground to deter unapproved access. Ladders should be locked to trees or belay benches when not in use. During periods of irregular use, belay hardware may be removed, and facilitators may have to climb via leading edge to set up the belay system.

Leading Edge Climbing

Facilitators should avoid climbing in leading-edge environments whenever possible by using dynamic belay systems. Rope ascension with prussik belays, cable ascenders, or LEAP anchors should be used when a dynamic belay is not available. Staples are not an appropriate anchor for leading-edge climbing. Participants should never climb in a leading-edge environment.

Ladder Access

Ladders are used by both facilitators and participants to reach the lowest level of staples when climbing poles. Participants must have a minimum of two spotters holding the ladder while climbing up or down. Instruct climbers to use every rung of the ladder and not step off early. The rope ladder may also be attached to various element structures and belayed as an additional means of access to high elements.

Equipment

1. Handle hardware carefully by not dropping or throwing hardware to prevent potential fatigue and stress fractures.
2. Yell "rock" in the event that something falls from height to alert people on the ground.
3. Place equipment on a ground cloth or tarp out of the way of participant and facilitator traffic.
4. Instruct participants in the proper use and care of equipment including, but not limited to, helmets, harnesses, static belay claws, belay ropes, and carabiners.
5. Teach the proper use of helmets to protect the head from bumps, scrapes, and falling objects including:
   a. Adjusting for proper fit;
   b. Wearing helmets within the "fall zone" (area within an element's guy lines).
6. Demonstrate to the participant how to put on and properly fit a harness.
7. Offer participants the option of using a chest harness and encourage it for participants who may desire or require more upper body support.
8. Require the use of a chest harness and a seat harness on elements that specify to do so.

9. Attach dynamic belay lines to the harness using a double figure 8 loop with a carabiner or a figure 8 follow-through directly into the harness.
10. Use static belays, called lobster claws, on static belay elements.
11. Demonstrate how to adjust lobster claws to lengthen or shorten as needed.
12. Girth hitch lobster claws onto carabiner and clip the carabiner to the seat harness according to the manufacturer's specifications.
13. Check harnesses for proper fit, attachment, and buckles prior to ascending the course.

Harness Types

The **Challenge Seat Harness** manufactured by **Edelweiss** can be used with both a dynamic belay line and static belays. The dynamic belay line can be clipped into the large black belay loop or tied into the belay loop. Static belay claws should be clipped into the belay loop.

The **Endurance Seat Harness** manufactured by **On Rope 1** can be used with both a dynamic belay line and static belays. The dynamic belay line can be clipped into the large yellow belay loop or tied into the waist and leg loops. Static belays should be clipped into the yellow belay loop.

The **Head Wall Chest Harness** is used in conjunction with either of the above seat harnesses. The seat-chest harness combination is clipped into a double figure 8 loop on the end of the belay line with a separate locking carabiner into each harness.

The **kid's and adults full-body harnesses** made by **Singing Rock** should be tied directly into the two front chest loops. These harnesses should not be used with a front clip-in and consequently cannot be used for the static course or zip line. The adult's full body harness may also be clipped into at the large metal ring on the back of the harness.

Belay Procedures

High challenge course elements include dynamic belay, static belay systems, and special element belay systems. Element descriptions are grouped according to belay systems.

Participant Belayers

1. The lead facilitator may elect to teach participants how to belay other participants. This decision should be based on, but not limited to:
   a. The number of facilitators available to teach, supervise, or provide belay systems;
   b. Participant readiness to participate as dynamic belay teams;
   c. Program length and design;
   d. Number of participants;
   e. Physical attributes of the element.
2. Teach participants belay techniques at Ground School.

3. Provide direct supervision for the belay system or perform a backup belay role to a participant belayer.
4. Ensure that participant belayers have both a backup belayer and an anchor (person or belay bench) prior to belaying.

Dynamic Belay Systems

1. Maintain a clear view of the climber from a place on the ground that is free from environmental obstruction and is accessible to backup assistance.
2. Inspect the climber for readiness to climb by doing a visual and/or tactile check prior to climbing, including:
   a. Ensuring that the harness and helmet are secured properly;
   b. Ensuring that the dynamic belay rope is secured to the harness using the appropriate knot that is properly tied in accordance with manufacturer specifications;
   c. Ensuring that carabiners are locked with a "squeeze check" and properly positioned;
   d. Ensuring that objects, clothing, or hair that affect the system are removed or tucked in.
3. Use proper spotting and climbing commands.
4. Review spotting and belay procedures and commands with participants as needed.
5. Remain attentive to a climber's needs, taking in or letting out slack as necessary.
6. Remind climbers to "follow their rope up" to prevent the belay rope from snagging on element structures and causing falls to result in swings.
7. Control descents when a climber descends an element for any reason.
8. In the unlikely event that a participant cannot be lowered via ground belay, a designated facilitator will initiate and manage rescue lowering procedures.
9. The primary belayer will be responsible for the safety of the climber until the climber communicates that s/he is "off belay."
10. Limit one participant to a single belay cable to enable a facilitator to move on any cable in an emergency.
11. Several dynamic elements have double belay lines allowing the element to be used with two participants at once. In this case:
    a. Element ropes are designated for use on the inner or outer belay cable;
    b. Belayer should be located inside or outside the respective belay cable (e.g., the Vine Walk outer cable should be belayed from outside the dynamic course);
    c. Care should be exercised when two contiguous "inner" elements are used at the same time to prevent confusion at the joining poles.
12. Dynamic elements on the high challenge course are typically "traversing" elements in which the participant moves from one pole to another; while those on the Tango Tower, the Pamper Pole, and the static course access are "ascending" elements in which the

participant climbs to the top of the element and is then lowered to the ground. Different techniques are utilized for traversing and ascending elements:

a. Ascending elements allow for the use of belay benches as at the Tango Tower. People are used as anchors for traversing elements or when belay benches are not accessible.

b. Pole climbs and lowering at the end of an element should be belayed as an ascending element. Falls while a climber is on a pole could lead to a pendulum swing due to the sag built into the belay cable. Belayers should position themselves to bring the belay system as close as possible to the starting pole while the participant is ascending and have the participant move back out onto the element approximately 8 to 10 feet to be lowered whenever possible.

c. Belayers should stay in line with the climber and move along the ground in front of the element. Ensure that this area is clear of obstructions, and coordinate with other facilitators to minimize contact between belay teams on contiguous elements.

Dynamic Belay Commands

Belayer	Climber/Rappeller	Meaning and Response Needed
	"on belay?"	Are you ready? Is the belay on?
"belay on"		All set. The belay will now catch you if you fall.
	"climbing"/"rappelling"	I am ready to climb/rappel.
"climb on"/ "rappel on"		Go ahead; the rope will be controlled by the belay.
	"slack"	The climber needs some slack in the rope. The belayer should feed out a small amount of rope. No verbal answer required.
	"tension"/ "that's me"	The climber has some slack in the rope. The belayer should take in rope until the climber communicates "that's me."
	"rope" or "rock"	A rope or another object is coming down—do not look.
"clear"		You may drop the rope; the area is clear.
	"off belay"	Take off the belay, I am secure and will no longer need the belay.
"belay off"		The belay is off, echoed to ensure there is not misunderstanding.

Static Belay Systems

1. Teach static changeovers at Ground School prior to climbing.
2. Use dynamic belay systems to access static elements.
3. Inform climbers of their responsibility for personal safety.

4. Review the use of spotting, climbing, and transfer commands used throughout the experience.
5. Secure the dynamic belay rope and static lobster claws to the harness as detailed in Section 6: Equipment in GCSU manual.
6. Limit three participants to a single belay cable at the same time to enable a facilitator to move on any cable in an emergency. Exceptions are the platform on the Tango Tower and the group elements, which may have four participants on a single cable.
7. Designate platform supervisor(s) to monitor climbers ready to commence a belay-assisted ascent or descent from a platform, including establishing a static belay prior to removing dynamic belay and vice versa.
8. Designate one facilitator "in the air" for every four participants "in the air" to supervise static belay transfers.
9. Position at least one facilitator on each level of the static course when both levels are being used.
10. Position facilitators comfortably "in the air" on platforms or other structures.
11. Require participants to execute the appropriate communication system for transfers between elements and to receive verbal authorization from the supervising facilitator for every transfer.

Static Transfer Commands

Participant to facilitator on platform:	"Will you watch me transfer?"
Facilitator to participant:	"Yes I will."
Participant to facilitator on platform:	"May I transfer first carabiner?"
Facilitator to participant:	"Transfer first carabiner. Please flip and squeeze-check gate."
Participant to facilitator on platform:	"Squeeze check. May I transfer second carabiner?"
Facilitator to participant:	"Transfer second carabiner. Please flip and squeeze-check gate."
Participant to facilitator on platform:	"Squeeze check. May I continue?"

Special Element Belay Systems

1. The Four-Way Pamper Pole makes use of a special belay technique called a Z-belay, which uses two permanently installed eyebolts on a pole for creating friction. The eyebolt on the very bottom of each pole is not part of the Z-belay system. (see Section Six: Dynamic Elements: Four-Way Pamper Pole).
   a. The Z-belay is set up by running the belay rope down the pole from the shear-reduction device on the belay cable, through the lower eyebolt, up through the upper eyebolt, and finally back down along the pole. The final setup should resemble a sideways "Z."

   b. The Z-belay is managed by a minimum of three participant belayers or two facilitators. The belayers alternate sides of the belay rope and use an alternating hand sliding technique to move rope through the belay system.
2. Ziplines utilize a tether attached to a steel double-wheeled cable pulley. The full use of this system is described below (see Section Six: Special Elements: Zip Line of GCSU manual).
3. Tango Tower and static access platforms often do not require participants to transfer from one static belay cable to another, such as when participants have a group debrief or are preparing to use the zip line. A static tether may be used in these situations.
   a. Static belay lobster claws are used "upside down" so that two participants may tether to each leg of the lobster claw.
   b. Up to four people may be attached to each belay cable on the top of the Tango Tower and the static access platforms.
   c. Designate one facilitator "in the air" for every eight participants "in the air" to supervise static tethers.
   d. One facilitator should remain on the ground to manage emergency situations.
   e. Participants using static tethers are not required to complete Ground School training if a facilitator directly supervises (hands-on) all transfers to and from the tether.

Climbing on Poles

Facilitator Responsibilities

1. Remind participants to climb staples and not poles.
2. Discuss potential hazards of climbing poles, including but not limited to:
   a. Splinters;
   b. Allergies to chemicals used to treat poles.

Rescue Procedures

1. Review general guidelines. *PPM Reminder:* Rescue Philosophy and Procedures.
2. Designate one facilitator to initiate and manage standard rescue procedures.
3. Locate rescue bags for dynamic course elements to enhance potential rescue requirements considering client assessment and program design; locate rescue bags for static course elements on the static course.
4. Inspect the contents of rescue bags prior to the program for the following contents:
   a. Belay rope;
   b. Rescue figure 8;
   c. Rescue knife or EMT shears;
   d. Etrier;

   e. 2 steel carabiners;
   f. 2 cordelette loops.

5. Encourage facilitators to carry personal rescue equipment, which may include shears or a knife, cordelette loops or slings, carabiners, and a belay device.
6. Provide calm, deliberate, and safe actions to provide help.
7. Rescue a stuck participant using a sequence of steps including:
   a. Move toward a participant who is unable to regain an element or needs to be lowered on dynamic belay with a rescue bag via the quickest route;
   b. Attach rescue equipment to the belay cable using a steel carabiner;
   c. Calm the participant with words of comfort and reassurance;
   d. Assist the participant to climb back onto the element (talking, tension, etrier, etc.);
   e. Continue to communicate with the participant throughout the completion of the element.
8. Rescue a participant in an emergency situation using a sequence of steps including:
   a. Move toward a participant who is unable to regain an element or needs to be lowered on dynamic belay with a rescue bag via the quickest route;
   b. Assess the severity of the situation and request that a ground facilitator call 911 if needed;
   c. Begin emergency take-down procedures immediately, including:
      - Communicate intentions clearly to ground crew.
      - Attach and lock carabiner with figure 8 device to belay cable.
      - Hook and lock the carabiner on the super figure 8 to the participant's harness.
      - Remove sheers from pocket of bag.
      - Make sure the ground is clear, and drop the rescue bag.
      - Select a lowering method and communicate the chosen method to other facilitators.
      - If available, a facilitator on the ground should manage the rescue belay.
      - Ensure that the rescue belay is on and that all possible slack is out of the rescue belay system.
      - Attempt to loosen and remove original belay system. If the initial belay system cannot be removed either from the harness or the belay cable, it will need to be cut with rescue shears.
      - Safely lower participant to ground on rescue belay rope.
9. Perform most rescues from the middle of the zip line by using a stepladder to access the participant.

10. Perform rescues at the far ends of the zip line by using the contents of one rescue bag to "lower" slowly down the zip line to prevent the rescuer from colliding with the participant, and a second rescue bag to perform a lower rescue as described above.

Tango Tower

Belay Benches

Belay benches will act as anchors for belayers on the Tango Tower. All belayers will be tethered to the belay benches and belay off of their harnesses. Attach the dynamic belay line to the harness using a double figure 8 loop with a carabiner or a figure 8 follow-through directly into the harness. Make a double figure 8 loop approximately 3 feet from the end of the rope and clip these loops into the belay bench eye bolts thus anchoring to the bench. The dynamic belay device will then be loaded with the rope between the climber and the belay bench.

Topping off

It may be necessary for participants to top off on the Tango Tower in order to access the zip line or to transfer to a rappel. The lead facilitator may also choose to have participants top off for processing. When topping off is an option for the Tango Tower, one facilitator should be belayed to the top of the tower and then transfer onto claws. Participants may then be transferred onto tethers and off of their dynamic belays by the facilitators on top of the tower. There must be one facilitator for every eight participants on the platform, and not more than four people on a cable. It may be necessary to belay from the top of the tower to get the last facilitator to the top of the Tango Tower platform. Belays on the top of the tower should be performed only by staff and should be securely anchored to the tower.

Charleston County Parks & Recreation		
	F	**Recreation**
	E	**Southeast Region**
	C	**General Population**
	S	**20.01–20.10**

Challenge Course Program Information

Mission

The Charleston County Parks & Recreation Commission Challenge Course Program will improve the quality of life in Charleston County by offering custom programs focused on the acquisition and application of knowledge through direct experiences as related to individual and group development.

Philosophy

The Charleston County Parks & Recreation Commission's Challenge Course Program is dedicated to experiential education in the provision of all programs. Through appropriate, hands-on experiences, participants will develop skills as they relate to the individual and group goals outlined at the beginning of each course. Utilizing the foundations of challenge course experiences, such as Full Value Contract©, Challenge by Choice©, goal setting, trust development, and sequencing, the program strives to develop ownership and responsibility in participants in terms of learning and strives to make the application of such skills and knowledge meaningful.

Goals

1. Provide appropriate, custom challenge course experiences.
2. Work toward the successful completion of group and individual goals.
3. Provide a secure environment for individual and group challenge.

Skills Proficiency Check Sheet for Challenge Course Facilitators

Facilitator Level 1 Skills Proficiency Exam

Low Challenge Course

	Processing/Debriefing Questions and Techniques
	Safety Requirements for 5 Elements
	Story Lines for Elements (at least 3)
	Spotting Techniques (demonstrate and teach)
	Benefits of Challenge Course
	Facilitators Role
	Perceived Risk vs. Actual Risk
	"Full Value Contract" (examples of, and when to use them)
	"Challenge by Choice" (examples of, and when to use them)
	Ability to Use Radio and Change Channels

Facilitator Level 2 Skills Proficiency Exam

This proficiency exam is to work high challenge course groups. If you do not wish to work high course groups you may go to Level 3 proficiency exam.

High Challenge Course Platform Facilitator

	Completed Facilitator Level 1 Proficiency Exam
	High Course and Alpine Tower
	Setup and Takedown of Alpine Tower
	Setup and Takedown of High Course (static and dynamic)
	Leading Edge Climbing on High Course
	Rescues from Alpine Tower
	Rescues from High Course (static and dynamic)
	Rappelling off High Course (where, when, and how)
	Ascending Pole with Prussik System
	Equipment/Hardware: (types, applications and safety)
	Carabiners (strength, types, and uses)
	Harnesses (how to put on, etc.)
	Helmets (helmet zones)
	Knots: (tie, teach, applications)
	Figure 8 Family (single, follow through, bight)
	Bowline on a Bight
	Prussik (double fishermans)
	In-Line 8
	Clove Hitch
	Waterknot
	Belaying: (demonstrate and teach)
	Devices (ATCs, Trangos, figure 8, rescue 8)
	Belaying and Climbing Commands

High Challenge Course Ground Facilitator

	Knots: Bowline on a bight, in-line 8, figure 8 family, prussik
	Rescue Procedure: Butt belay, belay commands, lowering procedure
	Belay Procedures: Belay commands, firemen's belay, monitoring clip-in
	Zip Line Procedures: Zip line commands, zip team operations
	Group Management Procedures: Managing participants on ground, helmet zones

Facilitator Level 3 Skills Proficiency Check Exam

Low Challenge Course

	Completed Facilitator Level 2 Proficiency Exam
	Safety Requirements for All Elements
	Story Lines for Elements (at least 5)
	Metaphors, Use
	Sequencing, describe and explain, examples
	Group Planning for a Challenge Course Day
	Group Planning for Persons with Disabilities
	Develop Contingency Plan (in case of bad weather)
	Group Development Models
	Conflict Resolution Models
	Individual Membership to AEE, ACCT, PA (or other recognizable organization)
	Plan Out a Full Day for a Corporate Client

Foundations of the Challenge Course Experience

Experiential Education

Experiential education is learning by doing. Challenging participants with an activity or initiative in which the process of solving it forces participants to use important teamwork skills. They can reflect on the experience and perfect the individual and team skills.

Known also as a ropes course, a challenge course consists of permanent structures of wood, cable, trees, and rope. These structures are called *elements*. They are located in a wooded, outdoor area. The elements, or challenges, are designed to be done with a group.

Initiatives or challenge course games introduce the group of participants to the challenge course idea, to each other, or help to stretch out, warm up, or "break the ice." Some initiative challenges can be passive in nature. They usually consist of mobile props.

The adult who introduces these challenges to a group, thereby facilitating group and individual change, is a facilitator. They monitor the safety and add fun to the challenge.

Full Value Contract© Project Adventure

This is an agreement among the participants of what they expect from one another for the duration of their challenge course. It is a listing of desired behaviors conducive to a safe, fun, and challenging experience. There are many ways in which a FVC may be written.

Challenge by Choice© Project Adventure

Participants often are concerned that they will be asked to engage in an activity that they do not want to do. Challenge by Choice simply means that the individual chooses to what extent they will participate.

There are many levels and forms of participation. Hopefully, there is something that they will feel comfortable doing, such as spotting, line judging, cheering, etc. All are important to the experience.

Sequencing

All challenges are selected for an individual group, according to what they want to accomplish. The challenges will increase in degree of difficulty so that groups deal with a manageable level of stress and challenge.

1. *Flow experience:* The challenges increase in a variety of areas; physical difficulty, level of trust involved, complexity of problem, emotional involvement, required level of leadership, etc.
2. *Observing growth:* Watch the group during processing to see what they have actually learned and what needs to be challenged again. This is a judgment decision on what they are ready for next.
3. *Connecting:* Often, one initiative naturally leads into another. The skills or logic needed to work toward the solution on one initiative may be taken to the next logical step on the next initiative. (For example: Initiative 1: building bridge and moving with 2 boards; Initiative 2: building bridge and moving with 3 boards and a bucket.)
4. *Successes:* Having success early is very important to group development. Sequencing and observing the group development will allow you to gauge how the group is progressing. After a very hard or frustrating initiative, or one in which they fail, an easy activity or one with a high rate of success is soothing. Please *avoid* activities that are too hard and are impossible for the group at their present level of development. This just breaks them down. Initiatives should be challenging, not impossible. You should never take the participants to a place from which you are not qualified to bring them back. Know your limits.

Story Lines

Using story lines in the presentation of group initiatives serves to grab attention; they relatc to the participants' imaginations. If presented respectfully and appropriately, story lines can bring cohesiveness and common purpose to an effort. They can be used *metaphorically* to fit the group's needs or life experiences, thereby drawing analogies to home, school, life, etc. They can create a scenario of "out of the ordinary," an adventure. Story lines should always be fun, motivating, and inspire ideas.

1. Length: As fun and useful as story lines may be, they are still just a "trapping." Therefore, keep it short. Your objective is to get as many of the rules and safety parameters into the story lines possible. Afterward, cover any rules and safety issues.
2. *Variations:* Try creating new story lines, co-facilitate with new staff, create a notebook resource of good themes and stories, combine events, make events harder, change the rules or goals, try new ideas from books, etc. Story lines that are based on the goals of the group and what they want from their experience are also beneficial.

Benefits of a Challenge Course

1. Builds self-confidence and personal leadership skills
2. Promotes fun in an outdoor environment

3. Teaches groups problem-solving skills, creative thinking, and initiative
4. Explores the value of diversity of individuals in a group
5. Increases group cohesiveness and trust
6. Fosters communication and decision-making skills
7. Encourages goal development and achievement
8. Develops responsibility for self and group
9. Enhances respect for individuals' unique abilities and limitations

Qualities of a Positive Challenge Course Experience

1. *Trust:* Participants can share, explore, and challenge themselves while feeling safe. It starts with role modeling by the facilitator.
2. *Communication:* In order to establish trust, people will need to share and communicate. You want participants to communicate with each other and with you.
3. *Cooperation:* Participants working, struggling, playing, and succeeding together.
4. *Fun:* Participants need time to play and learn to enjoy the group.

Expectations of a Challenge Course Facilitator

An effective *facilitator* provides the framework for an *effective* Challenge Course:

Boundaries

The facilitator is in charge of safety and rules, is goal directed, and creates an environment that is emotionally and socially safe.

Trust

The facilitator establishes and demonstrates trust, openness, and honesty.

Energy

The facilitator maintains momentum, keeping it fun and enjoyable for all.

Meaning

The facilitator helps the group to understand the lessons emerging from the experiences.

Ownership

The facilitator is not the sole leader, the leadership moves within the group. Sometimes you guide, sometimes you lead, and sometimes they move, lead, and process themselves.

Responsibility

As a challenge course facilitator, you are responsible for everything that happens at the challenge course during your shift. The position of a challenge course facilitator requires a great deal of responsibility because the daily operation of the challenge course is entrusted to your care, including the setup, equipment, paperwork, employees, problem solving, emergency procedures, and closing. You are responsible for the success of the challenge course and you must be capable of handling the duties assigned to you.

Commitment

Being a challenge course facilitator requires a great deal of commitment, especially when concerning your time. Simply the fact that you have been selected as a challenge course facilitator indicates that you have already shown a commitment to the program. By committing your time and effort, you are attempting to educate yourself and gain experience in order to become a better employee. Remember that this is your program and what you get out of it is what you put into it.

Attitude

Maintaining a positive attitude is essential to effective customer service. Your job will be as enjoyable as you make it. Remember that you must always be courteous and helpful when dealing with others, whether it is with participants or employees and especially in situations where someone is dissatisfied. Your attitude is a reflection of our program and hopefully it can be passed on to your fellow employees and participants. Ensuring that everyone has a positive experience is important so that they will keep coming back.

Communication

Practicing open communication in every aspect is necessary in order to maintain consistency and effectiveness. Two-way communication between the challenge course facilitators and the program coordinator is important so that daily operations run smoothly and consistently. Remember that you are the ones who manage the challenge course on a day-to-day basis, so your input is a great resource. Also be sure that you communicate with each other, whether it is at meetings or between and during shifts. Again, you can learn from each other and keep up program consistency. Finally, communication with participants is extremely important so that you can better serve their needs. Be sure that you communicate with them in a courteous and helpful manner. Remember that communication is the key.

Dedication

Again, our program is only as successful as its employees. We depend on you to provide us with a valuable service—your time and commitment. You serve as role models for other employees, and the experience that you gain is what makes our program work. Because you represent our program, you should want it to be a success. Remember to autograph your work with your performance.

Trustworthiness

Your duties require that you show tremendous responsibility. You are being entrusted with the security of the challenge course and various equipment, as well as with running the show when it comes to the daily supervision of the challenge course. We trust that you will perform your job to the best of your ability and will be responsible when carrying out your tasks. Your position is one of authority, so take pride in it. As an employee of the outdoor recreation program, you are representing the entire Charleston County Parks & Recreation Commission program and its staff. Whether you are answering a participant's question or instructing an employee, you must consider that everyone you come into contact with is important to our program. You are expected to be helpful and courteous at all times and to be polite and attentive to each individual. You are expected to exemplify the positive image of the CCPRC program that participants are expecting.

Facilitator's Role

Facilitators should structure the experience to meet specific objectives and goals of the group. The facilitator's function is to create situations and learning climates in which participants encounter challenge and growth. Facilitators should:

1. Be attentive to the group at all times
2. Listen and observe
3. Give verbal and nonverbal appreciation to others and receive it
4. Feel and express self-appreciation; role model what we teach
5. Defer judgment
6. Give useful feedback and observations and guidance for change
7. Lead and follow others
8. Accept individuals and feelings but not all behavior
9. Confront issues in a positive and constructive manner
10. Manage consequences, rules, and safety
11. Foster and role model accepting attitudes toward other opinions
12. Be flexible, customer-service oriented, and fun to be with
13. Create safe environments for challenge, change, and learning
14. Be an active spotter and supervisor of spotters
15. Explain clearly the goal, rules, story line, safety, and consequences of elements
16. Be an arbitrator of discussion and a sounding board
17. Be a presenter of challenges, elements, and insights for change

Facilitating the Experience

Numerous different factors must be kept in mind while working a challenge course. All of these come into play to provide for the needs of the participants. As a facilitator, it is your responsibility to ensure the quality of their challenge course experience. Keep these guidelines in mind as you plan for the challenge course.

1. Be flexible. Select an activity suited to the age and abilities of the group.
2. Clearly present the rules and guidelines. Ask if there are any questions before they begin. Then, step back and let them struggle through the activity. *Do not* give the answers away.
3. Use creativity, metaphors, or story lines to add further interest and tie in to daily life. Change or add consequences to add interest or challenge.
4. There is no "one way" to accomplish any activity, as long as it is done safely. The process of solving the challenge is more important than the outcome.
5. Sequence activities to progress from simple to more difficult.

6. At the conclusion of each activity, process or debrief the experience. The experience is worth more if they can learn from it.

7. *Intervene* if safety is jeopardized.

Behavior Management

Having control of the group in order for the challenge course experience to occur, as well as be of benefit, is very important. Knowing what to do will come with time and experience working with groups. There are some general guidelines to be aware of to manage the group.

1. Use positive rather than negative statements any time you intervene or try to tell the participants not to do something a certain way.

2. Align your participants so that you, and not the participants, are facing the sun squinting. Let them see your eyes and face—take off the sunglasses.

3. Use specific rather than general statements; "When you said, 'You suck,' that was when you hurt my feelings."

4. Use pleasant requests, calm and controlled, rather than scolding. Use thorough patient directions rather than stressed and rushed.

5. Be consistent in requests and rules and behaviors with all participants.

6. Give the participant choices and consequences up front.

7. Avoid making threats and avoid confrontations with them. Also, avoid getting angry over the issue.

8. Be flexible with different styles and approaches based on the client group you are facilitating.

9. Redirect hyperactive energies but stimulate the shy or withdrawn.

10. Behavior management is drastically different for youth and for adults. Be wise and think before you act.

11. Children especially may have short attention spans. If the group looks like they are bored, change the activity.

12. Talk to kids, not at them; get down to their level.

13. Role model having fun by smiling and laughing. Attitude is contagious.

14. Adapt the rules of an activity to have as many people participating as possible.

Spotting

Spotting involves one or more individuals in a position to prevent the head and spine of a participant from making contact with the ground. Falling off things is to be expected. Proper and alert spotting helps prevent falls from causing injury. Some basic rules of correct spotting are:

1. *Position:* The spotter must be taught proper form and be in a position to be effective.

2. *Attention:* The spotter watches the "faller" constantly.

3. *Anticipation:* The spotter's hands extend toward the "faller," anticipating a move or fall at all times.

4. *Listening:* The spotter must listen to the "faller" and the "faller" must communicate to his/her spotters.

Spotting varies considerably according to the event and changing positions by the "faller." Facilitators should place spotters in the best spot possible for each element and see to it that the group maintains this placement, or adapts and moves, properly.

Facilitators should encourage spotters to change around, take breaks as needed, perhaps with each new "faller." Make sure your first volunteer spotters don't burn out their energies by spotting the entire time.

Spotting techniques must be taught and practiced and constantly watched for correctness. Participants should understand that a spotter who breaks a fall, even though the spotter and the "faller" end up on the ground, has indeed performed his/her job.

Spotting is very serious. Never settle for poor spotting. This is not the time for silliness or stories. Good spotting is one of the most useful team-building aspects of a course. Each participant in turn assumes responsibility for the safety and well-being of each other. Individual confidence is heightened in this supportive atmosphere.

Keys to Teaching Spotting

1. Know the initiatives and the possibilities for accidents.
2. Provide an adequate number of spotters for the participant and the initiative.
3. Small or weak participants should not spot larger participants alone.
4. Remind participants to keep hands up and fingers together at all times.
5. Remind participants to stay close to the "faller," be attentive, but do not interfere with their movements. Effective spotters move through the element with the "faller."
6. Do not allow their attention to be diverted while spotting.
7. The facilitator should place themselves in a position to assist in some spotting as needed and supervise all spotting.
8. Participants should begin all activities that need spotting with commands: "Spotters Ready?" Spotters reply, "Ready!" Participant asks, "Falling?" Spotters reply, "Fall Away!" Same commands for all activities.
9. Be clear in explaining the importance of good spotting and how it develops trust.
10. Distinguish between spotting, catching, and assisting. Repeatedly emphasis that spotting is to be taken seriously.

Challenge Course Operating Procedures and Guidelines

The following are procedures and guidelines to be used in the instruction and leading of all Charleston County Parks & Recreation Commission Challenge Course programs. Facilitator's are expected to be familiar with, and abide by, all safety procedures and guidelines, and are expected to exercise the judgment and caution of a prudent professional operating within acceptable industry standards.

Participation: While participants may be encouraged to try activities that they may feel apprehensive about, direct coercion or force is not permitted. Except as required by an emergency situation, no participant shall be required to participate in any part of the program they do not wish. However, participants should be informed that they might be prohibited from future participation in any part of the program that requires such previous experience.

Ratios

1. *Low Challenge Course:* A group consists of 8 to15 participants. We require 1 staff for every group, minimally.
2. *High Challenge Course:* A group consists of 8 to 20 participants. We require 3 staff for the operation of the high course.
3. *Alpine Tower:* A group consists of 8 to 15 participants. Staff requirements are dependent on the age of the group participants as well as the size. A minimum of 2 staff members are required for operation of the Alpine Tower, with additional staff at the discretion of the program coordinator (ORC/ORS).

Low Challenge Course

Roles and Responsibilities of Staff

1. All participants must have a signed, completed Hold Harmless Form before entering the course. *There are no exceptions,* including individuals who will only be observing.
2. Review all Hold Harmless Forms. Make notes on any special cases that may require extra caution and/or observation in appropriate situations.
3. A first-aid kit and trained staff must be available on the challenge course.
4. Participants will be informed of the inherent risks involved in each activity.
5. Participants will be informed of the safety "Stop" procedure.
6. Participants will be informed of environmental hazards on the challenge course (ants, wet grass, gnats, etc.).
7. Spotting techniques must be taught before moving to trust initiatives that require spotting.
8. Sharp objects, jewelry, rings, and objects in pockets must be removed before participating.
9. Set parameters that are safe, challenging, thought provoking, and fun.
10. Meet with the other facilitators to ensure that everyone is familiar with his/her roles and the overall plan.
11. Review the group's goals and objectives.
12. Establish ground rules about safety including physical and emotional safety guidelines.
13. Participants will be informed of Leave No Trace ethics on the challenge course.
14. Walk the course and check it's overall condition, removing any hazards (downed branches, etc.) and visually inspect all elements.
15. Provide rest and water breaks.

High Challenge Course

Roles and Responsibilities of Staff

1. All participants must have a **signed, completed** Hold Harmless Form before entering the course. *There are no exceptions,* including individuals who will only be observing.
2. Review all Hold Harmless forms. Make notes on any special cases that may require extra caution and/or observation in appropriate situations.
3. A first-aid kit and trained staff must be available on the challenge course.
4. Participants will be informed of the inherent risks involved in each activity.
5. Participants will be informed of the safety "Stop" procedure.

Ground staff.

1. Monitor the radio.
2. Monitor the belay system and all ground clip-ins.
3. Monitor the zip ladder.
4. Create and monitor the "zip team."
5. Belay if a lower is necessary.
6. During belay, double-check harness, helmet, and carabiner.
7. Make sure zip team and all participants in the helmet zone have helmets on.
8. When Zip Staff says "Clear the zip!" this staff makes sure the Zip Team is in place and at least 5 feet to the side of the zip.

Platform/zip staff.

1. Perform crab claw clip-in and transfer from wall belay.
2. Monitor first transfer.
3. Send participants off the zip.
4. Maintain the flow of things, people going up and down.

The corner staff.

1. Observe entire course and assist the other staff.
2. Maintain constant visual checks on the participants during all transfers especially from the Burma Bridge to the Postman's Walk and to the Multiline.
3. When the participant reaches the Corner Staff, they should always visually check the carabiner at the harness and the harness buckle.
4. When the Zip Staff says "Clear the zip!" this staff makes sure participants are aware of the zip.
5. There is an eye bolt at this station for emergency rappel situations.

Extra platform staff.

1. This person will be available when the group size is 20 or more at the discretion of the program coordinator (ORC/ORS).

All staff.

1. You are in charge and you can stop things if you feel unsafe. *Do not hesitate—intervene.*
2. Make sure commands are being stated clearly for all transfers.
3. Monitor helmet zones.
4. Encourage the participants to challenge themselves and choose when to stop.
5. Allow participants ownership of their experience; provide the necessary direction and support, while allowing them the opportunity to make decisions.
6. Ensure only one participant is on each element at a time.

Helmets

1. All participants will wear helmets while within the high course perimeter or the Alpine Tower perimeter.
2. Helmets should fit snugly above the eyebrows. All helmets are adjustable by using the dials located on either side of the helmet. The chinstrap should be properly clipped and located approximately a ½ inch behind the edge of the chin. The helmet should never ride high on the participant's head.
3. Helmets are not to be used as seats on the ground.

Harnesses

1. All harnesses should be worn according to their standards and directions.
2. Waist belts should be tightened on the waist. Leg loops should be tightened. Two fingers should not be able to turn sideways in the waist belt or leg loops.
3. All harnesses and helmets should be double-checked by both staff before climbing begins.
4. All harnesses should be double-checked by the facilitator at the zip-line position before the participants exit the high course.

Rope

1. The high course and Alpine Tower both use static or low-stretch rope.
2. Although stepping on the rope does not severely damage the kerns inside the sheath, CCPRC would like to instruct all participants that misuse of equipment can lead to unneeded wear and tear. This will result in early retirement, thus an unneeded replacement expense. So, don't step on the ropes.

Setup

On the course.

1. When climbing poles, staff will use the prussik ascending system.

a. A triple wrap prussik is hitched to the ascending lanyard and clipped to an independent carabiner on the belay loop of the harness. Facilitator claws are carried to the platform where they are secured before the prussic system is disengaged.

2. Facilitators must wear a helmet at all times when participants are on the course. Helmets are optional when performing maintenance on top of the course and are highly recommended when assisting with maintenance underneath the course when some one is above.

3. Set up belay stations (flipped and clipped).

4. Set up zip pulley (flipped and clipped).

The wall.

1. The static belay rope goes through the spin static pulley and back to the ground.

2. Clip in for the wall is the double bowline that clips directly into the harness.

3. Run belay end of the rope through eyebolts.

    a. Approximately 3 feet from the eyebolt, tie an in-line figure 8; tie two more at 3-foot intervals. These are clip-in points for the belay team

4. A climber must have three belayers in order to begin climbing.

5. Use the belay commands, "On belay?" "Belay is on," "Climbing?" "Climb on!"

Ground School—Static Course

The purpose of Ground School is to have each participant practice using the crab claws, making a changeover, sitting in a harness, and going over the commands with their ground partner. The buddy system is introduced during Ground School. This continues to incorporate the teambuilding aspect of the challenge course we encourage. This is a very important aspect of the high course and involves great attention.

1. Commands:

    a. Participant: "Sam, unclipping one"

    b. Ground: *"Go ahead Dave"*

    c. Participant: "Clip, flip, twist, turn it back, squeeze"

    d. Participant: "Sam, unclipping two"

    e. Ground: *"Go ahead Dave"*

    f. Participant: "Clip, flip, twist, turn it back, squeeze"

    g. Ground: *"Thank you Dave"*

2. Each participant must physically go through the Ground School.

3. With adults you may want to set up the etrier so they see and use their aid.

4. Facilitators will watch each participant to make sure both participants are doing it correctly and to double-check the harness.
5. Some things to reinforce during Ground School:
   a. Hold claws together, in one hand.
   b. Do not twist too tight; explain the purpose of closing the gate.
   c. Explain the helmet zone.
6. Go over equipment care of the ropes, helmets, and crab claws.

Zip Line

1. Participant will come off the Burma Bridge and clip in to the low cable on the platform.
2. Participant walks around the zip pole to the platform and sits down.
3. Platform Staff attaches the lanyard to the belay loop of the participant. The participant is still clipped in with crab claws.
4. The participant may only go off in a sitting position.
5. The staff then explains what is going to happen: "I will yell 'Clear the zip' to inform the staff you are ready to go. Once I hear 'Zip is clear' from them I am going to unclip your crab claws at your waist. I will let you know it's okay to go. You will scoot up to the end and slide off the edge, holding the rope and sitting upright. Please do not jump. Any questions?"
6. Participants may be in the middle of any of the four events or climbing the wall when a participant zips.

Staff Exiting the Course

1. Staff may zip off the course.
2. The last staff may zip off the course if they can take the zip down while on the ladder.
3. The last staff member should make sure the equipment is cleared and then set up the rappel. They should take the belay rope and run it through the shackle. Tie the two ends together and send the ends to the ground. Descend at a safe speed with care.

Other Basic Uses and Thoughts

1. Each participant can only go through the course one time. More than that and it turns the tool into an amusement ride and it may belittle those that chose not to complete the course.
2. A participant may climb the wall and decide not to do the course. There are three options:
   a. Lowering on the wall belay system; ground staff belays and platform staff monitors and assists.
   b. Zip line.
   c. Lower with rescue bag. This takes the most time and is the least preferred.

3. At any point a participant may choose to exit the course.
   a. Ask them if they would like to go to the platform, in any direction. Platforms lowers off the wall are the most simple because the system is already there.
   b. If they do not want to go to the platform, ask them to go where the closest facilitator is located.
   c. If a lower is necessary, and it is not a life-threatening emergency, no one else should be entering the course or zipping.
      - Whichever staff member is the closest to the participant should prepare to do a rescue/lower. The staff on the course not involved in the lower should be monitoring the other participants on the course.
      - You may *not* set up a lower off a staple. An eyebolt or cable is the only acceptable place.

Weather

1. Realize that to exit the course takes time, especially if you have more than four participants on the course. If you hear thunder, do not wait for lightning to begin exiting participants off the course.
2. You should be ahead of the storm and all participants should head back to the platform safely and be lowered on the wall. Decisions should be made for safety.
3. Light rain is acceptable to continue. A downpour causes slick cable and holds, and the course should stop.
4. In an emergency weather situation:
   a. Participants are to go to the closest rescue bag, either on the corner or the platform.
   b. Staff may lower the participant from the rescue 8 directly or they can use a qualified person on the ground.
   c. The Ground Staff may be lowering from the wall. Thus, you could have three participants lowering at a time.

Alpine Tower

Roles and Responsibilities of Staff

1. Make sure that everyone on the Alpine Tower has signed a Hold Harmless Form, even if they are just watching.
2. Review all Hold Harmless forms. Make notes on any special cases that may require extra caution and/or observation in appropriate situations.
3. Participants will be informed of the inherent risks involved in each activity.
4. Participants will be informed of environmental hazards on the Alpine Tower (ants, wet grass, gnats, weather, etc.).

5. Participants and staff must wear helmets while on the Alpine Tower and/or within the Alpine Tower perimeter.
6. All staff members must be trained on the Alpine Tower rescue techniques.
7. Each rescue bag should be checked prior to program use to ensure proper packing and condition.
8. Staff should inspect the Alpine Tower prior to each use.
9. The Alpine Tower should not be used in high winds or approaching lightening.
10. Participants and staff must not climb without a belay system.
11. Staff should inspect all belayers, knots, harnesses, and back threaded buckles.
12. All belayers must be 14 years of age, unless participating in a CCPRC instructional program.
13. Shirts and shoes must be worn at all times.
14. Sharp objects, jewelry, rings, and objects in pockets must be removed before climbing.
15. A staff member must be on top of the Alpine Tower in order for participants to go to the top platform.
16. The first-aid kit will be on hand during Tower activities.
17. Review the group's goals and objectives.
18. Meet with the other facilitators to ensure that everyone is familiar with their roles and the overall plan.
19. Glasses worn should have a retaining strap.
20. Belay ropes must be positioned over the top of the belay rail from the outside.
21. Proper rope management is essential in order to avoid a pendulum situation.

Partner Events on the Tower

Either after a few ascents or initially you may want to suggest partner events. Examine the goals of the group and where they are attempting to go.

1. Frame the experience; discuss teamwork, physically helping each other, communication, etc.
2. Present the events:
   a. Team Beam
   b. Missing Link
   c. Corporate Ladder
   d. Floating Poles
   e. The Beanstalk
   f. The Diabolical Seesaw
3. Encourage participants to physically help each other.

Group Initiatives on the Alpine Tower

After everyone has done at least one route, consider presenting the group initiatives next. You may even attempt these first, prior to going up, especially if you have been doing low initiatives.

1. *The Jump*—after stretching out a bit, have participants practice stepping off and on the lower base rails. This will help later when they lose their balance. Use spotters.
2. *The Tower Pull*—This requires a lot of people. Have all belay stations and climbers suited up and ready to go (as many as six, as few as four). Take another belay rope and lay it on the ground circling the tower and tie the ends together. The objective is for all the climbers, with guidance and tension from the team, to work the giant rope circle all the way to the top rails of the tower.

Safety and Emergency Guidelines

The facilitator and the group members are responsible for safety. At any time an activity may be stopped to ensure the safety of all involved individuals. Participants as well as facilitators have the right and obligation to stop an activity.

General Procedures

Bloodborne Diseases

One of the major issues of concern that you will encounter when dealing with injuries is that of bloodborne diseases. It is inevitable that you will have to deal with an injured participant, who is bleeding, so you must use extreme caution when handling such a situation. The following guidelines should be used when dealing with a bleeding participant.

1. Remember, when dealing with blood, staff must always wear gloves.
2. If a participant is bleeding, s/he must stop participating immediately.
3. If a participant has blood on his/her clothing, s/he will be asked to stop participating upon detection. The participant is ineligible to continue to participate until the clothing saturated with blood has been removed.
4. Before any participant who has been bleeding will be allowed to continue participating, all bleeding must be stopped and any open wound or laceration must be covered.
5. Any blood on the equipment needs to be sprayed with bleach and water solution. If any blood is on the rope, the rope needs to be taken down, that portion washed, and the rope removed from use for at least 12 hours.

Emergency Lowering Procedure

Equipment will be present at the Alpine Tower and the high course for the purpose of lowering a participant. The high course must have a rescue bag at each facilitator location (zip line and pirate crossing).

Contents of Rescue Bag

1. Alpine Tower: One 150-foot static rope, 1 "fireman's" locking carabiner, 1 steel locking carabiner, 2 pieces of webbing, and trauma scissors.

2. High Course: 150-foot static rope with double bowline tied on one end and "fireman's" locking carabiner attached, 1 rescue figure-8 descender with steel carabiner, 2 prussik cords, 2 etrier, and trauma shears.
3. NOTE: Zip platform rescue bag will contain a dynamic pulley and prussik system.

When to Lower a Participant

1. Participant has fallen off an event and is unable to perform a self-rescue using the etrier. The facilitator cannot successfully assist and/or thinks that the participant is incapable of continuing.
2. Participant is incapable of continuing as a result of an accident. The accident must not be serious enough to warrant the use of a Stokes litter.
3. An emergency exit is required and lowering a participant(s) will remedy the evacuation.

Lowering from high course.

1. Thread the static rope through the figure-8 descender and attach the descender, using the steel locking carabiner to the overhead belay cable.
2. Toss the remainder of the rope in the rope bag to the ground facilitator. The facilitator should assume the belay position.
3. Clip the fireman's locking carabiner to the participant's harness.
4. Remove all the slack in the system.
5. After going through the belay commands, ask the participant to step up in the etrier to remove the weight from the lobster claws.
6. If the participant cannot step into the etrier to remove the weighted lobster claws, then the facilitator must cut the participant free.
7. *Always* ensure the ground belay system is secure before you disconnect and/or cut the participant's lobster claws.
8. The ground facilitator controls the rope and lowers the participant to the ground. The facilitator in the course helps control the rope from above.

Lowering from alpine tower.

1. Use the vector pull, fixed vector pull, pendulum or pick-off procedures as necessary.
2. Please see Appendices; ATI Rescue Procedures in CCPR manual.

Emergency Protocols

Weather Conditions

The challenge course will stop upon the sighting of lightning. During the summer when Splash Zone is operating, if they close for weather then so does the challenge course. For the off-season, refer to the Lightning Procedure in the CCPR manual.

Personal Injury

The following courses of action are appropriate in the event that a serious injury or life-threatening condition has occurred and an ambulance is needed:

1. Use the radio to notify JICP base that an ambulance is needed on the challenge course.
2. Notify outdoor land coordinator by radio, pager, or office or notify recreation base, during regular business hours to inform another program coordinator (ORC/ORS) or manager.
3. JICP will meet the ambulance at the front gate and guide them to the challenge course.

Equipment Care

Helmets

1. Keep helmets clean and dry.
2. Avoid dropping, tossing, or sitting on helmets.
3. Check helmets for any unusual wear such as cracks, missing rivets, or problems with the chinstraps or buckles.
4. Report any damage or concerns to program coordinator (ORC/ORS).

Harnesses

1. Keep harnesses clean and dry.
2. Inspect the stitching and specific wear areas for any damage or fraying.
3. Report any damage or concerns to program coordinator (ORC/ORS).

Ropes

1. Keep rope clean. Dirty rope can be washed with a mild soap in cool water. Do not put rope in a dryer. Air dry rope on a rack out of direct sunlight.
2. Do not put rope away wet. It can mildew.
3. Never step on a rope. Although stepping on the rope does not severely damage the kerns inside the sheath, misuse of equipment can lead to unneeded wear and tear. This will result in early retirement, thus an unneeded replacement expense.
4. Store rope in a bag in the challenge course barn. Never store the rope in direct sunlight. The UV rays can weaken the nylon fibers.
5. Always untie knots before storing the rope. This will prevent the same fibers from repeatedly taking the weight load.
6. Periodically check the rope for unusual lumps, depressions, or fraying. Excessive fraying, where the mantle is cut or ripped so that the core fibers are showing, is an indication that the rope must be retired or at least that section cut off and discarded.

7. Remove carabiners from lobster claws before storing them in the challenge course barn.
8. Report any damage or concerns to program coordinator (ORC/ORS).

Carabiners

1. Keep carabiners clean. Do not step on them or abuse them (such as dropping them from heights).
2. Lubricate the hinges (use a nonoil lubricant) at the hinge point when the gate becomes sticky. Remember to thoroughly wipe off all excess lubricant before using the carabiner. This will prevent contamination of the ropes. Remove tree sap from the carabiner with kerosene.
3. Check the integrity of the pins. If there is excessive side play in an open gate or if the pins are rusty, the carabiner must be retired.
4. Examine the carabiners for grooves caused by rope or cable. This is a sign of excessive wear and the carabiner must be retired. Aluminum carabiners are never to be used on the high course or the Alpine Tower.
5. Report any damage or concerns to program coordinator (ORC/ORS).

Pulleys

1. Keep all pulleys clean. Do not step on them or abuse them (such as dropping them from heights).
2. If a pulley feels sticky, lubricate all moving parts by using a nonoil lubricant. Remember to wipe off excess lubricant before using the pulley.
3. Severe rust on a pulley is cause for replacement of the pulley.
4. Never try to lubricate sealed bearings.
5. Avoid running an aluminum sheath pulley over a steel cable because this will quickly grind up the groove.
6. Never take a pulley apart.
7. Use only steel carabiners with steel pulleys and aluminum carabiners with aluminum pulleys.
8. Report any damage or concerns to program coordinator (ORC/ORS).

The Westminster Schools	*F* Education
	E West Region
	C High-School Students
	S 19.01–19.08

Challenge Course

Low Elements and Initiative Games

1. Safety rules and procedures for all events will be adhered to.
2. Events will be checked prior to use each day.
3. The staff will review the name, objective, procedures, and safety rules of the events prior to use each day.
4. The faculty and student staff will supervise all events and insure adequate spotting.
5. Participants are not allowed on events unless the group has been briefed and is performing that event.
6. Events for which spotting is inadequate due to height will use a belay. (See Challenge Course, High Elements in Westminster manual.)
7. The event site will be cleared of any hazards prior to use.
8. Instructors will stop the exercise and/or correct students to insure safe execution of the event.
9. Jewelry and sharp objects will be removed prior to participation in initiatives and games.
10. Only Discovery equipment will be used.
11. No gum chewing.

High Elements

1. Students will be hooked into a belay system continuously from the moment they leave the ground until they return to ground level at the completion of the event, except while in the tube net.
2. The hook-in procedure on the trapeze will be a locking steel carabiner on a figure 8 on a bight attached to the back of the full-body harness. Crab claws for self-belays on the zip wire and the pole course will be attached through the designated attachment loop on the harness.
3. High element events may be postponed because of unfavorable weather conditions at the discretion of the session director.
4. Staff will be anchored when on platforms or off the ground.
5. Rescue equipment will be available on platform events, pole course, and zip line.
6. Faculty will perform a hands-on check before the student is unhooked from a platform static belay (zip wire takeoff and giant swing).

7. Jumping off the zip line and giant swing platforms is not permitted.
8. Students will stay behind designated boundary lines unless they are doing the event or assisting with belays.
9. Students will wear helmets on all high element activities.
10. Mechanical belay devices will be used on high element activities requiring a belay from the ground.
11. The pole course will use a running belay with crab claws.
12. All switch-overs will be supervised by a staff member.
13. Only locking steel carabiners UIAA rated at 22 kN or above (longitudinal) will be used on running belays.
14. Students will not put their hands in the loops, or wrap the hand lines around their wrists on the giant swing.
15. All students will have completed Ground School under the supervision of a qualified staff person prior to entering the pole course.
16. A final harness and helmet check will be done by a qualified staff person prior to a student entering the tube net.
17. Helmets will be worn by everyone inside the safety area whenever anyone is on the course.
18. Crab claws will be of two slightly different lengths.

SECTION 21

SOLOS

Georgia College & State University	
	F Education
	E Southeast Region
	C University Outdoor Education Students and General Population
	S 4.10, 21.01–21. 08

Solos

Policy

Adhere to Land-Based Activities General Policy:

Solo	1:8 (minimum 2)

Facilitator Responsibilities

1. Select an area that has appropriate characteristics (terrain, access, isolation, communication, etc.) for the type of solo experience sought.
2. Scout area prior to the solo experience to identify individual locations that are free from obvious hazards (water, loose rock, debris, insects, etc.).
3. Select individual sites that are appropriate for participant skill level.
4. Check individual solo equipment and supplies (or intended lack of equipment), such as survival kits, special food that may be required, GPS or other communication needs, etc., based on goals of the solo experience.

Teaching

1. Guidelines for developing solo curricula are contained in policy; however specific curriculum should be developed on a per case basis and included in the appropriate program file.
2. Goals for using a solo experience as a component of an experience that focuses on a technical skill may include, but are not limited to:
   a. Creating opportunities for significant reflection;
   b. Applying skills learned in other components of the experience, such as primitive living, survival, emergency response, or land navigation.
3. Sequence activities to build on prior developed skills.
4. Use journals, cameras, or a check-in system to encourage reflection.
5. Use individual, small and larger groups to appropriately introduce techniques, permit individual skill acquisition, and build group leadership and problem-solving abilities.
6. Use teachable moments to reinforce skill development and take advantage of site-specific characteristics.
7. Debrief solo experiences to maximize transfer of learning as appropriate.

Safety and Environment

1. Select sites that minimize impact on native flora and fauna.
2. Teach specific communication and emergency response system to be used.
3. Introduce environmental considerations that may not be as acute on a trail (e.g., environmental hazards) relative to the setting.

Solo Setup System

1. Establish a base camp, with a clear trail or other location marker.
2. Ensure that all participants have base camp coordinates (Grid Ref or UTM) and proper equipment to ensure navigation to base camp (this will vary depending on the nature of solo experience).
3. Accurately locate and catalog (on GPS or map) by name and coordinates the location of each participant (this will depend on the type of solo experience).

4. Offer general supervision and check-ins as necessary in the least obtrusive manner.
5. Use the following procedures for trail-side solos of more than 3 hours duration (nuances in procedures should be made based on environmental factors):
    a. Travel approximately two-tenths of a mile along the trail;
    b. Mark this location with flagging tape or an alternative check-in device (e.g., film canister with paper inside);
    c. Have participant set a compass bearing perpendicular to the trail and travel a set distance (normally 25 to 50 paces) off the trail on said compass bearing;
    d. Designate or ask the participant to select the solo site and determine coordinates (mark GPS waypoint or UTM/Grid Ref);
    e. Remind participant of back-bearing to trailside check-in point and direction of base camp;
    f. Instruct participant not to travel more than 25 to 50 feet in any direction from solo site;
    g. Return to check-in point on trail;
    h. Travel one- to two-tenths of a mile further down trail;
    i. Repeat procedures for marking a solo site.
6. Use the following procedures for open area solos of more than 3 hours duration (nuances in procedures should be made based on environmental factors):
    a. Set a compass bearing in desired direction of solo sites;
    b. Travel approximately two-tenths of a mile away from base camp on the compass bearing;
    c. Mark this location with flagging tape or an alternative check-in device (e.g., film canister with paper inside);
    d. Remind participant of back-bearing to base camp;
    e. Instruct participant not to travel more than 50 feet in any direction from solo site;
    f. To set the next solo site, travel one-tenth of a mile further along original compass bearing or along a compass bearing that fits the terrain (if applicable, mark changes in bearings in GPS);
    g. Repeat procedures for marking a solo site.

University of North Carolina at Charlotte—Venture Center
F Recreation
E Southeast Region
C University Students and General Population
S 21.01–21.08

Solos

Purpose

1. To provide an opportunity for quiet reflection and self-appraisal.
2. Solo is not meant as a survival test; adequate food, shelter, and clothing should be available so students will be comfortable and safe.

Staff Responsibilities

1. Conduct a briefing so participants understand the purpose of the solo and how they might use their time, safety, and environmental concerns.
2. Staff writes on a map (or sketch) the participant and location of each site.
3. Staff will do a visual check of each person on solo at least once every 12 hours.
4. Staff will conduct a debriefing following the solo experience

Safety Considerations

1. When placing students at solo sites:
   a. It is usually appropriate to offer the site and let individuals volunteer.
   b. Students who may require additional supervision or support should be placed nearer to staff site.
   c. The specific boundaries of the site should be pointed out.
2. Fires will not be used on Venture solos except by special permission of the director.
3. All students will be briefed on:
   a. The location of the staff base or solo site.
   b. Use of whistles for emergency signals (3 blows, repeated over until response, means *need emergency assistance*, any students who hears whistle should go to site of signal).
   c. Not engaging in potentially dangerous activities (e.g., swimming, hiking, climbing).
   d. Not wandering around and visiting others on solo so as not to disturb others' experience; rather, if needing support, to come to the staff site.
   e. What to do if encountering a stranger (e.g., not engaging in conversation).

f. Participants are informed of pickup and check-in protocols, what to do if wanting to talk to a staff member during check-in (hang a bandanna), and what to do in an emergency.

g. Participants are encouraged not to read books.

h. Participants are encouraged to write in their journals.

i. Participants are encouraged not to use watches.

4. Each solo participant will have access to an adequate supply of potable water (this can be in water bottles for short solo's, or have a means of treating water on longer solos).

5. Equipment for solos depending on length of solo might include:

   a. All participants will have a whistle and know appropriate signals to use.

   b. Participants will have access to sleeping bags, ensolite pads, clothes, water bottles, flashlights, matches, and simple foods that do not require cooking (typically gorp and crackers).

6. For lightning protocols and lightning policy, see page 123 of UNCC Venture Center manual.

Santa Fe Mountain Center	*F*	**Therapeutic**
	E	**Rocky Mountain Region**
	C	**Youth and Families**
	S	**21.01–21.08**

Solo is a predetermined amount of time, usually 1 to 2 days, that participants spend alone, without traveling. A time for contemplation, introspection, self-appraisal, and rest.

Rules

1. All basic camping practices shall be maintained, especially those that pertain to campsite selection and land management agency regulations.
2. Participants shall be supplied with a whistle, adequate shelter, clothing, water, and the agreed-upon amount of food.
3. Each participant shall know the exact location of the instructor's camp and procedures to follow in case of extenuating circumstances.
4. At least one instructor shall be in camp, or otherwise on call at all times. Other instructors shall be available to respond to emergencies.
5. Clearly define the boundaries of the solo site and require that participants stay within them.
6. Climbing or swimming is not allowed on solo.

Procedures/Considerations

1. No fires or cooking allowed.
2. The duration of solos should reflect the age and maturity of participants and length of course. Consider your objectives.
3. Participants should be checked at least twice a day, or more often as the situation dictates. Once in the morning and once in the evening is a good practice. A system of visual checks may be used.
4. Participants should be placed relative to the degree of anticipated monitoring in considering emotional and physical readiness. Ensure that signals for help can be heard or seen.
5. Particular care should be taken to safeguard participants from sexual or other assault.
6. Select sites to provide greatest degree of safety from environmental hazards. Anticipate risk of flooding, rock fall, flora and fauna and enticing natural features that encourage climbing or swimming.
7. See that shelter construction is adequate to conditions.
8. Anticipate rule infractions: breaking solo, leaving boundaries, substance abuse, etc.

Briefing

1. Orient to safety and emergency procedures, how to signal for help, how to locate base camp, response to strangers.
2. Define solo site boundaries.
3. Brief on general rules.

SECTION 22
SERVICE PROJECTS

Prescott College	*F*	**Education**
	E	**Rocky Mountain Region**
	C	**University Students**
	S	**22.01, 22.03–22.08**

Service Projects

Many service projects conducted in a field setting engage students in activities for the purpose of mitigating environmental impact caused by outdoor recreational use. Examples include trail construction or repair, vegetation restoration, and installation of erosion control structures. These types of activities involve using tools, most of which are potentially hazardous in some way. The following is a set of general safety guidelines related to such activities.

1. At least one instructor or vehicle first-aid kit should be placed in a central location near the project site. The instructor(s) should communicate the location of first-aid supplies to everyone involved.
2. A safety briefing and tool use instructions should precede all projects involving the use of tools, with particular attention given to operation of cutting or power tools, and tools that are operated by swinging or prying motions. Instruction should include how to safely use, carry, and maintain tools and how to interact safely with other tool users. The project coordinator and/or the instructor(s), depending on the nature of the project and their qualifications, should give this instruction.
3. Protective clothing, footwear, safety glasses, gloves, and helmets should be used in accordance with accepted and appropriate safety standards as defined by the primary instructor. Rock climbing helmets are considered an acceptable substitute for construction helmets; durable hiking boots an acceptable substitute for work boots, and sunglasses an acceptable substitute for safety glasses. Open-toed sandals should not be worn while using tools or doing construction work.
4. Service projects involving the use of tools should be organized in such a manner that, in the event of an accident, immediate first-aid assistance and rapid evacuation will be possible.
5. Students proposing independent studies involving projects in which tools are to be used must demonstrate prior training in their safe and proper use as part of the Safety Committee review process.

Wilderness Treatment Center	*F* **Therapeutic**
	E **Northwest Region**
	C **Adolescent Males**
	S **4.10, 22.01–22.08**

Service Projects

Policy

It is the policy of the Wilderness Treatment Center, when volunteering for a service project, to provide a safe, positive, and achievable experience for the participants.

WTC's primary service project involves trail work in conjunction with the Bob Marshall Foundation during the summer wilderness trips. This work normally occurs June through September in the Bob Marshall Wilderness Complex.

Procedures

1. Staff-to-patient ratio will not exceed 1:4.5 with a minimum of two staff.
2. Always have a first-aid kit with the group.
3. Hard hats, gloves, full length pants, long sleeve shirts, and eye protection are required when doing service projects.
4. Brief the group prior to the service project to discuss project goals, therapy goals, safety, history, impacts, and cultural awareness. We follow U.S. Forest Service regulations and standards as our guidelines. Staff will carry a copy of the Trail Construction and Maintenance Notebook as a reference for all trail work specifications.
5. Instruction in proper use of tools and techniques will be taught. Staff will demonstrate the use of the tools and techniques first. Patients will then practice proper use of the tools and techniques while being monitored by the staff. Tasks should be sequenced appropriately to ensure the safety of the participants.
6. Monitor the group on a regular basis to ensure that safe work habits and attitudes are being practiced. Emphasize the distance to medical facilities.
7. Inspect the project area for hazards both prior to the starting of the work and as the project progresses. Communicate any hazards to the group.
8. Pace the group and take regular rest breaks to prevent exhaustion. Exhaustion can lead to unsafe work habits and accidents.
9. Monitor the group's food and water intake to ensure that proper hydration and energy needs are being met.
10. Monitor the group for proper clothing needs. Consider the variety of weather changes possible when conducting service projects.
11. Discuss each day's efforts at the evening leader burn-off session.
12. Reiterate to the patients the therapeutic value of service work regularly.

Georgia College & State University

F	Education
E	Southeast Region
C	University Outdoor Education Students and General Population
S	22.01–22.08

Service Learning

GCSU academic programs are committed to service learning across the curriculum. To this end, all outdoor education majors are required to complete a minimum of 15 service learning hours each semester for four semesters. In addition some ODED courses include service learning projects as course requirements. Outdoor education students take advantage of a wide range of opportunities for service learning in conjunction with student clubs and outreach programs supported by the university. A wide range of community organizations request assistance from the program, and the OEC depends on student volunteers for a variety of equipment and facility management needs.

Definitions

Service learning.

The National and Community Service Act of 1990 states that service learning:

1. Is a method whereby participants learn and develop through active participation in thoughtfully organized service experiences that meet actual community needs and that are coordinated in collaboration with the school and community.
2. Is integrated into the students' academic curriculum and provides structured time for students to think, talk, or write about what they did and saw during the actual service activity.
3. Provides students with opportunities to use newly acquired skills and knowledge in real-life situations in their communities.
4. Enhances what is taught in school by extending learning beyond the classroom and into the community and helps to foster the development of a sense of caring for others and the world in which we live.

Community service vs. service learning.

Community service and volunteerism stress service. Empathy, an ethic of service, moral development, and involvement in much-needed community programs and services are among the benefits associated with community service. However, these experiences differ from service learning in that they do not emphasize both service and learning outcomes in a way that both will occur and enhance each other. Most prominently, programs that emphasize learning always include a strong reflective component where students make sense of and enhance formal classroom learning from the service experience.

Facilitator Responsibilities

1. Identify and analyze the parameters of potential service learning experiences by including goals, roles and responsibilities, contact persons, safety and emergency procedures, equipment, food service, publicity, academic integration, etc.
2. Teach participants the skills and knowledge needed to perform the service.
3. Plan the service learning experience by:
   a. Involving participants in decision making as much as possible;
   b. Preparing agencies and individuals for the project by ensuring that logistics are complete and communicated to the appropriate people;
   c. Identifying ways to bring recognition to the project and the participants;

d. Informing participants about host site policies;

e. When appropriate, developing and implementing safety and emergency procedures;

f. Completing forms as necessary.

Environment

1. Inspect the area for potential environmental impact and hazards.
2. Develop procedures for removing garbage and debris to appropriate disposal sites.

Teaching

1. Challenge students to use vision to generate ideas for service projects in the community or environment.
2. Select a project and clearly identify its purpose.
3. Develop guidelines for completing the project.
4. Investigate potential cultural and environmental factors associated with successful completion of the project.
5. Allow time for reflection and discussion about the experience and how it can be applied to other settings or professional responsibilities.

Safety

1. Train students to use related tools and equipment.
2. Utilize challenge of and by choice.
3. Inspect the area for potential safety hazards.
4. Inspect and carry appropriate first-aid supplies and other relevant emergency equipment.
5. Comply with the PPM and CCFH relevant policy.

Clothing and Equipment

1. Inform students about appropriate clothing for the project.
2. Furnish and/or require the use of appropriate equipment.
3. Arrange for food and water to be provided or for students to bring lunch. Be sure there is an adequate water supply.
4. Arrange for access to restroom facilities.

SECTION 24
INCIDENTAL ACTIVITIES—LAND BASED AND WATER BASED

Prescott College	*F*	**Education**
	E	**Rocky Mountain Region**
	C	**University Students**
	S	**4.10, 24.01, 24.04, 24.06, 24.07, 24.09**

Swimming (Lake, Ocean, River)

Purpose

Swimming becomes a part of many courses. It can be a necessary part of course activities (as in rafting or canyoneering courses) or an enjoyable recreational activity in many courses (as in any course offered in Kino Bay).

Flat Water

Guidelines for flat-water (ocean, bay, lake, and calm eddies) swimming: Minimum staff-to-student ratios for flat-water swimming are as follows: 1:12 when all students have passed deep-water swim test and 1:1 when students are not accomplished deep-water swimmers

Skill Assessment

- Swimming skills should be assessed by the faculty member by means of a simple swim test prior to the facilitation of recreational or course-related swimming activities. The following is an example of an appropriate swim test:
  - Position two instructors (or trained lifeguards) 20 to 50 yards apart in waist-deep *calm* water.
  - Ask students to swim parallel to shore between instructors. No more then two students should swim at a time. Nobody should be forced or pressured to swim.
- A person should always wear a PFD and swim under direct instructor supervision when participating in swimming activities if s/he:
  - Touches the bottom.
  - Seems to be struggling.
  - Is very scared.
  - Refuses to participate in the test.
- A swim test can be conducted formally or informally at any point during a course in order to reassess swimming abilities.

Safety Briefing

The safety briefing prior to swimming should include:

- Environmental conditions including:
  - Bottom conditions: where are deep-water dropoffs, etc.
  - Current directions and dynamics
  - Flora and fauna hazards: sting rays, jelly fish, urchins, leeches, etc.
  - Water temperature considerations
- Specific requirements:
  - Students should be told how far from shore they may swim, based on student ability and environmental conditions.
  - Buddy systems should be established requiring students to swim in pairs.
  - A signaling system for calling students to shore should be established.
  - A check-in system should be established so that staff knows where swimmers are.
  - A lifeguard with rescue training should be on duty whenever students are swimming.
  - Proper rescue equipment should be available. For flat-water situations, any flotation device is acceptable.
  - No diving.

Surf

Guidelines for surf swimming: Minimum staff to-student ratios for surf swimming 1:6. These guidelines apply whenever wave action or currents (long shore, rip, or tidal) exist. All guidelines for flat-water swimming apply to surf swimming. All students should have passed deep-water swim test.

Specific requirements.

- An ocean swimming lifeguard, with rescue training (open-water rescue experience) should be on duty whenever students are swimming.
- Proper rescue equipment should be available. In surf conditions, a rescue buoy or paddle board and PFD should be available.

Kino Bay

Specific requirements.

- Accomplished deep-water swimmers (see Section S, Number 1 for swim test ideas) may swim without faculty supervision under the following circumstances:
  - Surf and currents are calm.
  - Students swim in groups of three.
  - Swimmers stay within 30 feet of shore.
  - Swimmers remain 50 feet away from the point at the north end of the beach.
  - Swimmers check out and in with faculty.

Georgia College & State University	
	F **Education**
	E **Southeast Region**
	C **University Outdoor Education Students and General Population**
	S **24.01–24.09**

Tree Climbing

(Adapted with permission from Tree Climbing USA Basic Technical Training Manual)

Policy

Adhere to Land-Based Activities General Policy:

Facilitator Responsibilities

1. Scout all climbing areas prior to program use to ensure that they are free and clear from obvious hazards (dead limbs, debris, insects, etc.).
2. Select climbs that are appropriate for participant skill level.
3. Use stable and appropriate anchor branches:
   a. Close to the trunk or main branches;
   b. Minimum of 6 inches in diameter.
4. Check staff and participant helmets, saddles, knots, and carabiners prior to each climb.
5. Check that staff and participants are wearing helmets within the climbing area.
6. Use appropriate backup belays for climbs, which may include, but are not limited to:
   a. Safety knots;
   b. Bottom or fireman's belays.
7. Emphasize problem solving, trust, teamwork, and challenge.
8. De-emphasize getting to the top at all costs.
9. Carry appropriate rescue equipment, including, but not limited to:
   a. Extra rope;
   b. Extra carabiners;
   c. Cordelette loops and slings;
   d. A friction device;
   e. Rescue knife or shears.
10. Teach and use specific verbal commands for tree climbing.

Teaching

1. Curriculum may include, but is not limited to:
   a. Physical and psychological demands of climbing and descending;

b. Proper fit, care, and inspection of helmets, saddles and ropes;

c. Rope ties and their uses (i.e. 5/3 Blake's hitch, figure-8 family, Prussik hitch, clove hitch, double fisherman, monkey fist family);

d. Bridge tying and clipping into saddle;

e. B.A.C.K. checks;

f. Use of weight bag to set route;

g. Proper spotting techniques;

h. Ascent to and descent from tree canopy, using double rope technique;

i. Use of backup safety systems (i.e., safety knots, fireman's belay);

j. Multipitch climbing;

k. Use of Cambium Savers;

l. Appropriate verbal commands.

2. Develop basic skill sequences based on instructional goals, client assessment, and the setting.

Safety and Environment

1. Select sites that minimize impact to native flora and fauna.
2. Protect trees used as anchors with Cambium Savers.
3. Select landing areas that are stable and without obstructions.
4. Permit only one climber on a route at a time.
5. Perform a B.A.C.K. check before ascending or transitioning from one pitch to the next.
6. Spot participants during initial climbing to minimize swinging.
7. Tie safety knots in the participant's rope once they have left the ground and ensure that participant continues to tie knots periodically during the climb.
8. Require a fireman's belay for any new or inexperienced climber while descending.
9. Locate first-aid and rescue equipment in an area accessible to all facilitators.
10. Locate a backboard at access point.

Clothing and Equipment

1. Avoid stepping on ropes or exposing them to excessive sunlight.
2. Prevent wear on ropes by using Cambium Savers.
3. Train participants to check ropes and other soft goods for damage during coiling or stacking.
4. Wear shoes that are closed at the toe and secure at the heel (i.e., no sandals).
5. Secure loose hair and clothing, and remove loose and cumbersome jewelry.
6. Secure all gear to climber to prevent equipment dropping from height.
7. Clip into saddle as per manufacturer recommendations.

Communication System

Climber Says:	Meaning and Response Needed
"Help"	Universal call for emergency assistance. No false alarms!
"Stop!" or "Whoa!"	Used to get attention. All unnecessary activity should cease until problem is resolved.
"Headache"	Used to warn others that something is falling or has been dropped from the tree. Keep head down and eyes covered.
"Clear"	Response to "Headache"—danger has passed.
"Complete"	Dangerous activity is finished.
"Climbing"	Climber is clipped in and ready to climb.
"On Rope"	Climber is clipped in and ready to climb.
"Off Rope"	Climber has completed the climb and has detached from the rope.
"Throwing"	Climber is about to throw weight bag into the tree to attempt a setting.
"Down Check"	Climber is calling for confirmation that rope is touching the ground before descending.
"Check OK"	Down check is good. Participant may descend to the ground.
"Descending"	Climber is descending.
"Free Rope"	Rope is to be pulled from tree. Stand clear.
"Gate Check"	Every participant should perform a squeeze check on their carabiner.

CHAPTER 8

TECHNICAL ACTIVITIES—WATER BASED

This chapter includes examples of policy and procedures that correspond to Chapter 5 in the Manual of Accreditation Standards for Adventure Programs, Fourth Edition. *Standards are applicable to the facilitation of specific water-based activities. An organization is required to demonstrate compliance with all standards that are applicable to its programming. If, for example, sea kayaking is conducted, compliance with standards in Section 41 of the standards manual is required. If an organization offers a wide gamut of water-based activities, it must demonstrate compliance with all of the standards associated for each section for every activity, regardless of how infrequently activities are conducted. These standards provide assurance that a program's field practices for respective activities are in alignment with or compare well to standard operating procedures of other similar and/or reputable organizations. As in previous chapters, readers will note a wide range of content, detail, structure, and integration of curriculum. Approaches vary across activities, settings, client and leadership characteristics, and desired outcomes. Examples of general water-based policy and procedures are integrated with specific activities in this chapter, as opposed to including them at the beginning of the land-based activities chapter, to demonstrate this format. Examples for snorkeling and SCUBA diving are not included, and an example of a water-based incidental activity is included in Chapter 4, Section 24.*

SECTION 40

FLAT AND WHITE-WATER CANOEING, KAYAKING, AND RAFTING

Charleston County Parks & Recreation Department	
	F Recreation
	E Southeast Region
	C General Population
	S 40.01–40.11

Kayaking

Description of Course Environment

1. Primarily rivers and lakes that begin, end, or travel through Charleston County, including all of the ACE Basin.
2. Paddling on water that does not exceed Class I on the International Scale of River Difficulty.
3. This is a four-season activity; however we will not paddle open water when two of the following three conditions are present: water temperatures are below 50 F., air temperatures are below 40° F, and wind speeds are greater than 15 knots.

Safety Concerns (specific to this environment or activity)

1. Participant/staff injury due to contact with local fauna (poisonous snakes, alligators, etc.), allergic reaction to toxins (bee stings, etc.), or poison ivy.
2. Participant loss of life due to drowning or other unforeseen accident.
3. Environmental problems related to program area (dehydration, hypo/hyperthermia, thunder, and lightning, etc.).
4. Equipment failure or lack of equipment maintenance.

Strategies for minimizing these safety concerns.

1. All participants will be provided with an appropriate sized and fitted PFD.
2. A qualified staff member will give a pretrip safety talk to participants. Participants who then wish to not paddle may choose so at that time.
3. Participants may have to paddle across boating channels while lake paddling. If this becomes necessary, they will cross as a tight group, moving at the pace of the slowest paddler with staff "corralling" participants on all sides. See below for applicable Nautical Rules of the Road.
4. All staff will be trained in and able to perform efficient rescues.
5. Practice standard participant management techniques (maintain hydration, take frequent breaks, check participant temperature/exertion comfort level frequently, etc.)
6. Staff will design and follow a program route that results in minimizing participants' exposure to hazards such as strainers.
7. Staff should check equipment while loading for unreported equipment problems.
8. Paddling at night will be avoided whenever possible, unless nighttime paddling is part of a specific program authorized by program coordinator (ORC/ORS). Program must also carry flashlights and strobes if paddling at night.

Equipment Requirements

These should be considered in addition to general equipment requirements addressed in Water-Based Activity Operating Procedures and Guidelines and elsewhere.

1. One appropriately sized and maintained canoe per participant(s), depending upon group configuration (solo or tandem)

2. Repair kit
3. Canoe will have 10-foot or longer bow and stern lines
4. One spare paddle per 3 boats
5. Minimum of two extra PFDs and paddles brought as spares (left in van/bus)
6. Extra dry bags for participant lunches/gear
7. Stirrup rescue rope
8. If paddling at night, one flashlight/strobe unit per person, with two spares

Supplemental Resource Information

Navigational Rules of the Road

1. Large vessels, which are restricted to a navigable channel, have right-of-way in that channel.
2. Unless contradicted by #1, nonmotorized craft have right-of-way over motorized craft.
3. Smaller, more maneuverable boats must yield right-of-way to larger less maneuverable boats (power boats must yield to sail boats, sail boats yield to kayaks, etc.).
4. Upstream boats shall not crowd downstream boats. Passing is best done on wide calm sections or when another boat eddies out.
5. More advanced boaters with better skills should be aware of the actions of less experienced boaters, and be prepared to assist or move out of the way as needed despite standard "etiquette" procedures.

In actuality, right of-way is a theoretical concept that has little practical value on the water with larger boats nearby. Realistically, gross tonnage wins! All paddlers, particularly PRC staff, should attempt to minimize confrontations when out paddling.

Rescue Guidelines

Swimming is a normal consequence of canoeing. Canoeists should expect to swim at some point. Staff must mentally and physically prepare themselves for this by wearing proper clothing (may include dry suits, wet suits, paddling jackets, polypro, etc.), carrying extra clothing, and being in the best physical condition possible. They must also have taken a canoe rescue class every other year that allows them to have practiced the appropriate rescues. Additionally, they must inform and instruct the participants/students about swimming and the potential dangers involved, including hypothermia, entrapment, drowning, etc.

Moving water rescue.

All trips on moving water should include a review of swimming in currents (self-rescue) and basic group rescue procedures (throw ropes, etc.) prior to launching.

Participants should be able to self-rescue by:

1. Swimming on their back with their head upstream and feet downstream; their feet kept near the surface to fend off obstacles and avoid entrapments.
2. Positioning themselves upstream of their capsized boat to avoid being pinned between boat and obstacles.

3. Backstroking aggressively with head pointed in the desired direction of safety. This is generally toward the closest shore or point of safety/assistance.
4. **In dealing with strainers, a different self-rescue is necessary.** Prior to reaching a strainer, participants should change to a headfirst position on their stomach and attempt to crawl up on the strainer. This position may also be used to swim more aggressively toward a desired area away from the strainer. **Avoid the temptation to stand up in moving water!** Upon reaching the shallows, log roll until in water less than knee deep before standing.

Group rescue guidelines for throw ropes.

Swimmers should:

1. Look for staff to throw him/her a rope and be prepared to aggressively reach for it if necessary.
2. Grab the rope, not the rope bag.
3. Stay on his/her back, feet up near the surface, and wait until s/he is in shallow water before standing up.

Staff should:

1. Hold onto free end of rope securely, but *never* attach it to yourself or an object!
2. Most beginners throw underhand most accurately.
3. Call "Rope!" to get the attention of the swimmer before throwing rope. Aim for his/her head or just downstream of the swimmer.
4. Stand in a secure location so that the swimmer will not pull you into the water and so that the staff person can swing swimmer into a protected area or eddy.
5. Assume a basic hip belay stance to pendulum swimmer into shore.

Santa Fe Mountain Center	*F* Therapeutic
	E Rocky Mountain Region
	C Youth and Families
	S 40.01–40.11

White-Water Rafting and Boating Activities on Moving Water

Rules

1. There shall be at least one experienced person in each boat.
2. There shall be at least one staff with swift-water rescue or equivalent training on all trips with Class 3 water and above.
3. Each float party shall carry a first-aid kit, pump, and repair kit in the sweep boat.

4. Each boat shall carry an extra personal flotation device (PFD) and paddle.
5. Each boat shall carry a minimum of 50 feet of throw line with a carabiner, extra paddles and/or an extra oar, and bailer (3 gallon minimum).
6. Approved PFDs (type I,II,V) shall be worn at all times on or in the water or when there is otherwise a risk of falling into swift water.
7. A safety briefing must be given to all participants before beginning any float trip (see briefing files for a copy).
8. There will be a two-boat minimum on all river trips.
9. All boats shall remain in visual contact of each other.

Procedures/Considerations

1. Abide by agency and permit stipulations; lead staff must carry a copy of the permit, and parking pass must be properly displayed in vehicle.
2. Consider two throw lines, rescue rope with extra carabiners, and extra bail buckets in sweep boat.
3. The sweep boat should not pass other boats in the party.
4. Scout unfamiliar rapids.
5. Consider chicken lines; otherwise, no loose lines on board.
6. Consider flip lines for big water.
7. Participants may float within an arm's length of boat in flat-water sections of the river (assuming participants have demonstrated ability to respond to instructor commands).

Briefing

1. Important points to consider when briefing participants for a float trip include:

Fitting the life vest.

1. Life vest must be worn at all times while in the raft or when there is otherwise a risk of falling into swift water
2. Life vest must be snug but comfortable.
3. Life vest collar must not be able to ride up above ears, test it.
4. Life vest must also be snug enough so it can be grabbed to rescue a swimmer.
5. Flotation collar must be free to float up in back.
6. Vests must not be worn under slickers or other garments. Buoyancy is significantly reduced.
7. Front opening of vest should draw together when fastened. This assures proper distribution of flotation foam.
8. Do not attempt to deliver safety talk while boaters are trying to adjust their vests.

Stepping into the boat.

1. The boat is dynamic, it's floating, it moves; be careful.
2. Please clean your feet so your boats last longer.
3. Be careful if the tubes are hot from the sun.

Riding in the boat.

1. Look around you, get comfortable and secure—you are responsible for keeping yourself in the boat. Stress personal responsibility here.
2. Look for hazards: Loose lines are bad; hard things like the frame and oars can be dangerous. If something is not comfortable or looks dangerous, ask the boat captain about it.
3. Riders in front get splashed a bit more.
4. Riders in back are in the catapult seat. Alert them and keep your eye on them.
5. Passengers are expected to bail.
6. Watch out for each other. If someone pops out, grab him/her quickly and pull him/her in.
7. Explain "high side" technique.
8. No alcohol.
9. No smoking in the raft.
10. Watch for hypothermia and sunburn.
11. Passengers should keep legs inside the raft at all times.

Human overboard.

1. Guides should anticipate factors that can bounce someone out. Example: If you are about to slam into a rock, tell your people to hold on.
2. When someone goes over, try to haul him/her in *immediately*.
3. Explain proper "white-water swimming" technique.
4. Explain danger of swimming downstream of the raft or under the raft.
5. Explain danger of foot entrapment.
6. Explain power of water and need to keep calm and aware of surroundings.
7. Explain throw line as possible means of rescue. Consider hazards of throw line.
8. In the event of a flip, every effort must be made to keep track of all swimmers. Swimmers should listen for instructions from the guides and get safely to shore if possible.

Leaving the raft.

1. Do not leave the boat unless guide says it is okay.
2. When stepping ashore watch for loose rock and deeply cut banks.
3. Bow person should be aware of possible strong pull on bowline when going ashore.
4. Watch for poison ivy and rattlesnakes.

SECTION 41
SEA KAYAKING

University of North Carolina—Carolina Adventures	
	F Recreation
	E Southeast Region
	C University Students and General Population
	S 41.01–41.10

Introduction

The following approved guidelines are adapted from the Hurricane Island Outward Bound School's Instructor Handbook and are to be used on all applicable Carolina Adventures sea kayaking courses. These guidelines are to be supplemented by the professional judgment of the expedition program manager and the instructors.

- Properly fitted Type III approved PFDs must be worn at all times by instructors and participants while in the kayaks.
- Staff should check participants PFDs prior to use by making sure they fit, all buckles and zippers are fastened, all compression straps are tight, and they cannot be pulled up over the head.

Cruising and Crossing Policies

- There will be no night paddling.
- Always travel in convoy.
- Unless making a crossing, kayaks should always be within 1 mile of shore.
- Crossings should not put kayaks more than 2 miles from shore with careful attention paid to weather, wind, and tide.

Capsize

- All kayaks used by Carolina Adventures are capable of providing adequate flotation to float full of water with one person aboard.
- All participants, prior to departing on an overnight expedition in a sea kayak, will have successfully completed at least one capsize, including reentry.
- This capsize will be supervised by instructional staff.
- A thorough briefing of the practice capsize procedure should be given by the instructor prior to this exercise.

- If a capsize should happen underway, all boats will group together in close convoy just downwind of the capsized boat. The designated staff rescue kayak will assist the capsized boat, with participant, if feasible.
- In the event of a multiple capsize:
  - The designated instructor will direct from his/her kayak the recovery of students and boats, assess the danger of trees, rocks or other hazards, tow if necessary, and determine whether to abandon kayaks and recover students only.
  - Hypothermia may well be a problem after the capsize. If so, use H rescues instead of T rescues to get the participants in the boats as soon as possible. The pumping and bailing process should keep people warm.
  - Immediately upon completion of re-entry and bailing, the convoy should proceed to the nearest safe refuge to address the needs of participants and equipment.

Staff

- All staff should have completed a basic staff training that includes capsize and rescue procedures (T and H assisted rescues and paddle float self-rescue), basic paddling instruction, towing, and, if possible, heavy weather paddling.
- Designate one instructor to be in charge if there is a capsize or other emergency on the water.

Expedition Skills

Packing and loading.

- Important items such as extra clothing, emergency equipment, map and compass, and water must be easily accessible. You can keep a dry bag in the cockpit with essentials for the day.
- Waterproof bags must be used to protect gear from the damaging effects of water and to provide flotation in case of capsize. Using more smaller bags versus fewer larger bags makes packing easier and less gear gets wet if a bag leaks.
- Gear must be well secured and distributed evenly so that your boat will maintain proper balance.

Convoy (group pacing).

- Boats should always travel in convoy and should be close enough so participants can talk easily with the boats in front and behind them.
- It is important to keep a close convoy, especially near channels, around headlands, and in fog.
- Traveling in convoy is both a safety feature and an important aspect of the expedition.
- It will test participants' communication skills, patience, and sense of responsibility for one another.

Communication.

- Communication between boats should not be a problem when convoy procedures are followed. When it is a problem, the following paddle and airhorn signals can be used.
- Teach participants to read paddle signals and practice before attempting a crossing, difficult landing, or paddling in to an area where communication could become an issue.
- Air horns should be used to warn other boats of the kayaks presence:
  - One prolonged blast every 2 minutes: for use in fog.
  - Four short blasts: if you can see the other boat and are in danger of collision.
  - Repeat until out of danger.

Navigation

Teaching navigation is a combination of land and sea techniques including:

Maps.

- What is a topographic map?
- Map features—margin references, colors, symbols, rivers, roads, structures, county lines, etc.
- Contour lines

Compass.

- Taking a bearing
- Triangulation

Plotting courses.

- Mileage/speed
- Hazards (including ship/ferry traffic)
- Refuges (from wind, current, tide)
- Trip log

Dead reckoning.

- DRT: Distance = Rate X Time
- Impact of current on speed
- Knowing paddling pace/speed

Tides and currents.

- Tide height must be known when planning to put in or land, because the tide determines how much beach will be exposed.
- Changes in tide can turn an easy landing into an impossible one.

Aids to navigation.

- Lights and their characteristics
- Buoys and channel markers
- Sound buoys: bells, whistles, gongs
- Day markers

Ferry Schedules

- Instructors should carry ferry schedules when crossing ferry paths and make participants aware of routes and times.

Winds and Tides

- Instructors must pay keen attention to changing weather and sea conditions. In particular, instructors should always be vigilant of the confused conditions caused by wind against tide.

Rules of the Road

- Stay out of the way of everything bigger than a kayak. Do not assume other boats see you, as it can be next to impossible to spot a kayak. *Stay together* and you are easier to see.

Kayak Care and Maintenance

Have participants follow these basic procedures to keep our kayak fleet in good repair for your expedition and for years to come.

- Never lift by the toggles or load lines, get an arm under the kayak.
- Avoid carrying kayaks while they are loaded.
- Never stand or kneel on the deck.
- Do not ram boats together playing tag games.
- Avoid banging kayaks when rafting up.
- Never drag kayaks over rocks.
- Be wary of hidden rocks along the journey and lift the rudder if shallow.
- Get out while the boat is still floating.
- Kayak hatches and cockpits should be rinsed with fresh water. Close lids securely before storing on trailer, even if hatches are still damp.
- Clean any dirt from paddling jackets, PFDs, and spray skirts.
- Scrub armpits and inside back of PFDs and paddling jackets with Simple Green solution and rinse thoroughly.

Safety Equipment

- During an expedition, each instructor should carry the following:
  - 1 freon horn
  - 1 throw line, with tow harness
  - Emergency knife
  - Paddle float
  - Bilge pump

- Instructors should carry between them:
    - Spare spray skirt
    - Spare paddle
    - First-aid kit
    - 1 waterproof weather radio
    - 3 red aerial flares
    - Hypothermia kit—sleeping bag, stove, hot cocoa, space blanket is in the first-aid kit (daytrips only)
    - Binoculars (for checking crossings)
- Each participant should carry the following personal items:
    - 1 spray skirt
    - 1 PFD with whistle attached
    - 1 paddling jacket
    - Warm layer and warm hat (kept in dry bag)
    - Paddle

Paddling Presentation Outline

Gear Introductions

- PFDs
    - Inspect and bring any concerns to instructors attention.
    - Make sure they are tight.
- Spray skirts
- Paddles—feathering
- Kayaks
    - Rudder
    - Deck lines
    - Fitting the boat

Wet Exit Walk-Through

- Make sure grab loop on spray skirt is exposed.
- Lean forward! (It's easier to wet exit, avoid hitting bottom.)
- Signaling trouble during exit: pounding on the bottom of the kayak.
- Releasing the spray skirt with one hand.
- Proper method of wet exiting the boat (lean forward, tight jeans metaphor).
- Checking for paddling partner.

- Recovering paddles.
- Moving to ends of kayak; hanging from the toggle.
- Righting the boat using the assist boat.
- Reentry procedure; staying low to the deck.
- Pumping out (H rescues).

Capsize Drill (overnight trips only)

Air Paddle—Holding the Paddle

- Knuckles
- Relaxed grip
- Paddler's box
- Torso rotation
- Pushing top hand

Launching

Paddle Lesson

- Push top hand instead of pulling bottom hand
- Forward
- Power
- Tour
- Sweep
- Demonstrate
- Distance of paddle to hull
- Hand position
- Follow-through
- Back
    - Same as above but in reverse, push bottom hand instead of pulling top hand.
- Turning
    - Sweep
    - Rudder
    - Pros/cons

- Side
    - Draw stroke
    - Keep paddle perpendicular to hull, wrist at forehead
- Stopping
- Side-to-side back paddle
    - Light touches, do not turn boat
- Landings
    - Rudder up
    - Forward landing
    - Side landing

Paddle Commands

- Forward
- Back
- Right
- Left
- Stop

Games

- Paddle commands "Simon says"
- Sharks and Minnows
- Follow the leader

Gear Clean-Up and Boat Care

Georgia College & State University	
	F **Education**
	E **Southeast Region**
	C **University Outdoor Education Students and General Population**
	S **4.10, 41.01–41.10**

General Water-Based Activities Policy

Staff/Participant Ratios

Swimming	1:10 (minimum 2)
Flat-Water Canoeing	1:8 (minimum 2)
Moving/White-Water Canoeing, Kayaking, or Rafting	1:6 (minimum 2)
Coastal Kayaking	1:6 (minimum 2)

Supervision

Water-based activities present facilitators with the added risks associated with being near, on, or in the water. Swimming in conjunction with canoeing, kayaking, and rafting is common, therefore participant swimming ability and level of comfort around water should be considered for participation in water-based activities. While it is recognized that, at this time, the American Canoe Association does not require instructors to be trained as lifeguards, it is recommended that facilitators are trained as lifeguards for the settings in which they are facilitating water-based activities. Outdoor education students are required to demonstrate swim proficiency, and encouraged to attain lifeguard training while at GCSU.

Activity Goals

1. Introduce unfamiliar and sometimes imposing environments in which participants confront and solve realistic problems.
2. Provide opportunities to apply newly acquired knowledge and skills.
3. Provide small group experiences.
4. Provide opportunities for leadership development.
5. Challenge participants physically, emotionally, intellectually, and socially.
6. Provide opportunities to set and achieve individual and group goals.
7. Provide group decision-making opportunities that have real and natural consequences.
8. Develop a sense of stewardship toward the environment, equipment, and facilities.

9. Teach skills for life-long recreation enjoyment.
10. Have fun while learning about oneself and others.
11. Promote trust, respect for diversity, team effectiveness, leadership development, and community.

Facilitator Responsibilities

1. Determine staff and participant swimming ability and comfort with the particular water environment.
2. Provide basic water safety instruction as appropriate, including PFD usage, buddy system, and other site-specific water safety topics before engaging in the activity.
3. Require staff and participants to wear appropriate PFDs while in natural water environments, and as deemed necessary by the lead facilitator while placing boats in or taking boats out of the water.
4. Provide supervision in and around water.
5. Determine if a lifeguard is necessary based on the setting and client characteristics.
6. Select PFDs that are appropriate to the type of activity and site characteristics, as well as water and air temperature, technical skill level, swimming ability, water dynamics, boat size and type, and participant size.
7. Require staff and participants to use Coast Guard approved Type III or Type V PFDs.
8. Determine that facilitators are experienced in general water safety and rescue.
9. Teach introductory skills before going on the water, or in a calm, controlled environment.
10. Brief staff and participants about rafting-up procedures and on-the-water communication.
11. Inspect equipment and note that boats are equipped with proper safety equipment.

Swimming

Swimming, though not specifically taught as part of outdoor education programs, may be an integral part of technical water skills or a complement to the main focus of a land or water program. Swimming may take place to refresh students and facilitators; for exercise, fun or relaxation; to develop or improve swimming skills or confidence in the water, or to teach water safety skills. Regardless of the setting or the purpose, follow these general guidelines and use good judgment:

1. Distinguish between "swimming" and "dipping":
   a. Dipping is any activity that takes place in calm, shallow (below waist height) water (a pool is acceptable provided hazards are not present and other criteria are met).
   b. Swimming is any activity that takes place in deep water (above waist level).
2. Require nonswimmers to wear a PFD at all times.
3. Require swimmers to wear PFDs if:
   a. A certified lifeguard is not present;
   b. Activity is conducted in Class I or higher white water;

   c. Activity is conducted in a coastal setting in which heavy surf or riptides are present.

4. Monitor all swimming activities.
5. Determine increases in the staff-to-swimmer ratio (10:1, minimum 2) based on context, activity, and participant characteristics.
6. Appoint a head lifeguard to determine appropriate safety procedures for the swimming activity:
   a. Establish a buddy system;
   b. Inspect areas for hazards and dangerous conditions;
   c. Ensure an unobstructed view of swimmers;
   d. Communicate safety procedures.
7. Locate first-aid and rescue equipment in an appropriate, visible location.
8. Conduct swimming only from sunrise to sunset.
9. Do not permit diving unless approved by the coordinator of outdoor education programs or designate.
10. Permit swimming in rapids when the following conditions are met:
    a. There is a pool below the rapids where swimmers can exit safely;
    b. Participants are instructed in the proper way to swim in rapids (i.e. feet up, on back, feet first, or tucked in a ball when a hydraulic is present);
    c. At least one facilitator is trained in swift-water rescue and positioned below the rapids, with a throw rope;
    d. The rapids are surveyed by the facilitation team in advance and deemed to be class I or II;
    e. Participants are able to swim (i.e., passed swim proficiency test) and are comfortable in moving water;
    f. Environmental conditions are assessed and determined to be manageable.

Coastal Kayaking

Facilitator Responsibilities

1. Maintain an appropriate distance between boats, based on context, program goals, and participant characteristics and skills.
2. Maintain vigilance to prevent common problems such as sunburn, motion sickness, and dehydration.
3. Determine beach camp selection to have minimal impact on fragile environments.

Teaching

1. Follow relevant American Canoe Association skills course curriculum based on context, program goals, and participant characteristics.
2. Teach prerequisite skills before going on the water or in a calm, controlled environment.
3. Design program and instructional sequence to accommodate appropriate methodology and practice/feedback opportunities.
4. Curriculum may include, in addition to ACA requirements:
   a. A rescue drill that emphasizes remaining calm, the importance of teamwork, and following directions and training such as wet exits, signaling, recovering equipment, righting the boat, and re-entry;
   b. On-land demonstrations, on-water demonstrations, and drills;
   c. Basic power, turning and bracing strokes;
   d. Basic maneuvers;
   e. Rescue techniques;
   f. Navigation;
   g. Coastal environment (weather, paddling in wind, waves, surf, and coastal ecosystems);
   h. Equipment.

Safety and Environment

1. Carry appropriate towing equipment, rescue sling, a spare spray skirt and paddle, hypothermia kit including spare clothing, appropriate charts and compasses, kayak repair kit, emergency signal kit, and a first-aid kit.
2. Inspect surf exits and landing areas for appropriate environmental hazards and conditions.
3. Plan program with consideration for environmental conditions such as tides and currents.
4. Warn participants about hazardous fauna such as sting rays and jelly fish.

SECTION 42
SAILING

Thompson Island Outward Bound
F Education
E Northeast Region
C Various Populations
S 42.01–42.11

Sailing Standard Operating Procedures

Sailing is part of Thompson Island's tradition. For years it was the only way that students and residents got to the island from the mainland.

General Procedures

- TIOBEC sailing courses and activities will be conducted according to all relevant USCG regulations.
- All TIOBEC pulling boats will be staffed with at least two TIOBEC staff and will have a certified wilderness first responder and a licensed USCG captain.
- All TIOBEC watch officers will be provided a copy of the TIOBEC Sailing Local Operating Procedures and will adhere to them on TIOBEC courses.
- In addition to the full complement of equipment for a standard pulling boat, a hand-held VHF and cellular phone, contained in a waterproof case will be carried.
- PFDs will be worn by all TIOBEC students and staff while underway and while swimming.
- All TIOBEC students will participate in a swim check prior to or during the first day of the sailing element. Those unable to complete the check in its entirety must always wear PFDs while on the pulling boat.
- All TIOBEC pulling boats will contact a TIOBEC designee (usually a course director) via NEXTEL phone every 24 hours at a predetermined time and extension. This time and extension will be clearly posted on the expedition plan and subject to additional contacts in the event of inclement weather, significant behavioral or medical situations, or other instances at the discretion of TIOBEC management.
- A boat inventory must be done before and after every expedition under the direction of the watch officer. No boat should leave on expedition missing any item from the inventory. In addition, the watch officer as part of the inventory check before going to sea should check all running and standing rigging.
- A fully stocked TIOBEC first-aid kit will be accessible on all TIOBEC pulling boats and will accompany groups on all shore excursions.
- All TIOBEC pulling boats will be in full lightning drill and anchored before lightning is within 3 miles.

Specific Procedures

Operating in Fog

In the fog, pulling boats will monitor VHF channel 13 and make security calls every 10 minutes. There will be no night sailing in fog. The required blast on the horn must take place every 2 minutes.

Island Use

An integral part of the sea program is the use of islands for expedition stops. The islands are owned by individuals, the Nature Conservancy, or the National Park System. It is imperative that staff understands correct island usage, instruct their students and monitor their use of the islands. Check with CD for permission and island guidelines, especially when considering group solo and individual solo sites.

Ship's Log

- At the outset of every sea program course, instructors must begin a logbook documenting all procedures, departure and arrival times, and events. This log is considered a legal document.

Sanitation

- The standard contained heads that are carried aboard the pulling boats will be used and properly disposed of at TIOBEC (see logistics policies) or another facility (see CD for off island sites). Composting toilets are available on most of the Boston Harbor park system islands.
- It is acceptable practice to pee overboard in deep, dark, moving water; with discretion.

Single Boat Policy

In addition to the full complement of equipment for a standard pulling boat, a handheld VHF or cellular phone contained in a waterproof case will be carried.

Swimming in Boston Harbor

It is recommended that students swim primarily in the outer harbor generally past Deer Island light and on the other side of Long Island. Hazards in the inner harbor include; pollution, jellyfish, and currents. In no instance shall students be allowed to swim in the inner or outer harbor for 48 hours following a hard rain due to potential hazard from a combined sewage overflow. The established LOPs for swimming will be followed.

Certificate of Inspection

Sailing vessels Aquinnah (30'), Marshall Dodge (30'), Sally Drew (30'), Frankly Bonnie (30'), Muriel (30'); vessels Joshua James (26'), and Madeline (26') are limited, coast wise, from Boon Island, Maine to Sandy Hook, New Jersey, and the Chesapeake Bay and tributaries not more than 3 miles from land and inside the boundary line as defined in 46 C.F. R. part 7 from May 1 to November 1 under reasonable operating conditions.

- When vessel operates in excess of 12 hours in any 24-hour period, an alternate crew shall be carried.

- To comply with FCC requirements, vessel operator shall radio in the vessel's position to a designated base station every 12 hours when vessel is in operation.

Going Ashore

- Islands are fragile ecosystems; soils are often shallow, easily eroded, and quickly compacted.
- Avoid eroded banks when climbing up from the shore.
- Use established trails where they exist.
- Stay on rock and avoid wet boggy areas, moss, and lichen patches.
- Forage only for your needs. Shelter-building materials should not be dispersed, but rather left for the next users stacked neatly.
- Do not use island as a bathroom site. Only use established facilities.

Solo

- No swimming is allowed on solo.
- Bathing will be allowed, but only in water less than knee deep, and students will wear life jackets while bathing.
- No bathing between dusk and dawn.
- Any youth groups participating in a shipwreck drill or group solo must have an instructor on land near them to fulfill 100% sight and sound requirements.

Solo Site

- Only dead wood may be used for shelter construction, scatter wood at the end of solo.
- Practice no-trace camping practices and leave the area cleaner than you found it.
- No fires.
- Students will be instructed in the function of the whistles and freon horn for emergency use.

Anchoring

Watch officers are expected to demonstrate competencies performing critical operating procedures and practice noncritical teaching techniques listed below. Considerations include:

Characteristics of anchorage.

- Forecasted weather conditions, wind direction, and state of tide.
- State of ground tackle. Check regularly for wear and tear. Make sure it's accessible and stowed properly at all times and that shackle is moused and bitter end fast.

Procedures.

- Sound out anchorage, under oars.
- Position the boat and throw the trip line and buoy over.

- Begin rowing astern and ease the anchor over the bow, paying attention to the length of the rode out.
- When a minimum 5:1 scope has been reached, set the anchor, make fast with sufficient turns around the cleat, continue rowing and grip the rode to "feel" the anchor take hold.
- If the anchor drags, let out more rode and try again.
- Allow more scope (7:1, 9:1, or more) in heavy winds, stronger currents or poor holding grounds.

Setting Anchor Under Sail

Considerations.

- Size of anchorage, area for maneuvering.
- Wind velocity. In heavy winds or in an emergency, anchoring under sail may be the only option and should only be done under the close supervision of the instructor, or by the instructor.

Procedures in heavy winds.

- Round up into the wind until the boat stops.
- Drop the anchor.
- Drop the main.
- Use the mizzen to make stern way.
- Set the anchor, using oars if necessary.

Procedures in light winds.

- Drop the anchor while still slowly making way.
- Snub anchor rode, using the momentum of the boat to set the anchor. Be careful not to put unnecessary strain on the bow cleat. This technique is not advisable in moderate winds because of the strain put on the bow cleat.
- Always drop anchor off windward side, if making way.

Going Ashore

Considerations.

- Type of bottom and shoreline, size of anchorage, existing weather conditions.
- Whether to anchor stern first or bow first.
- Preparation of ground tackle and organizing of details before anchoring.

Procedures.

- Set anchor in the direction of desired shore—best at right angles, unless it is windy.
- Row slowly toward shore using the set anchor as a brake. Position the rowers to face the shore for better maneuvering.
- Prepare shoreline, with danforth if on a beach, without if securing to a tree.
- Unship rudder if landing stern first.

- Control the movement of the boat in the surge by taking up or slacking off on the anchor rode, and by fending off with the butt of an oar. Don't allow the boat to hit the shore.
- Secure the line ashore.
- Unload and fend off so that the boat remains floating. Be alert to falling tides.
- Pull out to deep water with at least one person on board and secure bow and stern anchor ropes.

Rafting Up at Anchor

Considerations.

- In steady wind or current from one direction, two boats may fall back on the anchors set from that direction. Leave a wide angle to prevent crossing anchor ropes.
- In a small anchorage, set anchors in opposing directions so that when rafted up the boats stay securely between the two points.
- In a three-boat convoy the two outermost boats may anchor to windward, then fall back to join the middle boat anchoring to leeward.
- Effect of the sea on the boats, especially if rafting for a period of time.
- Watch for chafe.
- Alert students to the dangers of catching fingers or hands between the boats.
- Moderate or rough conditions may call for breaking the raft.

Procedures.

- The two boats should be facing in the same direction.
- Secure bow and stern lines to restrict the side-to-side motion of the boats.
- Make both spring lines fast to bow or stern and quarter cleat to restrict back and forward motion of the boats, trying to get a fair leas.
- Use at least two fenders, secured around the thwarts or across the knees and under the static lines and pulled up against the gunwales amidships for the best protection.
- Going ashore—two or three boats can effectively anchor along a beach close enough to raft up for meetings and/or meals, yet far enough apart to swing clear for the night.

Sheering Off

Often a stiff cross breeze makes it difficult to get to shore. In this situation, lead the rode aft to increase maneuverability. (Sheering off is a general term, but is used as a specific term here.)

Procedures.

- Anchor upwind.
- Begin rowing ashore, bow first.
- Re-lead the rode through an oarlock in the stern quarter, around a thwart, and secure to quarter cleat.
- Keep the helm over and continue rowing toward shore.
- Secure a line ashore.

Anchor Watch

- Anytime when a pulling boat is at anchor, an anchor watch must be maintained.
- Anchor watch is an important part of taking care of the pulling boats. Make sure that students understand the importance of this responsibility.

Concerns.

- Anchor dragging. Change in wind direction and/or weather may cause anchor to trip and drag.
- Grounding out due to miscalculation of tide or change in position of boat.
- Boat traffic.

Procedures.

- When students sleep on board:
  - One to two students per boat will maintain anchor watch.
  - Large boat light will remain with anchor watch.
  - Students will stand watch in such a place on board where they can readily evaluate the security of the anchor/boat and, if need be, respond effectively.
- When students plan to sleep on shore:
  - At least two people will sleep aboard, usually staff.
  - Two other people will keep watch from shore with freon horn, strong flashlight, and watch.
  - By day, a minimum of one student or two instructors will constitute an anchor watch.

Capsize Drill

The course director is responsible for the implementation of the capsize drill, to make sure the scheduling is feasible, the weather suitable, the support crew and divers available and the instructors prepared. A safety boat manned by two standby persons and two divers will support the drill.

The outline of a complete drill will be to capsize the boat, right it, bail it out, and swim ashore in pairs. This is a silent drill and only the instructors should be talking.

Objectives.

- To familiarize students with what to do in the event of a capsize underway.
- To challenge a watch's ability to work effectively as a team under stress.
- To emphasize the importance of remaining quiet and following directions in emergency situations.

Considerations.

- Brief students in a warm quiet place, not in view of an ongoing capsize.
- At least the senior diver should be present at the briefing given to the students.
- Watch officers (WOs), divers, and students should be clear and in agreement regarding procedures and responsibilities.

- WOs should advise divers of potential problem students and their positions for the drill.
- Shorter students and weaker students should be placed at the ends of the boat next to the instructors.
- Thought should be given to which students should go when for swim to shore: Weak swimmers should go with strong; those most likely to get hypothermia should go first.
- The instructor should not dive under the hull if students are caught underneath it unless requested to do so by the divers.
- Instructors should not wear life jackets.

Concerns.

- Life jackets should be cinched tightly and only in the case of the drill whistles should be removed from jackets/around necks.
- Students should remain facing the boat and straight-arm the high gunwale to avoid getting hit as it comes down.
- Students caught under the boat should not panic and wait for assistance from divers.
- It's important not to hold or to clamber onto the boat so as to maintain the maximum airspace under the boat.
- Count-offs need to be clear and deliberate.
- Fingers must be kept clear of centerboard slot when righting the boat.
- Be careful of slippery deck.
- Students should step off boat from amidships when leaving to swim ashore.

Drill.

- The instructor must await the diver's okay before capsizing the boat, demonstrating the airspace, and sending students ashore.
- Capsize by doing a layback with feet on the gunwale, legs straight, hands on the bench.
- Do not rock the boat.
- Reach up and straight-arm the high gunwale as the boat comes over.
- Make a conscious effort to step well back as the gunwale, reaching up for the keel, keeping weight high, out of the water, and out away from the boat.
- Have half the watch then swim back to the other side of the boat.
- Signal everyone to board the swamped boat from both sides.
- Start bailing the boat out, as soon as the buckets are aboard.
- Designate two students at a time to swim together to shore.

Emergency Procedures

- Following are the preferred principles to be undertaken in case of person overboard, capsize underway, and lightning.

Person overboard.

- Prior to getting underway for the first time, students must be briefed on person overboard procedures. In a real situation the watch officer or assistant should immediately take the helm after a "Person Overboard" has been declared.

****This is an urgent situation and the thought process should be to stop the boat immediately.****

Concerns.

- Maintain visual contact with victim.
- Minimize time of recovery.
- Do not further injure the victim with boat.
- Recover victim using the quickest course possible.

Drill.

- Shout, "Person Overboard"; two people point and maintain eye contact with the victim.
- Recover victim using quickest course possible. Push the tiller hard over (either for a tack or gybe). Do not adjust sails; the boat will come around fast and more effectively.
- Heave life ring (with light at night) in direction of victim.
- Approach the victim with enough room to allow the boat to slow down when rounding up into the wind, so that the boat stops alongside the victim.
- Pick up victim on the leeward side of the boat as this offers protection against the wind and sea and the boat will drift to leeward if you miss the mark.

Squall Drill

Procedures.

- Drop sails.
- Pull up the centerboard.
- Drop anchor.
- Let out all the rope if necessary.
- Put on foul weather gear and boots if time allows.
- Keep someone on the helm, or lash it down amidships.
- Sit everyone down in the bilge between the masts or in the cockpit.
- No one should be touching rigging or shrouds.

Capsize Underway

In the event of a capsize underway the other pulling boat(s) in the convoy must stay well away from the disabled boat until such time as she is righted and all the crew is aboard; they should then approach with the utmost caution. One boat should radio PAN.

Once the capsized boat is righted and craft is fully or partially bailed, if possible the standby boat(s) should switch crews and provide clothes, sleeping bags and warm liquid.

Considerations.

- Realize that with full gear on and a current or swell running, it is very difficult to maneuver in the water or return to the boat if separated from it.
- Be aware that duffels lashed to thwarts and loose gear afloat beneath the boat can limit the air space available.
- If righting does not work this way, unship spars and sails.
- Righting the boat by completing a full 360-degree roll is perfectly possible.
- Guard against hypothermia: The main concern once the boat is righted and bailed will be hypothermia.

Procedures.

- Stay with the boat.
- Count off immediately and search under the boat for those who fail to count off.
- Stabilize the hull; do not tilt or roll it.
- Uncleat all sheets before trying to right.
- Unlodge the stock anchor before righting, so boat does not sail away!
- Right the boat.
- Enter the boat per drill procedure.
- Sheet mizzen sail in (if it is still shipped) to bring boat into the wind; take mainsail down.
- Bail with everything possible (other boats in convoy offer gear).
- Head for nearest protected harbor.
- Accept help from others.

The Pulling Boat

The pulling boat is an impressive craft with a unique nautical history. They were specifically designed for Outward Bound, incorporating design elements from the Naval Academy pulling boats used to teach midshipmen teamwork and discipline, the lap strake Monomoy surf Boats of Cape Cod, and the whale boats used for harpooning from the great whaling ships. Our present craft is solid, seaworthy, and versatile—even lovable at times.

Vital Statistics.

- LOA—30 feet
- Net wt.—1 ton
- Sail plan—sprit sail rigged ketch
- Draught—18 inches empty, board up, rudder out; 24 inches, rudder in; 36 inches, board down

The first boat was built in 1965 for the Hurricane Island Outward Bound School. Cy Hamlin of Boothbay Harbor drew the design. Various builders along the coast, from Boothbay to the Eastern Shore of Maryland have built subsequent boats.

Construction material.

The original pulling boats were made of cedar stripe planks that were edge nailed and glued. Fiberglass boats unique to TIOBEC are made from a mold of those original pulling boats. On most of the boats the thwarts and deckboards are mahogany.

Escort Vessels and Towing

An escort vessel will not interfere with the operation of a pulling boat unless the situation is deemed dangerous by the licensed operator of the escort vessel or is requested to do so by the operator of the pulling boat. At such time, the escort boat operator is considered unquestionably in charge of and responsible for all equipment and passengers involved.

Towing Safety

The vessel-towing pulling boats must be able to clearly see signals from all boats being towed at all times Each vessel towed, except the last vessel in a line, will have a stern lookout at all times. The stern watch will have immediate access to the freon horn and (at night) the large flashlight. Whenever possible, towing lines will be made fast in such a way that they may be let go under tension in an emergency.

All personnel on board a pulling boat being towed will be seated in positions designated by the operator of the towing vessel. In most cases this will mean in the cockpit of the pulling boat. In no circumstances should staff or students be standing while the boat is under tow.

Expedition Procedures

Convoy

Traveling in convoy has evolved as both an important program element and an integral feature of safety on the water.

Objectives

To provide direct assistance to one another in emergency situations provides a structure that demands constant sailing and navigation skills, planning, and communication.

Requirements

Pulling boats will keep within maximum range 200 yards in conditions of mild weather and good visibility. The numbers on the other boats should be readable. By night, pulling boats will keep within a maximum range of 100 yards and in such proximity that navigational lights will be in view by every vessel at all times. On training expeditions, boats may separate briefly to sail train. This should be approved by the senior watch officer and in all instances boats should stay within sight of each other.

Captains and Navigators Meetings

Boats in a convoy should communicate regularly to ensure safe travel and program continuity, and morning captains and navigators meetings are a good vehicle for this communication. They should include:

- The condition and welfare of each watch
- The weather, including latest reports and forecasts
- Tides
- Destination for the day
- Routes to be sailed
- Rendezvous
- Choosing of command boat
- Choosing of harbors of safe refuge
- Departure time
- ETA
- Anchorages
- Briefing the convoy in a morning meeting

Communications

Watches have a responsibility, to maintain a convoy such that ready communication between the boats is possible and assistance timely rendered if need be. Signaling to close convoy facilitates this. A rendezvous is a planned communication between all the boats in a convoy, executed to confirm courses, destinations, etc. It is a useful tool that forces the students in each boat to be articulate and brief; it also is an opportunity, for instructors, often nonverbally, to check with each other on the status of their groups.

Signals.

- Close convoy: three long blasts
- Rendezvous: one short, one long, two short blasts
- Come up on VHF: swinging fender

Considerations.

- If bad weather or other emergency requires that a boat leave the rendezvous before the arrival of the others in the convoy, that boat should head for the nearest protected waters and stay there until conditions permit return to the rendezvous point.
- If communication by radio is necessary, swing large pink fender by day and at night illuminate fender with light, holding it high. The strobe light may be used if necessary.
- No boat should leave a rendezvous point until all boats have reached the point and until all business between boats has been taken care of, including the scheduling of the next rendezvous point.
- A rendezvous may be made underway; it need not necessarily be a stop.

Procedures.

- Any boat at any time may call for a "close convoy" or a "rendezvous" by signaling on the foghorn.
- Upon hearing the signal, all other boats must respond with the same signal.
- All boats must take whatever action necessary to close the convoy to acceptable limits.

Equipment Check

Equipment check before going to sea.

- Whenever a boat goes to sea for any length of time, a complete inventory of the following equipment must be checked and brought up to date if necessary, under the watch officer's supervision:
  - Boat inventory
  - Personal safety check must be made of: Foul weather gear, life jacket, boots, knife and whistle. Knife, especially instructors' knives, should be kept readily available for emergencies (i.e., belt a knife on the outside of foul weather gear).

Expedition Briefings

Instructors must meet with course director to discuss expedition plans, goals, convoy, signals, watch problems, safety issues, medical issues. Prior to leaving on training expedition or getting underway for the first time, students must be briefed on capsize and man overboard procedures.

Considerations.

- Tone setting
- Presentation of local knowledge
- Clarification of instructor roles
- Briefing is to include:
  - Weather
  - Time and tide (ETDs, ETAs, etc.)
  - Selection of routes and objectives
  - Rendezvous (including what to do when the other boats don't show up)
  - Student responsibilities (captain, navigators, etc.)
  - Island permissions list, if applicable
  - Watch locker gear
  - Equipment check prior to departure
  - Communications—day, night, sound, and light signals
  - Captains and navigators meeting, morning meeting
  - Local ferry traffic

Expedition Checklist

- Instructors meet with CD—discuss plans, goals, convoy signals, watch problems, safety issues
- Student expedition briefing
- Expedition plan—discuss and file with CD
- Boat inventory
- Food
- Update weather forecast
- Bring CG license and trip leaders/island permit

Medical.

- Belt packs
- Ana kits
- Student's medical form, copy of page 1

Boat Gear.

- Radios from waterfront
- Lights
- Charts
- Stoves and fuel

Miscellaneous.

- Island permission lists
- Instructor field manual
- Cruising guide
- Personal reading/library

Night Sailing

Subject to restrictions noted on LOPs night sails are permissible under the following conditions.

- There are no fewer than eight crew (students and instructors) for overnight cruising.
- By Coast Guard regulation, bow and stern lights will be lit and set in the proper positions commencing at sunset and continuing until sunrise.
- Pulling boats will keep within the maximum range of 100 yards of each other and in such proximity that navigational lights will be in view by all boats in the convoy at all times.
- One boat in a convoy will light up a sail every 15 minutes, with each other boat following suit. This signal will also be used when other vessels approach the pulling boats.
- Pulling boats will not operate at night in the fog.

Operation in the Fog

- Pulling boats will sound the following standard for signals on the foghorn every two minutes or less.
  - Underway, under oars: one long blast (same as power boats)
  - Underway, not making way: two long blasts
  - Under sail: one long, two short blasts
  - Under tow (last vessel only): one long, three short blasts
- Pulling boats underway in fog in areas where traffic is suspected (e.g., Long Island Bridge, Hingham High Speed Ferry route, Inner Harbor) will make security calls at 10-minute intervals while transiting this area. Consider not sailing through these traffic areas.

Group Solo

Group solo is an optional course element. For any group solo, the course director must give approval. That approval shall be based upon the level of responsibility demonstrated by the students, their level of first-aid training, their mental and physical condition, timing of the group solo, and weather conditions. The approval shall be given on the day of the proposed group solo drop. Students shall be thoroughly briefed prior to the group solo. Briefing shall include methods of contacting instructors in case of emergency, first-aid considerations, and safety consideration.

Objectives.

- Impel watch to work together, to deal with group problems
- Provide change in pace of course
- Give students and staff space from each other

Considerations.

- Thought should be given to whether a staff person should camp ashore, particularly with youth and standard watches and especially when there is a possibility of outsiders interacting with the group.
- Students must have clothing appropriate to conditions and the following gear:
  - Appropriate emergency kit
  - Watch
  - Freon horn
  - Foul weather gear and life jackets
  - Sleeping pads (if possibility of thunderstorm)
  - Whistles
- Staff must stay within sound-signaling distance of students left on group solo. The instructors will be the persons primarily responsible for the safety of the group solo.

Heavy Weather Sailing

Considerations.

- Appropriateness of going out given condition of all watches and condition/experience level of instructors.
- Likelihood of weather escalating, options for anchorage, course relative to wind direction.
- Running downwind in heavy weather, reduce the chances of broaching by dowsing the mizzen and letting the main pull you down wind. Put the mizzen back to work before tacking or reaching. Without the mizzen you cannot go upwind to pick up anything that might have fallen over.
- In a heavy following sea and deep water, you may want to tighten your rudder lanyard; the rudder tends to unship with the pitching of the boat. Remember to loosen it again in shallow water.

Precautions.

- Check and tighten shrouds.
- Make sure anchors are ready to go.
- Make sure sprits are tied properly.
- Make sure life ring is ready.
- Tie the rudder down.
- Feed the crew before going out: Bland foods that will tend to stay down and hot drinks. Make sure snacks are handy.
- Rig a safety line between the two masts for students to hold on to, not high enough to interfere with the sheets.

Squall procedures.

- Squall procedures should be followed in severe thunderstorms or line squalls (see Squall Drills this chapter) or when your boat feels out of control. Alternatively, run downwind to protection.

Shortening sail.

- Whether or not to shorten sail is all relative to the conditions and abilities of the crews on all the boats.

Upwind.

- The boat is consistently taking on water.
- There is too much weather helm.
- The crew is unable to handle sheets.

Downwind.

- When there is too much weather helm.
- The boat feels out of control.
- There's a danger of uncontrolled gybes.
- One boat is sailing away from the other, unable to keep convoy.

No wind.

- Get ready, it's coming.

Reefing

Particularly when beating to windward, reefing maintains optimum angle to wind and more control as the wind increases.

Procedures.

- If possible, come into the lee in an island.
- Round up into the wind, sheet in the mizzen.
- Lower halyard and extend sprit lanyard until the first cringle becomes the new tack.
- Secure to down haul cleat and tighten halyard.
- Rig sheets. If you are carrying two separate sheets, bend the lazy sheet onto the desired clew cringle. If you are carrying one continuous sheet cow hitched on, reeve both sheets through clew cringle.
- Lastly (and least important) furl excess sail along the foot and secure evenly with reef (square) knots.
- For a second reef, a monkey line could possibly be used to extend the sprit lanyard although this presents serious difficulties with the sprit hitting the gunwale, knocking the bow watch overboard, or catching the shroud. The mizzen could be scandalized and its sprit used in the mainsail. If you think you have to double reef, better to scandalize, or better yet, drop the hook.

Scandalizing

Scandalizing is most effective when sailing off the wind. Keep in mind that scandalizing the mizzen makes it difficult to point upwind, making for a potentially dangerous situation.

Procedures.

- Round up into the wind, sheet in the mizzen.
- Remove and stow main sprit.
- Pass peak lanyard around main mast and secure to mast.
- Proper leads for main will vary with sail shapes.
- Avoid scandalizing mizzen if possible to maintain maneuverability.

Knots and Rope Work

- Figure 8—as a stopper knot for sheet ends.
- Bowline—a secure knot for joining tow lines; attaching docking line to a piling or cleat; attaching anchor rode to mast and for securing a line around the body.
- Square or reef—for securing a furled sail or reef.
- Round turn and 2 half hitches—for securing an end to a spar, ring or piling.

- Double sheet bend—for joining two lines.
- Slippery hitch—to secure sprits and oars and wherever quick release is needed.
- Cleating—for securing sheets, halyards, anchor ropes, dock lines, etc.
    - The line is led to the far horn of the cleat. One complete turn is taken around the cleat, then a series of figure eights are made until it is possible to hold the free end with the thumb and forefinger, finishing off with a locking hitch *except* for sheets.
    - No locking hitches on sheets!
- Mooring pendant—The mooring pendant is taken over the gunwale and its eye firmly placed around the cleat. The eye is then closed up by the pendant lanyard, which is cleated on top of the pendant and finished off with a locking hitch. If there is no lanyard on the pendant, use a monkey line.
- Whipping and splicing—because you should know how to do it.

Licensing, Life Jackets, and Count Offs

Licensing.

- One instructor on board a pulling boat carrying students must be licensed by the Coast Guard to operate vessels carrying six or more passengers for hire and because it is an inspected vessel.
- The licensed operator aboard a pulling boat is, in almost all cases, the watch officer.
- The specific areas and limits of your license are set forth on the face of your certificate.

Life jackets (PFDs).

- Life jackets or personal flotation devices are required to be worn at all times by all personnel when on the water in TIOBEC vessels.
    - Exceptions to this policy are found in the LOPs or can be made in the following circumstances if approved by the staff in charge and if those involved have passed the TIOBEC swim test:
    - On board motor vessels
    - When tied up to a pier or float
    - Anchor in protected waters
    - When sleeping on the boats at night
- The second and third exceptions, when applied to students, may be made only when they have passed the TIOBEC swim test.
- Each staff member and student will be issued a life jacket that should be fitted and marked so that it can be identified.
- It is a staff responsibility to assure that students wear life jackets at all required times and to see that the life jackets are in good repair.
- Non-swimmers and students who lack confidence in the water will wear a life jacket at all times when in TIOBEC boats.

- As per Coast Guard regulations, all pulling boats carrying students will carry 15 USCG Type 1 PFDs in the 30-foot boats and 12 PFDs in the 26-foot boats and students will be instructed in their use.
- The Type 1 PFD (the orange "horse collars" with reflective tape) should be put on in emergency situation when, in the judgment of the staff, there is significant increase in the chance of losing students overboard.
- These circumstances could include a swamped boat awash in heavy sea, a capsized boat that for some reason cannot be righted, a boat run down by another vessel.
- The PFDs should also be put on when it becomes necessary to leave the boat under emergency situations, such as a boat breaking up on the rocks or on a lee shore.
- The buddy system will be used to ensure that when a student or staff temporarily removes his life jacket to take off or add clothing, he is carefully watched until he has replaced the life jacket.

Count off.

- Prior to leaving base site day one, each watch will be taught to use the count-off system and to be familiar with the situations in which it may be used (i.e., capsize, man-overboard).

Lookout, Groundings, and Collisions

Lookout.

- A bow lookout will be on duty whenever a pulling boat is being operated.
- A stern lookout will be on duty whenever a pulling boat is operated at night, in fog, or in any situation where such a precaution is warranted (see Towing Safety).

Groundings/collisions.

- All groundings of pulling boats (with the exception of sand or muddy bottom groundings) or escort vessels or collisions involving these vessels will be reported on the accident/incident report form and given to the course director as soon as practicable following the incident.
- Waterfront personnel should be notified as soon as possible.

Navigation Curriculum

Equipment Introduction and Use

- Chart, compass, courser or parallel rules, leadline, and logbook.
- Chart—symbols, scale (also use latitude: 1 min. = 1 nautical mile), compass rose (true and magnetic), soundings, contour lines.
- Piloting—laying out courses, measuring distances, calculating time and elapse.
- Logbooks—essential position record, including a record of rendezvous, watch changes and weather forecasts. The following information should be logged at the end of each watch: date, time position, course steered, course made good, speed, wind, sea, visibility, ETA, comments, initials.

- Fog Navigation—sound buoys methods of safe travel, horn signals, and attention to smells, foam and birds. Special attention to other vessels in the area (e.g., schedule ferries).
- Night Navigation—practice identifying lights, sounds, smells, distorted perception of distances, speeds.
- Speed Check for Pulling Boat—18/T = knots, where T = time elapsed as object passes from stem to stern (this is the reduced fraction from the old Rate X Time = Distance formula. Distance is the length of the pulling boat, 30 feet). NOTE: A fixed buoy will give true speed over the bottom; floating objects will speed through the water.
- Dead Reckoning—(abbreviation for deduced reckoning)—Updating position by using Rate X Time = Distance, and course steered.
- Rules of the Road—(refer to Coast Guard publications for details) keep to the starboard side of the main channel; port tack gives way to starboard tack; windward and overtaking boat keeps clear; vessels approaching each other pass port to port; large vessels in confined waters, vessels fishing, and vessels restricted in maneuverability are identified by special day shapes and lights and have right of way over sail and other powerboats, otherwise power gives way to sail. Pulling boats under oars is considered power rather than sail.
- Fixes, Lines of Position—sighting over compass (hand-bearing or even land compass if you have one) to take bearings on buoys, landmarks, lights, ranges.
- Additional Navigation Topics—bow and beam bearings, doubling the angle on the bow, running fixes, sound bearings in fog or at night.
- Tides and Currents— tide as vertical rise and fall of water, current as horizontal. Types of tides (diurnal, semidiurnal, mixed) and currents (tidal). Current described in terms of set (direction), drift (velocity), and measured by direction water moving toward.
- Rowing—students should be taught rowing skills as soon as possible in the course so that they have some capacity to control the boat. Stress the importance of teamwork and communication. Take the time to proactively practicing handling the oars (tossing and stowing).

Commands

- "Stand by the oars (or select oars)": oars are unlashed and selected, extra oars relashed.
- "Toss oars": oars are tossed upward in rapid succession from aft forward, blades positioned for and aft.
- "Ship oarlocks": position oarlocks in sockets.
- "Come to oars": oars are lowered into oarlocks and held parallel to water.
- "Prepare to give way": rowers lean forward and position oars to row.
- "Give way": together/port side/starboard side.
- "Backwater": together/port side/starboard side.

- "Hold water": together/port side/starboard side.
- "Stow oars": rowers lower and stow oars in succession from forward to aft.
- "Unship oarlocks": remove oarlocks from socket.
- "Cross oars": rowers slide oars inboard until oars rest on both gunwales. This position is only advisable while changing rowers in calm water, while the boat is not under sail.
- "Bench oars": rowers slide butt end of oars under king plank. Position is advisable while changing rowers or if you are sailing without putting the oars away.

Pulling Boat Maneuvers

Tacking

Tacking or coming about is the act of changing tacks by bringing the bow of boat through the wind. It's a committed, dynamic move.

Considerations.

- Pulling boats must move through 120 degrees of dead space between one close-hauled tack and the other. Therefore, it needs to be moving well with good way on before coming about.
- The centerboard needs to be down.
- In light winds or choppy seas, it may be necessary to push the mizzen to weather and back the main to bring the boat around.
- Forcing mainsail across prevents bow from coming through the wind.

Procedures.

- Sail close hauled, keeping the mainsail driving as long as you can.
- Push helm hard to the leeward gunwale.
- Release working sheet only when mainsail begins to bluff.
- Pull mizzen in a bow moves through wind.
- Sheet in to leeward quickly.
- Resume sailing close hauled. As sails fill, it may be necessary to fall off to regain speed before resuming a proper close-hauled course.

Gybing

This is the act of changing tacks by bringing the stern of the boat through the wind. It must be a controlled, cautious move.

Considerations.

- Always gybe slowly.
- Have a student (a.k.a. gybemaster) sit in the middle of the boat; back against the mizzen, to help control the mainsail.
- The centerboard should be up or no more than a quarter down to prevent tripping.

- When constantly gybing or having trouble keeping the sails full, go wing on wing or tack downwind—sailing on a broad reach, first on one tack and then on the other. In heavy weather, scandalize the main to take away the danger posed by the sprit.
- Go into a gybe fast and come out of it slow.

Procedures.

- Put the boat on a broad reach.
- Push the helm to weather.
- As the stern comes through the wind, the clew of the mainsail will begin to lift. Pull the working sheet in tight, pulling the sail down and into the center of the boat; the lazy sheet takes up slack.
- The student handling the mizzen should watch the clue of the mainsail and when it lifts or buckles, gybe the mizzen by pulling the sheet all the way in.
- As the stern comes through the wind, ease out the sails as they fill.

Sailing Backward

To go straight backward, tiller and mizzen are played back and forth, from side to side.

Procedures.

- Free or furl the main.
- Push the tiller opposite from the way you want the stern to go (can also be taught as pointing the tiller in the direction desired).
- Push the mizzen the opposite way from where you want the stern to go.
- Sailing without the rudder.
- When you remove your rudder, the mizzen takes over the steering function. It is easy to sail upwind with the mizzen but hard to go down wind, easy to tack but hard to gybe.

To Come About

- Sheet in the mizzen.
- Ease the main.
- Bring weight back to the leeward quarter.
- The main and/or the mizzen may have to be backed to bring the boat around.

To Gybe

- This is a difficult maneuver and requires plenty of sea room. It may be necessary to collapse the mizzen and/or bunch the mainsail up to the mast to get the boat to fall off.
- Bring all weight to weather as far forward as possible.
- Gybe the mizzen first, then the main.
- Force the sprit over and release the sail.

Powersailing

Even though this is a common practice on the pulling boats, it should be recognized that powersailing has the potential of being a dangerous maneuver. There is a time to sail and a time to row and they shouldn't be the same.

Heaving To

Heaving to is a method of keeping the boat as stationary as possible by balancing the sail plan and the rudder and centerboard. It is useful while waiting for another boat or in other conditions where you do not want to have much way on. This maneuver can be used anytime, in any situation. Heavy weather sailors' three rules of thumb: Never leave the boat; carry an EPIRB; and know how to hove-to.

Considerations.

- Make sure you have ample room to leeward, as you will move some.
- In heavy weather be very attentive to the potential of a knockdown.

Procedures.

- Sheet the main in on the weather side. This forces the bow away from the wind.
- Pull the mizzen in hard, forcing the bow into the wind.
- Hold the rudder hard over to leeward, steering the boat toward the wind.
- The centerboard would usually be all the way down, although this may be adjusted when balancing the boat.
- Note: A quick way to do this is when sailing to windward, tack without changing the sheets and then put the helm over to leeward when she comes through the wind. To get out of hove to quickly, release main and sheet to opposite side, ease mizzen and fall off.

Steering Oar

The steering oar is used in the event the rudder is broken or becomes ineffective (i.e., in shallow water or current).

Considerations.

- It is not necessary to have any way on for the steering oar to provide steerage.
- Oars/sails can be used to maximize effective steering.
- In heavy weather two steering oars may be rigged, one on each stern cleat.
- *Never* leave the steering oar in the water when rowing or sailing backward; it can snap right off.

Procedures.

- Rig with any number of knots; cat's paw, clove hitch, prussic, and constrictor.
- Cleat off tightly to a stern cleat.
- Use just like a tiller.
- Use rowing action to obtain greater steerage.

Docking

The most controlled means of docking is under oars. Landings under sail must be carefully supervised by an instructor and only in suitable conditions.

Procedures.

- Prepare fenders and bow, stern and spring lines in advance.
- Approach landing very slowly, with caution.
- Use an after-spring line to help stop the boat if necessary.
- When next to a pier, be sure to adjust the lines to allow for tide changes.

VHF Radio

The VHF radio can be a valuable piece of equipment, which provides weather information and communication with base sites, other vessels, or help. However, it is critical not to overestimate the reliability of electronic gear. The primary safety factor is the instructor. You are the one who has to make the correct decision to prevent an emergency situation. The VHFs are expensive pieces of equipment and should be treated with great care. The sets should be used for:

- Checking in with base.
- Emergency calls to base, Coast Guard, or other vessels.
- Security calls.
- Obtaining weather information.

If direct communication is required, or in the event of an emergency, use the following order:

- Telephone call to base using NEXTEL phone.
- VHF direct to base or MVOB.
- Marine operators can also amplify your transmission (patch it through) but this should only be requested for emergency or very important communications (there is a charge).
- U.S. Coast Guard—emergencies only.

Considerations.

- To operate these radios for other than an emergency situation, you need a third-class radio operator's license, obtained from the FCC.
- The higher the antenna, the better the reception. Moving the antenna may be helpful if it's handheld.
- Squelch should be adjusted such that you can begin to hear static.
- After each call, the following information should be logged in navigation log: date, time, vessel calling, and message.
- Radio traffic is monitored by the FCC; proper voice procedures should be observed, call signs always using the international phonetic alphabet (e.g., S = Sierra, I = India, R = Romeo, J = Juliet, A = Alpha) and profanity should never be used. Violations are noted and could lead to your license being revoked.

- Keep radio traffic clear and concise.
- Realize that everyone is listening.

Transmitting.

- Channel 16 is the international "Hail and Distress" frequency. It is only used in the event of an emergency. Do not carry on conversations on this channel.
- Channel 13 is for security calls only and is the standard frequency for harbor boat traffic.
- TIOBEC motor vessels monitor Channels 13,16, and 68.
- To transmit, use the following format:
  - Turn radio on.
  - Switch to proper transmitting channel.
  - Select highest power setting, hold the microphone 6 inches from your mouth, press the microphone key, speak slowly and don't shout.
  - Call the intended receiver three times, followed with your identification.
  - "Motor Vessel Outward Bound, Motor Vessel Outward Bound, Motor Vessel Outward Bound, this is Sail Vessel Muriel (call sign)."
  - Once you have established contact, switch immediately to alternate channel (09), indicating:
  - "Motor Vessel Outward Bound switch and answer 09."
  - Change to desired channel and repeat call.
  - When transmission is completed, sign off using your call letters and notify other traffic whether you will or will not be monitoring Channel 16.
  - "This is Sail Vessel Muriel (call sign) standing by on 16."
  - "Out" or "Clear" means you will not be monitoring Channel 16,
  - "Standing by" means you will be monitoring.

Emergency transmissions.

- Depending on the severity of the situation: *Security*—Precedes an announcement usually involving safety information such as weather warnings, large ship traffic, and Coast Guard search information.

Security calls.

This can be used to notify other vessels of your intention and is mandatory in fog. Examples of format:

- "Security, Security, Security, this is the sail vessel (State boat's name and call sign) operating between Thompson Island and Spectacle Island, course 150, speed 4 knots, any traffic in the area please respond."
- Upon making contact with another vessel, establish respective location and intention. Initiate calls on Channel 16 and then switch channel to a working frequency.

- "PAN"—Denotes urgent transmission concerning safety of life or equipment. PAN Calls:
  - If someone has fallen overboard, has an injury/illness, or if your boat has been dismasted, say: "Pan-pan, pan-pan (pronounced "pahn"), This is the sailing vessel (repeat boat's name 3 times), Pan-pan. My location is (state known position, then state type of emergency), There are (?) persons on board, (?) adults and (?) children. My vessel is (state boat color/type). This is the sailing vessel (state boats's name), Standing by, Channel 16." (Release microphone key and listen for response.)
- "*May Day*"—Emergency, grave danger, request immediate assistance. Use only if your boat is sinking, on fire, or you are abandoning ship. May Day Calls:
  - "Mayday, Mayday, Mayday. This is the sailing vessel (repeat boat's name three times), Mayday. My location is (state known position, then state type of emergency). There are (?) persons on board, (?) adults and (?) children. My vessel is a (state boat color/type). This is the sailing vessel (state boat's name), standing by, Channel 16." (Release microphone key and listen for response.)

References

Campbell, N. J. (1998). *Writing effective policies and procedures: A step-by-step resource for clear communication.* New York: AMACOM.

Gass, M. (1998). *Administrative practices of accredited adventure programs.* Needham, MA: Simon and Schuster, in conjunction with the Association for Experiential Education.

Hirsch, J. & Sugerman, D. (2005). *Association for Experiential Education Accreditation Program policy and procedures manual* (4th ed.). Boulder, CO: Association for Experiential Education.

Leemon, D., Pace, S., Ajango, D., & Wood, H. (2005). *Manual of accreditation standards for adventure programs* (4th ed.). Boulder, CO: Association for Experiential Education.

Page, S. B. (2002). *Establishing a system of policies and procedures: Printed, on-line, & web manuals.* Westerville, OH: Process Improvement.

Wieringa, D., Moore, D., & Barnes, V. (1998). *Procedure writing: Principles and practices.* Columbus, OH: Battelle Press.

Footnotes

1 Disclaimer: Risk and challenge are inherent in outdoor education experiences. While every effort is made to attend to the safety of participants and staff, it is not possible to control or anticipate all factors related to leadership, equipment and facilities, environment, and participant behavior that may contribute to emotional, physical, or social safety.

2 Wilkerson, J.A. (1992). *Medicine for mountaineering & other wilderness activities.* Seattle, WA: Mountaineers Books.

3 *Perspectives in Disease Prevention and Health Promotion Update: Universal Precautions for Prevention of Transmission of Human Immunodeficiency Virus, Hepatitis B Virus, and Other Bloodborne Pathogens in Health-Care Settings* 1988; 37:377–388

4 CDC. Updated U. S. Public Health Service Guidelines for the Management of Occupational Exposures to HIV and Recommendations for Postexposure Prophylaxis MMWR 2005; (No. RR-54): 1–17.

5 CDC. Updated U.S. Public Health Service guidelines for the management of occupational exposures to HBV, HCV, and HIV and recommendations for post exposure prophylaxis. MMWR 2001; 50 (No. RR-11):1–52.

6 CDC. Updated U. S. Public Health Service Guidelines for the Management of Occupational Exposures to HIV and Recommendations for Post exposure Prophylaxis MMWR 2005; (No. RR-54): 1–17.

7 Rescue Levels I–IV were developed by GCSU outdoor education faculty, Jeff Turner and Jude Hirsch, to provide a structure for teaching rescue strategies in GCSU outdoor education classes and OEC staff training.

8 Knapp, C. (1996). *Just beyond the classroom: Community adventures for interdisciplinary learning.* Charleston, WV: ERIC Clearinghouse. ED 388–485.

9 http://www.lnt.org/about/index.html, accessed on December 15, 2006.

ABOUT THE AUTHORS

Jude Hirsch, Ed.D., is a professor of outdoor education at Georgia College & State University, where she teaches in and coordinates undergraduate and graduate programs in outdoor education and directs the Georgia College Outdoor Education Center. Jude received the Association for Experiential Education (AEE) Outstanding Experiential Educator of the Year Award in 2001 and the Georgia College Teaching Excellence Award in 2002. In 2005, outdoor education accredited programs at Georgia College received the AEE Organization of the Year Award, followed by the Georgia College Program Excellence Award in 2006. Jude has been a member of AEE since 1977 and currently is the chair of the AEE Accreditation Council. She has helped to produce numerous books for the field, including *Essential Elements of Experiential Programming* with Simon Priest and the CD/DVD book and video training set *Developing Metaphors for Group Activities* with Lee Gillis. She has conducted numerous international and national workshops and trainings, and her writing has appeared in several books and professional journals. Jude was born in Toronto, Canada, and taught for many years at Acadia University in Nova Scotia, where she was the administrator of the recreation management program and coordinated the specialization in outdoor recreation. She attributes her passion for teaching and learning in the out-of-doors to years of working at youth camps in Ontario, Alberta, Quebec, and Nova Scotia. Her research and consulting interests encompass a wide range of pedagogical topics related to adventure and experiential education assessment and evaluation. Jude completed doctoral studies in curriculum and instruction with a focus on experiential education at the University of British Columbia. Jude, her husband Lee Gillis, and daughter Megan Gillis live on Lake Sinclair in Milledgeville, Georgia, where they are surrounded by boats, water, woods, and a community of friends and animals.

Deb Sugerman, Ph.D., has been teaching leadership development for the past 30 years. She taught outdoor education at the graduate and undergraduate level for 25 years, and now provides results-oriented program design, leadership training, and outcome evaluation designed to maximize the operational effectiveness of experientially based organizations through her consulting business, *Experiential Concepts*. Deb has been a member of AEE since 1981 and currently is vice-chair of the AEE Accreditation Council. In 2003, Deb received AEE's Outstanding Experiential Educator of the Year Award. She has written and presented extensively on the use of experiential methodologies with school-aged children, people with disabilities, and older adults, and is the co-author of *Reflective Learning: Theory and Practice.* Deb and her husband, Martin, live in Lee, New Hampshire, where they enjoy sea kayaking.

ASSOCIATION FOR EXPERIENTIAL EDUCATION (AEE)

AEE is a nonprofit, member-based, professional organization dedicated to experiential education. AEE provides professional development, skill-building, information resources, standards, and best practices.

AEE's vision is to contribute to making a more just and compassionate world by transforming education.

AEE's mission is to develop and promote experiential education. AEE is committed to supporting professional development, theoretical advancement, and the evaluation of experiential education worldwide.

The AEE Board of Directors developed the following Ends Statement to (a) portray how the world will be changed because AEE exists and (b) to provide guidance for association work. The Ends Statement reads:

Members of the Association for Experiential Education will be sought after and respected professionals for their ability to interweave a philosophy of experiential education through a variety of methodologies.

1. Experiential education is interwoven into many forms of professional practice, including but not limited to: education (K-12, higher education), outdoor adventure education, human service, corporate training.
2. Public policy is implemented that supports the philosophy of experiential education in professional practice.
3. Members have access to an advanced body of knowledge through the development, publication, and dissemination of new information, creative ideas, and ethical professional standards.
4. Members and consumers understand that experiential education occurs through a variety of methodologies.
5. Membership of the association reflects the many fields that utilize the philosophy of experiential education.

WHO AEE MEMBERS ARE

AEE members are students, professionals, and organizations engaged in the diverse application of experiential education in:

education • adaptive programming • recreation • leadership development
physical education • adventure programming • corporate training • environmental education
youth service • mental health • corrections

MEMBERSHIP BENEFITS

Scholarly Journal and Relevant Publications

AEE publishes the peer-reviewed, professional *Journal of Experiential Education (JEE)*, a collection of academic research, articles, and reviews; the *AEE Horizon* association newsletter; regional and professional group newsletters and publications; and other materials showcasing experiential education research, articles, reviews, initiatives, techniques, programs, and more. A subscription to the *JEE*, as well as discounts on AEE publications and educational tools, are included with membership.

Networking and Professional Development
Members enjoy discounted fees for annual and regional conferences, and can take advantage of AEE's online member directory.

Industry Standards and Risk Management
AEE works continuously with experts in outdoor and adventure programming to establish safety, efficiency, and general best practices. Organizational members who achieve AEE Accreditation provide evidence that their program meets the highest industry standards.

Leadership Development
AEE members are afforded the opportunity to learn leadership skills through volunteer training and development throughout the association.

Discounts on Events, Goods, and Services
AEE members receive discounts on all AEE-sponsored conferences and events, and on experiential education-related gear, tools, and services from a variety of vendors.

Career Services
The AEE Jobs Clearinghouse offers online job postings for experiential education employment, from internships to directorships. Additionally, AEE conferences offer career workshops, mentoring, résumé postings, and more.

HOW YOU CAN PARTICIPATE

Annual Conferences
Every November, the association convenes an annual conference of more than 900 attendees, with hundreds of workshops, internationally recognized speakers and presenters, and more. Our signature event provides professional development and renewal, skill-building, continuing education units, and unsurpassed networking and community-building opportunities.

Regions and Regional Conferences
AEE's eight Regions sponsor regional conferences, playdays, seminars, and other activities so members and the local experiential education community can participate and network in smaller, more accessible and intimate settings.

Professional Groups
AEE Professional Groups represent specific areas of practice, and offer opportunities for members to share knowledge and build skills with others who share similar professional interests within experiential education.

Involvement in any of the above activities, at any level, is a great way to become more involved in the association, expand your network, and get the most out of an AEE membership.

JOIN US!

Memberships are available at different levels and benefit structures.
See all the details and join online at:

www.aee.org